WORLD PEACE

VOLUME THREE

WAR AND PEACE

Suresh Chandra Mallick
Pritam Mallick

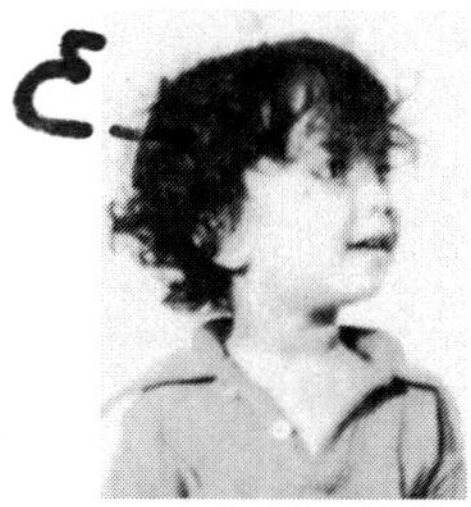

WAR AND PEACE

Institute of Development Studies and Policy research,
Pritam Bhawan, 93, Dharma Vihar, Khandagiri,
Bhubaneswar 751030 (Orissa), INDIA

ISBN: 978-81-924851-2-6

First Edition

2012

Price: US $

Dedicated to

Mr. Ban Ki-Moon
Secretary General,
The United Nations Organization

PROLOGUE

The manuscript on 'World and Peace' is intended to ascertain whether there is any possibility of reducing bloodbath of soldiers and civilians in different uprisings, wars, invasions, conflicts, insurgencies, crises, annexations, rebellions, violence, guerrilla warfare and bombings carried out by violent groups and warmonger countries. The study finds solutions for achieving long-term peace for the whole world. We are hopeful that world peace is achievable.

Wars are decided or caused by the governments. But the sufferers are young patriotic soldiers and innocent civilians. The First World War caused the deaths of 24,004,171 (24 millions) people, wounded 20,723,570 (20.72 million) people and the number of missing people was to the extent of 7,635,952 (7.64 million) people. The Second World War caused the killings of 60 millions of people including the annihilation of six million Jews in Nazi death camps. Each day one thousand people are killed in 2007 by war or violence. The world has reached a situation, where life of human beings, animals, birds and even plants are not safe. The most intelligent creature human being has become more selfish, vindictive, and inhuman. Man runs after peace; gives alms to the poor; donates food to the hungry; rears animals with care; enjoys the beauties of nature; joins prayers for world peace; but kills another man for fatuous cause.

The world has witnessed 722 high devastating and heinous historical warfare causing billions of deaths.

This speaks the barbarism of we-people, who have forgotten humanity. We are speaking ill of those who created or are now creating wars; but we do not dissuade them to stop war. We have to change our ill feelings, hatred and anger for others; we have the capacity to make others of any country or religion as our brethren and friends to achieve complementary and supplementary benefits. God resides in the heart of everybody.

The US has spent US $350 billion on nuclear, chemical and biological research for defense purpose only. But the developed countries donate only US $60 billion to the poor countries as aid. The world now produces arms and ammunitions to the extent of US $1058.90 billion per year and first 85 arms producing firms are located in United States, Russia, the United Kingdom, France, and Germany. Moreover, China, Brazil, India, Israel, Singapore, South Africa, and South Korea are now designated as arms producing countries. These firms undertake international trade mostly with the low-income countries.

The number of deaths by armed violence in the world is estimated to vary from 280,000 to 378,000 people per year.

So all of us should raise voice against the warmonger countries; pressurize the United Nations to pass resolution to stop international trade of arms and ammunitions. If the international Arms Trade Treaty is properly enforced, arms will not be transferred to those forces that use arms, and cause war, human rights abuse and poverty. Moreover, nuclear, chemical and biological researches for defense purposes must be completely banned for survival of people and civilization. We are confident that the developed and war monger countries will cooperate with the peace movements organized through out the world for survival and safety of human beings, flora and fauna.

In this manuscript we have discussed 'how we can avoid war and achieve peace' for the benefits of human society. The first chapter deals with 'urgency of world peace'. The second chapter incorporates the historical wars up to the end of World War II. The third chapter deals with the 'ongoing wars', which are continuing for decades and not yet solved. These wars are fought because of religion, insurgency, civil war, boundary issue, unrest, freedom struggle or insubordination. Chapter IV explains that the world faces a sever crisis. There is a fight between capitalism and communism, a fight between East and the West, a fight between a warmonger country and a Big Brother country. This chapter deals with defense preparedness of China and the US. We have incorporated 'Revitalization of the UN' to empower the UN for assuming the role of a world government in Chapter V. This organization should attempt to stop war, to focus on world peace, to promulgate international laws and to award UN Peace Prizes. Chapter VI has incorporated two important commission reports to free the world from nuclear war. The world can avoid catastrophe and can usher world peace. Chapter VII explains that world peace is achievable to save the world from destruction.

We are indebted to all authors, publishers; researchers cited in this manuscript. The authors are grateful to Wikipedia. Com, Google search, books, newspapers, journals, and Internet for collection of facts and figures. We acknowledge all the authors and have made authors' index. We are indebted to Ingram Content Group Inc for distribution. We are grateful to Mrs. Bina Mallick for her cooperation during preparation of the manuscript. We will appreciate for constructive criticism aiming at improvement of the subsequent editions of the book. We will be happy, if a small step towards world peace is contemplated through this endeavour.

October 8, 2012 Suresh Chandra Mallick

ACRONYMS

AEF	Aerospace Expeditionary Forces
AG	Assistance Group
A I C C R	All India Coordination Committee of Communist Revolutionaries
A L	Awami League (Bangladesh)
A O R	Central Command Area of Responsibility
A P H C	All Party Hurriat Conference
B E F	British Expeditionary Force
B D I	Backward Districts Institute
B R G F	Backward Regions Grant Funds
C A R	Central African Republic
C C S	Cabinet Committee on Security
C F E	Conventional Forces in Europe Treaty
C N S	Council of National Security (Thailand)
C P I	Communist Party of India
C P I (ML)	Communist Party of India (Marxist & Leninist)
C P N	Communist Party of Nepal
C R Z	Compact Revolutionary Zone
C S I C	Council of Somali Islamic Court
C T B T	Comprehensive Test Ban Treaty
ECOWAS	Economic Community of West Africa States
E E B C	Eritrea-Ethiopia Boundary Commission
E M R O	External Macedonian Revolutionary Organization

E P R D F	Ethiopian Peoples' Revolutionary Democratic Front
E P L F	Eritrea Peoples' Liberation Front
F A T A	Federally Administered Tribal Area
F A C T	Federation of Associations of Canadian Tamils
F I C N	Fake Indian Currency Notes
F I S	Islamic Salvation Front
F D I	Foreign Direct Investment
F F I	Foreign Funding Institution
F L N	National Liberation Front
F R U D	Front for the Restoration of Unity and Democracy
F U C	United Front for Democratic Change
G I A	Armed Islamic Group
G S P C	Salafist Group for Preaching and Call
H A L	Hindustan Aeronautics Limited
H C S	High council of State
H E U	Highly Enriched Uranium
I A E A	International Atomic Energy Agency
I C J	International Court of Justice
I D P	Internally Displaced Persons
I G A D	Inter-Governmental Agency for Development
I I G	Iraqi interim Government
I M R O	Internal Macedonian Revolutionary Organization
I N F	Intermediate-range Nuclear Forces
I R	India Reserve
I R A	Irish Republic Army
I R M O	State's Iraq Reconstruction and Management Office
I T AR(US)	International Traffic in Arms Regulation
J E M	Justice and Equality Movement
J K L F	Jammu and Kashmir Liberation Front
J V A	Java valley alliance
K E D O	Korean Peninsula Energy Development Organization
L D K	Democratic League of Kosovo
L E T	Laskar-e-Toiba
LTTE	Liberation Tigers of Tamil Elam

M A D	Mutual Assured Destructions
M E N D	Movement for the Democratic Forces of Casamance
M K	Umkhonto we Sizwe (South Africa)
M P V	Mines Protected Vehicles
NEPAD	New Partnership for Africa's Development
N P T	Treaty on Non-proliferation of Nuclear Weapons
NPTREC	Review and Extension Conference of the Treaty on Non-Proliferation of Nuclear Weapons
N W F P	North West Frontier Province
O N L F	Ogaden National Liberation Front
O N U B	United Nations Peacekeeping Mission (Burundi)
OPCW	Organization for the Prohibition of Chemical Weapons
O P D O	Oromo People's Democratic Organization
O S C E	Org. for Security and Cooperation in Europe
P C O	Project Contracting Office
P L O	Palestine Liberation Organization
P M L A	Prevention of Money Laundering Act
P S A	Public Safety act
R A F	Royal Air Force
R A F	Rote Armee Fraktion (Germany)
R N D	Re-assemblyment National Democratique
S A D C	South African Development Community
S E E D S	State Economic Empowerment and development Strategy
S I M I	Students' Islamic Movement of India
S L A	Sudan Liberation Army
S L F	Sudan Liberation Front
S L M / A	Sudan Liberation Movement / Army
S L P P	Sierra Leone People's Party
S N M	Somali National Movement
S O E	Special Operation Executive (British)
S P D C	State Peace and development Council (Myanmar)
S T A R T	Strategic Arms Reduction Treatise
T F G	Transitional Federal Government

T N G	Transitional National Government
T P L F	Tigrean People's Liberation Front
T S Z	Temporary Security Zone
UFDD	Union of Forces for Democracy and Development (Chad)
USAID	United States Agency for International Development
U N	United Nations
UNDPA	United Nations Department of Political Affairs
UNHCR	United Nations High Commissioner for Refugees
UNICEF	United Nations Children's Emergency Fund
UNISIL	U. N. Integrated Office in Sierra Leone
UNMIS	United Nations Observer Mission in Georgia
U N S C	United Nations Security Council
U S C	United Somali Congress Party
W T A	World Tamil Association
W T M	World Tamil Movement
W F P	United Nations World Food Program
W M Ds	Weapons of Mass Destruction

+++++

CONTENTS

INTRODUCTION

Nature has created rivers, oceans, mountains, forests, and has deposited vast mineral resources for the over growing human population. Bright sunlight, abundance of fresh air and water has sustained the human activity over thousands of years. The vast area of cultivated land has sustained human life for generations and has made life happier and healthier with production of flowers, sweet fruits, cereals, pulses and herbal medicines. The scenic wonders of nature fill our hearts with pleasure.

The modern world has achieved outstanding scientific progress. As a result, we are able to fly by aero planes; distance has been reduced through use of mobiles and computers; all books, reports, and newspapers have enriched our knowledge; the world is now connected with Internet; people enjoy events with television and enjoy cool air with air conditioner. We have achieved architectural grandeur with multistoried buildings and constructed high river dams. We have made the whole world a village through cultural exchange programs; can organize world events in cricket, football and other athletics. When natural hazards occur anywhere any time and we immediately assist the victims. But something has been missing continuously. Why we do not entertain other people as our friends or brothers or sisters? Why we do not believe in others? Why we treat others as our subordinates? Why we want to rule others? Why we hate other religion? We have inherited a culture of kings or monarchs, who were waging wars by sacrificing their soldiers to earn land, gold, prestige and woman. They enjoyed in observing the blood baths of soldiers and cries of civilians. A winner king enjoys satisfaction and pleasure by torturing the defeated royal family members, and killing the king and soldiers in the battlefield.

The inhuman activity of waging war continues even in the Twenty-first century. Why the United States of America and China are ready to face any military challenge? Why a country challenges the very survival of our human race and its civilization? Can the people tolerate nuclear war?

Perhaps the rulers of most of the countries kill their humanity as soon as they ascend to the thrones of President or Prime Minister of their countries. They are more worried for 'defense expenditure' rather than healthcare and education of unprivileged persons. In democracy too, the President and other ministers are accorded royal privileges. Even the state chief ministers need a fleet of 18 to 20 cars during his travel to the secretariat from his official residence, which is situated at a distance of one kilo meter only.

The governments of democratic countries know that assumption of power in each term is a difficult task. But the leaders also know that grabbing state wealth is the easiest way to amass large sums of money within a short span through defense deal, healthcare, education, irrigation and granting leases of land and mines to the industrialists preferably to foreign based companies. The ill-got money can be kept safe in foreign banks too. If government machinery becomes corrupt, it avoids transparency in the administration. This results in holocaust. People die through starvation; child sale becomes a common practice;

women die during maternity; children drop out from schools; and the administration avoids the public and bribes the media for advertisement. The grievances of the sufferers remain unsolved. This causes mass resentment, dissatisfaction and mass support for a revolt.

The poor and unprivileged people in low-income countries bear all the sufferings and accept the sufferings as God's punishment. But the brave, strong, frustrated and educated youths take up the challenge to fight against the government. They convince other unemployed boys and girls with noble ideas for helping all the distress people and bring them to their folds. These boys hide themselves in jungles; carry weapons; take military training; attack police stations, moneylenders and police informers and create terror to destabilize the government. The government spends more funds to suppress the Terrorists, Maoists and Naxalites. In short, the elected government wages a war against the revolutionaries. The Terrorists, Naxalites and Maoists challenge the governments through guerrilla warfare, as their number is small; they cannot wage a war against an army of police officers with guns.

This book aims at reduction of arms and arsenals, ban of international trade of arms and ammunition to decrease the horrors of war. The governments and people should accept humanity for strengthening world peace. All governments should implement arms trade treaty, stop nuclear, chemical and biological researches for defense purposes. The UN should be revitalized and act as the World Government. The UN Peace Council should be strengthened to render justice to the people.

People of all countries, religions, faiths, cultures do need peace, safety and happiness. And it is possible even today.

Chapter I

URGENCY OF WORLD PEACE

Man invents war. Man discovers peace. He invents war from without. He discovers peace from within. War man throws. Peace man sows. The smile of war is the flood of human blood. The smile of peace is the love, below and above.

Sri Chinmoy, 'Songs of the Soul', Verses 72

Man needs peace in family, society, and country and desires to live in a safer and peaceful world where he can work, live and sleep peacefully. But people of more than 112 countries defer peace because of insurgency at home for political and economic reasons. The governments incur higher expenditure on internal security and war. These countries are unable to meet the basic needs of the people, but the political leaders divert the attention of the masses for their own survival in vote politics. The psychological and political activities of leaders have made the planet – a battlefield and a mass burial ground. But the world needs its survival through peace, progress and prosperity of all people.

The world witnessed 722 fierce fighting wars. The most important wars are: The Kalinga War, War of American Independence, Russo-Turkish War, French Revolution, Peninsular War, Italian Independence War, Crimean War, War of Greek Independence, American Civil War, Passim War, Battle of Waterloo, Austro- Prussian War, Franco-German War, Seven Years War, First Balkan War, Second Balkan War, Serbo-Bulgarian War, Graeco-Turkish War, Pig War, Russo-Japanese War, **First World War, Second World War,** Boer War, Anatolian War, Spanish Civil War, Anglo-American War, Opium War, Vietnam War, Sino-Japanese War, Korean War, Iraq War, Indo-Pak War, and Afghanistan war etc.

These wars have changed the country boundaries, made millions of inhabitants nomads, millions dead, scratched human rights of hundreds of millions of civilians, millions as captives, and added sufferings to billions of innocent persons.

On an average, one thousand people die every day as a direct result of armed violence.

In most of the cases wars could have been avoided, as these wars were not caused with valid reasons. The present world lacks efficient arbitrators and negotiators, who could have taken steps to stop wars. The UN is hibernating and delaying to meditate between war-monger countries. Involvement of the UN observers prolongs the conflicts.

War is costly. War is unproductive. Yet powerful kings, monarchs, military rulers or warmonger Presidents of different countries take unilateral decisions to declare wars against other countries, which defy them or don't support them cent percent. Even today, all the democratic governments incur huge defense expenditure to protect their land or wage war against their rivals.

In short, our culture, civilization, education and scientific endeavor would not render peace to the world unless the United Nations and member countries promulgate, activate and work for peaceful solutions of uprisings, wars, invasions, conflicts, insurgencies, crises, annexations, rebellions, violence, guerrilla warfare and bombings. In this chapter, Crises in World Scenario, Conflicts Situations, Ongoing Wars, International Arms Trade, Global Trade, Nuclear Weapons, The Geneva Declaration, Christian Peace Witness, The World Peace March and the Obama Peace Factor have been discussed and Conclusion has been drawn for a solution.

Crises in World Scenario

The world faces a minimum of 20 wars daily and innumerable stray fights among the countrymen or fights between the government and people.

The International Crisis Group[1] has reported that about 60 countries are at war intermittently or at war-like situations that can flare up any time.

These countries can be classified into three categories, such as:

(a) Deteriorated Situation: Chechnya (Russia), Niger, North Caucasus (non- Chechnya), Senegal and Yemen

(b) Unchanged Situations: Afghanistan, Algeria, Armenia, Azerbaijan, Bangladesh, Basque country (Spain), Belarus, Bolivia, Bosnia, Burundi, Cameroon, central African republic, Chad, China (internal), Colombo, Cote d' Ivorie, Cyprus, democratic republic of Congo, Ecuador, Egypt, Eritrea, Ethiopia, Fiji,

---

[1] Crisis Watch, International Crisis group, September 1, 2009, No. 73

Gabon, Georgia, guinea, guinea-Bissau, Haiti, Honduras, India, Indonesia, Indonesia, Iran, Iraq, Israel/ Occupied Palestine Territories, Kazakhstan, Kenya, Kosovo, Kyrgyzstan, Lebanon, Liberia, Macedonia, Madagascar, Mauritania, Moldova, Myanmar,/ Burma, Nagomo-Karbakh, (Azerbaijan), Nepal, Nigeria, Pakistan, Peru, Philippines, Rwanda, Saudi Arabia, Serbia, Somalia, Somaliland, (Somalia), Sri Lanka, Sudan, Syria, Taiwan strait, Tajikistan, Thailand, Timor-Leste, turkey, Turkmenistan, Uganda, Ukraine, Uzbekistan, Venezuela, Western Sahara, Zimbabwe

(c) Improved Situations: Armenia/Turkey, Mali and North Korea

Conflict Situations

In Somalia, full-scale war erupted between the Council of Somali Islamic Courts and the Ethiopian-backed Transitional Federal Government, with fighting estimated to have killed hundreds of people and displaced tens of thousands. In Darfur, the humanitarian and security situation deteriorated while international negotiations continued over the deployment of a strengthened peacekeeping force. The Occupied Territories saw their worst factional clashes in a decade as Fatah and Hamas battled over the formation of a unity government. Tensions over Iran's nuclear program rose after the UN Security Council voted unanimously to impose sanctions.

The sudden death of Turkmenistan's authoritarian leader, Saparmurat Niyazov, prompted fears of a destabilizing struggle to fill the power vacuum left behind. In Fiji, military commander Frank Bainimarama in a bloodless coup deposed the government of Laisenia Qarase. The situation also deteriorated in the Basque Country, Bolivia, Egypt and Kyrgyzstan. One situation showed improvement in December. In Guinea, supporters of President

Conte and the opposition reached consensus on conditions for organizing legislative elections in June 2007. For January 2007, Crisis Watch identifies Lebanon as a Conflict Risk Alert, or situation at particular risk of new or significantly escalated conflict in the coming month. A Conflict Resolution Opportunity is identified for Uganda.[2]

On-going Wars

Wars are caused without valid reasons. It is simply caused to frighten the neighboring countries. Most of the political leaders are more worried for annexation of foreign land for their political mileage in their home countries. **These political leaders want to be immortal.** Some of the on-going wars would continue for years; jeopardize the essential services; wipe out peace and harmony in the region, and cause immense sufferings to the people. The wars which would not ceasefire in coming years are: Algerian Insurgency, Civil War in Georgia, Boundary Issue in Kashmir, Sri Lanka–Tamil Separatists, Sudan–Darfur, Religion-based War, Chechnya War, Iraq –US War, Unrest in Nigeria, annexation of Tibet by China, entry of Communists into Nepal and military rule in Myanmar/ Burma. The political leaders of these countries induce wars and the sufferers are the soldiers and the people.

International Arms Trade

The uncontrolled arms transfer has increased human suffering immensely; it has challenged the existence of human civilization.

Countless more are injured, bereaved, abused and displaced by state security forces, armed groups, criminal gangs and other armed individuals. Between

---

[2] Crisis Watch N°41, 2 January 2007/ UNITED NATIONS - / www.MaximsNews.com UN/ - 14 September 2006 –

one-third and three-quarters of all grave human rights violations and 85 per cent of killings reported by Amnesty International over the past decade have involved the use of small arms and light weapons. Massive numbers of people – men, women, older people, and children – die indirectly from the effects of armed conflict. The human suffering caused by collapsing economies, devastated health and security infrastructures, disease and famine is horrifying. Many more people are made refugees or internally displaced, injured, abused and bereaved, and lose the chance to lead prosperous and peaceful lives in a safe and secure environment.[3]

The Israel has used attack helicopters, combat aircraft and air-to-surface missiles in the Occupied Territories, which resulted in hundreds of deaths and thousands of injuries in apparent violation of international humanitarian law. At the same time, Palestinian armed groups have used rockets, explosive belts and other bombs to kill and injure hundreds of Israelis, and the Lebanese armed group Hezbollah has fired rockets at civilian areas in northern Israel.

Easy access to weapons not only contributes to violations of human rights and humanitarian law, it also increases the threat from armed groups and organized crime. This is especially the case with small arms and light weapons. For example, hand grenades bearing the markings of an Austrian company and reportedly manufactured under license, in all likelihood in Pakistan, have been used by armed groups in numerous attacks in India, Bangladesh and Pakistan, leaving scores dead and hundreds injured. Furthermore, there are other huge costs associated with the arms trade. Government arms purchases can

---

[3] Arms without Borders, Control Arms Campaign, October 2006; Oxfam International; The International Action Network on Small Arms, Controlarms.org

exceed legitimate security needs, diverting substantial amounts of money from health and education. There are many measures that governments must take to address the causes of conflict, since weapons themselves do not create violence. But the availability of weapons contributes greatly to the scale of killing, suffering and fear. Control of arms transfers is therefore an indispensable element in the effort to make a more peaceful world.

Need for action:

If based upon existing international human rights and humanitarian law, an Arms Trade Treaty will prevent arms transfers into conflict zones where they are likely to be used to facilitate serious violations of those laws, including torture, enforced disappearances, and war crimes, crimes against humanity or genocide. It will also help prevent the supply of arms to law enforcement agencies that use them to commit grave and persistent violations of human rights, including extra judicial executions, enforced disappearances and torture. The Treaty will also help to prevent violations of key economic, social and cultural rights, reduce the diversion of human and economic resources from sustainable development and poverty reduction efforts, and reduce the flow of weapons to criminals and terrorists.

The worldwide Control Arms campaign, with the support of hundreds of civil society organisations and more than a million people via the 'Million Faces Petition', has raised awareness, changed public opinion, and pressured parliaments and governments to set up an Arms Trade Treaty. So far more than 50 governments have publicly stated their support for such a treaty and more have stated their support for legally binding transfer controls. The Arms Trade Treaty that will create minimum global standards for arms transfers, in order to prevent the transfer of those arms likely to be used to seriously violate human rights, fuel conflict or hold back development. Argentina, Australia, Costa Rica, Finland, Japan, Kenya and the UK have circulated a draft UN resolution to start this process. Arms Trade Treaty refers to better respect for international law, including the UN Charter and international humanitarian law. This treaty should also include international human rights law to save a significant number of lives.

A Global Trade

Global trade in arms increases since 1999; global military spending has reached an unprecedented $1,058.9 billion, which is roughly 15 times annual international aid expenditure. In 2005, estimated global spending on arms alone was 34 per cent higher than in 1996. Global military spending is increasing and expanding the market for the global arms trade. This growth shows no signs of reversal as the United States and other countries have started the 'war on terror'. The conflicts in Iraq, Afghanistan and the Middle East among others, and the increased military spending by all the low-income countries would increase the global trade in arms and military spending. **Botswana, the Democratic Republic of Congo, Nigeria, Rwanda, Sudan and Uganda are among those that doubled their military spending between 1985 and 2000**.[4]

In 2002–03, the governments of Bangladesh, Nepal and Pakistan incurred more expenditure on military than on healthcare. In Angola, the proportion of GDP devoted to military spending was doubled in two years rising to 4.2 per cent after its 27-year-long war ended in 2002.

---

[4] Smith D. (2003), "The Atlas of War and Peace", London: Earth Scan, P.25

In 2004, the US Congressional Research Service estimated that Asia, the Middle East, Latin America and Africa spent $22.5 billion on arms, 8 per cent more than they did in 2003 ($20.8 billion). This sum would have enabled those countries to put every child in school and to reduce child mortality by two-thirds by 2015. Overall, the international trade in arms, having shrunk in the 1990s, has been growing in parallel with the growth in total military spending. Between 2000 and 2004, the approximate value of arms exports increased from $35.6 billion to $53.3billion in 2003 at constant prices. This does not include most of the fast-growing trade in weapons components. Between 2000 and 2004, the top 100 companies reportedly increased their domestic and international sales of conventional weapons from $157 billion to $268 billion, an increase of nearly 60 per cent. 85 out of 100 top arms companies of the world were headquartered in the industrialized world in 2003. The Chinese arms companies were not included for want of sufficient data. The USA-based Boeing and Lockheed Martin topped the list with arms sales of $27.5 billion and $26.4 billion respectively.

The impact on human rights and development:

Without the international arms trade, many governments - without their own arms industry - would be unable to equip their armed forces and law enforcement agencies to meet legitimate defense and policing needs. But unlike most other legitimate trades, the arms trade has devastating consequences when it is not adequately controlled.

Despite a drop in the number of conflicts following the end of the Cold War, at least 35 conflicts are currently ongoing. The global trade maintains arms supplies to all of them, despite the serious and widespread violation of human rights and international humanitarian law by many belligerents. While weapons do not cause these conflicts, the continuing supply and misuse of easily available arms and ammunition fuels their continuation, and makes them more deadly. For example, while some weapons are manufactured in Sri Lanka, the steady international supply of weapons to both sides has significantly prolonged the country's internal conflict, which has claimed the lives of an estimated 65,000 people.[5]

Estimates of the annual number of deaths caused by armed violence range from 280,000 up to 378,000.[6] This takes into account non-conflict deaths caused by the use of arms by state security forces, as well as firearm homicide, firearm suicide and accidental shootings. In armed conflicts, there are almost invariably civilian deaths on all sides. Helicopters, combat aircraft and air-to-surface missiles supplied to Israel primarily by the USA, but often incorporating components supplied by other countries, have been used in the Occupied Territories resulting in hundreds of deaths and thousands of injuries, in apparent violation of international humanitarian law. Unlawfully killing including deliberate and reckless shooting, or attacks in densely populated residential areas is a common feature in this war-ravaged territory. At the same time, Palestinian armed groups have used rockets, explosive belts and other bombs to kill and injure hundreds of Israelis.

The global trade in weapons supplies arms to many of those who commit serious violations of human rights, such as extra judicial executions, torture, rape and sexual violence, and enforce displacement. Human rights standards including those binding in treaties and in international customary law apply both during armed conflict and during peacetime, but the

---

[5] Chris Smith, "In the Shadow of a Ceasefire: The Impacts of Small Arms Availability and Misuse in Sri Lanka", Small Arms Survey Occasional Paper No. 11, October 2003
[6] Small Arms Survey 2005, P. 230

proliferation and poor regulation of arms contributes to serious human rights violations by armed forces, police, security services, militias and other armed groups in many countries both before and after conflict. These violations often occur widely where small arms are readily available.

Recent research findings show that between one-third and three-quarters of all grave human rights violations and 85 per cent of killings reported by Amnesty International involve the use of small arms and light weapons.[7] Men, particularly young men, constitute the majority of both those who use and are killed with firearms. It is not just men who are the victims. Large numbers of women and girls suffer directly and indirectly from armed violence. Women are particularly at risk of certain crimes because of their gender – crimes such as violence in the home and rape. From Liberia to Cambodia, easy access to guns has reportedly increased the incidence of rape.

In Haiti, a high number of rapes are directly linked to the proliferation of arms. Rape, a crime is committed at gunpoint. Both exporters and importers of arms have a duty to behave responsibly. In addition to irresponsible sales contributing to serious human rights violations, irresponsible arms purchases waste the resources of poor countries whose governments should be prioritizing poverty reduction.

In 2002, some of the poorest countries in the world spent more on their military than on health: an average of 3.7 per cent compared to 2.4 per cent of GDP. The same trend is seen in most of the low-income countries even in 2009.

---

[7] Amnesty International Documentation from a sample of ten countries for 12 years (1991 – 2002): Algeria, Brazil, Chechnya / Russia, Colombia, DR Congo, East Temor, Egypt, France, Jamaica and Nepal

Nuclear Weapons

Writing as far back as June 1957, well before he strode the Washington Beltway, Henry Kissinger cautioned that "except for the two explosions of now obsolete weapons over Hiroshima and Nagasaki, no nuclear weapons have ever been set off in wartime; there exists therefore, no body of experience on which to draw. To a considerable extent the impact of the new weapon on strategy, on policy, indeed on survival, depends on our interpretation of their significance."

The empirical experience and related database about nukes are very limited and almost all extrapolations are made from Hiroshima and the experience of deterrence during the cold war. It is one of the ironies of the nuclear age that righteous certitude is inversely proportional to actual experience and the interpretative aspect gets even less attention.

World Peace is possible if the following countries control their land acquiring appetite. Those possess nuclear arms are designated as super powers. They claim membership in all world organizations; try to make international laws and rules to suit their aspirations; detect terms to the United Nations; follow dubious roles in all the low-income countries through funding and encouraging Public Private Partnership Projects, and encourage nongovernmental organizations to interfere in administration; and poke their noses in others' internal affairs for their own gain at the cost of the poor people and indebted countries.

If the super power countries reduce their defense budgets by 5 percent only and donate the amount to the indebted countries, the world can do away with hunger, poverty, illiteracy, diseases, war, annexations, and terrorism.

These countries are well equipped with Weapons of Mass Destruction. Some of them are in possession of nuclear arms and ammunitions. For example:

Weapons of Mass Destruction: The countries which possess Weapons of Mass Destruction are: Albania, Algeria, Argentina, Brazil, Bulgaria, Canada, PR China, France, Germany, India, Iran, Iraq, Israel, Japan, Netherlands, Pakistan, Poland, Romania, Russia, Saudi Arabia, South Africa, Sweden, Syria, Taiwan (ROC), United Kingdom, United States

The Nuclear–armed States are: The United States, United Kingdom, China, Pakistan, South Africa, Russia, France, Israel and North Korea

Nuclear Club Countries: The United States, Russia, the United Kingdom, France and China

Nuclear Explosions have thundered the humanity, states and the world. It challenges the very existence of people, plants and animal kingdom. It is a difficult task to identify the causes of these anti-human activities of the governments and scientists, who have planned for destruction of this beautiful world. The countries, which have made nuclear explosions to test their power, are:

(a) **The United States of America** has undertaken 1054 tests (involving 1151 devices and 331 atmospheric tests). The US has 2623 active warheads and a total number of 9400 warheads.
(b) **Soviet Union** has conducted 715 tests involving 969 devices. Russia has 13, 000 warheads.
(c) **France** has completed 210 tests including 50 atmospheric and 160 underground tests. The country possesses 300 warheads.

(d) **United Kingdom** completed 45 tests including 21 tests in Australian territory. The UK has 185 warheads.
(e) **China** has completed 45 tests including 23 atmospheric and 22 underground tests. China has 240 warheads.
(f) **India** has completed six under ground tests. It has 60 – 80 warheads.
(g) **Pakistan** has confirmed two underground tests.
(h) **Israel** possesses nuclear weapons. It has 80 warheads.
(i) **South Korea** possesses nuclear power.
(j) **North Korea** has less than 10 warheads and has already test fired twice.
(k) **Iran** claims that it possesses nuclear power.

Geneva Declaration

In June 2006, 42 governments, ranging from Brazil to Indonesia, Japan and Nigeria to South Africa, signed up to the 'Geneva Declaration on Armed Violence and Development', resolving to 'promote sustainable security and a culture of peace by taking action to reduce armed violence and its negative impact on socio-economic and human development'. The suggestions are:

Armed violence destroys lives and livelihoods, breed's insecurity, fear and terror, and has a profoundly negative impact on human development. Whether in situations of conflict or crime, it imposes enormous costs on states, communities and individuals. It closes schools, empties markets; burdens health services, destroys families, weakens the rule of law, and prevents humanitarian assistance from reaching people in need. It threatens permanently the respect of human rights.[8]

---

[8] The Geneva Declaration on Armed Violence and Development, June 7, 2006

The signatories resolved to 'take further action to deal effectively both with the supply of, and demand for, small arms and light weapons promoting the development of further international instruments, including legally binding ones.' Many developing country governments such as Bangladesh, Costa Rica and Kenya are now saying that one such instrument is an international Arms Trade Treaty.

The arms trade is not just larger, but now more 'globalize' than ever before, as a result of the continuing and cumulative transformation of the industry since at least the early 1990s. The top 100 arms companies no longer simply build weapons. They integrate components made all over the world. The global spread of arms power has become potentially catastrophic. Like products in most other industries, very few pieces of military equipment are now manufactured entirely in one country. Instead, components are sourced from across the globe, production facilities are set up in new, often developing, countries, brokers and dealers flourish, technology is traded, and arms companies produce their branded weapons in many locations. When major Western arms companies co-operate with partners in other countries they can develop and penetrate new markets, while their partners can gain access to cutting-edge technology.[9]

In the middle Ages, it took two centuries for cutting-edge arms technology (gunpowder) to be transferred across the world, from China to Europe. In the twenty-first century, it is very much quicker. Globalization of arms trade has created globalization of war, mass killing, mass poverty and obstructed world peace. Hence, international Arms Trade Treaty must be implemented among all the member

---

[9] Trends in Arms Marketing, Jane's Intelligence Review, 1 May 1997

countries of United Nations to usher permanent world peace. And it is imperative.[10]

Christian Peace Witness

Matt Guynn, a coordinator of peace, expressed that Church of the Brethren members from as far away as California and as close as Virginia traveled to Washington, D.C., for the Christian Peace Witness on the evening of Friday, March 16, 2007. Brethren also traveled from Kansas, Indiana, Ohio, Pennsylvania, Vermont, and New York, among other states. The witness marked the fourth anniversary of the US invasion of Iraq.

More than 210 Brethren participated in the events of the weekend, among some 3,500 Christians from other traditions. The group gathered to repent of their complicity with the war and to seek the end of the US occupation of Iraq. A hand holding a candle in the darkness was the central image for the witness. On Earth Peace, a Church of the Brethren agency, and the Brethren Witness/Washington Office of the Church of the Brethren General Board, was among the organizations sponsoring the witness. On Earth Peace staff Matt Guynn and Susanna Farahat provided logistics for peacekeeper training before the event.

The Christian Peace Witness[11] began with an ecumenical worship service at the National Cathedral. Candles shone as they were carried into the cathedral's immense stone hall by representatives of 15 denominations and more than 30 partner

---

[10] Oxfam International; The International Action Network on Small Arms; Control Arms Campaign (2006)

[11] News line: Church of the Brethren Members Attend Christian Peace Witness, April 2, 2007 Church of the Brethren News Service Cheryl Brumbaugh- Cayford, News Director 800-323-8039 ext. 260 -- cobnews@brethren.org

organizations, including Phil Jones, director of the Brethren Witness/Washington Office, and Verdena Lee, a physician representing On Earth Peace. Testimony and messages from US soldiers, Iraqi citizens, Abu Ghraib detainees, and members of Christian Peacemaker Teams were shared. "Hear what the Spirit is saying to the churches," was the refrain repeated again and again. In a four-mile candlelight procession down the hill from the cathedral and surrounding the White House, participants expressed support for soldiers, a desire to end the occupation, and a prayer for the just rebuilding of Iraq. In nonviolence training before the procession, participants spiritually prepared themselves to surround the White House with the light of Christ, and some prepared to risk arrest by entering restricted space around the White House.

At the White House, 222 people were arrested including at least four members of the Church of the Brethren--Esther Moller Ho, Phil Jones, Phil Rieman, and Illana Naylor.

At least 60 Brethren and friends joined together for breakfast following the witness, organized by the Brethren Witness/Washington Office at Washington City Church of the Brethren. Art Gish, recently returned from working with Christian Peacemaker Teams (CPT) in Iraq, was the keynote speaker. He and his wife Peggy Gish have rotated in and out of Iraq and Hebron as members of CPT. Brethren at the breakfast collected more than $480 for the work of CPT and $120 in support of the fines given to the four Brethren who were arrested. While major events like the Christian Peace Witness can be moments of media focus, spiritual formation for nonviolent followers of Jesus requires long term organizing and prayer at the congregational level. The trip to Washington was the culmination of such a process for Jan Long, pastor for congregational life at Beacon Heights Church of the Brethren in Fort Wayne, Ind., who accompanied a delegation of 10 members and friends of her congregation.

In the months leading up to the invasion of Iraq in 2003, Beacon Heights formed a group called Persistent in Prayer for Peace. The Beacon Heights group studied the work of theologian Walter Wink, participated in local groups with witnesses related to the Iraq war, and participated in other community peace events. The Church of the Brethren is a Christian denomination committed to continuing the work of Jesus peacefully and simply, and to living out its faith in community. The denomination is based in the Anabaptist and Pietistic faith traditions and is one of the three Historic Peace Churches. It celebrates its 300th anniversary in 2008. It counts about 130,000 members across the United States and Puerto Rico, and has missions and sister churches in Nigeria, Brazil, the Dominican Republic, Haiti, and India.

The World Peace March

Thousands of activists would undertake Peace March for a period over three months to demand an end to war. The World March for Peace and Non-violence began on October 2, 2009 in New Zealand with symbolic acts all over the world.

The Peace March coincides with the birth anniversary of Mahatma M. K. Gandhi who preached 'Nonviolence and Peace' to the world community and showed the path of achieving independence without war and bloodshed.

Organizers expect that the Peace March will continue for 98 days, cross 90 countries and 100 cities in five continents. The march, which ends on January 2, 2010 in the Aconcagua snow peak in Argentina, would cover 160,000 kilometers. Participants will cross various climate zones and seasons, from hot summers in the tropical regions and deserts to a

Siberian winter. A permanent group of 100 participants will do the complete route. The participants are scheduled to meet with political leaders, organizations, and civil societies to demand dismantling of nuclear arsenals, immediate withdrawal of troops from occupied countries, and the progressive disarmament of conventional weaponry as well as the signing of non-aggression pacts, and the renounce to war to resolve conflicts.

The World-Without-War group will include Uruguayan writer Eduardo Galeano, US linguist and philosopher Noam Chomsky, Presidents of Argentina, Bolivia, Chile and Ecuador and artists like Juanes, and several Nobel Peace Prize winners. It will be a part of the Humanist movement and will participate in the march. Students, human rights advocates, artists and other citizens launched an inauguration of the march in Lima, Peru, on October 2, 2009 in the Pueblo Libre district.

Madeleine John, a Peruvian and a member of World Without Wars says that the greatest demand of this march is for dismantling of nuclear arms, end of wars and the reduction of conventional arms because they are completely disproportionate.

Another member, Galeano says that while three children die every minute from a curable disease, US $3 million is spent per minute on the military industry. While we see rampant poverty and so much money are spent on weapons to kill others.

We must undertake peace-marches though out the world and chant: **No more violence and no more war between ourselves.**

The Obama Peace Factor

The United States Arms Control Association has expressed deep satisfaction for the 'Nobel Prize for

Peace 2009' on Barrack Obama, the President of United States of America.

The communiqué says: "The Peace Prize is a recognition of the need to transform - not simply tinker with - outdated thinking - about nuclear weapons, unless the President Obama and other world leaders succeed in significantly reducing the role and number of nuclear weapons to better fit the realities of the 21st century, we will not succeed in preventing the use and spread of the world's deadliest weapons".

Senior and bipartisan national security leaders in the United States and abroad have praised the decision of the Nobel Committee. It is because Mr. Barrack Obama's call for nuclear disarmament, non-proliferation and nuclear materials security initiatives has been considered as the concrete steps towards world peace.

A growing bipartisan consensus is that we can only reduce the degree of nuclear weapons with bold, concrete US leadership to reduce the role of these weapons and to strengthen global nonproliferation rules.

The Nobel Committee attached special importance to Obama's vision of and work for a world without nuclear weapons. Beginning with his April 5, 2009 speech in Prague outlining his concrete action agenda to his leadership in achieving the unanimous UN Security council Resolution on nonproliferation and disarmament on September 24, 2009 Obama has put the goal and the task of eliminating the nuclear weapons threat front and center on the national and international agenda.

The ACA has highlighted the importance of results on steps begun by Obama to reduce the role of nuclear weapons in US national security strategy; restart talks with Russia on further verifiable reductions in the two countries bloated Cold War nuclear stockpiles; aggressively pursue OS Senate's ratification of the Comprehensive Nuclear Test Ban Treaty, jumpstart efforts to negotiate a new, verifiable treaty to end the production of fissile materials; and engage in direct diplomacy with Iran and north Korea to bring their nuclear programs into compliance with their treaty obligations and compliments.

The United States Arms Control Association (USACA) expresses that in selecting President Obama for Nobel Peace Prize, the Nobel Committee reminds them of the work that still needs to be done to reduce and eliminate the nuclear weapon threat. [12]

Conclusion

In short, there are crises in most of the countries because of political and religious rivalry, political ambition, corruption, boundary disputes, corrupt election practices, military coup, poverty related issues, black money, constitutional amendments and foreign funding. These factors have created crises and wars, which could be politically and economically addressed for ushering peace everywhere. The arms trade has put the entire globe for an emerging catastrophe. But world peace can be achieved through sanction of Arms Trade Treaty and conferring more power to the United Nations.

The United Nations is now working as a voluntary organization; an organization with begging bowls, and is controlled by big bosses. It acts as an advisor without the power of awarding punishment. This highest organization of the world can be successful in

---

[12] US Arms Control Body Now Expects Nobel Laureate Obama to Push Non-proliferation, the Pioneer, Bhubaneswar, October 12, 2009, P16

rendering its duties through amendments of its charters and full support of industrialized countries.

The **'World Peace Council'** should be a part of the United Nations to organize peace movement, award peace prizes and make dialogues with the heads of different countries. The UN should appoint Peace Representatives or open branches in all countries and states to advise the governments and collect feedbacks.

Most of the UN organizations are working just as NGOs and their work does not help to the United Nations, countries or people. So these organizations should be audited, evaluated, dismantled or be made independent organizations; these cancerous outgrowths debars the working of the United Nations. The United Nations should prioritize in solving war and stabilizing peace process.

The UN should be the 'leader of the leaders' in the twenty-first century in establishing ONE WORLD FAMILY for securing peace, security, happiness, progress and should ensure that none should be a victim of hunger, disease, injustice and war.

The Nobel Committee has rightly awarded the Nobel Peace Prize to Mr. Barrack Hussein Obama, the President of the United States of America in October 2009. He is capable of attempting the peace process for securing WORLD PEACE.

The world needs peace, progress and prosperity. And, it is possible even today.

+++++

Chapter - II

HISTORICAL WARS

Peace cannot be kept by force. It can only be achieved by understanding. -- Albert Einstein

The World history includes Java man and astronauts, arrows and computers, wars and treaties, discoveries and inventions, monarchy and democracy; it also includes from evolution of religions and faiths to religion-based wars and terrorism, social life to individuality and Dark Age to globalize world. Man discovered the art of living through identifying seeds for raising plants near river valleys, domesticated cow, sheep, goat, pig and dog; discovered water, air, fire, soil and light for peaceful living and worshipped Sun and Moon. The Neolithic period witnessed development of agriculture, religion, family and state.

Majority of people in the twenty-first century desire to live in peace, prefer brotherhood and exchange technology and culture but a small number of people particularly the fundamentalists, governments, reformers and youths are acting against world peace either to garner political power or for hatred ness for other faiths. All religions are based on sound principles and dictums. All persons are good and they need world peace. But there exist some misgivings, wrong interpretations or too much aspiration to occupy power, which cause turmoil in the society, state, country, and world. Permanent peace is possible in our planet if religious fundamentalists soften their anger over other faiths, the states delay the decisions to wage wars and youths are employed or engaged in peace-building processes. The real danger in this century comes from corporate world; which needs to occupy all the land and water masses for their own gain. The international organizations and world organizations should be neutral to caste, creed, colour, or religion. These organizations should work for the people, society and culture. None should be deprived of human rights, legal rights, and feel suffocated. Hunger and injustice must be scrapped from dictionaries to usher world peace.

In this chapter, Great Wars That Challenged World Peace, World War I, Peace Treatise, New National Identities, Blood Bath of Soldiers and Civilians, World War II, Chronological Events, World War II Casualties, and Thus Speak Historians have been discussed.

Great Wars that challenged World Peace:

The world has witnessed both sporadic and long term wars since the last ten thousand years. Each day war is fought between rival groups or countries. Wars and treaties are common through out the last two thousand years. Some of the wars are fought for a longer period or for a number of times for the same cause. The world history has incorporated 722 important war fares that had caused more casualties and created unprecedented havoc for both the rival groups. These wars have changed the boundaries of kingdoms or countries. Wars are being fought between countries in this twenty-first century too.

Wars are not fought with the approval of people. The governments are responsible for all wars. But the victims are the innocent people and young soldiers. The soldiers sacrifice both family life and in some cases they dedicate their life for the country.

The mythological wars between Sri Rama and Ravan in Sri Lanka, Battle of Kurukshetra (Maha Bharat War) in India, Battle of Zhuolu, and Trojan War were also fought much before historians started writing about wars. These wars are reported by great scholars, poets, and authors and were accepted by the archaeologists, historians and the general public as true events.

The mythological wars teach us value of life and conclude that peace cannot be achieved through war.

Prehistory - 1000 BC:

The world history has recorded 12 war fares from pre-history to 1000 BC such as border dispute between Umma and Lagash, Xia-Shang war in China, Shang-Zhou War in China and other seven wars as conquests, attacks or invasions from 2450 BC to 1046 BC.

999 BC - 1 BC:

During this period **34 wars** were fought out of which the Sicilian War was fought for thrice during 480 BC – 307 BC, Samnite War for thrice during 343 BC – 290 BC, the Syrian War for four times during 274 BC-200 BC, the Punic War for thrice between 264 BC – 146 BC, Macedonian War for thrice during 215 BC – 168 BC, Roman – Syrian War for five times during 191

BC–188 BC and Servile War for thrice during 135 BC–71 BC. Similarly, the Mithridatic Wars were fought thrice (89 BC - 63 BC), and the Roman Civil War for five times during 44 BC - 30 BC and Julious Caesar's Gallic wars were fought during 58 BC - 50 BC and Julious Caesar's Roman invasion of Britain during 55 BC–54 BC.

AD 1 - 999 AD: During the first Millennium the world witnessed **46 fierce battles** in Britain, Rome, China, North America, Korea, Arab, Italy and European countries. The Jewish- Roman wars caused heavy tolls during three fights during 66 AD –135 AD. Similarly the Parthian war was caused thrice from 161 AD to 217 AD. The Perso–Turkic war also occurred for thrice during 588 AD, 619AD, and 627AD. This Millennium also witnessed Islamic Civil War and Islamic Conquests thrice during 633AD-651AD, 639AD-641AD and 711AD-718AD. War of Three Kingdoms (220AD-265AD) and War of Eight Princess (291AD-306AD) were fought in China. Moreover, there occurred Civil War in China (Five Dynasties and Ten Kingdoms) during 907 AD - 960 AD. The Korean Civil War occurred during 660–677 AD and 892–936 AD.

1000 AD– 1099 AD: The World witnessed **13 wars** during 1000 –1099 including second Goryeo-Khitan War in 1010, third Goryeo-Khitan War in 1019, the Battle of Clontarf, Ireland in 1014, Early Nine-Years' War in 1051-1063 and Spanish Reconquista during 1081–1492. Moreover, the First Crusades started in 1096 till 1099.

1100 AD - 1199 AD: The Crusade War continued till 1291 in other words this war continued for almost two centuries and was fought for nine times between 1096 and 1291. Perhaps the Twelfth Century was preferably a peace century with only six wars.

1200 AD – 1299 AD: The world witnessed **18 wars** during the thirteenth century. The Mongols carried out invasions to China, Cental Asia, Rus, Volga Bulgaria, Korea, Europe, Japan, and Poland. The Mongol invasion of China continued from 1211 to 1276. The Mongol invansion of Central Asia (1218-1222), Mongol invansion of Rus (1223-1480), Mongol invansion of Volga Bulgaria (1223-1236), Mongol invansion of Korea (1231-1273), Mongol invansion of Europe (1241-1242), Mongol invansion of Japan (1274-1281) and Mongol invansion of Poland (1287) clearly speaks bravery but war-mongering attitude of the people of Mongolia.

In short, the Mongolians were very powerful and phisically strong to venture to fight most of the countries accessible to their countries. There were also two Baron' war (1215-1217, and 1264-1267), Conquest of Estonia (1208-1227), Russo-Swedish War (1240), Teutonic-Novoqorod War (1242), French conquest of Sicily (1266-1268), War of the Sicilian Vespers (1284-1302) and War of Scottish Independence (1296-1328) in this century. Of course, two wars continued during the next century.

1300 AD– 1399 AD: There were **16 fierce fighting wars** in the world during fourteenth century. It witnessed Swiss War of Independence (1315), Iris War of Independence (1315-1318), and the Second War of Scottish Independence (1332-1333). It means that people wanted self-respect and wanted to free themselves from the misrule of kings or monarchs. During this century, the Peasant Revolt in Flanders (1323-1328), War of Eight Saints (1375-1378), Ottoman-Serbian War (1386-1389) and Muscovite-Mongol War (1380) were also other important fierce fighting battles. Moreover, Byzantine- Ottoman War (1301-1453), Hundred Years' War (1337-1453), Nanbuko-Cho period (1336-1392), Breton War of Succession (1341-1364) and Tokhtamysh-Timur War (1385-1399) were fought for decades or even for a century. That indicates that war continues from grandfather to grand children.

1400 – 1499: There were **25 war fares** in the fifteenth century such as Ottoman- Timurid War (1400-1402), Chinese Conquest of Vietnam (1405-1427), Teutonic-Polish War (1409-1410), Oei Invasion (1419), Hussite War (1420-1436), Ottoman siege of Constantinople (1422), War in Lombardy (1425-1454), Albania resistance against the invading Ottomans (1443-1468), Fall of Constantinople (1453), Thirteen Years' War (1454-1466), War of Roses (1455-1485), Ottoman siege of Belgrade (1456), Ottoman- Wallachian War (1460-1462), Onion War (1467-1477), Wars of Senqoku Period in Japan (1467-1603), First Swedish-Danish War (1471), Burgundian Wars (1474-1477), Moscow-Novgorod War (1478), Ottoman siege of Rhodes (1480), War of Ferrara (1482-1484) and Italian Wars (1494-1559). The Italian Wars include Charles VIII's Italian War and Louis XII's War with Milan. Moreover, there were First Russo-Swedish War (1496-1499), Swabian War (1499), Ottoman-Venetian War (1499-1503), and Third Turkish-Venetian War (1499-1503). In short, history speaks that victory in wars was treated as achievements and earned prestige to the emperors but loss in wars was treated as inefficiency, mismanagement of the weak rulers and loss of kingdom in the hands of the enemy. Moreover, countries like China, Japan, Italy, Russia and Turkey were involved in wars during this century. The Ottoman Wars were instituted in fifteenth, sixteenth and seventeenth century.

1500-1599: There were **61 important wars** in the sixteenth century. The countries involved in wars during this century were Italy, Poland, Spain, Sweden, Hungary, France, Switzerland, Peru, Japan, Korea, Ireland, Fin land, Mexico, and Demark. This century witnessed Ottoman Civil War (1509-1513), Hungarian Civil War (1526-1528), Swiss Civil War

(1531) and Swedish War of Liberation (1521-1523). Moreover, there were Wars of Religion in France eight times during 1562 - 1598. The wars continued for two–three years in six occasions, the Seventh War of Religion (Lovers' War) was fought in 1580 and the Eighth War of Religion continued from 1585 to 1598. The Dutch War of Independence continued during 1568–1648, which is known as Eighty Years' War. The Japanese invasion of Korea and China during 1592-1598 is regarded as a great war in Asia. The Mogul conquest of India through First Panipath War (1526) has made Muslims' dynasty in India. During the twentieth century, the increasing population of Muslims in India caused the division of India into three countries (India, Pakistan and Bangladesh).

1600 - 1699: During this century **83 wars were** fought and particularly countries like Poland, Sweden, Turkey, Russia, Denmark, China and Mongolia had fought fierce fighting wars and as result of a number of kingdoms have been conquered or annexed through wars. In two cases, the wars ended within a year but in 81 cases, wars continued for a number of years. For example, the Polish-Swedish War (1600-1611), Turkish-Persian War (1602-1612, 1616-1618), Manchu Conquest of China (1620-1659), Franco-Spanish War (1635-1659), Catalan Revolt (1640-1656), Portuguese War of Independence (1640-1668), Mauritanian Thirty Years' War (1644-1674), Sixth Turkish-Venctian War (1645-1669), and Russo-Turkish War (1676-1681, 1686-1700) were fought for more than a decade. Moreover, the British Civil Wars continued from 1639 to 1652. The Deluge / Northern wars (1648-1660) continued involving Poland, Sweden, and Braden burg, Russia and Transylvania, Denmark and Norway. In short, these wars changed the boundary of most of the countries at cost of peace and human sacrifice.

1700-1799: The eighteenth century also witnessed **82 fierce fighting** wars in the world leaving aside small warfare among small states. This century witnessed wars, campaigns, rebellions, revolts, civil wars, uprisings, and wars of succession and revolutionary wars. Some of the important wars were Great Northern Wars (1700-1721), Fox Wars (1712-1714, 1728-1737), Austro-Turkish War (1716-1718, 1787-1791), Russo-Persian War (1722-1723), Turkey-Persian War (1722-1727, 1730-1736, and 1743-1747) and Franco-Russian War (1798-1799, 1799-1801). The Cape Frontier Wars occurred for nine times during 1779 to 1879 and it continued for 110 years.

Similarly War of Spanish Succession was fought twice (1701-1714, 1702-1713), and War of Austrian Succession was fought in seven places (1739 – 1748), War of Polish Succession (1736-1739, 1737-1739) was fought in two places and War of Bavarian Succession was fought during 1777-1779. Moreover, the American War of Independence (1775-1783) constitutes Anglo-French War, Anglo-Spanish War and Fourth Anglo-Dutch Wars. The French Revolutionary Wars (1792-1802) covered War of the First Coalition, Franco- Prussian War, Franco-Austrian War, Franco-Spanish War, Franco-Dutch War and Franco-British War. The Dutch Civil War took place during 1785-1787.

1800-1899: During the nineteenth century **202 major war fares** were fought in the world. The Napoleonic Wars (1803-1815) could explain that a single man could also aspire to be the monarch of mankind. All wars are important as they can change the geography of nations. The wars destroy peace and incur heavy expenditure on arms and ammunitions; defense expenditure, which could have been utilized for productive purposes, causes heavy casualties. The Bolivar's War (1811-1825), Seminole Wars (1817-1858), Several Maori land Wars in News land (1843-1872), and Arcola War (1873-1904) were some of the historical wars fought in the century.

The century witnessed 'war of independence' in many kingdoms / countries. The War of Haitian Independence (1802-1805), Vellore (India) Battle of Independence (1806), Bolivian Independence War (1809-1825), Colombian War of Independence (1810-1819), Argentina War of Independence (1810-1816), Mexican War of Independence (1810-1821), Venezuelan War of Independence (1371-1812), Chilean War of Independence (1814-1826), Greek War of Independence (1821-1831), Peruvian War of Independence (1824), Italian War of Independence (1848-1866), First War of Independence of India (Indian Mutiny) of 1857-1858 and Cuban First War of Independence (1895-1898) were fought during this century.

In this century, fierce fighting had happened in Anglo-Russian War (1807-1812), Russo-Turkish War (1806-1812, 1828-1829, 1877-1878), Russo-Persian War (1804-1813, 1825-1828) and Russian Conquest of Central Asia (1860-1873). There were civil wars, uprisings, revolutions, and revolts in different countries. Moreover, there were War of Oranges (1801), Gunboat War (1807-1814), Black War (1804-1835), Punjab War (1810-1820), Liberal Wars (1828-1834), Black Hawk War (18320, Pastry War (1838), Honey War (1839), Snake War (1864-1868), Red Cloud's War (1866-1868), Red River War (1874-1875), Black Hills War (1876-1877) and Gun War (1880-1881). In short, people fought for independence or at least expressed their desire to live in peace through out the globe.

1900 – 1999: The twentieth century witnessed growth of inventions, communication, education, and transport, flow of goods, knowledge sharing, and mushrooming of international organizations. This century witnessed massive growth in agricultural sector, industrial sector and services sector. Hence, the world became smaller day by day. It was expected that humanity would grow faster; the rich should extend assistance to the poor and the downtrodden and ill-fated people around the globe. Perhaps our intelligence and activities have been mis-utilized and we have become more selfish and arrogant.

There occurred 240 major wars during the twentieth century including 35 ongoing wars, which the United Nations or world bodies could not solve even during the first decade of the twenty-first century.

The twentieth century witnessed two WORLD WARS and gave rise to guerrilla warfare, terrorist movement, Naxalites movement and Maoist attack, which had thundered the very existence of humanity and the whole world. In short, seven billion people, environment, forest, animals, and property all over the globe are not safe. This twenty-first century has made world peace at a stake.

We can have lasting peace in this world provided if we try to breath, think, aspire, and live peacefully and donate few minutes for the welfare of people living unknown and unseen and leading painful life away from us.

The past losses cannot be restored but we have the ability to secure permanent world peace through perseverance, friendship and sacrifice today and tomorrow.

There is no need to surrender but there is need to delay anger, hatred, quarrel and action against other faith, religion, region or country.

The world witnesses wars, civil wars, invasions, uprisings, conflicts, insurgencies, revolutions, crises, emergencies, troubles, annexations, armed conflicts, rebellions, violence's, and bombings in different countries of the world in this century. Moreover, the world now faces strikes, road blockades, firings, flag marches, and killings of innocent people by the radical groups. We are living in a world, where none is safe including the Presidents / Prime Ministers of sovereign independent countries.

The road to peace is not closed forever. We can convert horrible situations into an 'abode of peace' even today.

There were **51 civil wars** during 1900 – 1970. These were: Persian Civil War (1908-1909), Nicaraguan Civil War (1909-1911, 1927-1933), Mexican Civil War (1911-1914), Russian Civil War (1917–1922), Finnish Civil War (1918), Portuguese Monarchist Civil War (1919), Irish Civil War (1922-1923), Chinese Civil War (1927-1937, 1945-1949), Afghan Civil War (1929, 1989-1992, 1992-1996, 1996-2001), Ecuadoran Civil War (1932), Spanish Civil War (1936-1939), Greek Civil War (1946-1949), Paraguayan Civil War (1947), Palestinian Civil War (1947-1948), Costar can Civil War (1948), Indonesian Civil War (1950-1961), Laotian Civil War (1962-1975), Cambodian Civil War (1967-1975), Sudanese Civil War (1955-1972, 1983-2005)), Columbian Civil War (1958-1987), Guatemalan Civil War (1960-1996), Yemen Civil War (1962-1970), Dominican Civil War (1965), Chadian Civil War (1965-1993), and Nigerian Civil War (1967-1970).

There were other **25 civil wars** from 1970 to 1999. These are: Ethiopian Civil War (1975-1991), Angolan Civil War (1974-2002), Lebanese Civil War (1975-1991), Mozambican Civil War (1977-2002), Chadian Civil War (1979-1982), El Salvador Civil War (1980-1992), Sri Lankan Civil War (1983-2009), Second Ugandan Civil War (1987-2008 ongoing), Somali Civil War (1988-2008 ongoing), Liberian Civil War (1989-1996, 1999-2003), Rwandan Civil War (1990-1994), Togolese Civil War (1991-1992), Djiboutian Civil War (1991-1994), Algerian Civil War (1991-2002),

Georgian Civil War (1991-1993), Sierra Leone Civil War (1991-2002), Tajikistan Civil War (1992-1997), Burundi Civil War (1993-1999), Yemen Civil War (1994) and Nepal Civil War (1996-2006).

Some of the invasions that took place in the twentieth century were: Red Army Invasion of Georgia (1921), Japanese Invasion of Manchuria (1931-1932), Hungarian Invasion of the Carpatho – Ukrain (1939), Italian Invasion of Albania (1939), Chinese Invasion/ Occupation of Tibet (1950-2007 ongoing), Bay of Pigs Invasion (1961), Turkish Invasion of Cyprus (1974), Israeli Invasion of Lebanon (1978, 1982), Soviet Invasion of Afghanistan (1979-1989), USA Invasion of Grenada (1983) and USA Invasion of Panama (1989-1990).

The USA undertook bombings in Afghanistan, Sudan and Iraq in 1998. The USA also attacked Iraq and arrested Saddam Hussein, the deposed President and dictator of Iraq on December 13, 2003 and he was executed on December 30, 2006. USA has deputed 1, 40,000 defense personnel in uniform to establish democracy in Iraq and to depose Saddam Hussein. In this war 3,000 USA soldiers died in Iraq from March 2003 up to 2006-year end.

During the Twentieth century, there were 11 wars in the first decade (1900-1909), 29 wars in second decade, 21 wars in the third decade, 17 wars in fourth decade, 17 wars in '50s, 33 wars in '60s, 24 wars in '70s, 30 Wars in '80s, and 43 wars in the '90s. In the Twenty-first century six wars have fought and other 42 wars are ongoing wars, which are now in force.

This century witnessed two fierce fighting wars namely World War I (1914-1918) and World War II (1939-1945), which were fought by a number of countries and were more disastrous. Both the wars challenged the very existence of our survival. The

World War II even used Atomic Bombs to win over the enemies.

Peace achieved through wars disappears within a short period because the winning country wages war against another country or countries till it looses its existence. But we strongly feel that peace can avoid war always.

In short, as civilization advanced, the researchers invented war weapons and equipped the military establishment with destructive war equipments and arsenals. This caused the rich and powerful countries to acquire the art of conquering low-income countries and poor people for exploitation.

It is this world, where slave trade was treated as a profitable business for centuries. Now also rich countries play with the life of hungry people of low-income countries. Can't we find ways for avoiding wars in this beautiful world? Can't we make attempts to stop wars forever for the benefits of human beings?

World War I (1914 – 1919)

Europe was divided into two armed camps: the Entente Powers and the Central Power. The most sinister interpretation is that Germany planned an aggressive war. In December 1912 the Kaiser held a meeting at which some historians believe it was decided to go to war and the coincidence with the actual outbreak of war in August 1914 is remarkable.

In 1914 fate seemed to have offered Germany the opportunity to turn dreams into imperial reality. The gamble failed and the Germans were themselves defeated by the Western Allies. Having played for everything, the German leadership lost everything. Britain went to war because it saw a German victory as a threat to its security.

An Allied victory led to the maintenance and even extension of liberal democracy in Europe. The old European empires were under strain, and would soon collapse. Based on the encouragement of democracy and nationalism, accompanied by liberal capitalism, Wilson's timing was perfect. The old European empires were under strain, and would soon collapse. The Bolsheviks seized power in Russia only weeks before the 14 Points speech and Marxist-Leninism was to prove a powerful, similarly universalism, and rival to liberal democracy for the rest of the 20th century.

Far from being fought over trivial issues, World War I must be seen in the context of an attempt by an aggressive, militarist state to establish hegemony over Europe, extinguishing democracy as a by-product. A world in which Imperial Germany had won World War I would have been even worse.[13]

About 8 million men surrendered and were held in POW camps during the war. All nations pledged to follow the Hague Convention on fair treatment of prisoner of war. In general, a POW's rate of survival was much higher than their peers at the front.[14]

Individual surrenders were uncommon. Large units usually surrendered en-mass. At the Battle of Tannenberg 92,000 Russians surrendered. When the besieged garrison of Kaunas surrendered in 1915, 20,000 Russians became prisoners. Over half of Russian losses were prisoners (as a proportion of those captured, wounded or killed); for Austria 32 per cent, for Italy 26 per cent, for France 12 per cent, for

---

[13] Gary Sheffield, "The Origins of World War One", Early signs in Europe, British Broadcasting Corpora ration, March 1, 2002, web: http://www.bbc.co.uk/history

[14] Zieger, Robert H. (2001). *America's Great War: World War I and the American experience*. Lanham, Md: Rowman & Littlefield Publishers, 50. ISBN 0-8476-9645-6

Germany 9 per cent; for Britain 7 per cent. Prisoners from the Allied armies totalled about 1.4 million (not including Russia, which lost between 2.5 and 3.5 million men as prisoners.) From the Central Powers about 3.3 million men became prisoners.[15]

Germany held 2.5 million prisoners; Russia held 2.9 million and Britain and France held about 720,000. Most were captured just prior to the Armistice. The U.S. held 48,000. The most dangerous moment was the act of surrender, when helpless soldiers were sometimes gunned down. Once prisoners reached a camp, in general, conditions were satisfactory (and much better than in World War II), thanks in part to the efforts of the International Red Cross and inspections by neutral nations. Conditions were terrible in Russia, starvation was common for prisoners and civilians alike; about 15-20 percent of the prisoners in Russia died. In Germany food was in short supply, but only 5 percent died. [16]

The Ottoman Empire often treated POWs poorly. Some 11,800 British Empire soldiers, most of them Indians, became prisoners after the Siege of Kut, in Mesopotamia, in April 1916; 4,250 died in captivity.[17]

Although many were in very bad condition when captured, Ottoman officers forced them to march 1,100 kilometers (680 miles) to Anatolia. A survivor said: "we were driven along like beasts; to drop out was to die."[18] The survivors were then forced to build a railway through the Taurus Mountains. The most curious case occurred in Russia, where the prisoners

---

[15]Coast Guard in the North Atlantic War

[16] Gilbert, Martin, "The First World War: A Complete History", Clearwater: Owl Books, 306. ISBN0-8050-7617-4

[17] Jones, H. (2001), "Crucible of Power: A History of US Foreign Relations since 1897", Wilmington, Del: SR Books 80, ISBN 0-8420-2918-4

[18] Nova Scotia House of Assembly Committee on Veterans' Affairs

from the Czech Legion of the Austro-Hungarian army, were released in 1917. They re-armed themselves and briefly became a military and diplomatic force during the Russian Civil War.

Armenian Genocide: The ethnic cleansing of Armenians during the final years of the Ottoman Empire is widely considered genocide. The Turks accused the (Christian) Armenians of preparing to ally themselves with Russia and saw the entire Armenian population as an enemy. Most estimates are between 800,000 and 1.5 million.[19] Turkish governments have consistently rejected charges of genocide, often arguing that those who died were simply caught up in the fighting or that killings of Armenians were justified by their individual or collective treason. These claims have often been labeled as historical revisionism by western scholars.

Rape of Belgium: In Belgium, German troops, in fear of French and Belgian guerrilla fighters, or *francs-tireurs,* massacred towns people in Andenne (211 dead), Tamines (384 dead), and Dinant (612 dead). The victims included women and children. On 25 August 1914, , the Germans set fire to the town of Leuven, burned the library containing about 230,000 books, killed 209 civilians and forced 42,000 to evacuate. These actions brought worldwide condemnation.[20]

Economics and Manpower Issues: In Britain, conscription put into uniform nearly every physically fit man, six million out of ten million eligible in 1917-18. Of these, about 750,000 lost their lives and 1,700,000 were wounded. Most deaths were to young unmarried men; however, 160,000 wives lost husbands and 300,000 children lost fathers. Britain

---

[19] Greek American Operational Group OSS, Part 3

[20] Price, Alfred, "Aircraft versus the Submarine" (London: Wiliam Kimber, 1973)

turned to her colonies for help in obtaining essential war materials whose supply had become difficult from traditional sources. Geologists, such as Albert Ernest Kitson, were called upon to find new resources of precious minerals in the African colonies. Kitson discovered important new deposits of Manganese, used in munitions production, in the Gold Coast.[21]

There was chemical warfare and aerial bombardment, both of which were outlawed by the 1907 Hague Convention. Both were of limited tactical effectiveness.

The widespread use of chemical warfare was a distinguishing feature of the conflict. Gases used included chlorine, mustard gas and phosgene. Only a small proportion of total war casualties were caused by gas. Effective countermeasures to gas attacks were quickly created, such as gas masks.

The most powerful land based weapons were railway guns weighing hundreds of tons a piece. These were nicknamed Big Berthas, even though the namesake was not a railway gun. Germany developed the Paris Gun that was able to bombard Paris from a distance of over 100 km, though shells were relatively light at 94 kilograms (210 lb). While the Allies had railway guns, German models severely out-ranged and out-classed them.

Fixed-wing aircraft were first used militarily during the World War I. They were initially used for reconnaissance and ground attack. To shoot down enemy planes, anti-aircraft guns and fighter aircraft were developed. Strategic bombers were created, principally by the Germans and British, though the former used Zeppelins as well. Towards the end of

---

[21] Fromkin, David (2001), "A Peace to End All Peace: The Fall of the Ottoman Empire and the Creation of the Modern Middle East" New York: H. Holt, 119. ISBN 0-8050-6884-8

the conflict, aircraft carriers were used for the first time, with HMS Furious launching Sopwith Camels in a raid against the Zepplin hangars at Tondern in 1918. Trenches, the machine gun, air reconnaissance, barbed wire and modern artillery with fragmentation shells helped bring the battle lines of World War I to a stalemate. The infantry was armed mostly with magazine fed bolt-action rifles, but the machine gun, with the ability to fire hundreds of rounds per minute, blunted most infantry attacks. The British sought a solution with the creation of the tank and mechanized warfare.

The first tanks were used during the Battle of the Somme on September 15, 1916. Mechanical reliability became an issue, but the experiment proved its worth. Within a year, the British were fielding tanks by the hundreds and showed their potential during the Battle of Cambrai in November 1917, by breaking the Hindenburg Line, while combine arms teams captured 8000 enemy soldiers and 100 guns. Light automatic weapons also were introduced, such as the Lewis Gun and Browning automatic rifle.

Opposition to war:

The trade union and socialist movements had long voiced their opposition to a war, which they argued, meant only that workers would kill other workers in the interest of capitalism. Once war was declared, however, the vast majority of socialists and trade unions backed their governments. Many countries jailed those who spoke out against the conflict. These included Eugene Debs in the United States and Bertrand Russell in Britain.

No other war had changed the map of Europe so dramatically — four empires disappeared: the German, Austro-Hungarian, Ottoman and the Russian. Four defunct dynasties, the Hohenzollerns, the Habsburg, Romanovs and the Ottomans together with all their ancillary aristocracies, all fell after the war.

Belgium was badly damaged, as was France with 1.4 million soldiers' dead, not counting other casualties. Germany and Russia were similarly affected. The war had profound economic consequences. In addition, a major influenza epidemic that started in Western Europe in the latter months of the war killed millions in Europe and then spread around the world. Overall, the Spanish flu killed at least 50 million people.[22]

Peace Treaties:

After the war, the Allies imposed a series of peace treaties on the Central Powers. The 1919 Versailles Treaty ended the war with Germany. Germany was kept under blockade until it signed the treaty, which declared that Germany was responsible for the war. The treaty required Germany to pay enormous war reparations, which it did by borrowing from the United States, until the reparations were suspended in 1931. The "Guilt Thesis" became a controversial explanation of events in Britain and the United States. The Treaty of Versailles caused enormous bitterness in Germany, which nationalist movements, especially the Nazis, exploited. The treaty contributed to one of the worst economic collapses in history of Germany, sparking runaway inflation.

The Ottoman Empire was to be partitioned by the Treaty of Sevres in 1920. The treaty, however, was never ratified by the Sultan and was rejected by the Turkish republican movement. This led to the Turkish Independence War and, ultimately, to the 1923 Treaty of Lausanne. Austria-Hungary was also partitioned, largely along ethnic lines. The details

---

[22] Armenia National Assembly's Letter dated December 3, 1918 to Paris Peace Conference, 1919 and Triple Alliance

were contained in the Treaty of Saint- Germain and the Treaty of Trianon.

New National Identities:

Poland reemerged as an independent country, after more than a century. Yugoslavia and Czechoslovakia were entirely new nations. Russia became the Soviet Union and lost Finland, Estonia, Lithuania and Latvia, which became independent countries. The Ottoman Empire was soon replaced by Turkey and several other countries in the Middle East. Some people think that the Allies opened the way to more colonization with their policy, because with it the Allies could colonize territories owned by the Ottoman Empire and Austro-Hungarian Empire, by making them independent.

Postwar colonization in the Ottoman Empire led to many future problems still unresolved today. Conflict between mostly Jewish colonists and the indigenous, mostly Muslim, population intensified, probably exacerbated by the Holocaust, which stimulated Jewish migration and encouraged the new immigrants to fight for survival, a homeland, or both.

However, a new homeland for immigrants would cause hardships for the indigenous population, especially if the former displaced the latter. The United Nations partitioned Palestine in 1947 with Jewish approval but without Arab and Muslim approval. After the creation of the state of Israel a series of wars broke out between Israel and its neighbors, Egypt, Jordan, and Syria, in addition to unrest from the indigenous Palestinian population and terrorist activity by Palestinians and others reaching to Iran and beyond. Lasting peace in the Near East is an elusive goal even almost a century later.

This effect was even greater in Canada. Canadians proved they were a nation and not merely subjects of a distant empire. Indeed, following the Battle of Vimy Ridge, many Canadians began to refer to Canada as a nation "forged from fire". Canadians had proved themselves on the same battlefield where the British and French had previously faltered, and were respected internationally for their accomplishments. Canada entered the war as a Dominion of the British Empire, but when the war came to a close, Canada emerged as a fully independent nation. [23]The World War I witnessed horrible human disasters; it buried humanity; and the catastrophe was seen never before.

Blood Baths of Soldiers and Civilians:

Austria: In this war Austria engaged 7.8 million soldiers, out of which 2.2 million soldiers were taken as prisoners or reported missing; 3.62 million soldiers were wounded; and 1.2 million soldiers were killed.

Britain (including Empire): Britain engaged 8,904,467 soldiers, out of which 191,652 soldiers were taken as prisoners or reported missing; 2,090,212 soldiers were wounded; and 908,371 soldiers were killed.

France: France engaged 8.410 million soldiers, out of which 537 thousands soldiers were taken as prisoners or reported missing; 4.266 million soldiers were wounded; and 1.3578 million soldiers were killed.

Germany: Germany engaged 11 million soldiers, out of which 1.1528 million soldiers were taken as prisoners or reported missing; 4,216,058 soldiers were wounded; and 17.737 million people were killed. (This speaks that not only soldiers died in the battle field but also civilians were also killed. The excess

---

[23] Wikipedia, the free encyclopedia

was about more than 12 million. It further denotes that there might be errors in reporting.)

Italy: Italy engaged 5.615 million soldiers, out of which 0.6 million soldiers were taken as prisoners or reported missing; 947 thousands soldiers were wounded; and 0.65 million soldiers were killed.

Russia: Russia engaged 12 million soldiers, out of which 2.5 million soldiers were taken as prisoners or reported missing; 4.95 million soldiers were wounded; and 1.7 million soldiers were killed.

Turkey: Turkey engaged 2.85 million soldiers, out of which 250 thousands soldiers were taken as prisoners or reported missing; 400 thousand soldiers were wounded; and 325 thousand soldiers were killed.

United States: United States engaged 4.355 million soldiers, out of which 4500 soldiers were taken as prisoners or reported missing; 234,300 soldiers were wounded; and 126 thousand soldiers were killed.

Now, we should evaluate the effects of our past deeds; we should do something to do away with the wars; we should at least try to find out some ways to stop war and we should execute a plan for permanent WORLD PEACE that saves the humanity and all living beings. The wars are not caused by the people; these wars are created by the governments and strengthened by the media. In the twenty-first century, the United Nations should promulgate international laws to restrict or stop wars. The press, too, creates panic to the people and creates loss of peace by publishing war reports.

World War II (1939–1945)

World War II was the largest, worst, deadliest and most violent armed conflict in human history. The Second World War, a protracted, total war fought for unlimited aims, was a global struggle between two powerful coalitions. The amalgamation of two separate conflicts, one beginning in Asia in 1937, as the Sino-Japanese War and the other beginning in Europe in 1939 with the invasion of Poland increased the devastations. For six years, the war unleashed atrocities on a scale never before seen, including the annihilation of six million Jews in Nazi death camps. Before it was over, more than **60,000,000** people lost their lives. And the world entered the nuclear age when the United States dropped two atomic bombs on Japan in August 1945.

Three events helped usher in World War Two: Japan overran Manchuria; Italy, under fascist dictator Benito Mussolini, invaded Ethiopia; and - most important -- Adolf Hitler came to power in Germany. He rearmed the country, in violation of a treaty signed after World War One, and soon began to threaten other European nations.

The Great War, the war that "made the world safe for democracy," had created tremendous dislocations, which laid the groundwork for the collapse of democratic institutions in Europe, and set the stage for a second German attempt at conquest. The experience of the Great War compelled the Western democracies to develop alternative strategies and policies to support their national-security interests. The United States sought security through arms-limitation treaties, strict isolationism and neutrality laws. France, morbidly obsessed by the prospect of German resurgence, negotiated a web of alliances and tried to maintain its military preeminence (at least on paper.) Great Britain pinned its hopes for post-war security on participation in an activist League of Nations and a new European concert system. When these failed, both Britain and France turned to appeasement.

World War II engaged more than 100 million military personnel. It utilized both civil and military resources and activated economic, industrial, and scientific capabilities for the purposes of the war effort; nearly two-thirds of those killed in the war were civilians. For example, nearly 11 million of the civilian casualties were victims of the Holocaust, which was largely conducted in Eastern Europe, and the Soviet Union. The conflict ended in an Allied victory. As a result, the United States and Soviet Union emerged as the world's two leading superpowers, setting the stage for the Cold War for the next 45 years. The effects of World War II caused mass movement for independence in Asia and Africa. Europe was integrated after World War II.

The war termination strategies adopted by the United States remain controversial despite the passage of more than fifty years. Germany and Japan were determined and resourceful adversaries. Bringing about their complete defeat, while holding down American casualties and managing the United States' relationships with allies, posed difficult strategic choices for American decision-makers. Nothing better illustrates these difficulties than the decision to use nuclear weapons to force Japan's surrender. With the atomic attacks on Japan, the Second World War thus became the first nuclear conflict.

With a combined American air bombardment and naval blockade, Japan had been defeated by the summer of 1945, if not earlier. But even in defeat the Japanese Army intended to fight in defense of the homeland. Both sides still expected the allies to launch a final invasion into Japan itself. But the United States dropped an atomic bomb on the Japanese city of Hiroshima on 06 August 1945, and another on Nagasaki on 09 August 1945.

More than one hundred thousand persons were killed in Hiroshima and Nagasaki.

While individual firebomb raids had actually inflicted heavier casualties than either atomic bomb attack would, the psychological effect of a single weapon of such explosive force had the desired effect, spurring the precipitate surrender of the Japanese government. The Soviet Union entered the war against Japan, and Tokyo surrendered within days, with V-J Day declared on 15 August 1945.

On 2 September 1945 World War II ended when representatives of Japan signed the instruments of surrender aboard the battleship USS Missouri (BB 63) in Tokyo Bay.

Suddenly, sooner than expected, the war ended. Germany and Japan were defeated. The Soviet Union was strong in much of Eastern Europe. And the United States found it had become the world's strongest military, economic, and political power. World War II was a watershed in the history of the United States. Wartime developments in science and technology provided new tools for the solution of prewar problems that had been put aside and new ones created by the exigencies of the war. The contribution of science to the security and prosperity of the Nation was more widely recognized than ever before. World War II was fought between the Axis Powers and the Allies Powers.

The Axis powers constituted Germany, Italy, Japan, Hungary, Romania, and Bulgaria.

The Allies included U.S., Britain, France, USSR, Australia, Belgium, Brazil, Canada, China, Denmark, Greece, Netherlands, New Zealand, Norway, Poland, South Africa, and Yugoslavia.

Chronological Events:

1939:

(a) Germany invades Poland and annexes Danzig.
(b) Britain and France give Hitler ultimatum (Sept. 1) and declare war (Sept. 3)
(c) Disabled German pocket battleship *Admiral Graf Spee* blown up off Montevideo, Uruguay, on Hitler's orders (Dec. 17)
(d) Limited activity ("Sitzkrieg") on Western Front

1940:

(a) Nazis invade Netherlands, Belgium, and Luxembourg (May 10).
(b) Chamberlain resigns as Britain's prime minister; and Churchill takes over (May 10).
(c) Germans cross French frontier (May 12) using air/tank/infantry "Blitzkrieg" tactics.
(d) Dunkerque evacuation: about 335,000 out of 400,000 Allied soldiers rescued from Belgium by British civilian and naval craft (May 26–June 3).
(e) Italy declares war on France and Britain; invades France (June 10).
(f) Germans enter Paris; city undefended (June 14).
(g) France and Germany sign armistice at Compiègne (June 22).
(h) Nazis bomb Coventry, England (Nov. 14).

1941:

(a) Germans launch attacks in Balkans.
(b) Yugoslavia surrenders—General Mihajlovic continues guerrilla warfare
(c) Tito leads left-wing guerrillas (April 17).
(d) Nazi tanks enter Athens; remnants of British Army quit Greece (April 27).
(e) Hitler attacks Russia (June 22).
(f) Atlantic Charter—FDR and Churchill agree on war aims (Aug. 14).

(g) Japanese attacks on Pearl Harbor, Philippines, Guam force U.S. into war;
(h) U.S. Pacific fleet crippled (Dec. 7).
(i) U.S. and Britain declare war on Japan. Germany and Italy declare war on U.S.; Congress declares war on those countries (Dec. 11).

1942:

(a) British surrender Singapore to Japanese (Feb. 15).
(b) Roosevelt orders Japanese and Japanese Americans in western U.S. to be exiled to "relocation centers," many for the remainder of the war (Feb. 19).
(c) U.S. forces on Bataan peninsula in Philippines surrender (April 9). U.S. and Filipino troops on Corregidor Island in Manila Bay surrender to Japanese (May 6).
(d) Village of Lidice in Czechoslovakia razed by Nazis (June 10).
(e) U.S. and Britain land in French North Africa (Nov. 8).

1943:

(a) Casablanca Conference—Churchill and FDR agree on unconditional surrender goal (Jan. 14–24).
(b) German 6th Army surrenders at Stalingrad—turning point of war in Russia (Feb.1–2)
(c) Remnants of Nazis trapped on Cape Bon, ending war in Africa (May 12).
(d) Mussolini deposed; Badoglio named premier (July 25).
(e) Allied troops land on Italian mainland after conquest of Sicily (Sept. 3).
(f) Italy surrenders (Sept. 8).
(g) Nazis seize Rome (Sept. 10).

(h) Cairo Conference: FDR, Churchill, Chiang Kai-shek pledge defeat of Japan, free Korea (Nov. 22–26).
(i) Tehran Conference: FDR, Churchill, Stalin agree on invasion plans (Nov. 28–Dec. 1).

1944:

(a) U.S. and British troops land at Anzio on west Italian coast and hold beachhead (Jan. 22).
(b) U.S. and British troops enter Rome (June 4).
(c) D-Day—Allies launch Normandy invasion (June 6).
(d) Hitler wounded in bomb plot (July 20).
(e) Paris liberated (Aug. 25). Athens freed by Allies (Oct. 13).
(f) Americans invade Philippines (Oct. 20).
(g) Germans launch counteroffensive in Belgium—Battle of the Bulge (Dec. 16).

1945:

(a) Yalta Agreement signed by FDR, Churchill, and Stalin — establishes basis for occupation of Germany, returns to Soviet Union lands taken by Germany and Japan
(b) USSR agrees to friendship pact with China (Feb. 11).
(c) Mussolini killed at Lake Como (April 28).
(d) Admiral Doenitz takes command in Germany;
(e) Suicide of Hitler announced (May 1). Berlin falls (May 2). Germany signs unconditional surrender terms at Rheims (May 7).
(f) Allies declare V-E Day (May 8).
(g) Potsdam Conference—Truman, Churchill, Atlee (after July 28),
(h) Stalin established council of foreign ministers to prepare peace treaties.
(i) Plan German postwar government and reparations (July 17–Aug. 2).
(j) A-bomb dropped on Hiroshima by U.S. (Aug. 6).
(k) USSR declares war on Japan (Aug. 8).

(l) Nagasaki hit by A-bomb (Aug. 9).
(m) Japan agrees to surrender (Aug. 14).
(n) V-J Day—Japanese sign surrender terms aboard battleship Missouri (Sept. 2).[24]

World War II - Casualties

The statistics of World War II has elaborated the killings of humans which could be an ugly example for all time to come. The countries, which were entangled in this war lost millions of brave people as they were killed.

Total causalities' during the World War II were 52,199,262 including military personnel and civilians. Reports also speak that the causalities' crossed even more than 60 million.

The countries, which suffered most by sacrificing the soldiers and civilians, were as follows:

(a) USSR: During the World War II, 20.6 million people were killed in USSR; out of which, the military deaths were 13.6 million and civilian deaths were 7 million and the country lost 10.4 per cent of her pre-war population.
(b) China: China lost 10 million of people during World War II, which accounts for 2 per cent of pre-war population
(c) Germany: 6.85 million people were killed in the war in Germany; (the military deaths were 3.25 million, civilian deaths were 3.6 million) and the country lost 9.5 percent of its pre-war population.
(d) Poland: 6.123 million people were killed in the war in Poland; (the military deaths were 123 thousands, civilian deaths were 6 million) and

[24] Information Please Database, Pearson Education, Inc. 2007

the country lost 17.2 per cent of pre-war population.

(e) Japan: 2 million people were killed in the war in Japan; and the country lost 2.7 per cent of pre-war population.

(f) Yugoslavia: Yugoslavia lost 1.706 million people, who were killed in the war; and the country lost 10.9 per cent of pre-war population.

(g) France: France lost 0.81 million people, who were killed in the war; (the military deaths were 0.34 million, civilian deaths were 0.47 million) and the country lost 1.9 per cent of pre-war population.

(h) Greece: 20.6 million people were killed in the war in Greece; (the military deaths were 13.6 million, civilian deaths were 7 million) and the country lost 10.4 per cent of pre-war population.

(i) United States: United States lost 500 thousand people, who were killed through military action and the country lost 0.4 per cent of her pre-war population.

(j) Austria: Austria lost 480 thousand people, who were killed in the war; and the country lost 7.2 per cent of her pre-war population.

(k) Romania: Romania lost 460 thousand people, who were killed in the war; and the country lost 3.4 per cent of pre-war population.

(l) Hungary: Hungary lost 420 thousand people, who were killed in the war; and the country lost 3.0 per cent of pre-war population.

(m) Italy: Italy lost 410 thousand people, who were killed; the military deaths were 330 thousands, civilian deaths were 80 thousands and the country lost 0.9 per cent of pre-war population.

(n) Czechoslovakia: Czechoslovakia lost 400 thousand people, who were killed in the war; and the country lost 2.7 per cent of pre-war population.

(o) Great Britain: Great Britain lost 388 thousand people, who were killed in the war; the military deaths were 326 thousands, civilian deaths were 62 thousands and the country lost 0.8 per cent of pre-war population.
(p) Netherlands: Netherlands lost 210 thousand people, who were killed in the war; the military deaths were 198 thousands, civilian deaths were 12 thousands and the country lost 2.4 per cent of pre-war population.
(q) Belgium: Belgium lost 88 thousand people, who were killed in the war; the military deaths were 76 thousand, civilian deaths were 12 thousands and the country lost 1.1 per cent of pre-war population.
(r) Finland lost 84 thousand people or 2.2 percent of pre-war population,
(s) Australia lost 39 thousand people or 0.3 percent of pre-war population;
(t) Canada lost 34 thousand people or 0.3 percent of pre-war population;
(u) Albania lost 28 thousand people or 2.5 percent of pre-war population;
(v) India lost 24 thousand people or 0.01 percent of pre-war population;
(w) Norway lost 10,262 people or 0.3 percent of pre-war population;
(x) New Zealand lost 10 thousand people or 0.6 percent of population;
(y) Luxemburg lost 5000 People or 1.7 percent of pre-war population in the World War II.[25]

Again we neglected our duties and organized another World War and allowed killings of 70 million of soldiers and civilians, who did not start or plan for wars. Why the leaders create wars? We, people have to answer at least for our future generations. Who killed them? Why they were killed?

---

[25] The History Place TM

Thus Speak Historians:

The Germans killed 2.8 million young, healthy Soviet POWs mainly by starvation in less than eight months of 1941- 42 before the decimation of Soviet POWs ... was stopped.[26]

The total number of prisoners taken by the German armies in the USSR was in the region of 5.5 million. Of these, the astounding number of 3.5 million or more had been lost by the middle of 1944 and the assumption must be that they were either deliberately killed or done to death by criminal negligence. Nearly two million of them died in camps and another million disappeared while in military custody either in the USSR or in rear areas; a further quarter of a million disappeared or died in transit between the front and destinations in the rear; another 473,000 died or were killed in military custody in Germany or Poland. This slaughter of prisoners cannot be accounted for by the peculiar chaos of the war in the east. ... The true cause was the inhuman policy of the Nazis towards the Russians as a people and the acquiescence of army commanders in attitudes and conditions, which amounted to a sentence of death on their prisoners.[27]

Existing sources suggest that some 5.7 million Soviet army personnel fell into German hands during World War II. As of January 1945, the German army reported that only about 930,000 Soviet POWs remained in German custody. The German army released about one million Soviet POWs as auxiliaries of the German army and the SS. About half a million Soviet POWs had escaped German custody or had been liberated by the Soviet army as it advanced westward through Eastern Europe into Germany. The

---

[26] Daniel Goldhagen, *Hitler's Willing Executioners* (p. 290)
[27] Peter Calvocoressi, Guy Wint "*Total War*"

remaining 3.3 million, or about 57 percent of those taken prisoner, were dead by the end of the war.[28]

Conclusion:

When we can't give life to the dead, we have no right to kill the innocent civilians and deploy the brave soldiers to die. The soldiers should be recruited to protect the country from enemies.

Let the philosophers, saints, intelligentsia, planners and University Professors find ways to stop the on-going wars completely and make suggestions for a world free of wars for enjoying peace everywhere.

The boundary disputes of the countries must be finalized by the United Nations with a high-powered committee consisting of five Ex-Presidents and five Ex-Prime Ministers and five Noble Laureates in the committee. The committee may recommend to the United Nations the justified boundary line of all the countries as on New Year day of 2014.

History should not repeat in waging wars. Much blood has already flown into the rivers and oceans. No country should aspire to rule the planet, environment, time and people as Germany has failed and suffered.

There should be ban on nuclear, biological, chemical and radiological defense research for all the countries. All nuclear, biological, chemical and radiological weapons manufactured and stored should be immediately destroyed. Defense budget should be reduced by 10 percent each year as compared to the last year.

People of different faiths or religions must practice **humanity** for a safer and peaceful world. The

---

[28] Nazi Persecution of Soviet Prisoners of War, United States Holocaust Memorial Museum

ultimate goal in religion is God-realization. So each individual is related to each other.

The United Nations, all countries, all states, all conglomerates and even hamlets should constitute PEACE FORUMS to seek permanent peace in each human settlement.

Any country facing military attack from another country should be assisted by the United Nations politically, legally, financially and physically. The decision could be taken at once.

Let the whole world remain in peace. No individual should be allowed to declare himself as the man with supreme power. No country can remain in safe by waging war against another country or other countries. Partnership in war / defense collaboration must be declared anti-human policies.

History speaks that military forums encourage war and do suppress peace. If we can award power to the United Nations, military forums would be of no use and cannot create war like situations.

The United Nations and the Governments should take all steps to stop wars because this war might be more dangerous than the former World Wars. It is better to discuss the differences between countries in the presence of the Boundary Commission of the UN and all issues should be settled amicably and amiably.

+++++

Chapter – III

ONGOING WARS

The chain reaction of evil - wars producing more wars – must be broken, or we shall be plunged into the dark abyss of annihilation.

Martin Luther King, Jr.

The ongoing wars are the permanent peace-breaking wars, which are caused because of unsolved problems. The world now faces 42 trouble spots where sporadic war is caused for years. These ongoing wars are caused mainly because of absence of international boundaries, insurgency, civil war, civil disturbances, civil conflicts, uprising or grabbing land of weaker states for acquiring natural resources, free labour or to exhibit super power over the enemies. Both the military persons and the general public have expressed their anger over war as it causes causalities of both military and civilians. The reasons are neither genuine nor approved by the people, but it continues even with successive governments. The budget earmarked for defense could be better utilized for welfare programmes.

The United Nations has failed in combating ongoing wars. The lists of ongoing- conflicts continue in as many as 31 countries. The countries are: Angola, Burma- Myanmar, Central African Republic, Chad, Democratic Republic of Congo, Eritrea, Ethiopia, Nigeria, Rwanda, Somalia, Sudan, Uganda, Afghanistan, India, Indonesia, North Korea, South Korea, Pakistan, Philippines, Georgia, Russia, Spain, North Ireland, Iran, Iraq, Israel, South Arabia, Turkey, Yemen, Colombia, and Venezuela- Colombia.

The United Nations defines **major wars** as military conflicts inflicting 1,000 battlefield deaths per year. In 1965, there were 10 major wars under way. The new millennium began with armed conflict or cultivating an uncertain peace. As of mid-2005, there were eight Major Wars under way, with as many as 24 lesser conflicts ongoing with varying degrees of intensity. Most of these are civil or intrastate wars, fueled as much by racial, ethnic, or religious animosities as by ideological fervor. Most victims are civilians, a feature that distinguishes modern conflicts. During World War I, civilians made up fewer than 5 percent of all casualties. Today, 75 percent or more of those killed or wounded in wars are non-combatants.

The African continent is afflicted by war. Africa has been marred by more than 20 major civil wars since 1960. Rwanda, Somalia, Angola, Sudan, Liberia, and Burundi are among those countries that have recently suffered serious armed conflict. War has caused untold economic and social damage to these countries of Africa. Food production is impossible in conflict areas, and famine often results. Widespread conflict has condemned many of Africa's children to live in misery and, in certain cases, has threatened the existence of traditional African cultures. Conflict prevention, mediation, humanitarian intervention and demobilization are among the tools needed to underwrite the success of development assistance programs. Nutrition and education programs, for example, cannot succeed in a nation at war. Billions of dollars of development assistance have been virtually wasted in war-ravaged countries such as Liberia, Somalia, and Sudan.[1]

In this chapter, ongoing wars such as War in Libya and after, Algerian Insurgency, Civil War in Georgia, Sri Lanka–Tamil Separatists, Sudan–Darfur Conflict, Iraq–United States War, Civil war in Syria, Unrest in Nigeria, Cries for Freedom in Tibet, China and Tibet, Chine proposes war in Tibet, Recent Development in Nepal are discussed, which could have been solved by the United Nations. But the UN is not in a position to solve the wars and could not attempt for ensuring world peace.

War in Libya and After

Responsibility to Protect Libyans:

In 2005, world leaders unanimously and solemnly declared that where governments were manifestly failing in their sovereign duty, the international community, acting through the United Nations, would take "timely and decisive" action to honour the collective responsibility to protect people against atrocity crimes. Libya today is the place and time to redeem that pledge.

The UN's record on the Arab world is no less patchy than the West's. Having degenerated into internal security states backed by the US national security state, one after another Arab regimes were politically exhausted and morally bankrupt. It was the UN that, almost a decade ago, provided the moral compass and intellectual leadership with the Arab Human Development Report, written mainly by Arabs themselves. Yet Libya was also elected to the UN's main human rights watchdog.

---

[1] www.globalsecurity.org/military/world/war/index.html

Even more shameful was the UN's inaction, led by the most powerful countries of the world, in the Rwanda genocide and the Srebrenica massacre. Both happened on Kofi Annan's watch as the top UN official for peacekeeping. When he became secretary-general, his instinctive humanitarianism was stiffened by the memory of these two searing experiences and he pushed for a doctrine to take effective action. With the help of Canada, an international commission formulated the innovative principle of the responsibility to protect, commonly known as R2P.

Annan later described R2P as one of his most precious achievements. He used its preventive pillar as a prism through which to mediate the post-election crisis of violence in Kenya in 2008: our only successful R2P marker to date. Fortunately, Ban Ki-moon has put his full weight behind R2P as well.

The language of R2P refers to state inability or unwillingness to discharge its responsibility to protect as the catalyst to the collective international responsibility being activated. Because it would have been impolitic, we did not explicitly say that the most critical and offensive situation is when the state itself is the perpetrator of atrocity crimes, when the security forces, meant to protect their people, are instead let loose in a killing spree by predatory rulers.

That is the situation we face in Libya. Not satisfied with 42 years of autocratic rule, the erratic Colonel Muammar Gaddafi is using deadly violence to crush and kill his people in open revolt against his brutal regime. He has vowed to fight to the last drop of his blood. The UN should grant him his wish.

R2P provides the normative tool of choice and political cover to deal robustly, promptly and effectively with the threat that Gaddafi poses to his people. Doing so will also help both the UN and the West to cleanse their conscience of the stain of being passive spectators in Rwanda and Srebrenica, and of complicity in privileging stability over freedoms for the Arabs, in effect declaring all of the Arab world as a democracy- and human rights-free zone.

R2P is narrow - it applies only to the four crimes of ethnic cleansing, genocide, crimes against humanity, and war crimes - but deep: there are no limits to what can be done in responding to these atrocity crimes. In a matching symmetry, support for R2P so far has been broad but shallow. Libya is the perfect opportunity to convert the noble sentiments and words of R2P into meaningful action through deeds.

On February 22, the Security Council issued a press statement calling on Libya "to meet its responsibility to protect its population". The UN Human Rights Council did the same on the 25th while suspending Libya's membership. Ban and his special advisers on genocide prevention and R2P have issued statements warning of egregious violations of human rights and international humanitarian law as well as reminding Libya of its R2P obligations.

On the 26th, the Security Council voted unanimously (Resolution 1970) to impose sanctions on Libya, forbidding the sale of arms and freezing the assets of its leaders. It also referred Gaddafi to the International Criminal Court (ICC) for breaches of human rights and international humanitarian laws. Trouble is, those who reject the ICC but refer others to it – China, India, Russia, and the US - violate natural justice and are guilty of gross hypocrisy.

The crisis in Libya has escalated to beyond the point of return. Calls for restraint are no longer enough. When Gaddafi says that the protesters deserve to die and his son - he who has cultivated an international image of moderation - warns of a river of blood, the world must meet the challenge, not duck it yet again.

Helped by so many Libyan diplomats defecting en masse and joining calls for international intervention, the Security Council must forthwith implement R2P and declare and enforce a no-fly zone - if Libyan officers fly, they die.[29]

For Gaddafi's trial at the ICC to be morally credible, it must be backed by criminal investigations of the foreign banks that have parked his ill-gotten gains in violation of global anti-corruption agreements, and public shaming of Africans who elected Libya to the Human Rights Council and westerners who armed his thugs.

US intervention in Libya

This was a unique experiment with covert warfare. Obama maintained throughout the seven-month-long "European" campaign in Libya that the US was "not involved". Yet, America did everything to make it succeed, and will be reimbursed full costs.

In May 2011, an important issue confronted the United States Congress. Lawmakers demanded to know why President Barack Obama was involving their country into another costly overseas military adventure without even bothering to seek Congressional sanction.

The NATO campaign in Europe was then already into its second month. The American people were already angry with the disastrous effect that the Afghan and Iraq campaigns were having on their society and economy. Naturally, legislators wanted to know about the goals, methods, costs and, above all, the administration's projection of the outcome of the Libyan intervention.

---

[29] Ramesh Thakur (2011), " Responsibility to Protect", The Times of India, Bhubaneswar, Mar 4, 2011

The top Republican on the Senate Foreign Relations Committee, Richard Lugar, expressed strong misgivings about President Barack Obama's failure to seek congressional consent to launch war operations over Libya. "The president should have come to Congress seeking authority to wage war in Libya. And I believe that Congress and the American people would still benefit from a debate on this matter," he said.

The Obama regime consistently maintained the façade that Libya was not a military campaign along the lines of Afghanistan or Libya. It was only giving "support" to its European allies. When the war in Libya began, the US government convinced a large number of war supporters that America was only out to achieve the very limited goal of creating a no-fly zone in Benghazi to protect civilians from air attacks.

In March, the Pentagon announced it had spent about $550 million. In mid-May, Robert Gates, the Defense Secretary, said the expenditure on the Iraq front had grown to $750 million. In end-August, John Barry, the respected American journalist, wrote that the US military has spent about $1 billion on Libya's revolution, and secretly helped NATO with everything from munitions to surveillance aircraft. Barry argued that the Obama government's cover that it was a peripheral participant in the NATO operation was simply not acceptable. The Europeans were hugely divided over Libya and simply lacked the wherewithal to conduct an operation spread over seven months.

An international naval force gathered off Libya. To lower the US profile, the administration elected not to send a super-carrier. Even so, the dozen US warships on station were the biggest contingent in this armada. In the opening hours of the campaign, an American submarine, the USS Florida, launched 100 cruise missiles against Libyan air defenses, crucially opening an entry corridor for the airstrikes that followed.

American tanker aircraft refueled European war planes constantly. The Europeans have tanker aircraft, but not enough to support a 24/7 air offensive averaging, by NATO count, around 100 missions a day, some 50 of them strike sorties. The US flew 30 of the 40 tankers. When the Europeans ran low on precision-attack munitions, the US quietly resupplied them. Says Barry: "That explains why European air forces flew F-16s — those of Norway, Denmark, Belgium — carrying out a disproportionate share of the strikes in the early phase of the campaign. The US had stocks of the munitions to resupply them. When Britain and France, which fly European-built strike aircraft, also ran short, they couldn't use US-made bombs until they had made hurried modifications to their aircraft.

To target Gaddafi's military, NATO largely relied on American 'JSTARS' surveillance aircraft, which, flying offshore, could track the movements of rival forces. When more detailed targeting information was needed — as in the battles for Misrata and other towns defended by Gaddafi's troops — the US flew Predator drones to relay a block-by-block picture.

US Air Force targeting specialists were in NATO's Naples operational headquarters throughout the campaign. They oversaw the preparing of "target folders" for the strikes in Tripoli against Gaddafi's compound and the headquarters of his military and intelligence services. It may be pointed out that organizing precision strikes by high-speed jets is not a task for novices. The attack routes over Tripoli and the release times of bombs had to be precisely calibrated so munitions released even a second late by a strike aircraft would have the best chance of avoiding civilian homes.

American AWACS aircraft, high over the Mediterranean, handled much of the battle-management task, acting as air-traffic controllers on most of the strike missions. Again, the Europeans have AWACS, but not enough crews to handle an all-hours campaign lasting months. Eavesdropping by US intelligence — some by aircraft, some by a listening post quietly established just outside Libya — gave NATO unparalleled knowledge of what Gaddafi's military planned.

What the world witnessed through the success of the "revolution" against Gaddafi, was the latest form of war-waging by the world's only superpower. President Obama was literally true to his word — he did not put America's "boots on the ground in Libya". What's more, most of the costs incurred will be reimbursed by the Europeans. The US will be repaid for its assistance to the Europeans — everything from fuel for the aircraft to munitions and spare parts — which according to the Pentagon's estimates cost about $222 million. Compared with Afghanistan, which is still costing the American taxpayer roughly $10 billion a month, Gaddafi's overthrow has been a bargain.

In return, Obama has delivered a huge gift to American oil interests. The deceased Gaddafi had made Libya difficult terrain for US oil companies. When, in 2004, Bush lifted sanctions on Libya, optimism was widespread among oil tycoons that one of the world's biggest oil reserves was theirs for the asking. But soon the relationship soured. Gaddafi had begun to demand tough contract terms. Now, thanks to the Arab spring, they are dreaming again.[30]

[30] Shahoz Tarique Raza (2011), " Libya saw a different kind of US intervention", the Pioneer, November 5, 2011

Libya after Gaddafi — a big future

The North African oil major is at a tremendous crossroads today but much will depend on how the transitional regime overcomes the awesome challenges which confront the troubled nation at the present time. Of utmost importance is the need to balance its Arab identity with its European future

The 'liberation' of Libya is one of the few bits of good news in today's world. However, it is clear that while the Gaddafi regime has been overthrown, a number of challenges remain to confront the new Libya. Great care must now be taken to prevent the prospects of a dark, chaotic future being realized in the oil-rich North African country.

The biggest questions are — will the positive changes in Libya be sustained? Will these changes lead the Libyan people towards a prosperous and democratic future? Will these changes in Libya lead to greater stability in its adjoining regions?

Libya's future trajectories can best be understood by looking at its core physical characteristics.

When we think of Libya, the most visible feature is its vast oil reserves. Libya has around 50 billion barrels of oil reserves and an estimated 50 trillion cubic feet (Tcf) of natural gas reserves. These huge reserves not only give Libya the potential for prosperity but also make it potentially one of the more important players in the energy market. Unlike other states liberated by the Arab Spring, Libya's economy is heavily dependent on oil. Libya is the world's 17th-largest oil producer. Revenues from the oil sector account for 95 per cent of its export earnings, 25 per cent of its GDP, and —most significantly — 80 per cent of its government revenue.

Libya is literally covered by the Sahara Desert. The only exception is the narrow 1,200 mile coastline bordering the Mediterranean Sea, where almost 80 per cent of its population resides. Apart from its reserves of oil and gas, Libya's desert, which receives abundant sunshine through the year, is crucial for the success of a proposed "Deserted" - a $ 550 billion scheme to harness solar power by installing giant mirrors in the Sahara desert which spreads over Egypt, Morocco, Sudan, Tunisia and, of course, Libya. The Sun's rays would power turbines which would generate electricity for not only local markets, but also the entire European continent. The Arab Spring this year has given a boost to the world's most ambitious solar project, which could be producing green electricity in the desert by 2015.

The critical fact, however, is that Libya, along with its huge energy potential is located in fairly close proximity to Europe — this means that much of the market in the foreseeable future will be in Europe. Thus, Libya will become increasingly tied into the European system. At the same time, there will be a tension between this movement towards Europe and Libya's natural linkages with the Arab world. Libya's new rulers would need to navigate these opposing pressures very carefully.

Another aspect of Libya's future will be focussed on Libya's location — Libya is located strategically at the northern tip of Africa and close to Southern Europe. This geographic location together with the sparse population has made Libya a passageway for migrants seeking to move from sub-Saharan Africa into Europe. Left unmanaged, such migration has the potential to destabilize several European nations; thereby creating the basis for conflict between Libya and Europe. Given the multiplicity of issues involved, migration through Libya will need to be closely watched and managed by future Libyan governments.

Then again, in demographic terms, Libya has a tiny population of around 6.5 million. However, like many of the Arab countries in its region, Libya has a particularly youthful population. Given the nature of the Gaddafi regime, large sections of Libya's population have been economically and politically marginalized for a very long period.

What these facts mean in practice is that significant sections of the already religious Libyan population have, over the years, gravitated towards religion as an identity and as a channel of expression. A few Libyans from within this constituency even participated in the Afghan Jihad and now form a part of the forces that overthrew the Gaddafi regime. Expectedly, like all other Libyans they are now articulating their own vision of the future Libyan state — in which they see Islamic law as the guiding principle.

Thus, Libya has a large constituency that believes in a positive role for tradition and religion in their government. This will inevitably create opportunities for tension between modernity and tradition. Libya's future constitution will need to take cognizance of and manage this tension in order for Libya to have a stable future.

The National Transition Council (and successor Governments) will thus be under constant pressure — not only from Islamic groups and parties but also from the various factions till now held together by the objective of getting rid of the Gaddafi regime. Each of these groups will now begin wanting to determine the course of Libya's future. In the process, they will want to lessen the role of other factions and the age-old processes of nepotism and corruption will have as much room to flourish as they did before — only the faces would have changed.

Overcoming these potential problems would require huge efforts towards creating a national identity and sense of purpose. The manner in which this tension is managed will also determine the success of Libya's Democracy in the future.

More than the importance Libya has as an energy producer, these huge reserves would also translate into vast revenues for the state. It is precisely at this point that Libya's problem began the last time round when the essentially tribal Gaddafi regime captured control over the state and over its resource wealth. This control was not vested in a transparent — equitable governance mechanism but in the hands of the Gaddafi family and of its cronies. Given this access to untold wealth, the regime consolidated its strangle hold on the country through patronage to its supporters and brutal repression of its opponents and challengers.

Thus, Libya's wealth would require the government to make strenuous efforts to ensure that all sections of the population partake of the country's prosperity. Moreover, the mechanisms of sharing this prosperity will also be important. If Libya remains trapped in the rentier frame of mind then the benefits will be short-lived. If however, the wealth is used to create infrastructure, facilities and economic opportunities, then Libya can look forward to a stable and prosperous future.[31]

Algerian Insurgency

After a century of rule by France, Algeria became independent on 03 July 1963. The fundamentalist FIS (Islamic Salvation Front) response has resulted in a continuous low-grade civil conflict with the secular

[31] Ashok Singh (2011), "Libya after Gaddafi — a big future", The Pioneer, November 5, 2011

moderate religious-based parties. FIS's armed wing, the Islamic Salvation Army, although disbanded since January 2000 still continues residual fighting.

France declared Algeria independent on 03 July 1963. On September 8, 1963, a constitution was adopted by referendum, and later that month, Ahmed Ben Bella was formally elected president. On June 19, 1965, President Ben Bella was replaced in a bloodless coup by a Council of the Revolution headed by Minister of Defense Col. Houari Boumediene who was elected president of the republic on December 10, 1976. He died 5 years later. Following nomination by an FLN Party Congress, Col. Chadli Bendjedid was elected President in 1979 and re-elected in 1984 and 1988. A new constitution was adopted in 1989 that allowed the formation of political associations other than the FLN. It also removed the armed forces, which had run the government since the days of Boumediene, from a designated role in the operation of the government. Among the scores of parties that sprang up under the new constitution, the militant Islamic Salvation Front (FIS) was the most successful, winning more than 50 percent of all votes cast in municipal elections in June 1990 as well as in first stage of national legislative elections held in December 1991.

Faced with the real possibility of a sweeping FIS victory, the government canceled the second stage of elections in January 1992. This action, coupled with political uncertainty and economic turmoil, led to a violent reaction on the part of the Islamists. A campaign of terror in the country included assassinations, bombings, and massacres. Charging the FIS with supporting or encouraging such actions, Bendjedid declared a national state of emergency, resigned, and appointed five-member High Council of State (HCS) to run the government. The HCS officially dissolved and outlawed the FIS in 1992 and began a series of arrests and trials of FIS members that reportedly resulted in over 50,000 members being jailed.

Despite efforts to restore the political process, violence and terrorism characterized the Algeria landscape during the 1990s. In 1994, Lamine Zeroual was appointed Head of State for a 3-year term. During this period, the Armed Islamic Group (GIA) launched terrorist campaigns against government figures and institutions to protest the banning of the Islamic parties. A breakaway GIA group - the Salafist Group for Preaching and Call (GSPC) - also undertook terrorist activity in the country.

Government officials estimate that more than 100,000 Algerians died during this period.

Zeroual called for presidential elections in 1995, though some parties objected to holding elections that excluded the FIS. Zeroual was elected president with 75 percent of the vote. By 1997, in an attempt to bring political stability to the nation, the Re-assemblymen National Democratic (RND) party was formed by a more progressive group of FLN members. Zeroual announced that presidential elections would be held in early 1999, nearly 2 years ahead of the scheduled time.

Algerians went to the polls in April 1999, following a campaign in which seven candidates qualified for election. On the eve of the election, all candidates except Abdelaziz Bouteflika pulled out amid charges of widespread electoral fraud. Bouteflika, the candidate who appeared to enjoy the backing of the military, as well as FLN and RND party regulars, won with an official vote count of 70 percent of all votes cast. He was inaugurated on April 27, 1999 for a 5-year term.

President Bouteflika's agenda focused initially on restoring security and stability to the country.

Following his inauguration, he proposed an official amnesty for those who fought against the government during the 1990s unless they had engaged in "blood crimes," such as rape or murder. This "Civil Concord" policy was widely approved in a nationwide referendum in September 2000. Government officials estimate that 85 percent of those fighting the regime during the 1990s have accepted the amnesty offer and have been reintegrated into Algerian society. Bouteflika also has launched national commissions to study education and judicial reform, as well as restructuring of the state bureaucracy. His government has set ambitious targets for economic reform and attracting foreign investment.

Three years into Bouteflika's mandate, the security situation in Algeria has improved markedly. However, terrorism has not been totally eliminated, and terrorist incidents still occur, particularly in remote or isolated areas of the country. An estimated 100-120 Algerians are killed each month, down from a high of 1,200 or more in the mid-1990s. In 2001, Berber activists in the Kabyle region of the country, reacting to the death of a youth in gendarme custody, unleashed a resistance campaign against what they saw as government repression. Strikes and demonstrations in the Kabyle region have become commonplace as a result and some have spread to the capital.

The 2002 elections in Algeria suffered from widespread public disillusionment. The killing of 23 people in Sendjas marred the eve of the election. Many of the Berber speaking populace boycotted the election while expressing anti-governmental views. Some secular parties did not participate, citing their belief that the government was based on fraudulent results in reference to the 1997 and 1999 elections. The 47 percent voter turn out was the lowest since 1962. The National Liberation Front (FLN) won 199 out of the 389 seats. The nationalistic RND fell from having 156 seats to a mere 47.

The widespread disenchantment was attributed to a dismal economy; also housing and medicine continue to be pressing problems in Algeria. Failing infrastructure and the continued influx of people from rural to urban areas has overtaxed both systems. According to the UNDP, Algeria has the highest occupancy rates for housing, and government officials have publicly stated that the country has an immediate shortfall of 1.5 million housing units. Rachid Abu Turab took over as leader of the GIA after the death of Antar Zouabri in February of 2002. The change in leadership marked an increase in terrorist activities carried out by the GIA. Turab pledged to continue the increased pace, and committed the GIA to non-reconciliation.

The civil unrest continued and in March of 2002 the planned presidential pardoning of 5000 criminals caused a riot at Algeria's largest prison. The prisoners were protesting their exclusion from the pardoning, which was issued by President Bouteflika in honor of the Prophet Mohammed's birthday. Police resorted to tear gas in order to quell the uprising. The prison is the site of a 1995 attack by the GIA which led to the escape of 1000 criminals, and still houses many convicted terrorists.

The Algerian government blamed a January 2003 ambush of security forces on the GSPC, and connected their actions with Al-Qaeda. The attack represented the largest such incident since 1992, reportedly between 20 and 40 people were injured. In February of 2003, the Salafist Group for Preaching and Combat kidnapped 32 tourists while they were traveling through the Sahara. Reportedly, the tourists were being held for ransom. The kidnapping prompted German Foreign Minister Joschka Fischer to visit Algeria on March 12th to hold talks concerning the missing Europeans. Algerian authorities raided the compound where the tourists were being held on May 14th 2003, freeing 17 people. The raid resulted in the deaths of at least 9 GSPC members, and wounded several others. The country's 11-year civil conflict has pitted self-proclaimed radical Muslims against moderate Muslims.

Approximately 150,000 civilians, terrorists, and security forces were killed up to the end of 2003.

Extremist self-proclaimed Muslims have issued public threats against all "infidels" in the country, both foreigners and citizens, and have killed both Muslims and non-Muslims, including missionaries. Extremists continued attacks against both the Government and moderate Muslim and secular civilians; however, the level of violence perpetrated by these terrorists continued to decline during the period covered by this report. There were 183 civilian deaths due to terrorism in the first 6 months of 2003, compared with 313 civilians killed in the same period in 2002. These figures contrast with more than 1,000 killings per month several years earlier. The majority of the country's terrorist groups, as a rule, do not differentiate between religious and political killings. During the period covered by this report, the majority of cases of security force and civilian deaths at the hands of terrorists were a result of knifings (particularly throat-slitting) and shootings. Terrorists, often claiming religious justification for their actions, set up roadblocks to kill civilians and security force personnel.

In February of 2003, Human Rights Watch reported, "state-sponsored disappearances have virtually stopped in Algeria." The 2004 US State Department Report on Human Rights Practices claims that, while the country's record remained "poor," the government took "notable steps to improve human rights." Foreign observers certified that elections that have taken place over the last few years have been, generally, free and fair.

In 2006, sporadic, low-intensity fighting continued between the government and the GSPC. In March of 2006 Hassan Hattab, a former leader of the GSPC, called for members to disarm and accept government offers of amnesty. On September 14th, Ayman al-Zawahiri, Al Qaeda's second-in-command, called for the GSPC to remain resolute and declared a "blessed union" would unite the two groups in a fight against French and American interests. Since this alliance was forged, two attacks have taken place. On October 30th, two near-simultaneous car bombs exploded outside police stations in two towns east of Algiers. The next attack, the first against foreigners in over two years, took place on December 10. Gunmen ambushed two buses, carrying British, American, Canadian, and Lebanese employees of oil company Brown & Root Condor following a roadside explosion. There has been no claim of responsibility, but the nature of the attack suggests an Al Qaeda influence. Algeria has been a valid ally of the US in the War on Terror. While certainly diminished in activity, the GSPC, which is a US designated terrorist organization, remains active in the southern area of the country, with the same area known to harbor a few hundred Al-Qaida operatives.[32]

The rising of tide of violence in Algeria is unfortunate and has again claimed the life of 19 people and injured 100 people on December 11, 2007. The two truckloads of bomb explosion in Algiers on this date, which followed an attack on a police convoy, are the handiwork of a group allied to Al Qaeda. Specifically Al Qaeda Islamic Magreb has claimed responsibility

---

32

http://www.globalsecurity.org/military/world/war/algeria-90s.htm

for it. This is a group of Islamic militants working to overthrow the Algerian government, which is engaged in counter-insurgency operations for some months against it. Though terrorism has had a presence in Algeria, this is the first time that a UN building was targeted. Moreover, this incident was targeted on the life of Algerian President Abdelaziz Bouteflika, which has, fortunately, failed.

It is therefore necessary that all political parties should try to solve the problem of terrorism politically. Perhaps the youths in West Asia are not satisfied with the present policy of their governments. Perhaps unemployment, poverty and frustration of the youths have resulted in conversion of young minds to the terrorist activities. The 'war on terror' is now guerrilla warfare between the government and terrorists in most of the least and low income countries.

Civil War in Georgia

Georgia is of vital strategic interest to Russia and the west, because it sits in the path of potentially lucrative oil routes. By early 2003 it appeared that the political situation in Georgia had stabilized after years of civil strife. It had a leader, President Shevardnadze, who commanded support from home and had a high profile abroad. Georgia had friendly relations with all of its neighbors - rare in a region torn with conflict. In addition, it had also been able to institute a series of economic reforms and position itself as a regional trading hub.

Russia has sought to retain a military presence in Georgia. Moscow asked for lease renewals on two other Soviet-era bases -- one in Batumi in the Ajaria region, the other in Akhalkalaki in the Javakhetia region. Georgia wanted the two bases vacated by 2004, but Russia wants 15 years to fulfill its pledge to pull out, by 2016.

Stability in Georgia has been a recent phenomenon, and several underlying problems remained. These boiled over in late 2003. Regional ethnic distribution is a major cause of the problems Georgia faces along its borders and within its territory. Under Soviet rule, a large part of Georgian territory was divided into autonomous regions that included concentrations of non-Georgian peoples. Russians, who make up the third largest ethnic group in the country (6.7 percent of the total population in 1989), but they do not constitute a majority in any district. The highest concentration of Russians is in Abkhazia.

Georgian government has no effective control over Abkhazia or much of South Ossetia. The Georgian state is highly centralized, except for the autonomous regions of Abkhazia and Ajaria, which are to be given special autonomous status once Georgia's territorial integrity is restored. Those regions were subjects of special autonomies during Soviet rule and the legacy of that influence remains. The political status of the breakaway provinces of Abkhazia and South Ossetia is unresolved. Sporadic outbreaks of violence continue to erupt in Abkhazia. About 300,000 people displaced by these conflicts have yet to return to home.

Gamsakhurdia, the president of Georgia was virulently anti-communist politician ever elected in a Soviet republic. He moved quickly to assert Georgia's independence from Moscow. Once the Soviet Union collapsed at the end of 1991, Georgia refused to participate in the formation or subsequent activities of the Commonwealth of Independent States. Following its independence from the Soviet Union in 1991, Georgia suffered from a civil war in 1992 following the overthrow of Zviad Gamsakhurdia, its first democratically elected president. In addition, Georgia was divided by separatist struggles in Abkhazia (northwest Georgia) and South Ossetia (North central Georgia). South Ossetia wants to join with North Ossetia, which is a part of Russia, and Russia has backed both separatist struggles. About 250,000 people were displaced by the civil wars in Georgia.

The UN Observer Mission in Georgia (UNOMIG), consisting of about 115 military observers monitoring the ceasefire lines and a civilian component, was established in 1994 after an accord reached in Moscow. This ended fighting that had forced nearly 300,000 people to flee. The Russian-enforced ceasefire in 1994 brought an end to the armed conflict in Abkhazia, and resulted in the permanent stationing of Russian troops in Abkhazia. A Russian peacekeeping force was engaged in South Ossetia since 1992. Both Abkhazia and South Ossetia have remained adamant in their separatist demands, and have refused any sort of autonomy that would mean remaining a part of Georgia. Georgia has been striving to reach a peaceful solution with the separatist regions. The instability in Georgia during the early 1990s led to the postponement of elections until November 1995, when President Shevardnadze and his ruling Union of Georgian Citizens party won the presidential elections with over 70 percent of the vote.

President Shevardnadze narrowly escaped an assassination attempt just prior to the elections on August 29, 1995. The assassination attempt resulted in a crackdown against opposition forces such as the Para-military Mkhedrioni (horsemen), led by former ally Saba Joseliani. The 1998 trial of Joseliani and 14 other alleged conspirators was characterized by the same violations of due process found in other trials with political overtones. The Government consistently violated due process both during the investigation and the trial. Torture, use of forced confessions, fabricated or planted evidence, denial of legal counsel, and the government adapted expulsion of defendants from the courtroom. In February 1998 between 10 to 15 assailants unsuccessfully attempted to assassinate President Shevardnadze. During the exchange of gunfire, two of his bodyguards and one of the attackers were killed, and four bodyguards were wounded seriously. Both assassination attempts in 1995 and 1998 were linked to disputes over construction of oil pipelines through Georgian territory. Moscow is also suspected of being behind the two assassination attempts on President Shevardnadze.

On 19 October 1998 army forces put down a small scale mutiny led by Colonel Akaki Eliava, a supporter of deceased former President Gamsakhurdia. The mutiny resulted in the deaths of one soldier and two mutineers and generated almost no popular support. Since surviving assassination attempts in August 1995 and February 1998, President Eduard Shevardnadze consolidated his leadership and declared an ambitious reform agenda. Elections on November 5, 1995, described as the freest and fairest in the Caucasus or Central Asia gave him the presidency and resulted in a progressive parliament led by sophisticated reformers. Since 1998, however, the reform process encountered serious obstacles and made limited progress.

The parliament instituted wide ranging political reforms supportive of higher human rights standards, including religious freedoms enshrined in the constitution. Problems persisted, however, largely as a result of the unwillingness of law enforcement and criminal justice officials to support constitutionally mandated rights. Violence against religious minorities and mistreatment of pretrial detainees are significant and continuing problems, as is corruption. The coup attempt in October 1998 led the chairman of the National Independence Party to call for NATO or the United States to station a military contingent in Georgia to protect Caspian oil transport. In December 1998, representatives from the GUAM Group

(Georgia, Ukraine, Azerbaijan, and Moldova) held talks about setting up a special peacekeeping force to protect the oil export pipelines. Proposals were made to work with NATO to set up this force within the framework of the Partnership for Peace Program, which was established by NATO to strengthen ties with former Eastern Bloc and former Soviet states.

Renewed fighting in the neighboring Chechnya (Russia) has generated concerns that the conflict will spill over into Georgia. Several thousand Chechen refugees moved into Georgia's Pankisi Gorge in late 1999, adding to the refugee/internally displaced population. The Abkhaz separatist dispute absorbs much of the government's attention. While a cease-fire is in effect, about **300,000** internally displaced persons (IDPs) who were driven from their homes during the conflict constitute a vocal lobby. The government has offered the region considerable autonomy in order to encourage a settlement, which would allow the IDPs, the majority of whom are ethnic Georgians from the Gali region, to return home, but the Abkhaz insist on independence.

On 27 September 2006, Georgian-Russian relations deteriorated further when the Georgian government detained four Russian military officers on charges of espionage. Both nations engaged in a back-and-forth series of shows of military and diplomatic force. These included the surrounding of Russia's military headquarters in Georgia, the withdrawal of the Russian diplomats, and reprisal raids against each other's business interests.

On 6 October, the Russian Duma ratified a treaty that would guarantee a withdrawal of Russian forces from Georgian territory and assure Russian access to Armenian bases via Georgia. Georgia continued war against Russia/ Abkazia/ South Ossezia in 2008. Tensions at border countries continue in 2010.

Sri Lanka – Tamil Separatists

Liberation Tigers of Tamil Elam (LTTE), World Tamil Association (WTA), World Tamil Movement (WTM), and Federation of Associations of Canadian Tamils (FACT), are the actors in the Sri Lanka insurgency and Tamil separatists' movement.

Tamil rebels began an armed uprising in 1983, after they complained of discrimination against the minority Tamil community. The rebels say they want wide-ranging autonomy for Tamil-dominated areas under their control in the north and the east. Although a ceasefire signed in 2002 is still in force, peace talks have been on hold for more than a year. Norwegian envoys have shuttled between the government and the rebels in a bid to revive talks, but neither side can agree on an agenda to resume discussions. In 2004 the ruling party won local elections, which could strengthen the government's hand and pave the way for it to restart talks with the rebels. In July 2004 Tamil Tigers threatened to resume a civil war halted by a peace process that began two-and-one-half-years ago. The Tigers accuse the Sri Lankan military of trying to weaken the rebel movement by using the rival rebel faction against them. The army and the government deny the charges, saying they are abiding by a ceasefire agreement signed in 2002. Several Tamil Tiger cadres had been killed in the east recently, and a suicide-bomb attack ripped Colombo, killing four policemen.

The Tamil people of the island of Ceylon (now called Sri Lanka) constitute a distinct nation. They form a social entity, with their own history, traditions, culture, language and traditional homeland. The Tamil people call their nation Tamil Elam'. Founded in 1976, the LTTE is the most powerful Tamil group in Sri Lanka and uses overt and illegal methods to raise funds, acquire weapons, and publicize its cause of establishing an independent Tamil state. The LTTE began its armed conflict with the Sri Lankan Government in 1983 and relies on a guerrilla strategy that includes the use of terrorist tactics. The group's elite Black Tiger squad conducts suicide bombings against important targets, and all rank-and-file members carry a cyanide capsule to kill themselves rather than allow them to be caught. The LTTE is very insular and highly organized with its own intelligence service, naval element (the Sea Tigers), and women's political and military wings.

Approximately 10,000 armed combatants in Sri Lanka; about 3,000 to 6,000 form a trained cadre of fighters. The LTTE also has a significant overseas support structure for fundraising, weapons procurement, and propaganda activities. The LTTE also has its own naval wing designated the Sea Tigers.

The Tigers control most of the northern and eastern coastal areas of Sri Lanka but have conducted operations throughout the island. Headquartered in the Wanni region, LTTE leader Velupillai Prabhakaran has established an extensive network of checkpoints and informants to keep track of any outsiders who enter the group's area of control.

The LTTE's overt organizations support Tamil separatism by lobbying foreign governments and the United Nations. The LTTE also uses its international contacts to procure weapons, communications, and bomb making equipment. The LTTE exploits large Tamil communities in North America, Europe, and Asia to obtain funds and supplies for its fighters in Sri Lanka. The Liberation Tigers of Tamil Elam are involved in numerous trans national criminal activities, including partnerships with Pakistani heroin producers/traffickers, alien smuggling, extortion from Tamil families living abroad, and various forms of fraud. All this in order to raise funds for their insurgent activities in Sri Lanka

The LTTE has integrated a battlefield insurgent strategy with a terrorist program that targets key government and military personnel, the economy, and public infrastructure. Political assassinations include the suicide bomber attacks against Sri Lankan President Ranasinghe Premadasa in 1993 and Indian Prime Minister Rajiv Gandhi in 1991, which is the group's only known act outside Sri Lanka. The LTTE has detonated two massive truck bombs directed against the Sri Lankan economy, one at the Central Bank in January 1996 and another at the Colombo World Trade Center in October 1997. The LTTE also has attacked several ships in Sri Lankan waters, including foreign commercial vessels and infrastructure targets such as commuter trains, buses, oil tanks, and power stations. The LTTE prefers to attack vulnerable government facilities then withdraw before reinforcements arrive, or to time its attacks to take advantage of security lapses on holidays, at night, or in the early morning. In the past several years, the LTTE has also attacked several commercial ships flying foreign flags in the waters off the north and east of the country. In 1998, threats were directed at domestic air carriers flying between Colombo and Jaffna, and in September of that year, a domestic civilian aircraft flying from Colombo to Jaffna crashed, killing everyone on board. The cause of the accident is still unknown.

Bomb attacks remain the greatest terrorist hazard. The LTTE has attempted or carried out numerous political assassinations or attempts. In 1999, suicide bombings resulted in the death of 30 persons and injury to 143 others in Colombo, Trincomalee, Batticaloa, Jaffna and Medawachchi. In January 2000, a suicide bomber killed more than a dozen and wounded several passers-by when she detonated her bomb outside the Prime Minister's Office after being detected by security personnel. In March 2000, as many as eight LTTE terrorists attacked a government motorcade traveling on a major Colombo thoroughfare, killing 25 people and wounding many others. In June 2000, a suicide bomber assassinated the Minister for Industrial Development in a Colombo suburb. Twenty-one others were killed and 60 people were injured in the attack. In October 2000, two American and one British women and their Sri Lankan driver were seriously injured in their vehicle in Central Colombo when an LTTE suicide bomber confronted by police exploded his device rather than surrender. Three policemen were killed. In October 2001, an LTTE suicide bomber stopped by police in the vicinity of an election rally in Colombo detonated his device rather than surrender, killing five people and injuring 16 others.

In May 2000, the Sri Lankan Government activated provisions of the Public Security Ordinance, giving certain government authorities sweeping powers to deal with threats to national security. The next month the LTTE gained a significant victory in taking the Elephant pass army garrison, located in a town on the Jaffna Peninsula. In February 2002 the LTTE and the Sri Lankan government signed a ceasefire agreement brokered by Norway. As of June 2003 the agreement appeared to be dissolving. The LTTE claimed the government has done little to address rebel concerns and deliver on the promises made during the six rounds of peace talks. The LTTE wanted to draft an independent Tamil administration, while the Sri Lankan government was willing to go only as far as granting financial autonomy. The impasse came as involved parties planned to meet in Tokyo for a Sri Lankan financial aid conference.

Skirmishes between LTTE rebels and government forces were decreasing until April 2006 when riots broke out in the northeast and explosions killed 16 people. On 11 May 2006, the LTTE attacked a naval convoy. The attack was seen as the most blatant violation to date of the 2002 peace agreement. On 16 October 2006, a LTTE suicide attack on a Sri Lankan naval convoy killed 93 sailors and wounded 150 others. Peace talks ceased, and attacks by LTTE rebels and government forces have resumed. The LTTE followed up this strike with a suicide attack on a Sri Lankan naval base on 18 October. In Colombo, on 23 October, the Sri Lankan President, Mahindra Rajapakse, inked a deal with the United National Party, the opposition, for a common policy for dealing with the LTTE.

With a unified policy in place, Rajapakse entered two-day talks with the LTTE in Geneva on 28 October. The talks, which were the first in eight months, covered the humanitarian crisis in Sri Lanka. The first day of the negotiations was dominated by back-and-forth recriminations. The second failed due to disagreement on access to the Jaffna peninsula. The talks were deemed a failure and, on October 30, Sri Lankan forces clashed with the LTTE in Jaffna. November saw higher intensity fighting between the two sides. On 1 November, the Sri Lankan air force struck rebel targets. Seven days later, the Amnesty International accused Sri Lanka of killing 45 civilians in an artillery strike. Sea clashes occurred on 10 November resulting in the sinking of two Tamil boats. That same day, unknown gunmen murdered a pro-LTTE Sri Lankan MP. On 21 November, Sri Lankan aircraft struck a LTTE camp.

On 23 November, a Tamil website revealed that Anton Balasingham, the LTTE's top negotiator, had been crippled by an advanced-state cancer that had spread over much of his body. A Tamil newspaper described his situation as incurable. Balasingham died on 14 December. Jon Hanssen-Bauer, Norway's peace envoy in Sri Lanka, agreed on 4 December to a government request to delay negotiations scheduled for the next day. As part of the agreement, Sri Lanka asked the Norwegians to contact the LTTE only with its approval. In the midst of this decision were signs that the government may again ban the LTTE and designate it as a terrorist organization. The government stopped just short of designating the LTTE as a terrorist organization. Instead, the cabinet enacted anti-terror measures against the LTTE that would give security forces the increased power to search, arrest, and question. Approximately 3,400 people have died since late 2005.

About 80,000–100,000 people have died in Sri Lanka's civil war.

Sri Lanka Government forced 300, 000 refugees into camps after fleeing the final months of the government's decade-long war with separatists LTTE cadre.

Killing of Pravakaran in 2009

On May 18, 2009 the LTTE supreme Velupillai Pirabhaharam (popularly called Pravakaran) was shot dead by the army of Sri Lanka Government. The Tiger supremo ruthlessly tried a separate state inside Sri Lanka for equal rights of the Tamils. The LTTE assassinated Rajiv Gandhi, the Prime Minister of India in Sriperumbudur near Chhenai (India) at 10.21 pm on May 21, 1991. As a result the Tamils in India, which supported Tamil guerrillas openly or covertly, were put in dilemma. The chauvinist Singhalese Army Chief General Sarath Fonseka has requested the President of Sri Lanka Mahindra Rajapaksa to give equal status to the Tamils in Sri Lanka. This island country inhabits Singhalese majority and Tamils minority. The law of the land indirectly treats the Tamils as second-class citizens. The leader is dead but the root cause of the problem is not yet solved. The Tamils in Sri Lanka must be awarded human rights and the international community around the world expects that the government should take immediate step.

LTTE has a new leader

Mr. Selvarasa Pathmanathan, who was head of the international affairs of LTTE, has been appointed as the 'Leader' and Pravakaran - the leader who was killed by the army was, is and will be the leader of Tamil Nationhood forever. The organization will follow a modified procedure to achieve the goal of a free Tamil Elam. The LTTE has revitalized to undertake a duty that has been left in their hands by their leader, martyred heroes and civilians who have given their lives in defending their soil. They have formulated sector-based working groups and requested the Tamils to assist to their future plans. They have vowed to achieve an independent Tamil Nation through actions. They say that the fire for freedom awakened by their great leader V. Pravakaran continues to burn in the hearts of all Tamils, and that only a freedom has the power to extinguish it.

The Sri Lanka government would release 1, 36, 000 Tamil war refugees on December 1, 2009 and others by January 31, 2010.

General Sarath Fonseka has claimed in an interview in December 2009 that the surrendering LTTE leaders were killed on the orders of Defense Secretary Gotabhaya Rajapaksa. Perhaps this mass killing of POWs resembles the killings of Jews or Russians by the Nazis during the Second World War. The United Nations Organization is silent over this matter and is searching for human rights of the Tamils.

Election in Sri Lanka: January 26, 2010

President Mahindra Rajapaksa and Army Chief Sarath Fonseka were the war heroes of Sri Lankan victory over LTTE in 2009. But both of them were the Presidential candidates for the 2010 Election in Sri Lanka. The Army Chief resigned to contest the Presidential Election and was supported by the opposition parties. In a bitterly-fought contest, the President Mahindra Rajapaksa won the second term with 6,015,934 votes while Sarath Fonseka bagged 4,173,185 votes. The former chief of Army has requested India for his safety and complained that the President Rajapakse has played foul play in the election. Fonseka accused also Rajapaksa of using the state media to attack him and of misappropriating public funds for his campaign and of preventing displaced minority Tamils from voting. He would initiate legal proceedings to have the January 26 election annulled. Sri Lankan army surrounded the hotel where Fonseka was staying with his supporters on January 27, 2010. Now the question is, "Why the ex-Army Chief feels that he is unsafe? How a losing Presidential candidate finds himself under siege?"

Urgent Action by the United Nations

The Ex-Army Chief Sarath Fonseka is already booked under martial law by the elected President Mahindra Rajapaksa. A false allegation has been made that Fonseka had plotted an attempt to murder the President. Mr. Fonseka is tortured in jail and martial court punished him another term of 3-year term in 2011. Why then he was not arrested before the election and his candidature was not rejected by the President before election? Why he was charged with allegations after the result was declared?

If the defeated Presidential candidate bagging 4,173,185 votes in the election is booked and might be punished by the winning President, the United Nations must take up the matter at the earliest to save Mr. Sarath Fonseka. He was the Ex- Army Chief and Ex- Presidential candidate. Where is the Human rights Commission? Mr. Fonseka was elected as a Member of the Parliament in March 2010 and was released from jail custody in May 2012.

This suggests that democracy must be redefined. Can a winning Presidential candidate defame and imprison his contender (the failure Presidential candidate of the opposition) with false allegations? There should be an international law for election of the President of a country.

Sudan – Darfur Conflict

Darfur region is located in the western part of the Sudan. Darfur is situated with border of Libya in the North, Chad in the West and the Central African Republic in the South West. Kordofan and Bahr El-Gazal regions border the eastern and the southern parts of Darfur respectively. The estimated population of Darfur is around 4 million; approximately 60 percent of them are subsistence farmers. The major ethnic group is the Fur, hence the name Darfur. The rest are either nomadic or semi-nomadic herders. The majority of farmers live close to subsistence level. There are some small traders and local merchants, but their economic impact is insignificant. The Fur, largely peasant farmers, occupies the central belt of the region, including the Jebel Marra massif. Also in this central zone are the non-Arab Masalit, Berti, Bargu, Bergid, Tama and Tunjur peoples, who are all sedentary farmers. The northernmost zone is Dar Zaghawa, part of the Libyan Sahara, and inhabited by camel nomads: principally the Zaghawa and Bedeyat, who are non-Arab in origin, and the Arab Mahariya, Irayqat, Mahamid and Beni Hussein. The general sense of antagonism toward Khartoum was reinforced by the drought and the near-famine conditions that have afflicted Darfur since 1984. Khartoum failed to cope with the social and economic consequences of the environmental disaster, a situation that increased alienation from the central government. By the early 1990s, much of Darfur was in a state of anarchy.

Historically, Darfur has suffered recurrent droughts. Crop yields have remained low and unpredictable due to erratic rainfall, pest infestation and the lack of agricultural inputs. The livestock has also dwindled due to pasture and water scarcity. The local labor force has continued to migrate in search of employment leaving behind children, women and the elderly. A combination of these factors over several years has systematically eroded the coping capacities of communities. The government of Sudan maintains that conflict in this region of Darfur is primarily a tribal one, centered on the competition for land between pastoralists and crop farmers in the area. However, leaders of the Four- tribe insist that the depopulation of villages and consequent changes in land ownership are part of a government strategy to change the whole demography of the region of Darfur.

Fighting between two main opposition groups -- the Sudanese Liberation Movement/Army (SLM/A) and the Justice and Equality Movement (JEM) faction of the Sudan Liberation Movement/Army (SLM/A) -- the Government of Sudan (GOS) military, and GOS-supported militia groups collectively known as Janjaweed intensified in the three states of Darfur, the western region of Sudan, during late 2003. Insecurity has steadily increased since the Darfur-based opposition SLM/A attacked GOS military forces at El Fasher, North Darfur, on April 24 and 25, 2003. The humanitarian emergency in Darfur is a direct result of violence toward the Fur, Zaghawa, and Massalit civilian groups by GOS forces and the Janjaweed. Conflict-affected populations describe recurrent and systematic attacks against towns and villages, burning of buildings and crops, arbitrary killings, gang rape, and looting. The GOS has used aerial bombardments to terrorize civilians, who the GOS claims are harboring SLM/A. and JEM forces.

The main cause of this conflict is the widespread feeling of being consistently socio-economically marginalized and the sense of being left out of the peace negotiations particularly in the context of self-determination and power sharing. Over five-dozen people from the Fur tribe were arrested and detained during July and August 2002, from the towns of Zalingei, Tour, and Nyartati and Golou in Jebel Mara province. None of the 66 people had been formally charged, but the Government stated that those arrested were suspected of working to form an opposition group calling themselves the 'Darfur Liberation Front'. Darfur had experienced a marked increase in levels of tribal conflict, with at least 65 people, all from the African tribes, confirmed killed in attacks by Arab militia since May 2002. Hundreds of houses had also been destroyed and thousands of livestock lost.

By early 2003 exiled Sudanese rights activists claimed that the conflict in Western Sudan's Darfur region was developing from ethnic cleansing into genocide. The Khartoum government allegedly supports Arab militias in their massacre of Fur and other indigenous people termed "slaves". Khartoum however claims its neutrality and says it is fighting "banditry" in Darfur. The United Nations estimated that up to 600,000 people had been displaced by the conflict since February 2003. Hundreds of thousands of people have been forced to flee their homes since fighting broke out in April 2003 between the rebel Justice and Equality Movement and government forces. The situation of women and children is particularly desperate.

There are two main rebel groups:

The Sudanese Liberation Army is backed by Eritrea. Until 2003, the group was known as the Darfur Liberation Front. Rebels in Darfur emerged in February 2003 under the name of Darfur Liberation Front. The Darfur Liberation Army announced no connection with the southern rebels, but it called in the middle of March 2003 for "an understanding" with the opposition forces which fight the Islamists government in Khartoum. In March 2003 the Darfur Liberation Front announced it had downed a helicopter that was carrying an official in the province. On 14 March 2003 Darfur Liberation Front announced that the movement would be called the Sudan Liberation Movement and the Sudan Liberation Army (SLM/SLA). The Darfur Liberation Front was a secessionist organisation calling for the secession of the area from Sudan. The SLA, led by Mini Arkoi Minawi, says it wants to "create a united, democratic Sudan."

The Justice and Equality Movement (JEM) faction of the Sudan Liberation Movement/Army (SLM/A) appears to have received support from Chad, and some captured rebels were found to have Chadian identification and arms. It is also possible that Hassan al-Turabi, a Sudanese opposition leader backed this war. Turabi, the former speaker of Sudan's parliament and the ideologist of its Islamists revolution, was removed from office in May 2000 and imprisoned by Sudan's military. During the late 1970s he had worked with Sadiq al-Mahdi, the leader of the Mahdist political party and grandson of The Mahdi.

The Sudan Liberation Army began battling an Arab militia called Janjawid as well as government troops in the Darfur region of western Sudan. The Janjawid have been pushing local farming communities off their land in a bid to have access to the resources. Critics accuse the Sudanese government of manipulating traditional ethnic tensions and pursuing a policy of "Arabization" in Darfur, in order to maintain a support base there. The government has denied backing the Arab militia and said it wants to bring them under control. The Sudanese government strongly denies backing the militias. It says it has urged all tribes in Darfur to "defend" themselves against rebels in the region.

Reports indicate more than 600,000 civilians have been internally displaced, 75,000 refugees began fleeing to Chad in April 2003, and as many as 3,000 unarmed civilians have been killed in the region's spiraling conflict.

Many more have been prevented from planting or harvesting crops. Humanitarian access continues to be inhibited by ongoing insecurity and the Government of Sudan's denial of travel permits to humanitarian workers.

The government has denied all humanitarian agencies access, so UNICEF and other UN agencies are complaining to the government about this. UNICEF fears that the acute malnutrition among children less than five-years-old will increase dramatically due to a lack of food, due to displacement, due to lack of access from humanitarian agencies, and also, already very poor sanitary conditions and access to safe water. The authorities might be embarrassed that fierce fighting is going on in this remote corner of Sudan at a time when a peace deal ending 25 years of civil war is almost concluded. Hostilities in Darfur between indigenous opposition groups and the Sudanese Armed Forces and its allied militias have caused non-governmental organizations and the UN to curtail needed humanitarian assistance programs. This is an invisible emergency that does not get a lot of attention around the world, but it is something of extreme concern. UNHCR is concerned about security along Chad's eastern border with Sudan, and planned to begin relocating the Sudanese refugees from that area to sites deeper inside Chad.

On May 25th 2004 the United Nations Security Council responded to widespread human rights violations and a deteriorating humanitarian situation in the Darfur region by condemning attacks on civilians and calling on the Khartoum government to prevent the Janjaweed from carrying out strikes on the black African population. The resolution expressed concern at reports of large-scale violations of human rights and international humanitarian law such as "indiscriminate attacks on civilians, sexual violence, forced displacement and acts of violence, especially those with an ethnic dimension" and demanded that the perpetrators be held accountable. While the Council welcomed the humanitarian ceasefire agreement signed in April in Chad, it reiterated its call for the Government of Sudan to respect its commitments and ensure that the Janjaweed are neutralized and disarmed. Earlier in May, Sudan was re-elected as a member of the UN Commission on Human Rights, prompting a walk out by the American envoy in protest of the Khartoum-government's backing of atrocities in Darfur.

On June 24th the US Congress approved a humanitarian aid package for Sudan's western Darfur region as an amendment to a defense-spending bill. The measure included $70 million for the US Agency for International Development's disaster and famine programs in Darfur, and $14 million to assist refugees in Chad. A few days later, on June 29th US Secretary of State Colin Powell visited Sudan to urge Khartoum authorities to reign in Arab militiamen accused of human rights abuses in the Darfur region. He met with President Omar el-Bashir and visited displaced people in Darfur, threatening unspecified UN Security Council action unless the government brought an end to militia violence. The United Nations has described the 15-month Darfur conflict as the world's worst humanitarian crisis, and UN relief groups estimate that up to 2 million people are in need of food, while a million more have been forced to flee their homes. The US government claims that the casualties of fighting between the Janjaweed and black Africans range from 10,000 to 30,000 people thus far. The Islamists Khartoum government denies links to the Janjaweed, but continues to block aid workers, journalists, and independent human rights monitors from entering Darfur to assess the situation, in violation of earlier agreements.

African Union military observers in Darfur reported that Sudanese militias have burned civilians alive. The AU's peace and Security Council announced in a meeting in Addis Ababa on July 27th that it is actively considering expanding the military observer mission into a multinational peacekeeping force with particular emphasis on disarming the Janjaweed if the Sudanese government does not do so. This would be the AU's first military intervention in a member state. The AU will also expand its ceasefire-observer mission, which originally would be protected by a small force of 300 troops, to a much larger contingent with the specific job of disarming the militiamen. The United Kingdom raised the possibility of sending troops to Darfur, but US Secretary of State Colin Powell insisted it was premature to speak of military intervention. Sudan's Foreign Minister Mustafa Osman Ismail warned that Sudanese solders would repel any advance by foreign troops in Darfur. Khartoum went on to summon UK and German diplomats to protest EU-sponsored sanctions on the Darfur conflict.

The UN Security Council was also to discuss possible sanctions against Sudan. On July 27th, the United States circulated the latest version of a resolution that sets deadlines for the Sudanese government to stop the Janjaweed's campaign of terror and promises unspecified sanctions as a consequence of noncompliance. EU foreign ministers supported the resolution, but veto powers Russia and China argued that the Sudanese government should have more time to comply with the earlier joint communiqué to crack down on the militiamen and allow aid to reach starving Darfur. Pakistan and Algeria were said to also oppose immediate sanctions, but US diplomats said they were confident that a majority of UN Security Council members would back the draft. There has been resistance to a Council vote on the issue. The Arab League told the Security Council to "avoid precipitate action" and give Sudan more time to honor its pledges. African leaders seek an "African solution" to Darfur at a special summit in Ghana on July 29th called by the AU Chairman, President Olusegun Obasanjo of Nigeria. The AU requested British and Dutch assistance in airlifting 300 African troops to Sudan.

In mid-July 2004, Human Rights Watch obtained copies of Sudanese government documents that described an official policy of support for the Janjaweed militia. Thus far, aid agencies had estimated the death toll at 50,000 and warned that it might eventually run into hundreds of thousands. More than a million people had fled their homes. On November 19 Sudan's government and southern rebels signed a pledge to commit them to ending Sudan's 21-year civil war. The pledge was signed in front of the 15 Security Council members in Nairobi, remarkable for the fact that it is the first time in 14 years and only the fourth time ever that the Security Council has met outside of its New York home. While the two groups have made similar, failed pledges in the past, the presence of the Security Council members may give this pledge added credibility. Officials also hoped that the agreement could be later applied to the situation in Darfur. However, human rights groups such as Oxfam and Amnesty International expressed skepticism with the agreement, claiming it to be little more than empty words and promises. While the Security Council promised that it would consider taking appropriate measures should either side fail to follow through on its commitments, both China and Russia have said that they are opposed to any penalties.

On September 21, SPLM/A rebels overtook the government - fortified town of Shareya, northeast of Nyala in south Darfur. The violence drove out humanitarian agencies working in Shareya and nearby Mohajuria, leaving behind nearly 77,000 people who had been receiving assistance. These actions were predicted to provoke government reprisals. As of September 23, 2005 the situation in Sudan remained dire. Since the eruption of violence in the Darfur region in February of 2003, the ongoing battle between the rebel forces and government backed Janjaweed has driven an estimated 2 million natives from their home with some 200,000 fleeing into neighboring Chad. The fighting as well as the killing of civilians and the miserable conditions of refugees has been responsible for 180,000 deaths. That number is an approximation since the circumstances do not allow for a more accurate death toll, and the true number could very well be much higher than that.

Despite the best efforts of the United Nations Mission in Sudan (UNMIS), the African Unions Mission in Sudan (AMIS), and the humanitarian NGOs, supplies remain scarce and securities insufficient to guarantee a safe return home for the survivors. The signing and implementation of the Comprehensive Peace Agreement created the interim government integrated with the rebel group SPLM/A, ending, on paper, the country's 21-year civil war. The new national unity government in conjuncture with the ongoing peace talks with the remaining rebel groups provides the potential for peace and stability in the region. However, the fragility of Sudan's cease-fire remains painfully apparent in the wake of continued engagements drawn along ethnic and political lines. There also seems to be increasing division and dissent in the ranks of the rebel militias, leading to further chaos and violence preventing the peace process. The longer the country remains embattled, the further these conditions will degrade, creating conditions for even more suffering.

As of October 2005, the African Union, with the support of the United Nations had a contingency of approximately 6000 AU soldiers to monitor a ceasefire. At that time it was estimated that there were 1.8 million people in camps in Darfur, with another 200,000 refugees in Chad. Despite the ceasefire and AU force, it is widely reported that the security situation deteriorated significantly. Not only were refugees and AU members attacked and victimized, but aid and humanitarian workers were also attacked, raped and looted. As a result international aid and its workers had virtually ground to a halt.

As of the beginning of February 2006, the UN Security Council asked Kofi Annan to "initiate contingency planning" and to produce various options in consultation with the AU, for UN peacekeeping operations. Around the same time, which helped spur on the UN Security Council initiative, was the fact that 70,000 people fled the town of Mershing, after militiamen attacked. Talk of NATO reinforcements had also been expressed at this time. After many delays and missed deadlines, the slow negotiations between the Sudanese government and the largest rebel movement active in Sudan's Darfur region, struck a deal in the Nigerian capital, Abuja, on May 5th, 2006. Despite the optimistic deal, two other significant rebel groups refused to sign it. While not all the parties agreed, the agreement affords a political breach which made it possible for the UN to send stronger, better-armed peacekeeping forces into Darfur, to support and replace the existing AU forces. Additionally the agreement called for the disarming of the Janjaweed. As of the end of July 2006, the Khartoum government has been slow to approve and grant permission to let UN officials and troops into Darfur, Sudan. The prospects of UN peacekeeping forces remain grim, unless the Sudanese government relinquishes their obstinate stance.

In August 2006, the Sudanese government rejected a UN resolution authorizing a peacekeeping force in

Darfur on the grounds that it would be a violation of Sudanese sovereignty. The plan would enlarge the current force from 7,000 to 20,000. On September 3, Khartoum asked the African Union force to leave the country when at the end of its mandate. At a 22 September emergency international meeting on the Darfur conflict, US Secretary of State Condoleezza Rice said that "time is running out." She called upon those in attendance to continue to press Sudan to accept a larger peacekeeping force. In 6 October, Sudan sent a letter to the Security Council declaring its view that any contribution to a peacekeeping force would be considered "a hostile act." The US' ambassador to the UN, John Bolton, said the letter demanded "a strong response."

On 22 October, UN envoy to Sudan, Jan Pronk was expelled from Sudan. Khartoum claimed that Pronk was asked to leave because he had violated his neutrality on the situation. The Sudanese army was suffering from low morale due to defeats in Darfur. The UN interfered and announced that he would keep his position.

The Darfur crisis threatened to become a regional conflict on 7 November when Chad accused Sudan of "exporting the genocide." In the week prior to this announcement, 200 people were killed attacks on villages just inside the Chad border. Chad declared a state of emergency on the 13th and was backed by a UN warning against the incursion. On the 17th, Sudan said it would welcome a hybrid UN-AU force as long as the UN was not in command. Specifically, the Sudan said it would accept "all financial, material, logistic, or technical assistance from the UN in order to strengthen the AU mission in Darfur." On the same day, Chad proposed an anti-Sudan alliance with the Central African Republic (CAR). Both nations have accused Sudan of backing rebels fighting against the CAR government. Hopes of a deal between the UN, AU, and Darfur were put in jeopardy on 18 November when the AU accused Sudan of launching a new ground and air offensive in Darfur. Although details were few, the AU said that there had been heavy casualties. On 30 November the AU voted to extend the peacekeepers' mandate for another six months after January. The United States, on 14 December, proposed a no-fly zone over Darfur to prevent attacks against civilians. The State Department proposed other UN-sanctioned options including a naval blockade or air strikes. Meanwhile, the UN Human Rights Council agreed to send a team of experts to Darfur to investigate allegations of abuse.

Top envoys from the United Nations and the African Union chairing talks in Libya on the troubled Darfur region of Sudan welcomed the Khartoum Government's unilateral declaration of a cessation of hostilities and called on all parties to the conflict to make a similar commitment without delay.

The UN envoy Jan Eliasson and his AU counterpart, Ahmed Salim in a joint statement expressed that the parties cannot talk and fight at the same time, without tragic consequences to the population of Darfur. It is critical that all parties do their utmost to improve the security and humanitarian conditions of the people in Darfur. This was a turning point in the long search for a lasting political solution to the crisis in Darfur. The envoys were happy that the first stage of a three-phased peace process was possible with the attendance of the Government of Sudan, leading personalities and representatives of the movements, as well as representatives from civil society.

This first phase of the talks included two lively plenary debates where representatives from the Government of Sudan, the movements, civil society, including women, regional partners, and international observers exchanged views and discussed key issues pertaining to the peace process. Closed meetings were then held with the parties, regional partners, and international observers. The second phase will play out over the next few weeks as the envoys continue to engage in intensive discussions with the parties on the substantive issues to be addressed in the third stage of negotiations. The peace process is irreversible. The conflict-affected Sudanese deserves peace. The committee owes it to the people of Darfur to make every effort to end their suffering and allow them to live their lives in peace and dignity.

The conflict has killed more than 200,000 people and displaced more than 2,500,000 people in Darfur region only.

Ashraf Qazi, the Secretary-General's Special Representative for Sudan, has also welcomed the peace talks in Sirte. He opined:

(a) Peace can only be achieved through an inclusive political process supplemented by recovery and development programmes.
(b) Peace and stability in all of Sudan is crucial to resolve the humanitarian emergency in the war-ravaged and impoverished said
(c) Sustained peace throughout Sudan is the key to ending the humanitarian crisis in Darfur and to moving towards a more holistic goal of recovery and development throughout Sudan

Darfur humanitarian operation remains an enormous challenge. Humanitarian community remains concerned about the suffering and insecurity in Darfur, where the population faces continued displacement and ongoing insecurity.

A successful humanitarian response is dependent on widespread respect for the basic humanitarian principles of impartiality, humanity and independence of humanitarian actors, and I would like to take this opportunity to appeal to all parties involved in the conflict to adhere to these principles.

Ameerah Haq, the Deputy Special Representative for Sudan and UN Humanitarian Coordinator told:

(a) Funding to meet humanitarian needs will surge from $650 million this year to $825 million next year.

(b) Aid workers are worried about the insecurity in camps for internally displaced persons (IDPs), particularly in South Darfur, as well as the proliferation of arms in camps and rising levels of violence.

(c) All parties to cease arming camp residents and to respect the principles of voluntary return and security camps as neutral humanitarian spaces.

(d) The UN intervention in peace process must yield better results, but it is too late. We opine that the UN Peace Building Council should take up immediate steps to start peace process in all the conflict-affected regions with representatives of the countries. The peace workers, peace organizations and peace researchers should be associated in the peace process. Sudan has forgotten peace and fights for its own survival. Fights continue in Sudan in 2010 as follows:

- (a) Fight between Islamic North Sudan Government against Christian South Sudan since 2005
- (b) Government fights Darfur population from 2003
- (c) Government is continuing clashes with rebels of Justice and Equality Movement (JEM) since 2006. Government is fighting against Sudan Liberation Army (SLA) since 2002.
- (d) In 2006 JEM and SLA formed Alliance of Revolutionary Forces of West Sudan.[33]

---

[33] UN: Darfur: African Union envoys urge all parties to press ahead for peace: 30/10/2007 (Maxims News Network), - 30 October 2007 -

Iraq–USA War

In March 2003 coalition forces entered Iraq, forcing an end to the rule of the Ba'athist regime. The resulting conditions for the Iraqi population after the Iraq war were different than what had been speculated in the months leading up to the conflict. An acute humanitarian crisis did not materialize as anticipated. The predicted influx of refugees spilling over into neighboring Kuwait, Jordan and Turkey and the projected degree of internal displacement due to the military campaign by coalition forces simply did not transpire. As a result, emergency preparedness efforts were ultimately applied not towards responding to emergency humanitarian needs due to military action and forced population movement but rather to humanitarian needs resulting from increased civil insecurity, looting and years of neglect, isolation and oppression.

From May 2003 through June 2004, the CPA, led by the United States and the United Kingdom, was the UN-recognized authority responsible for the temporary governance of Iraq and for overseeing, directing, and coordinating the reconstruction effort. In May 2003, the CPA began the process of recreating Iraqi security forces. Multinational force commanders eventually assumed responsibility for recruiting and training Iraqi security forces in their areas of responsibility. The Department of State is responsible for all U.S. activities in Iraq except security and military operations. The Iraq Reconstruction and Management Office (IRMO) are responsible for planning and prioritizing reconstruction requirements, monitoring spending, and coordinating with the military commanders. The U.S. Army Corps of Engineers provides engineering and technical services to USAID, State, and military forces in Iraq. In December 2005, the responsibilities of the Project Contracting Office (PCO), a temporary organization were merged with those of the U.S. Army Corps of Engineers.

On June 28, 2004, the CPA transferred power to an interim sovereign Iraqi government, the CPA was officially dissolved, and Iraq's transitional period began. Under Iraq's transitional law, the transitional period included the completion of a draft constitution in October 2005 and two subsequent elections—a referendum on the constitution and an election for a permanent government. The Iraqi people approved the constitution on October 15, 2005, and voted for representatives to the Iraq Council of Representatives on December 15, 2005. The Independent Electoral Commission of Iraq certified the election results on February 10, 2006. After much negotiating and many attempts to form a national unity government, Nuri al-Maliki was chosen to fill the Prime Minister post and choose a cabinet to be approved by the Council of Representatives. Maliki had taken the post previously occupied temporarily by Ibraham al-Jaafari. On June 8, 2006, Iraq's Council of Representatives approved the final members of Maliki's cabinet.

Military Operations have continued to occur despite the end of major combat operations on 01 May 2003. Iraqi opposition forces show some signs of organization. Continuing conflict seems to be contained in the areas surrounding Fallujah and the Baghdad-Tikrit corridor. Attacks are opportunistic and show signs of organization leading DoD officials to believe the attacks to be conducted by "dead enders" loyal who continue to be loyal to Saddam Hussein.

In August 2003 Lt. Gen. Ricardo Sanchez, the commander of US ground forces, decided to minimize the large military sweeps to the north and west of Baghdad. While the sweeps, conducted in June and July 2003, rounded up hundreds of Iraqis, they angered residents who complained of mistreatment, arbitrary arrests and humiliation at the hands of US soldiers. The release of 30,000 felons in the fall of 2002 by the former regime has placed a criminal element on the street that has fought hard to ensure instability and take advantage of the lack of an effective security organization. Well-funded drug gangs unchecked for nearly a year are committing random murder and mayhem against US forces and the populace.

An influx of known third country nationals combined with remnants of the Saddam Fayadeen, have constituted the bulk of the ambush teams that have attacked convoys and individual soldiers. They have used incidents at Fallujah (3 ACR in April 2003) and Baghdad (1 AD in June 2003) to incite incidents by planting instigators with AK-47s to fire on Army soldiers then let the human shields in the crowd absorb the lethal response. This response though "legally correct" under the force protection rules of engagement is depicted as "morally wrong" under the CNN spin effect that did not detail the presence of the AK-47 gunmen.

There were initially unrealistic expectations for the resumption of normal life support services and the immediate Americanization of the country on the part of the Iraqi people. This has lead to dissatisfaction and a lack of cooperation in combating the insurgents, as the people believed that if we could defeat Saddam in three weeks we should get them to a decent standard of living quickly, even with infrastructure that has been neglected for a decade. The local police, state police, and federal law enforcement, and their various jurisdictions and strengths are unknown to Iraqis. The previous regime deconstructed the proactive police force of the 1970s and that which remained did not actively patrol or interact with the population. They were neither situation ally aware of crime nor trusted by those they ostensibly protected. The police force protected the regime first and the populace second.

US Forces:

This is a "best available" listing of US forces deployed to the Central Command Area of Responsibility (AOR) for Southwest Asia and for US forces deployed to European Command's locations in Turkey, Romania and Bulgaria. It does not include forces deployed exclusively for operations in Central Asia though it may at times list units that are involved in both Operations Iraqi and Enduring Freedom. This listing also does not account for US or Coalition forces involved in operations in the Horn of Africa.

The task of developing a comprehensive listing of US forces present in the area is particularly difficult as the number of units rotating in and out of Southwest Asia is substantial. The events of Sept. 11, 2001 and the Global War on Terrorism have made such an effort significantly more difficult as the military seeks to improve operational security (OPSEC) and to deceive potential enemies and the media as to the extent of American operations. The significant number of troops that have been mobilized or activated in the United States for unspecified duties, whether they are in support of Operation Iraqi Freedom or in support of homeland security also complicates matters as it is not entirely clear which units are going where. Increasing reliance on the part of the Department of Defense on the mobilization of small-sized units to fill its manpower needs further compounds this. These can range from individual companies, batteries, to even smaller-sized groups of troops rather the mobilization of entire battalion-sized units. This being the case, mistakes, misidentifications, or ignorance regarding specific units being in the region, or not being in the region will occur.

Troop levels:

Initial war plans for Iraq had an initial American invasion force of about 130,000 soldiers and Marines, which would drop quickly to as few as 30,000 to 50,000 by the end of 2003. As of October 2005 80,000 of the Guard and Reserve forces were deployed in 40 nations. The largest portion was in Iraq, where Guard units accounted for eight of 15 Army combat brigades. As of 01 March 2006 there were 133,000 US troops in Iraq, down from about 160,000 in December 2005 during parliamentary elections. The Pentagon cut Army combat brigades to 15 from 17. The 25th Infantry Division from Hawaii, along with seven other major military units is scheduled to deploy as part of the summer 2006 troop rotation. The Pentagon hoped to reduce the US presence in Iraq to less than 100,000 by the end of 2006.

By March 2006 some 7,000 Schofield Barracks soldiers were preparing for deployment in August 2006. The soldiers deployed in April 2006 to the National Training Center at Fort Irwin, California. The 25th Infantry Division would command Multinational Division North-Central operations in northern Iraq, with four to five brigades, one of which will be the 3rd Brigade Combat Team from Hawaii. At that time, more than 1,000 Marines of the 3rd Battalion, 3rd Marine Regiment, and Marine Heavy Helicopter Squadron 463 were already on their way to Iraq. On 15 March 2006 it was reported that a battalion of about 700 soldiers from the 2nd Brigade, 1st Armored Division would deploy into Iraq from their base in Kuwait to provide extra security during the holiday of Ashura, which ended 20 March 20006. The unit is one of the three battalions that were originally were scheduled to deploy to Iraq but were held in Kuwait as a standby force. Nearly 4,100 soldiers in the 34th Brigade Combat Team left for Iraq in late March 2006. The soldiers were from Iowa, Kansas,

Kentucky, Nebraska and New Jersey. The deployment included 2,600 from Minnesota's National Guard, the largest contingent from the state to see combat since World War II.

By June 2006 the US had 14 combat brigades in Iraq, and a total of 127,000 troops. According to a 25 June 2006 report in the New York Times, a draft plan calls for significant reductions in the American military presence in Iraq by the end of 2007.

The Department of Defense announced on four separate occasions the units that would rotate into Iraq during mid and late 2005. As part of the OIF-4 rotation, the Department of Defense announced (on the following dates) that the following major units would deploy to Iraq:

On August 3, 2006 Secretary of Defense Donald Rumsfeld testified that **133,000** US personnel were deployed in Iraq. At the same hearing, the number of troops in the Central Command AOR was officially estimated at **200,000** by General John Abizaid.

As of August 22, 2006, over **17,000** coalition personnel from 23 nations were deployed in Iraq. Inside the Horn of Africa there were around 1,200 personnel that dedicate or focus themselves on the Horn of Africa. In Afghanistan there were around 22,000 personnel.

The US Air Force's Expeditionary Air and Space Force (EAF) concept and organization sets a guideline for Air Force deployments to operational locations. The EAF is comprised of 10 Aerospace Expeditionary Forces (AEF) each with lead combat and support wings including on-call wings that could be deployed if required. While deployments for active duty units generally lasts roughly 90-days, Reserve and Guard units deploy typically for 30-60 days. In testimony before the House Armed Services committee on June

13, 2006, General D.W. Corley, USAF reported that in Iraq, the Air Force had flown over 237,000 sorties. The Marine presence in Iraq is centered on the I Marine Expeditionary Force and the 1st Marine Division. One Marine Expeditionary Unit, the 15th MEU is deployed to Kuwait. One Marine Expeditionary Unit is also in the region, though it is currently supporting operations in Afghanistan [and are thus not included in this tally]. On June 30, 2005, General Michael W. Hagee, Commandant, USMC, testified that about 23,000 Marines were deployed in Iraq and would remain there into 2006. General Hagee also testified on the same day that 27,000 Marines were deployed in the Central Command AOR.

There were about 152,000 US troops in Iraq during October 2005. It is reported that as many as 3784 US military personnel were killed from March 2003 to August 2007 and as many as 27,004 US troops were wounded during the same period.

Iraqi Insurgency Groups

The insurgency in Iraq has grown in size and complexity over the course of 2004. Attacks numbered approximately 25 per day at the beginning of 2004, and averaged in the 60s by the end of the year. Insurgents demonstrated their ability to increase attacks around key events such as the Iraqi Interim Government (IIG) transfer of power, Ramadan and the January 2005 election. Attacks on Iraq's Election Day reached approximately 300, double the previous one day high of approximately 150 reached during Ramadan 2004.

The pattern of attacks remains the same as in 2004. Approximately 80 percent of all attacks occur in Sunni-dominated central Iraq. The Kurdish north and Shia south remain relatively calm. Coalition Forces continue to be the primary targets. Iraqi Security

Forces and Iraqi Interim Government (IIG) officials are attacked to intimidate the Iraqi people and undermine control and legitimacy.

Attacks against foreign nationals are intended to intimidate non-government organizations and contractors and inhibit reconstruction and economic recovery. Attacks against the country's infrastructure, especially electricity and the oil industry, are intended to stall economic recovery, increase popular discontent and further undermine support for the IIG and Coalition.

In 2010, there are fights between regular army and American/English army against Islamic militias (Ba'athists, Salafi Islamists, Shi'a militias), which continues since 2003.

Syrian and Iranian involvement

Syria: In December 2004 US General George Casey warned that sympathizers of the insurgency within Syria had been allowed to provide funding, weapons and information to Iraqi insurgents and continued to be a source of infiltration by foreign volunteers. The following February, Iraqi television broadcast taped confessions of alleged insurgents, who claimed to have been trained in Syria, possibly by Syrian intelligence officials. Yet while coalition forces often suspect Syria of assisting insurgents, Syrian denials are adamant and hard evidence is lacking.

Also in February, after continued American pressure, Syria delivered Sabawi Ibrahim Hassan, a half-brother of Saddam and a financial backer of the insurgency. US officials reported some improvement in co-operation against the insurgency from Syria, whose border forces are too few to police the porous Iraqi border effectively. While coalition-aided Iraqi border controls are strengthening, Iraq's borders, totaling 3,650 kilometers in length, remain difficult to control. As with Syria, the Iranian presence in Iraq is difficult to gauge, although it certainly exists. Several Shi'ite political parties (including SCIRI and al-Da'wa, both members of the United Iraqi Alliance, the country's dominant political coalition) have ties to Iran. The Interim Iraqi Government repeatedly expressed concern over Iraqi influence, Defence Minister Hazem Sha'alan claiming in mid-2004 that there was "clear interference in Iraqi issues by Iran" and that the latter supported terrorism in Iraq. The recalcitrant cleric Muqtada al-Sadr is widely perceived as an Iranian proxy, while in a television interview, Muayed al-Nasseri, commander of Saddam's "Army of Muhammad," said his group received weapons and cash form both Iran and Syria.

Iran: Iran too has strenuously denied involvement. But Iranian actions often diverge from Tehran's official policy: The Iranian polity is fractured, with various power bases supporting their own interests. This was clearly apparent in the aftermath of the capture by Iran in June 2004 of a British patrol boat. After a number of contradictory statements, likely reflecting disagreement between Iranian elements, the crew was released. At the same time, sources within the hard-line Iranian revolutionary made plain that restraint in Iraq was contingent on international treatment of Iran in other aspects of policy, such as Iranian nuclear ambitions. Internationally isolated, Iran maintains links with dissidence groups, such as the Lebanese Hezbollah, as useful levers in foreign policy negotiation.

Iran is a nuclear country

Iran's hard-line President Mahamoud Ahmadinejad declared that 'Iran is a nuclear state' on February 11, 2010. Teheran claims that its nuclear program is devoted solely to civilian nuclear power and research purposes. But the contention is contradicted by the following facts, such as:

(a) Iran has built an extensive and expensive nuclear infrastructure that is much larger than what would be necessary to support a nuclear civil power program
(b) Iran sought to buy technology from A Q Khan's nuclear weapon proliferation network, which also provided assistance to Libya and North Korea.
(c) Iran continues to conceal and lie about its nuclear weapons efforts.
(d) Iran rejected a nuclear deal that would have advanced its civilian nuclear efforts, belying its claims that civilian purposes are its only motivation.

In short, Iran is now a nuclear state and has maintained economic and military cooperation with North Korea. Both the countries share a common hostility to the United States of America. Iran is more interested to wipe Israel off the map.

Civil War in Syria

The stalemate over Syria in the UN Security Council is leading the beleaguered country in one direction: a civil war. It was as if the double veto exercised by Russia and China was preordained because Moscow was acting on its belief that it was an assault on Syrian sovereignty, the Assad regime was fighting for its life and a newly invigorated Arab League, despite its fissures, was proposing that President Bashar Assad step down in favour of his deputy and form a national unity government.

The Syrian Army and security services are, of course, the main strength of the Assad regime. It is largely officered by the minority Alawites to which the family belongs and the powerful security services are headed by the President's younger brother. The short point is that the future course of action is not the President's alone but that of the close family and clan and they know that any other course but suppression means their death or banishment.

What lent drama and urgency to Saturday night's Security Council session was news from the city of Homs in which hundreds of civilians were reported to have been killed by a major Syrian Army offensive with heavy weapons? US President Barack Obama issued a strong statement and as Russia stuck to its guns, all other members barring China (India had its own earlier reservations but voted in favour) were convinced that the least bad option to stem the massive killings of civilians was to back the only plan on the table, that of the Arab League.

What had been haunting Russia and China, and to a lesser extent India, was the Libya precedent in which the Security Council authorization to save civilians was converted by Western Powers and NATO into a license to tilt the balance in favour of the beleaguered rebels on the point of defeat through a massive air intervention and some smuggling of weapons and mentoring of rebels. By any impartial count, it was a great stretch of the original resolution.

In Syria's case, regime change was factored into the UN Security Council's resolution although the actual deposition of President Assad was not specifically mentioned to respect Russian sensitivities. The pattern followed was the Yemen formula devised by members of the Gulf Cooperation Council led by Saudi Arabia, although President Abdullah Saleh prevaricated for long before agreeing to cede power and go to the United States for medical treatment.

However, there are other geopolitical factors riding on the Syrian crisis. Syria has been the only traditional Arab ally of Iran and provides Tehran access to both the Hezbollah movement in Lebanon and Hamas on the Gaza Strip. Besides, there is the Israel factor and the inevitable full support Washington offers to anything Tel Aviv might choose to do to safeguard its perceived self-interest. Over the decades, American ability to influence Israel in line with US interests has diminished greatly and, more often than not, it is led by the nose by Israelis, conscious as they are of their power to demolish a US President through their power over Capitol Hill, the Christian Right and the influential American Jewish lobbies.

As the gale force winds of the Arab Spring have buffeted the region, Israel has felt that its best policy would be to behave like a porcupine because anything it would do would hurt its interests. But Tel Aviv has been plotting the alternatives it has with an eye on the future. It was, of course, sorry to lose Hosni Mubarak because he was the kingpin of the whole Post-Camp David structure, the Egyptian Army receiving an annual subvention of $ 1.3 billion. In a sense, Israelis will be sorry to see President Assad go because he has been equally assiduous in refraining from rubbing Israelis the wrong way, discounting the rhetoric.

It is now pretty clear that though the UN Security Council stalemate dooms Syria to a further period of massive blood-letting, the days of President Assad are numbered. Russian foreign minister Sergey Lavrov is planning to visit Damascus to persuade his host to begin a new initiative more mindful of the lives of his citizens. But President Assad's hands are tied. The only way he can retain his throne is by force and with the bulk of his countrymen and women having decided that they have had enough, there is nowhere the President can hide.

Unlike Libya, Syria is very much the heart of the Arab world with its strategic location and Syrian Golan Heights remaining under Israeli occupation. There is also the ethnic and tribal nature of the country with the minority Alawites living with majority Sunnis and a substantial Christian population. It was the strong dictatorial hand of the Assad family that has kept the peace among the different sects while keeping the family Shia sect at the top. The non-Sunni sects are feeling nervous over the future shape of things. The Russia-US rupture over Syria, which has led to sharp exchanges between them, is unlikely to have a long-term impact on their relations but it has brought about a temporary freeze. In a sense, Russia backed itself into a corner. It is no longer credible — if it ever was — to buy the Syrian government's argument that the turmoil was entirely due to "foreign-armed bandits", and there seems little scope to persuade President Assad to find a new opening because anything less than his departure will no longer satisfy the majority of his people.

The temper of the Arab world and much of the rest of the world can be gauged by the demonstrations — many of them violent — held outside (and sometimes inside) Syrian embassies around the world. Despite the many setbacks the Arab Spring has encountered since a fruit vendor in Tunisia set himself alight, the Arab world has changed irrevocably. It cannot be patched up and put back in place. Syria's friends must make President Assad understand the new reality — the sooner the better.[34]

SYRIA
Full-scale Civil War in Syria

Syria's 15-month uprising has grown into a full-scale civil war where its president Bashar al-Assad's forces are trying to recapture swathes of urban territory lost to rebels, the UN peacekeeping chief said today.

"Yes, I think we can say that," UN under-secretary general for peacekeeping operations Herve Ladsous

---

[34] S. Nihal Singh (2012), "U N veto takes Syria nearer civil war", Deccan Chronicle, February 6, 2012

said when asked if the Syrian crisis could now be characterized as a civil war.

"Clearly what is happening is that the government of Syria lost some large chunks of territory in several cities to the opposition and wants to retake control of these areas," he said. His remarks, the first time a senior UN official has declared Syria's conflict is a civil war, came as the International Red Cross said the situation was deteriorating in several parts of Syria simultaneously as fighting intensifies.

Many hundreds of people, including civilians, rebels and members of Mr. Assad's army and security forces, have been killed since a ceasefire deal brokered by international mediator Kofi Annan two months ago was supposed to halt the bloodshed.

"Now we have confirmed reports of not only of the use of tanks and artillery but also attack helicopters," Mr. Ladsous said in an interview. "This is really becoming large scale."

Last week, the head of the International Committee of the Red Cross said the fighting in Syria has been so intense in parts of the country that at times it has qualified as a localized civil war, though he stopped short of saying that it was a full-scale civil war.

An ICRC declaration of the Syrian crisis as an "internal armed conflict," would have legal implications in terms war crimes and compliance with the Geneva Conventions. Mr. Ladsous' declaration may not have any legal implications, though it could carry political weight, possibly making some countries on the UN Security Council less inclined to renew the UN observer mission's mandate next month.

U.S. and European officials have repeatedly said the escalation of the conflict in Syria occurred because Russia used its UN Security Council veto to prevent the 15-nation body from imposing sanctions on Damascus to force it to halt its assault on an uprising that began as a peaceful pro-democracy movement.

Syrian Free Army rebels withdrew today from the besieged Sunni Muslim town of Haffeh under pressure from bombardment by forces loyal to Mr. Assad, a rebel spokesman said.

"Heavy shelling by field artillery has forced the remaining 200 rebels defending Haffeh to leave. There are several thousand civilians left without anyone to protect them from the Alawite militias surrounding the town," Selim al-Omar said by phone from the coastal city of Latakia, 30 kms west of Haffeh.

United Nations observers overseeing Mr. Annan's ceasefire deal were turned back from Haffeh earlier by angry crowds throwing stones and metal rods. As they left, three of their vehicles were fired on, although the monitors were unhurt.

The monitors have been trying since Thursday to visit Haffeh where activists say the army is battling hundreds of rebels and the United States has warned of another potential massacre.

Activists say Syria's army and pro-Assad militia have committed two mass killings in the last three weeks, in the Houla region and the farming hamlet of Mazraat al-Qubeir. Syrian authorities blamed the killings on "terrorists".

The killings have hardened sectarian divisions between the mostly Sunni Muslim rebels and supporters of Mr. Assad - from the country's Alawite minority - in a conflict whose dynamics are also shifting as rebels become increasingly well-armed. At least 51 civilians were killed across Syria today, the Syrian Observatory for Human Rights reported, including 13 who were killed by mortar bombs fired by security forces on a protest in the eastern city of Deir al-Zor.

Twelve soldiers also died in clashes with rebels, the body said. Syria TV reported that "terrorist groups" had seized two buses in Homs province and kidnapped all the passengers. It gave no other details.

The International Committee of the Red Cross, the only international agency to deploy aid workers in Syria, said today the situation is worsening in several parts of the country simultaneously.

"Our priority is to be able to reach as many people in as many fighting-stricken areas in the shortest delay possible. However, due to the increasingly deteriorating situation, we are unable to answer all the needs at the same time," spokesman Hicham Hassan said.

He said hundreds of people had fled this week from parts of the city of Homs, which activists say has come under the heaviest bombardment since Mr Annan's tattered ceasefire was supposed to come into force on April 12th.

Mr. Annan's spokesman said he hoped to convene a meeting of an international contact group on Syria soon, saying he was encouraged by broad support for the idea. But he gave no date for the meeting and said no venue or list of participants has yet been set.

The United States and some Western allies have resisted proposals for Iran to take part, accusing Tehran of "stage-managing" Mr. Assad's crackdown on the uprising.

US secretary of state Hillary Clinton said Washington was worried Russia may be sending Syria attack helicopters and views Moscow's argument that its arms transfers to Syria are unrelated to the conflict there as "patently untrue".

The fighting in Haffeh started last Tuesday when rebels clashed with security forces setting up checkpoints to tighten their grip on the town, which lies close to the Mediterranean port city of Latakia as well as the Turkish border.

Twenty-nine civilians, 23 rebels and 68 soldiers have been killed since then and state forces appear intent on seizing control of the rebel-held town. "The question is, at what price?" the Observatory's director, Rami Abdulrahman, said.

Rebels said they were trying to smuggle trapped civilians out of Haffeh, a Sunni Muslim town in the foothills of the coastal mountains which form the heartland of the ruling minority Alawite sect. They said hundreds of their fighters were facing a tank and helicopter-backed assault by forces loyal to Mr. Assad. "Every few days we manage to open a route to get the wounded out, so some families were able to escape yesterday," said one rebel in Haffeh, who called himself Abdulwudud.

"The situation is dire. Forget the weapons, people need medicine and food. As you know, we're in a state of war in Syria. The army could enter Haffeh in minutes if it wanted but it is trying to crush it instead," said rebel commander Abdulaziz Kanaan, speaking from Turkey.

State television said security forces were continuing "their pursuit of remnants of the terrorists who attacked residents". A foreign ministry statement also reiterated that Syria was committed to Mr. Annan's peace plan, but said the agreement gave Damascus the right to prevent attacks on the army and on state institutions.

A United Nations report into children in armed conflict said that children as young as nine had been victims of killing, maiming, arbitrary arrest, torture, sexual violence and use as human shields.

"In almost all recorded cases, children were among the victims of military operations by government forces, including the Syrian Armed Forces, the intelligence forces and the Shabbiha militia," it said. There were also credible reports of children being recruited by the rebel Free Syrian Army, it said, and in one incident in March the army and Shabbiha placed children aged 8 to 13 in front of the windows of buses carrying military personnel raiding a village.[35]

SYRIA AND IRAN

Middle East cauldron Syria and Iranian Missile Test

The Middle East cauldron continues to bubble. Fighting in Syria has become more intense and the pressure on the Assad regime has increased.

Simultaneously, the Russian military presence in the seas off Syria has significantly enlarged with the deployment of a naval fleet and detachments of marines for land operations. It is not that this build-up presages any clash directly involving Russian forces: what seems to be intended is to deny the Western opponents of Assad the unimpeded ability to strike at the dictator as they had in Libya, and of which they took full advantage. The Russian presence will be expected to discourage direct involvement in Syria's military situation by others from outside the region.

In Syria itself, apart from major outbreaks around Aleppo, fighting has been reported from the

---

[35] Www. Irish times Com, June 12, 2012

Damascus region, with heavy guns being brought into use.

While the situation there deteriorates further, there have been developments in and around Iran that have added considerably to the region's difficulties. The test firing of a new short-range missile, billed as a fourth generation weapon, has been announced even while the virtual civil war in Syria gathers momentum.

According to the announcement from Tehran, the new missile has a range of 300 km., which is comparable to that of the earlier generation of weapons but the new one is more accurate and it can be aimed at naval as well as land targets. At 300 km, the range is sufficient to reach potential adversaries in the region, including Israel. It can, therefore, have a destabilizing effect in a region that is already afflicted by dangerous strife and warfare.

The Iranian claim of having developed a fourth generation missile will no doubt claim the attention of defence specialists, and it is likely to add to the uncertainty and loud name-calling that are part of the region's affairs. It is not something to be seen in isolation, however.

For quite some time, periodic threats of pre-emptive strikes against Iranian nuclear installations have been made by its foes, and there have even been times when such an event has appeared imminent. It can be surmised that Iran would have seen, as has the rest of the world, that a helpless quarry of the "international community" is greatly vulnerable, as was Libya and, earlier, Iraq.

On the other hand, a country that is believed to be able to hit back, or at least make it uncomfortable for the attacker, can better hope to escape aggressive strikes. Thus Iran has been upgrading its defence capacity over the last few years, including naval vessels and, much more daunting, missile capacity, evidently in order to ward the kind of attack with which it is threatened. Warnings and threats from both sides have also escalated, with no drawing back by the opponents of Iran from expressions of readiness to exercise the military option should they consider it necessary.

Iran has not bowed before these threats and, on the contrary, has issued threats of its own, including its readiness to block the Straits of Hormuz if subjected to attack, thereby bringing to a halt the movement of oil from the Gulf to consumers across the world. All these developments underline the fact that the situation in the region remains as fraught as ever, which adds to the dangerous implications of the latest Iranian missile test.

Apprehensions about what may come next have been made more marked by a flurry of high-level visits between the US and Israel. Senior officials who have recently made the trip from Washington include the Secretaries of State and Defence, and the National Security Adviser; presidential candidate Romney has also been there.

Statements by these and other officials give the impression that Israel could be preparing a unilateral military initiative which the US is anxious to discourage. In some respects, these exchanges are reminiscent of more than one such discussion in recent times, the difference being that those who favour an attack argue that the time is currently propitious, before the US election campaign with its unpredictable outcome gets into full swing.

Reports from Washington suggest that the US Administration, while not precluding a military option at some stage, does not wish to see anything of that sort take place now: however, Israel may have a different calculation. Such war talk can only stir the already bubbling cauldron.

One of the important factors that threaten the regional peace is the ambiguous Iranian nuclear programme. Iran insists that this is peaceful in intention and to persist with it is its sovereign right. But others see its real purpose as that of producing a nuclear weapon, which they are determined to prevent.

The prolonged international effort to introduce restraints on Iran have had little effect, leading some to believe that they are being dragged on to ward off unfriendly action and to provide cover for the accelerating enrichment programme that will enlarge Iran's options. Within the Middle Eastern region, only Israel is armed with nuclear weapons, and it is determined to keep it that way.

The International Atomic Energy Agency has made repeated efforts to engage Iran in talks and to institute an acceptable inspection regime on that country's nuclear facilities, and there have been occasional indications that a measure of progress may be possible, but nevertheless the deadlock that has existed for many years seems irremovable. As a result, the precarious balance within the region is under constant strain and can readily be upset by unilateral measures by any of the major players.

The UN has a big role to play in the region: its agencies have been closely engaged in Iran from the start and it is currently greatly preoccupied with the effort to halt hostilities in Syria. Its latest endeavour, following more than one failed attempt to pass a minatory resolution through the UN Security Council, was to bring the matter before the General Assembly. Even though General Assembly resolutions are non-binding, the expectation was that this initiative would add to the pressure on Assad and make his position less tenable.

In the vote in the General Assembly, India decided to abstain while a small group opposed the resolution and a larger number supported it.

Thus the weight of opinion is against Damascus, including most of its Arab neighbours. India's abstention was explained in New Delhi as a carefully considered decision reached after late-night discussions where the mandarins pondered at length before the government eventually decided to abstain. No fresh initiative at the UN may be on the cards for now, but India has to be alert to the potentially dangerous developments in this contiguous region.[36]

Unrest in Nigeria

A potent cocktail of poverty, crime and corruption is fuelling a militant threat to Nigeria's reliability as a major oil producer. Since January 2006, fighters from a new group, the Movement for the Emancipation of the Niger Delta (MEND), have fought with government forces, sabotaged oil installations, taken foreign oil workers hostage and carried out two lethal car bombings. MEND demands the government withdraw troops, release imprisoned ethnic leaders and grant oil revenue concessions to Delta groups. The Nigerian government needs to forge far-reaching reforms to administration and its approach to revenue sharing, the oil companies to involve credible, community-based organizations in their development efforts and Western governments to pay immediate attention to improving their own development aid. The root causes of the Delta insurgency are well known. Violence, underdevelopment, environmental damage and failure to establish credible state and

---

[36] Salman Haidar (2012), " Middle East Cauldron", The Asia News Network, August 07, 2012

local government institutions have contributed to mounting public frustration at the slow pace of change under the country's nascent democracy, which is dogged by endemic corruption and misadministration inherited from its military predecessors. Nigeria had estimated oil export revenues of $45 billion in 2005 but the slow pace of systemic reforms and the lack of jobs, electricity, water, schools and clinics in large parts of the Delta have boosted support to insurgents such as MEND. Militants appeal to the kind of public disaffection that prompted ethnic Ogoni leader Ken Saro-Wiwa to protest the military-led government and Royal Dutch/Shell before his execution in November 1995.

A decade later, the potential consequences of this conflict have escalated in both human and economic terms across a swathe of territory 30 times the size of Ogoni land. Nigerian and international military experts have recognized that the crisis requires a negotiated political resolution. Any attempt at a military solution would be disastrous for residents and risky for the oil industry. Most facilities are in the maze of creeks and rivers that are particularly vulnerable to raids by well-armed militants with intimate knowledge of the terrain. But inaction risks escalating and entrenching the conflict at a time when tensions are already rising in advance of the 2007 national elections. MEND increasingly serves as an umbrella organization for a loose affiliation of rebel groups in the Delta. It has not revealed the identity of its leaders or the source of its funds but its actions demonstrate that it is better armed and organized than previous militant groups. Observers warn that a worst-case scenario could lead to a one to two-year shutdown of the oil industry in the Delta, where most of Nigeria's 2.3 million daily barrels of crude oil originate.

Illegal oil "bunkering" – theft – has accelerated the conflict and provided militant and criminal groups with funds to purchase arms. Another source of funding are the discreet payments oil companies make to militant leaders in return for "surveillance" and protection of pipelines and other infrastructure. This practice, frequently cloaked as community development, has fueled conflict through competition for contracts and by providing income to groups with violent agendas. Oil companies also pay allowances, perks – and sometimes salaries – to "supernumerary police", as well as regular duty police and soldiers deployed to protect oil installations. Security forces consider these plum postings and are alleged to use excessive force to protect company facilities and their jobs.

President Olusegun Obasanjo's government has begun important reforms but these must be deepened if peace is to succeed. Yet, his government has downplayed the seriousness of the insurgency. Senior officials have dismissed the militants as "mere" criminals and defended security crackdowns that have embittered locals, making it easier for armed groups such as MEND to gain new recruits. In an effort to deflect growing public impatience, government officials have demanded oil companies spend ever-larger amounts on community projects. Oil industry officials counter that, after taxes and royalties, the federal government collects the vast majority of earnings on a sliding scale – 90 per cent of industry profits when oil prices are above $60. The companies rightly place the primary responsibility for political solutions to the crisis – including increased development – on the government but they also chafe at the suggestion that their own development strategies have failed.

Transparent and participatory development schemes can foster hope and accountability in Delta communities. Development efforts led by the European Commission and Pro-Natural International provide models for an approach that could reverse the cycle of poverty and violence – but only if their scale is significantly broadened to include a wide range of groups in oil producing areas. Government must also tackle corruption by making development initiatives more transparent. Otherwise, even dramatic increases in spending will be wasted.

Call for new Nigerian poll

A group of Nobel Prize winners, including Peace Prize Laureates Archbishop Desmond Tutu and the Dalai Lama, have called for new elections in Nigeria, saying the country's recent poll was not free and fair and fell far short of acceptable international standards.

A statement by the New York-based Elie Wiesel Foundation for Humanity, and signed by 49 Nobel winners, said a "lack of legitimacy" on the part of the new national government "increases prospects for violent conflict with serious consequences for Nigeria and the region". [37]

In 2010, Nigerian army fights against MEND (Movement for the Emancipation of the Niger Delta. It is a fact that in all low-income countries, few individuals, families or rich people controls democracy. Election is manipulated in favour of the ruling party and black money controls the election process.

Cries for Freedom in Tibet

The Chinese have sealed off all the monasteries in Lhasa and their Buddhist monks placed under house arrest. Barred from seeking alms, the monks are being supplied with army rations. All religious and social interactions have been banned. It is a total and brutal clampdown in Tibet. Despite measures like

---

[37] Ecumenical News International, News Highlights, May 25, 2007

incapacitating Internet servers, blocking foreign websites reporting on the situation in Tibet, jamming the broadcasts of *Radio Free Asia* and the *Voice of America* and blocking overseas telephone calls, the Chinese have not yet been able to enforce a total isolation of Tibet. Lhasa continues to be a closed city with all shops shut down on the orders of Chinese troops on March 15 and 16, 2008.

The Chinese troops are emulating the methods followed by the military junta in Myanmar (Burma) last year to suppress the agitation by the monks. On March 14, 2008, 20 young monks are killed and many more are injured in violence. China uses to refer this violence as the 'violence by separatism, extremism and terrorism'. China is wrestling with the unrest in Tibet, which has erupted on a scale not seen in the last two decades.

Han Chinese invaded Tibet in 1950. They are oppressing local Tibetans, are murdering and ethnically cleansing Tibetans and are practicing civilization genocide. Moreover, Chinese communism is wiping out an Indic faith – Tibetan Buddhism. The Chinese government is not willing to accept the Johnson or McMahon Boundary Line. China first snatched Aksai Chin and gained land access to Tibet. Then it invaded Tibet. Now China claims North- East (Arunachal Pradesh) and North - West (Jammu-Kashmir) of India as a part of Tibet. But the Tibetans need complete independence of their present territory and India is silent over the issue.

According to the Dalai Lama, "these protests are a manifestation of deep-rooted resentment of the Tibetan people under the present governance. Unity and stability under brute force is at best a temporary solution. Force is not conducive to finding a peaceful and lasting solution. Tibetans should not resort to violence.

The protest in Lhasa is because China is carrying out a sort of cultural genocide in Tibet, intentionally or unintentionally.

China's Economic Policy Reinforces Poverty in Tibet

The Canada Tibet Committee (CTC) alleges that China's economic policies are reinforcing poverty, inequality and underdevelopment in Tibet. The Economics of Discrimination in Tibet uses China's own statistics to challenge claims that the occupation of Tibet is motivated by economic and social development for the Tibetan people. Instead, systemic economic discrimination imposed through central policies that violate fundamental human rights principles.

Andrew Fischer, a development economist has authored 'The Economics of Discrimination in Tibet'. Its release was scheduled to coincide with the UN World Summit on Sustainable Development (WSSD), in Johannesburg. Thubten Samdup, President of the Canada Tibet Committee said, "It is time for western governments and international development agencies to face the fact that China's presence in Tibet is not benevolent. When they participate in China's development strategies for Tibet, they risk contributing to discrimination and endemic poverty in Tibetan communities.

The Economics of Discrimination in Tibet reveals that economic growth during the 1990's has by-passed most Tibetans:

(a) Tibet's economy is characterized by a state-controlled industrial and service sector that is excessively concentrated in urban areas, unrelated to productive activities, and superimposed on the Tibetan, non-industrial agrarian economy;

(b) In rural areas where most Tibetans live, the economy has stagnated, diversification has been ignored, and incomes have dropped during the past decade;
(c) There is a severe under-supply of social services in Tibet and education spending is neglected relative to national shares - 46% of all Chinese have received a post-primary education compared to only 8.6% of Tibetans;
(d) Chinese settlers are lured to Tibet by subsidized salaries approximately 46.9% higher than elsewhere in China, and by school fee waivers not available to the local Tibetan population;
(e) Tibet's rural economy is excessively dependent on a few commodities such as barley, rapeseed, wheat and wool, and is particularly vulnerable to falling prices resulting from WTO accession.[38]

The tragic history of Tibet: A chronology of events:

1911 – Tibet is declared an independent republic after decades of rebuffing attempts by Britain and China to establish control.

1935 – The man who will later become the 14th Dalai Lama is born to a peasant family in a small village in Northeastern Tibet. Two years later Buddhist official declare him to be the reincarnation of the 13 previous Dalai Lamas.

1949 – Mao Zedong proclaims the founding of the peoples republic of China and threatens Tibet with liberation.

---

[38] Canada Tibet Committee (2002), "China's Economic Policy Reinforces Poverty in Tibet", Johannesburg & Montreal, August 28, 2002

1950 – China invades eastern Tibet. The Dalai Lama now aged 15 officially becomes head of the state.

1951 – Tibetan leaders are forced to sign a treaty dictated by China. The treaty known as the 17-point agreement professes to guarantee Tibetan autonomy and to respect Buddhist religion but also allows the establishment of Chinese civil and military headquarters at Lhasa.

1950 October 17 – The Red Army attacked Tibet with 40,000 soldiers and entered in to Tibet and occupied 410 Kilo Meters and occupied the Tibet completely in 1951. Mounting resentment against Chinese rule leads to outbreaks up arms resistance.

1954- The Dalai Lama visits Beijing for talks with Mao. But China still fails to honor the 17-point agreement.

1959 March – Full-scale uprising breaks out in Lhasa. 60 thousands Tibetans were killed by Chinese Army. Moreover, Chinese Army arrested 11, 000 Tibetans and tortured them in prisons. The Dalai Lama and most of his ministers flee to northern India to be followed by some 80,000 other Tibetans. Nearly 5,000,000 Chinese people were resettled in Tibet immediately, who tortured the Tibetans too.

1963 – Foreign visitors are banned from Tibet.

1965-Chinese government establishes Tibetan autonomous reign.

1966 – The Cultural Revolution reaches Tibet and results in the destruction of a large number of Monasteries and cultural artifacts. Foreign visitors are again allowed to enter the country.

1970s – End of Cultural Revolution leads to some easing up repression though large-scale relocation of Han Chinese into Tibet continues.

1980s – China introduces open door reforms and boosts investment while resisting any move towards greater autonomy for Tibet.

1987 – The Dalai Lama calls for the establishment of Tibet as a **zone of peace** and continues to seek dialogue with China with the aim of achieving genuine self-rule within China.

1988 – China imposes martial law after riots.

1989 – The Dalai Lama is awarded the Noble Prize for Peace by Sweden Academy of Sciences.

1993 – Talks between China and the Dalai Lama break down.

1995 - The Dalai Lama names a six-year old boy, Gedhum Choekyi Nyima, as the true reincarnation of the Panchen Lama, the second most important figure in Tibetan Buddhism. The Chinese authorities place the boy under house arrest and designate another six-year old boy, Gyanciain Norbu, as their officially sanctioned Panchen Lama.

2002 – Contacts between the Dalai Lama and Beijing are resumed.

2006 July – A new railway linking Lhasa and the Chinese city of Golmud is opened. The Chinese authorities hail it as a feat of engineering, but critics say, it will significantly increase Han Chinese traffic to Tibet and accelerate the undermining of traditional Tibetan culture.

2007 November – The Dalai Lama hints at a break with the century-old tradition of selecting his successor, saying the Tibetan people should have a role.

2007 December – The number of tourists travelling to Tibet hits a record high up 64 per cent per year at just over four million, Chinese state media say.

2008 March 14 – Chinese troops killed 20 Buddhist monks and injured many Buddhist monks.

2009 November 27 – Mr. Barack Obama, the President of United States said in Beijing that Tibet is a part of China.

2009 December 5 –The government of Nepal is under intense pressure of China. The military delegation from Tibet led by Lt Gen Shu Yutai reached Nepal to hold bilateral talks. Another team would reach Nepal in mid-December to study Tibetan activities. All the 59 Tibetan monasteries in Nepal are under scanner to check pro-Tibetan activities.

The Chinese government and CPC can try to suppress dissidence in Tibet, but they will fail to silence the cry for freedom. The US, UK, Germany, Japan, Australia and other countries have already condemned the incident and voiced their concern over the incident. The death toll may increase in future street violence. The Amnesty International demands that the Chinese authorities should allow an independent UN investigation into the events for the cause of sealing off the region and the long-term restrictions on human rights monitoring there.

The US speaker Nancy Pelosi has demanded that Beijing should allow independent international monitors to observe the situations in the Himalayan outpost. It is expected that the UNSC will send an observer to study the situation in Lhasa. Long-term grievances surfacing March 2008 include perceived exclusion from the benefits of economic development, restriction on religious practice, weakening of Tibetan culture and ethnic identity through government policies. All these small countries must be saved through UN intervention, as these buffers states would stand as walls between two great powers.[39]

China and Tibet

This week, China's heir apparent to succeed Hu Jintao as President, Xi Jinping, is on a "coming out" diplomatic visit to the United States where he'll hold wide-ranging discussions on bilateral ties between the world's two greatest powers. In light of the transition at the top of the Chinese Communist Party (CCP), this visit is being monitored for the kind of first impressions that Mr. Xi will leave on the international stage.

Is he another hardliner like President Hu? Will he continue China's assertiveness towards southeast and northeast Asia, which have ignited fears of the return of a 21st century Middle Kingdom? As the scion of an elite CCP family with leadership in his bloodline, will he be more liberal and daring in reforming China's ossified political structure? Does the fact that he headed the CCP in a booming metropolis like Shanghai imply that he is more global in orientation than his predecessor and hence open to foreign opinion?

Such questions are boggling China watchers right now because Mr. Xi has kept policy cards close to his chest throughout his cautious rise within the politburo of the CCP. The typical opaqueness of CCP power transitions has led to a guess work about what kind of continuities and changes China is in for during the 18th Party Congress, scheduled for later this year, which will witness the passing of the baton from Mr. Hu to Mr. Xi.

---

[39]BBC, London and The Pioneer, Bhubaneswar

Yet, for all the speculation about the direction Chinese policies will take under Mr. Xi, it is certain that Beijing's repressive rule in Tibet will remain in place or even intensify. Central governments in China have always been convinced that Tibet must be subdued with force and that its stubborn Buddhist natives must be "re-educated" to become patriotic Chinese. The coming Xi era in Chinese history is unlikely to veer away from coercion and intimidation, especially as controlling mechanisms in the face of a spirited newer generation of Tibetans which is more radical and seething with dissatisfaction against one of Asia's last instances of orthodox colonial rule.

Over the years, Beijing has accumulated enough confidence that it can clamp down on Tibetan aspirations without paying a heavy cost. In a reprise of previous decades, when mainland China used its diplomatic clout to severe Taiwan's linkages with the wider world, Beijing is making its foreign aid, outward investment and political relations with most countries conditional upon the latter boycotting the Dalai Lama and fastening the lid on political activism of Tibetan refugees.

The refusal of South Africa, a close partner of China within the BRICS group, to grant a visa for the Buddhist spiritual guru late last year was just one instance of China's effective pressure tactics. Far from critiquing China's appalling human rights record in occupied Tibet, many governments which do business with China or have strategic partnerships with it are now unwilling to even permit peaceful actions of Tibetan émigrés that help to keep their cause in international consciousness. This trade-off between the economic and military benefits of associating with China and the moral duty of assisting Tibetans who are being browbeaten and marginalized in their homeland is, of course, explained by a real-politik world where material self-interest trumps normative ideals. China is basically getting a free pass on Tibet these days in the capitals of the world which are inferior to Beijing and are afraid of rubbing it the wrong way.

In the case of countries that are equal to or materially stronger than China, Tibet does get mentioned and raised in diplomatic settings as a problem that needs to be addressed. On Mr Xi's US trip, he is being reminded by high-level American interlocutors that China must exercise restraint and safeguard human rights for Tibetans. That these appeals would fall on deaf ears is obvious, but the needle between China and the US in the Asia-Pacific region and the atmosphere of great power competition between the two means that there is enough political will in Washington to keep reminding China that it must relax its iron hand in Tibet.

For the sake of the persecuted Tibetan people, who are a shining example of non-violent resistance, it is essential that other countries also tell China that its behaviour in Tibet is unacceptably violent and soul-crushing. Tiptoeing around the gravity of Tibet today is proving impossible after nearly 20 self-immolations by monks over the last one year and a discernible sense of mass unease on the eve of the Tibetan New Year and the anniversaries of the March uprisings of 1959 and 2008.

The double standards of condoning Chinese excesses in Tibet, while harshly denouncing regimes for brutality in Syria or the Palestinian territories, reveal the stark hypocrisy underlying international politics and are not surprising since we are talking about priorities in statecraft. But what happened to the news media and to civil societies in democratic societies? Why are they underplaying the Tibetan tragedy when there should be headline stories and a barrage of petitions about it? Time magazine recently called the self-immolations of Tibetan monks the most unreported story of 2011. Are concepts like the "free media" and civil society mere window dressing for opinion making which takes cues from state and business elites who are partying with rising China?

Burma's democracy icon Aung San Suu Kyi wrote recently that "passion" (i.e. the degree of commitment to a cause) is more capable of ushering in durable historical change than raw "power". Tibetans should not be punished for preserving the flame and the passion for freedom against the headwind of a China-dominated international system. Taking Tibet off the agenda is not an option for those who desire non-violent solutions to global injustices. In the words of the African American civil rights hero, Malcolm X says: If you want something, you had better make some noise. Let Xi Jinping hear it, even if he ignores the voices of conscience.[40]

China plans for war in Tibet

Describing the situation in Tibet as grave, China has ordered authorities there to prepare themselves for a war against secessionist sabotage by the Dalai Lama amid reports that security forces shot dead two Tibetans protesters.

Officials in the Tibet Autonomous Region have been ordered to recognize the grave situation in maintaining stability and to ready themselves for a war against secessionist sabotage, Chen Quanguo, regional Communist Party chief of Tibet told official Tibet Daily.

The orders come ahead of the February 22 Tibetan New Year and this year's Chinese Communist Party Congress to elect new leaders. The Congress would elect new leaders replacing the President Hu Jintao

---

[40] Sreeram Chaulia (2012), "Tibet and Xi who must be obeyed", Deccan Chronicle, February 14, 2012

and Prime Minister, Wen Jiabao who are set to retire later this year.

Chen and other top officials called for extra vigilance to foil any attempts by the Buddhist Monks and supporters of the Dalai Lama pointing out that the Tibetan spiritual leader has a spoken of a decisive battle to be launched ahead of this year's Communist Party Congress, likely to be held in November this year.

Meanwhile, US based broadcaster Radio Free Asia on Friday said that two Tibetan brothers, who have been on the run after protesting against Chinese rule have been shot dead.

Yeshe Rigsal, a 40-year monk, and his 38-year-old brother, Yeshe Samdrub, had been pursued by the authorities after they participated in January 23 protests against Chinese rule. The two brothers had been on the run for more than two weeks, and had been hiding in the hills in a nomad region when they were surrounded and fired upon. The fight against the Dalai Lama clique is a long-term, complicated and sometimes even acute one, Chen was quoted as saying.

Xu Zhitao, an official with the United Front Work Department of the Communist Party Central Committee, told state-run Global Times that secessionists led by the Dalai Lama appeared more determined to plot conspiracies this year. The Dalai Lama clique had claimed that they might carry out some schemes to wreck the upcoming Tibetan New Year, which falls on February 22 this year, Xu said. This year the region saw self immolations by Buddhist Monks calling for the return of Darla Lama from his self exile in Dharmashala. So far 17 monks and nuns have attempted suicides.

So far 17 monks and nuns have attempted suicides. Many of these attempts were confined to the Sichuan province, neighbouring Tibet and the Tibetan officials fear that the restive monks would attempt some thing big during the New Year celebrations in Lhasa, the provincial capital. Global Times which carried the Tibet story today with banner headlines 'Tibet officials prepare for war' also mentioned discussions on Tibet during External Affairs Minister S M Krishna's just concluded visit here to inaugurate the new Indian Embassy building.[41]

China claims that Arunachal Pradesh of India was a part of Tibet; hence it belongs to China. In other words, China is fully prepared to fight against all Asian countries and claim that China stands for Asia and all countries in Asia are subordinate to China.

War by Cyber means

When Pakistani groups sent morphed images and videos over mobile phones and social networking sites to incite a riot in Mumbai and panic across the country, they opened a new front in their war on India — the cyber front. It's a dangerous new phase in religious radicalization and terrorism, warns A.K. Verma.

As evidence mounts that the morphed images of atrocities against Muslims in Assam and Myanmar first came from the websites of Pakistan-based groups close to that country's intelligence agency, the ISI, the uneasy feeling that Pakistan's proxy war against India has entered a new and dangerous phase is almost inescapable.

---

[41] KJM Varma, "China plans for war in Tibet", PTI News, February 10, 2012

It's the result not only of Pakistan's failures so far, through both conventional wars and terrorism, to achieve its goals vis-à-vis India, but also of the realization in Pakistan that digital technologies such as the Internet and mobile phone communications now provide easy tools of subversion and radicalization of populations, on the cheap and with deniability.

There has been no time since its birth in 1947 when Pakistan has thought of a durable peace with India. The tribal incursion in Jammu and Kashmir was engineered within months of the country's creation. Major wars followed in 1965 and 1971.

The Kargil incursion in 1999 could also have flared into a major war but for American intervention. Meanwhile, Pakistan tried other strategies, too. In the late 1980s, subversion was introduced in J&K. When that failed, terrorism was added to the mix. When even that failed, Pakistan did not give up, but expanded subversion and terrorism to the rest of India.

All through, as Pakistan has increasingly become mired in a battle for survival against itself, its anti-India ambitions only increased, and it finds new ways and channels. The August 11 riots in Mumbai indicate that the Pakistani campaign is now entering a new phase -- digitalized subversion.

The Internet and social media such as Face book and Twitter have enormous influence. If one single instrument is to be identified for the electrifying upheavals in the Arab world, the so-called Arab Spring, it is social media. Millions could be reached in real-time, mobilising and galvanizing them into following a programmed agenda.

A similar development had begun to take shape in China, but the alarmed Chinese authorities shut down

Face book and Twitter and placed heavy restrictions on the Internet.

Digital subversion

What caused turmoil in the Arab world and China was indigenous to those countries, but electronic communications do not respect national frontiers. Pakistan recognises this, and sees new opportunities to mount a sophisticated onslaught against India through digital subversion and cyber warfare. It is an exercise that is easily deniable.

All that is needed is a set of computers and a band of technically savvy operators who can function from very small spaces, very difficult to pinpoint.

Such groups can hack into the computer systems of a targeted country, disturb the electronic systems and perform any of these functions - steal data, including classified data, disrupt stock markets, immobilize transport systems that are electronically controlled, degrade missile offensive and defensive configurations, interfere with power production and transmission, disrupt space-based assets and activities, and so on.

In other words, they can paralyze cities and infrastructure, wreak economic havoc and even jeopardize a country's offensive and defensive structures. These, of course, need sophistication and deep penetration capabilities.

But when the aim is to simply create terror, mere morphed images and videos sent over the Internet and mobile phones serve very well, as the August 11 riots and the panic and mass exodus of north-easterners from Bengaluru and Pune showed recently.

Pakistan has for long been studying India's fault lines. It has zeroed in on radicalization as a strategy. Terrorism and radical Islam work hand-in-glove, as events in the tribal regions of Pakistan have well demonstrated.

It was such plans that led to the founding of the Indian Mujahedeen, to operate at an ideological level. The IM is expected to develop on the lines of Al Qaeda, which also has a presence in several countries. The units function autonomously and are not interlinked.

The Al Qaeda ideology is the only common link. Pakistan hopes to achieve the same phenomenon in India. It expects that the IM virus will erupt in splotches all over the body politic of India, like cancerous cells, without any local history or prior warning. The game plan is to loosen centralized control once it becomes self-perpetuating. By any yardstick, the growth of a virus of this kind is highly dangerous.

Cyberspace extends limitless opportunities for digital subversion, exacerbating the problem greatly. Using cyber technology and appealing in the name of radical Islam, even a non-state enemy can become a source of explosive damage, and he can do so while cloaking himself in deniability. With support from a nation-state, his ability to cause damage rises phenomenally.

A non-state actor like Hafiz Mohammed Saeed, the chief of Jamaat-ud-Dawa, who wants to see the Islamic flag flying all over India, will undoubtedly try to attract millions in India to his insane ideology through cyberspace. That the combined forces of arms of the Pakistani state and non-state actors have so far failed to bring about the disintegration of India is a tribute to the Indian ideals of democracy, secularism and pluralism. But digitalised subversion and radicalization add a whole new dimension, and call for an urgent strategy to combat these dangers.

Pakistan's radicalization

Consider what has happened to Pakistan's own civil society between 1947 and now. Its founder Mohammed Ali Jinnah dreamt of a secular nation following the traditions of the British era, constitutional government and strong institutions. What Pakistan has become since is quite the opposite of such dreams.

As it searched for an anchor and a foundation, Pakistan's early ruling elites, although themselves mostly a coalition of feudal, British-trained bureaucrats and a professional military, declared it an Islamic republic in 1956, a concession to the religious groups that had already entered the political fray and were demanding acceptance of Sharia as the law of the country.

A losing battle for the secular principle continued up until General Zia-ul-Huq became the country's ruler. By the time of his death in a mysterious plane crash in 1988, the modernist approach in the Pakistani constitution that had survived till then was finally overcome by the heavy ideological overload that Zia placed on all the functional systems of the country.

Zia's Pakistan saw a growth of conflicting strands of thinking among the Pakistani people. Zulfiqar Ali Bhutto's hanging angered the Shias, whose morale was otherwise bolstered by the Iranian revolution of Ayatollah Khomeini.

Jihad in Afghanistan against the Soviets, mostly a Sunni phenomenon, and the flow of Saudi money to wage that war boosted the Sunni profile. With arms freely flowing in for jihadis, sectarian militancy took shape in Pakistan, polarizing people in Pakistan differently in different regions.

Yet, as sectarianism grew, there was no public alarm, because public discourse could not imagine the end result of such polarization. The loss of liberal values in the body politic was largely left uncommented upon in the media. The prevailing psychology and the absence of intellectual scrutiny of the new atmosphere in the country caused confusion in the public mind.

The moderates left all issues of religion to be decided by fanatic clerics. There was no longer one clear, acceptable idea throughout the country as to the purpose and meaning of the State. Identity, so necessary for citizens, got mired in conflicts engineered by multiplicities of clashing claims of ethnicities, sub-nationalisms and resource allocation.

Zia was also responsible for giving the entire spectrum of education in Pakistan an anti-India twist and an ideological religious orientation that fed into the jihadi culture set in motion to fight the Soviets. Madrasa education injected a new thrust to religious extremism already sponsored by the increasing sectarianism and produced graduates whose xenophobia was an antithesis to modernity, pluralism, tolerance and scientific temperament.

The religious political parties saw in the Madarassa-trained an invaluable asset, making them opposed to the reforms that Parvez Musharraf, after seizing power, and wanted to introduce to modernize the system. The reforms also failed because there was little public and media support and also because the government machinery and politicians did not display adequate political determination. Intended mosque reforms to stop venomous sermons went nowhere.

The jihadist discourse has produced a new amalgam of religious activism, misplaced security and xenophobic patriotism that charges the agenda of the clergy, land-owning gentry and the establishment, none of whom really care for new socio-political reforms in the country. Lip service is paid for the evolution of a democratic system, but ground conditions hobble it. Free thinking is taboo.

The civil society faces an oppressive environment with growing restrictions on dress, music and the pursuit of the arts. Women and minorities are treated as less than citizens. Blasphemy laws cannot be tinkered with for fear of retribution, as the killing of Punjab Governor Salman Taseer showed. Chillingly, Taseer's killers were feted for the act, then Prime Minister Yousaf Raza Gilani refused to attend his funeral for fear, and almost no one in civil society condemned the act.

Cyber command and control

The radicalization of large sections of Pakistan proceeded over decades, but for most of that time, there were neither instantly-accessible social media websites nor the now ubiquitous mobile phone. The danger that India faces, as the morphed images that created mass panic among north-easterners earlier this month showed, is that today those technologies could well compress that process of subversion, radicalization and terror of sections vulnerable to propaganda from decades into real-time, instant, and uncontrollable, do-it-yourself attacks on the Indian social fabric.

It's time India began to think doctrinally about, and prepare for, a new age of cyber terror and cyber warfare. In this, we must learn from the Americans and the Chinese. The US, for instance, has created a whole new arm called Cyber Command, whose head is the Director of the National Security Agency. The

Cyber Command ensures that no electronic transmission enters the US without it knowing. When one is faced with light-speed offensive measures, counter-measures, too, have to be instantaneous.

India unprepared

The US established a separate Cyber Command in 2009 for offensive and defensive operations. Headed by the Director of the National Security Agency, it ensures that no electronic communication reaches a device in the United States without the Cyber Command knowing about it.

The Chinese army graduates dozens of cyber warriors every year. China is said to have tested its capabilities to launch cyber attacks on other countries' infrastructure and war fighting assets.

India's approach to cyber defense has been scattered and lacks doctrinal and organizational coherence. There are multiple agencies, military, civilian and intelligence, with tasks split between them, and no real co-ordination. India has been the victim of hundreds of cyber attacks, including on the External Affairs ministry and the Indian Navy.

The US-Israel cyber attack with the Stuxnet virus on Iran's Natanz uranium enrichment plant set back the latter's nuclear programme by years. Stuxnet also affected thousands of Indian computers, including industrial assets. [42]

Conclusion

In short, the ongoing wars involving 31 countries are acting as the peace-breaking devices for the people of the whole world. Insurgency, civil war, border

---

[42] A K Verma (2012), " War by Cyber Means", Deccan Chronicle, August 26, 2012

issue, religion-based war, separate identity, ethnicity, military rule, unrest or cries for freedom and weakening of culture are the reasons for these ongoing wars. The United Nations Peace Council and UNSC should solve all ongoing wars on priority basis and establish peace process in these troubled states.

If necessary the United Nations should use forces to punish the warmonger countries for greater cause of achieving WORLD PEACE. The United Nations should not wait for indefinite period for a decision and allow these countries to wage wars.

Peace is mightier than war. We can solve all complicated problems by mutual understanding and respect. The war monger country must be requested to come to negotiating table for a discussion. If all discussions fail, stringent political, trade and economic sanctions must be followed with warnings to the war-monger nation. The United Nations must take steps to stop war anytime anywhere.

The United Nations needs to monitor its activities on boundary disputes between countries. The ultimate aim of the United Nations is to bring and stabilize peace in the World. There should not be two categories of states or members in this august organization.

Hence, the VETO power of the highly militarized countries must be abolished; yet these countries would be powerful and their decisions would count most of the decisions.

Syria is nearer to civil war because Russia and China have exercised VETO, which is an assault on Syrian sovereignty.

+++++

Chapter IV

A WORLD IN CRISIS

My country has suffered appallingly from the effects of the uncontrolled arms trade – and continues to suffer... We don't manufacture these guns, yet they end up in our country, erode our security and have terrible consequences for our development.

----Florella Hazeley, Sierra Leone Action Network on Small Arms, 9 July 2006

The greatest threat before humanity today is the possibility of secret and sudden attack with chemical or biological or radiological or nuclear weapons...What has changed in the 21st century is that, in the hands of terrorists, weapons of mass destruction would be a first resort -- the preferred means to further their ideology of suicide and random murder. These terrible weapons are becoming easier to acquire, build, hide, and transport. Armed with a single vial of a biological agent or a single nuclear weapon, small groups of fanatics, or failing states, could gain the power to threaten great nations, threaten the world peace...America, and the entire civilized world, will face this threat for decades to come. We must confront the danger with open eyes, and unbending purpose. I have made clear to all the policy of this nation: America will not permit terrorists and dangerous regimes to threaten us with the world's most deadly weapons.

--- **President George W. Bush**, February 11, 2004

The greatest threat before humanity is war and war related issues. Of course the thinkers of the world visualize different factors for the cause of crises of the world. We feel that the twenty-first century is burdened with wars, crises, killings, revenge, corruption, power exercise, diseases and poverty of masses. But all religions teach us that divine power can change this world into an abode of Peace Empire of Humanity.

The world has witnessed bloodbaths of our brave heroes during wars in the past, witnessing killings today and if we do not take any positive actions now, the world would not only loss the brave heroes but the entire plant and human kingdoms would be destroyed/killed without any reason. So the question is: why there is a rush for war, arsenals, nuclear war or arms trade?

We feel there are many crises in the world. A crisis can be solved; a crisis can be challenged; a crisis can be rooted out in the budding stage; but when the crisis is more powerful than the control of a man or a government or even the United Nation; it becomes a dangerous crisis for the humanity and the world. But the crisis can be solved or at least be tried for a solution. An unsolved issue could challenge the 'WORLD PEACE' today or tomorrow.

The present chapter incorporates two issues, which could be better managed to solve the problems of humanity. But if these issues are mis-handled or mis-utilized, the world would face the worst catastrophe in this century. So the United Nations should be reorganized and empowered to manage the issues judiciously for achieving peace, prosperity and progress in the world. The issues are:

(a) The China Factor of Communism and Annexation
(b) The United States as a Big Brother

(A). CHINA
Factor of Communism and Annexation

After the defeat of Japan in World War II, the Communists brought the whole country under their control and Mao Tse-tung established the People's Republic of China on October 1, 1949. China attacked Tibet first and brought the country under China's control. Mao launched the great proletarian Cultural Revolution to eradicate 'revisionism'. Mao died in 1976. The country passed through turmoil and Deng Xiaoping became a dominant force in the party, who drove China for modernization and economic restructuring. The country took stern steps to control population growth and economic progress. The funeral of HU on April 15, 1989 sparked mass student unrest and the whole world was shocked the way the sit-in strike was controlled by bullets.

China possesses the largest population in the whole world. The country is highly advanced in science, technology, economy, agriculture, defense, and self-dependent in food. China possesses nuclear power, well equipped with arms and arsenals and desires to spread communism (Maoism) to other countries. It has entered Nepal in 2007 through Maoist leader Pusps Kumar Dahal Prachand and has overthrown the Monarch of Nepal and has driven out the monarch from the palace. China attacked India in 1962 and occupied a large forest and hill areas in the Indian Territory.

China has become a Super Power because its military has employed the highest number of troops and its defense expenditure consists of double-digit percentage. The country dislikes democracy and tries to popularize communism in neighbouring countries. The country would pose a problem to Asia or even to the world if United Nations does not prohibit the warmonger activities of China. Human rights are violated in the country openly. China has borders with the Russia, Mongolia, North Korea, Vietnam, Laos, Myanmar (Burma) India, Bhutan, Nepal, Pak-occupied Kashmir and Afghanistan. China has border issues with Japan and main land china. This has caused a crisis in the region; it creates problems that result in a war and killings of soldiers and common people. The first attack may be on Taiwan.

Breaking all norms of diplomacy, China on October 13, 2009 used very strong words to protest against Prime Minister India visiting Arunachal Pradesh, a State in India and has asked, "Not to trigger disturbance (in the disputed region). China claims the state is a disputed region and said, "It was dissatisfied with the visit of Prime Minister Dr. Man Mohan Singh, who had addressed election rallies in the State on October 3, 2009.

China and India had never officially settled demarcation of their boundaries. They share a disputed boundary (Line of Actual Control) of more than 5,000 Kilo Meters long for the last four decades. The Armies of both the countries are deployed at LAC since then. The LAC is divided into three sectors, including western sector (Ladakh), middle sector (Himachal Pradesh and Uttarakhand) and eastern sector (Arunachal Pradesh). The Arunachal Pradesh is an integral part of India and the state government runs under Indian constitution.

In order to avoid conflicts or war both the countries are engaged in dialogue through special representatives. But China records airspace violations and Chinese army is intruding Indian Territory repeatedly. India is only lodging protests against these incursions. China and India are the most populous countries in the world. China has a population load of 1400 million and India has population of 110 million (calculated) by 2009. Both the countries had fought in 1962 and there was fierce fighting between the countries, although before that India and China were called as brothers. The common slogan was Hind-China brother and brother. If there is a war between India and China, more than one-third of human population of world would directly be affected. This war could do immense harm to the sufferers. It is the duty of the United Nations to solve the problem and establish peace in the Asian countries.

China is illegally occupying 43,180 sq. km. in the state of Jammu and Kashmir. China accuses that India is possessing about 90,000 sq. km. of Chinese Territory mostly in Arunachal Pradesh. Moreover, China has made roads in inaccessible hilly areas through the Himalayas through Tibet, Pak occupied Kashmir and to other bordering states of India. China now makes trilateral cooperation with Japan and the Republic of Korea.

China's defense spending is far outpacing that of other nations in the region, and its aggressive development of ballistic and cruise missiles and attack of submarines threatens to upset the balance of power in Asia and beyond, according to a Pentagon report.

A report indicates that uncertainty over Beijing's intentions in modernizing its military is a source of concern. Given the apparent absence of direct threats from other nations, the purposes to which China's current and future military power will be applied remain uncertain. China's People's Liberation Army is acquiring large numbers of "highly accurate" cruise missiles and modernizing its long-range ballistic missile force by making it more mobile and, therefore, more secure.

China has the most active land-based ballistic and cruise missile program in the world. China continues to build up an arsenal of short-range missiles along its coast opposite Taiwan, despite what the report described as an easing of tensions across the Taiwan Strait over the past year, said a Pentagon official, who spoke on the condition of anonymity according to ground rules set by the Pentagon. The longer-range DF-31A missile, deployed in 2007, has a range of almost 7,000 miles and can target any location in the continental United States, although the defense official said China has publicly committed to a policy of no first strike.

Naval forces are another area that China is seeking to develop to project military power farther from its shores. For example, it is conducting research and training related to a program to develop aircraft carriers, with construction of an indigenous ship possible by the end of the decade. China is also expanding its fleet of attack submarines.

The Pentagon mentions that construction of a naval base on the southern island of Hainan would accommodate a large number of ballistic missile submarines and advanced surface combatant ships, which could be used for a war by China. The port, which has underground facilities, would provide the PLA Navy with direct access to vital international sea-lanes, and offers the potential for stealthy deployment of submarines into the deep waters of the South China Sea. China's emerging cyber war capabilities are also troubling to the Pentagon. The report notes that in 2008, computer system intrusions that appeared to come from China targeted U.S. government computer systems as well as others around the world. Although these intrusions focused on infiltrating information, the accesses and skills required for these intrusions are similar to those necessary to conduct computer network attacks.

The U.S. government is also investigating whether Chinese officials secretly copied the contents of an American government laptop computer during a visit to China by the U.S. commerce secretary.

China is an aggressive country and is a super power. So the Asian countries are at risk and can face war-like situations in near future. Russia is silent; Tibet is occupied by China since 1951 and the religious Head, His Highness Dalai Lama is residing in India in exile; Myanmar is under military rule; Nepal faces the greatest shock as Maoists claim to join Nepal military in the country; Bangladesh faces natural hazards, political turmoil and wide spread poverty, hunger, corruption and debt overhang. [43]

In this sub-section, China's preparedness of war is discussed. Unless the public opinion grows against defense attitude of war monger countries, the world could be at risk. Hence, the world forums should activate the peace process in the world.

China - A Republic sans People

Claude Arpi (2009) has reported that 'Amid much fanfare that marked the 60th anniversary celebrations of the People's Republic of China on October 1, 2009; the main absentees were the 'people', who were told to stay inside their homes. Even today ordinary people in China have no say in the system of governance and succession'.

---

[43] Ann Scott Tyson, the Washington Post, Washington Post Staff Writer Thursday, March 26, 2009

Xinhua news agency reported: A total of 52 types of new weapon systems, all Chinese-made, including new generation tanks, missiles and warplanes were displayed. Ninety per cent of the weapons were paraded for the first time. The Second Artillery Force stole the show with a display of five types of missiles, 'China's core strategic deterrent. The gigantic weapons in camouflage colors roll by on long-bed trucks, which trigger cheers from spectators. Experts already knew that that the dreaded DF21 medium range ballistic missiles could be well camouflaged and launched from trains (from the Qinghai-Tibet train, for example), but to see them all at the same time was awesome.

It was followed by 151 warplanes which flew over Tiananmen Square, including China's most advanced J-10 and J-11 fighter jets, airborne early warning and control aircraft, bombers and aerial tankers.

No judgment about Chinese military capabilities can be rendered simply by watching this parade (Dennis J. Blasko). And more importantly, based on the weapons on display no judgment can be rendered as to the Chinese intention behind the deployment of these weapons," but one can guess what the probable targets are.

If there was Glamour Award, it would have gone to the ladies of female militia unit; they were clad in red miniskirts with white jackboots carrying the latest submachine guns.

The kitsch part of the grandiose parade was President Hu Jintao reviewing the troops in an open roof 12-cylinder Red Flag limousine dating from Mao's times. For the occasion Mr Jintao was dressed in a high-collar Mao-style jacket (while other members of the Standing Committee of the Polit Bureau and former President Jiang Zemin wore ordinary suits and ties). During the review, the President stood stiffly in front of four microphones fixed on the limousine, shouting "Greetings, comrades!" with the troops answering "Serve the people!"

In his speech, Mr. Jintao proclaimed that the Chinese people "cannot be prouder of the development and progress of our great motherland," however observers noted the main absentees at the celebrations, the people of China. Apart from a few thousands apparatchiks, some foreign diplomats and journalists and 100,000 extras, **where were the Chinese people?**

They were told to remain inside their homes and not emerge. To make sure that the party's instructions were followed to the letter, some 800,000 volunteers had been engaged. Such tight security had not been seen during the last six decades. What else to conclude? Sixty years after its foundation, the 'Republic' is not for the 'public', but for a party. China is still not a 'republic'. This is the tragedy of modern China.[44]

Military Strength of China

China announced a further sharp increase in military spending; a day after the United States renewed its warning that a lack of openness surrounding the rapid buildup of China's armed forces posed a threat to stability in Asia.

China's military budget for 2008 will increase by 17.6 percent to 417.8 billion Yuan, or about $58.8 billion, Jiang Wenzhou, spokesman for the National People's Congress, China's legislature, said at a news conference. Military experts in the United States and elsewhere say Beijing's real military spending is at least double the announced figure.

---

[44] Claude Arpi (2009), "A Republic sans People", The Pioneer October 13, 2009 P.9 /

China has increased annual defense outlays by double-digit percentages most years in the past two decades to pay for an array of modern weapons, better training and conditions for the 2.3 million people in its military, the world's biggest standing force.

China's main objective is to develop the firepower to overwhelm Taiwan in the event of a conflict while deterring or delaying any American forces sent to help defend the island.[45]

Beijing Does Not Bother

A more accurate picture would take note of China's noncompliance with its pledges to the World Trade Organization; its failure to use its leverage with North Korea to end Pyongyang's game of nuclear Russian roulette; its continuing refusal to abide by human rights and refugee conventions it has signed; its less-than-stellar nonproliferation record; its use of Chinese nationalism to browbeat Japan; its refusal to cooperate with the other great powers in the Proliferation Security Initiative; its obstructionist policies on Iran, Sudan, Zimbabwe, and Burma; and of course its repeated threats to use military force to unify Taiwan with the mainland - and, if need be, engage in nuclear brinkmanship to prevent the United States from intervening to stop a forcible reunification. It is this fuller - but unstated - account of Chinese behavior that fits with the substantive heart of the report, documenting China's rapid and dramatic improvements in military capabilities.

Ballistic Missiles

What's new in this year's report is the finding that China's military buildup has begun to have serious

[45] David Lague, From Beijing, *The New York Times*, 3/5/08, p. A6

implications not only for the cross-strait balance of power but also for the region as a whole.

The People's Liberation Army possesses a growing fleet of nuclear and diesel submarines, has **650-730 mobile ballistic missiles**, and is working on aerial refueling for a significant percentage of its 2,600 combat aircraft.

Japan Recognizes the Problem

Toss in new and improved command, control, and communication systems and over-the-horizon targeting capabilities, and the picture that emerges is a China with military capabilities that are not just Taiwan-centric. While the report suggests that these capabilities 'could pose a credible threat to other modern militaries operating in the region ... over the long term, if current trends persist,' most regional militaries are already worried. When Chinese ships and subs begin making clandestine trips into Japanese home waters – as they have – the signal being sent to Japan and the region is clear enough.

Taiwan Knows Beijing

Beijing does not believe a full-fledged invasion would be necessary to accomplish its goal. Rather, the PLA leadership, according to its own doctrinal papers, thinks a combination of ballistic-missile, special-operation, and aerial strikes could be sufficient to shock Taiwan's population and leadership into accepting Beijing's version of 'one China'.

For similar reasons, China is working hard to develop the capacity to blockade Taiwan. The submarine modernization program is extensive. Eight new quiet KILO-class diesels will soon be added to the four already in the arsenal; China's indigenous SONG diesel is now in serial production; and a new diesel submarine, the YUAN class, was launched last year.

Chinese naval journals indicate a deep interest in blockading operations, and pay close attention to the vulnerabilities of Taiwan's island economy. ...

U.S. Aircraft Carriers targeted

China's military knows that it must be able to prevent, or, at least severely complicate, the American Navy's use of its aircraft carriers. To this end, as the new report spells out, China's anti-ship cruise missile force is growing by leaps and bounds. It has begun to field high-end, supersonic and subsonic cruise missiles on its new destroyers, attack boats, and submarines. It has even experimented with use of maneuverable, multiple-entry MRBMs and SRBMs to hit carrier battle groups. Once China solves the problem of longer-range detection and targeting, it will pose the most serious threat to American carriers in the world.

PRC'S ICBMS More Dangerous than Katrina

The report also details China's programs to upgrade its intercontinental ballistic missile force with new solid-fuel, road-mobile missiles and new sea-based, submarine-launched systems. The net effect will be a more survivable, more accurate, and more lethal nuclear strategic capability – aimed primarily at the United States. As General Zhu Chenghu, dean of China's National Defense University, not so subtly reminded American visitors recently: Should the United States intervene in a conflict between China and Taiwan, 'the Americans will have to be prepared that hundreds -- of [their] cities will be destroyed by the Chinese' nuclear weapons.

Combine the PLA's fascination with 'carrier killing,' its ability to degrade severely the operational utility of U.S. air bases in Japan through missile strikes, its aggressive pursuit of space and counter space capabilities, and its upgraded nuclear arsenal, and you have a military that believes it has or is close to having the means to make any American president think twice before going to Taiwan's rescue.

But rather than face the facts presented in the report about the character and scope of China's military buildup, the tendency in the senior ranks of the administration is to wash over them with sound bites about our relationship with China being 'good but complex.' Or it may be worse. The day after the report was issued, in response to a question about the cross-strait military balance, Marine general Peter Pace, vice chairman of the Joint Chiefs, said:

There's lots of countries in the world that have the capacity to wage war but few have the intent to do so; There's absolutely no reason for us to believe there is any intent on China's part.

General Pace had better hope his statement doesn't go down in history alongside George Tenet's now infamous, 'It's a slam dunk, Mr. President.' [46]

War Inevitable

It flows from this basic insight that we must be concerned about such developments as:

The persistent assertion by the Chinese leadership to their political cadre and military officers that America is the 'main enemy' and that war with the United States is 'inevitable.'

Official Chinese efforts to secure energy resources from all over the world to meet its yawning needs (notably for oil, coal and natural gas) in a way that seems meant to deny such resources to the U.S. and other global competitors.

---

[46] Gary Schmitt and Dan Blumenthal, *The Weekly Standard*, August 8, 2005, pp. 14-16

The PRC's predatory trade practices and intellectual property rights continued in violation of past commitments and World Trade Organization obligations. In part, the result is a bilateral trade deficit that has increased 'over 140 percent in only four years.' The wealth thus garnered by China is used – among other things – to fuel the plundering of America's remaining high-technology industrial base and the utter liquidation of our manufacturing sector.

Wealth transfers from the United States are underwriting Beijing's ominous build-up of its armed forces, as well. The commission says: 'China is engaged in a major military modernization program, the motives of which are opaque and unexplained. It is building a modern navy and air force, upgrading its nuclear-armed ICBM force and beginning to operate in a power-projection mode. It has markedly expanded its information warfare operations to a level that is clearly designed to disrupt American systems.

Finally, China is engaged in activities that pose a more immediate danger. Two of its nationals were recently arrested trying to sell Chinese-made QW-2 man-portable surface-to-air missiles in this country. Had they done so, the result could have given rise to a potentially grave threat to American airliners. And Chinese micro-satellites are being readied to attack our space assets as another, potentially devastating manifestation of Beijing's pursuit of what the Pentagon calls 'asymmetric warfare' capabilities against the United States.[47]

Red China's Spy:
Networked in US Grows Rapidly

---

[47] Frank Gaffney, Jr., author of *War Footing: 10 Steps America Must Take to Prevail in the War for the Free World* Naval Institute Press, November 2005, available at *The Washington Times*, 11/15/05, p. A20

Back in the 1980s, David Szady was among the premier a Soviet spy catcher at the Federal Bureau of Investigation, studying every aspect of the Kremlin's mole network. Today, he's a mobilizing agent across the country to sniff out spies from a new rival: Beijing. China is the biggest espionage threat to the U.S. today,' says Mr. Szady, Assistant Director of the FBI's counterintelligence division.

In one of their biggest initiatives after the fight against terrorism, the FBI and Justice Department have sent hundreds of new counter intelligence agents into the Bureau's 56 field offices, many with a specific focus on China. There is a cloak-and-dagger element to some of this: A principal FBI team focusing on Chinese economic espionage, including some undercover operatives, occupies an unmarked floor in a Silicon Valley office park near a popular Chinese restaurant.

Thousands of Chinese nationals regularly come to the U.S. as students and businessmen, some working for major U.S. defense contractors – something the Russians could only have dreamed of during the Cold War. They are welcomed with open arms by universities and companies who prize their technical acumen and links to capital and low-cost labor back home.

The vast majority of them are here innocently working or studying. Counter-espionage experts say the trouble often starts when they are contacted by Chinese government officials or one of the more than 3,000 Chinese 'front companies' the FBI alleges have been set up in the U.S. specifically to acquire military or industrial technologies illegally. Sometimes they are wooed with cash, but often the motivation is nationalism.

Mr. Szady says that they work at many levels, so China may prove more difficult to contain than the

Russian threat. The FBI's Business Alliance, established a year ago, and has been meeting regularly with leading defense contractors to understand what technologies they're developing and what potential threats company employees pose. The participants include Lockheed Martin Corp., General Dynamics Corp. and Raytheon Co.

The FBI reports that about 150,000 Chinese students are currently studying in the U.S and the number of new admissions has been rising. The U.S. Immigration and Customs Enforcement department reports that nearly 64,000 Chinese students entered the U.S. in 2004 as against 55,000 in 1998. About 700,000 Chinese tourists and business executives visit the U.S. each year.

In addition, the Beijing government runs an extensive, informal, decentralized spy network, counter-espionage experts allege. In most cases, Beijing's spy agencies don't send trained agents to the U.S. to penetrate companies and government agencies, but rather simply seek to glean information from the hundreds of thousands of Chinese who visit and study in the U.S. every year. They also try to get Chinese-Americans to provide information, appealing to their desire to help uplift China's economy.[48]

Democratic Centralism

China's government issued a report on October 19, 2005 stating why the Marxist system will not be changed to allow for Western-style democracy and why democracy is limited to within the ruling Communist Party dictatorship.

China's democracy is a democracy guaranteed by the people's democratic dictatorship. Under that

---

[48] Jay Solomon, *The Wall Street Journal*, 8/10/05, pp. 1, A4

dictatorship, 'democratic centralism' is used to rule collectively by party leaders.

The Politburo Standing Committee of the Communist Party of China, which has five to nine members, holds real power in the country. President Hu Jintao, who serves as party general-secretary, leads the committee. The Communist Party also controls the Chinese military through the Central Military Commission. In building socialist political democracy, China has always adhered to the basic principle that the Marxist theory of democracy be combined with the reality of China.

The report states that the Communist Party regards itself as a 'vanguard of the working class.' The party has rejected copying the 'Western bourgeois political system' because it 'would lead them nowhere,' the report said.[49]

Underwater Warfare

There are 400 submarines in the world today; about half are friendly. China has a larger submarine force than the United States. China is building at least five new nuclear fast attack submarines – and two new ballistic-missile nuclear submarines greatly enhancing Chinese capabilities.

Nineteen submarines were launched last year worldwide – nine of them in China. But the American military history records many instances of poor readiness or non-availability of war-fighting equipment when conflicts broke out. American submarines perform many missions – but serve as the premier anti-submarine weapons platform in the U.S. Navy inventory today. And the United States has

[49] From Beijing, Bill Gertz, *The Washington Times*, 10/20/05, p. A13

launched just four submarines in the last five years.[50]

China Challenges other Asian Countries

Vietnam: China poses problems to all the Asian countries. China launched an unprovoked attack on Vietnam and forcibly occupied the Paracel islands in 1974, the Johnson Reef in 1988, and Da Lac Reef in 1992. China made its first military presence in the occupied area since 1988.

Malaysia: China claims that it's territorial engulf three million sq. km. out of the total area of 3.5 million sq. km. in the South China Sea. China has created maritime disputes with Philippines, Malaysia, Vietnam, Brunei, Indonesia, Japan, North Korea and South Korea. China claims a land and other two islands of Malaysia, although all three belongs to Malaysia.

Philippines: China occupied Mischief Reef in the Spratlys Islands but the Philippines destroyed the Chinese markers within a month. Both Vietnam and Malaysia have appealed the UN Convention on the Law of the Sea, China's claim and definition of continental self.

Japan: China has spread fears about a revival of World War II Japanese militarism and put Japan on the defensive by protesting about the visits of Japanese leaders to the Yasukuni shrine, which is dedicated to the memory of soldiers killed in service of the country.

---

[50] Vice Adm. Albert Konetzni Jr. (served as Deputy commander and Chief of Staff, U.S. Fleet Forces Command, 2001-'04, and Commander, Submarine Force, U.S. Pacific Fleet, 1998-'01), *New York Post*, 7/5/05, p. 27

Having emerged as the largest trading partner of Asia's three largest economies – Japan, South Korea and India – and a major trading partner of the ASEAN countries, China appears determined to combine its economic clout and its military potential to emerge from using maritime power to emerge as Asia's dominant power. China issues press notes that its land is occupied by other countries and then fights against that country. China has tried successfully with all neighbor countries.

India: China claims Arunachal Pradesh - a State, which is situated in India. China has grabbed land in other countries. China fought with India in 1962 and occupied a vast area in the Himalayas. The boundary line (the McMahon Line) was accepted as on November 7, 1955, but now China claims that it should be November 21, 1962 because by that time it had captured thousands of sq. km of hilly forest area of India after the October 1962 invasion. China has put India on the defensive diplomatically and militarily because of His Holiness Dalai Lama is living in India for the last five decades as a guest.

India and China are the most populous countries in the world and both the countries possess nuclear arsenals. They are neighbor countries and rich in ancient civilization.

Both countries can prosper in international trade with mutual understanding and partnership; both of them can award peace to the whole world; but both the countries can perish together by waging war.

So China and India should be friendly countries for their safety, stability, prosperity and welfare of the humanity.

Tibet: China has already annexed Tibet since 1951. But it killed and beheaded many Tibetan Buddhists because they undertook a march through Tawang Street in March 14, 2008.[51] Many Tibetans are being tortured in Chinese jails and all the Tibetans are passing hard times both inside Tibet and outside the country. In one year (2011-2012), more than 20 young Tibetans have committed suicides by burning them to liberate Tibet from clutches of China.

Nepal: China has sent Lt Gen Shu Yutai to Nepal on December 5, 2009 to hold bilateral talks with the government of Nepal. China advises the Nepal government to watch all the 59 Tibetan monasteries situated in Nepal to check pro-Tibetan activities. China has invited Prime Minister Madhab Kumar Nepal to visit China to avail generous economic and military aid from China including military training.

Pakistan: China assists Pakistan in supplying arms and ammunitions to raise the Kashmir issue against India. It wants to reach Pakistan through Pak Occupied Kashmir.

Beijing Gets Ready for Attack on Taiwan

Beyond warships armed with missiles, the building and deployment of amphibious lift ships is one of the clearest signs of what U.S. defense officials say are Beijing's intentions to attack Taiwan, located about 100 miles from the Chinese mainland.

In the past three years, China has more than doubled its fleet of amphibious landing and troop-carrying ships, a key indicator of such an assault, said officials who spoke on the condition of anonymity. For example, intelligence officials told *The Washington Times* that since 2002, China has deployed at least eight tank-carrying Yuting II LST transport ships, at

---

[51] G. Parthasarathy (2009), "A Rising China Bares Its Fangs", The Pioneer, October 29, 2009.P.8, Bhubaneswar

least 10 Yunshu LSM ships and at least five Yubei LSU ships.

China has two Russian-made Sovremenny-class guided-missile destroyers, and two others are being built in Russia. The ships will carry large numbers of SSN-22 supersonic anti-ship cruise missiles that are designed to sink U.S. aircraft carriers and warships.

It also is building three new classes of destroyers. Two Luzhou guided-missile destroyers are under construction, along with two Luyang II missile destroyers that are undergoing sea trials. Two other Luyang I destroyers are operational or undergoing sea trials.

The fact that you have three destroyer classes being built in China at the same time also implies a higher degree of sophistication in shipbuilding capability and overall project management.

The defense officials are describing the Luyang II as China's answer to the U.S. Aegis-equipped destroyers, which form the backbone of the U.S. Navy warship fleet. The Luyang II also has advanced air-defense missiles. In addition to destroyers, China has built two new Jiangkai frigates and two-Jiangwei frigates since 2002. The new Jiangweis are in addition to the eight Jiangweis built before 2002.

It also has built at least three fast-attack patrol boats with a radical catamaran design that allows for high speeds. The wave-piercing design is aimed at making the ships less vulnerable to enemy radar and targeting. To service its new warships, China is building numerous support ships, including a minesweeper, two Fuchi surveillance ships, and at least 15 tankers, logistics and service ships.

As for naval training, intelligence and policy officials said one troubling development is China's use of commercial freighters in military exercises, which they view as a sign that it plans to move large amounts of troops and equipment across the Taiwan Strait in a future war.[52]

On April 4, 2009 TV cameras recorded a Chinese Riot Control Police outfit, wearing the 'Blue Berets of the U.N.' marching across the airport tarmac in Port-au-Prince, Haiti. It is one of many examples of China projecting itself to the far corners of the world.

Beijing Prepares for Future

The Chinese military budget, oil demand and standoff with Taiwan and the United States, ignores long-term implications. With its centrally controlled government, China can closely monitor and influence its military, economic and socio-political development and could plan 20 to 100 years into the future. The real budget of China is a secret deal.

But America's political leaders too often look only at four- to eight-year terms, ignoring China's enormity. For example, people dismiss the simple idea 1 in 3 of the world's people could be Chinese by 2050, all over the globe. Further, Americans especially do not see how a large portion of our conventional military is retooling to deal with low-intensity asymmetrical threats. This, while China's conventional military power expands every year and concentrates on macro strategic warfare, including even outer space.

Immediate concerns over rising world oil prices have obscured the indirect role of China moving into economic high gear with booming oil demand and industrialization. Meanwhile our foreign policy focuses

[52] Bill Gertz, *The Washington Times*, 6/26/05, p. A4, Excerpted from Howard Phillips Issues & Strategy Bulletin of July 31, 2005

on combating terrorism and spreading real and ersatz democracies.

Examining these situations and trends stimulates serious concern. Last year, China's military budget visibly increased 12 percent, with similar upsurges each year over the last decade. Each annual expansion is only a small concern, but this development is ominous and doesn't include China's commercial military-industrial performance. China's money has poured into improving strategic capabilities, including its blue-water navy, air capabilities and modern space communications, reconnaissance and attack systems. These increased capabilities have moved China's army to shed its militia roots and adopt Western doctrines that integrate technology, joint operations and information warfare. So, as China's military capabilities become comparable to those of America, conflict could erupt on sea, in the air and in space.

Twenty-First Century Will Belong to China

At the current level of growth, China will surpass the United States as the world's largest economy in 30 years or less. Huge cash reserves and lucrative markets allow China to forge worldwide commercial ties by enticement and pressure.

These same economic moves dictate political and diplomatic relationships. In any sort of conflict, it would be very easy for China to leverage its power and coerce nations to its side, as in the classic Sun Tzu adage: 'The next best plan is to attack the enemy through alliances, forcing the enemy to capitulate.

Recent developments show China follows that advice and is slowly moving toward a goal of sole superpower Dom. It recently signed an economic partnership with the **Philippines and Vietnam** to develop the natural resources of the Spratly Islands, sidestepping turmoil there. These islands are an important center of a long-sought Chinese domination of the South China Sea's trade routes and resources, a goal that directly challenges U.S. interests in the area. This, coupled with new negotiations with India, shows a new direction in thought. Chinese officials say they do not wish to challenge U.S. superpower status, but the scenario above illustrates a strategy of dominance through slow, subtle influence. ...

American military strategists must address future global and space developments by the Chinese military to counter any potential intimidation. We should curtail trade with the Chinese until they make a commitment to lasting sociopolitical liberalization, while we control our own hemorrhaging trade deficit with them. Trade agreements between China and other nations must be monitored to prevent economic blackmail.[53]

CIA Report

China's military buildup is 'tilting the balance of power in the Taiwan Strait' in ways threatening to the United States, say U.S. intelligence officials, whose blunt comments contrast sharply to past intelligence assessments of the communist country's capabilities.

Improved Chinese capabilities threaten U.S. forces in the region,' CIA Director Porter J. Goss told the Senate Select Committee on Intelligence Wednesday.

China continues to develop more robust, survivable nuclear-armed missiles, as well as conventional

---

[53] F. Andrew Messing Jr. (U.S. Army Special Forces retired major and executive director of National Defense Council Foundation (NDCF) and Daniel Perez (NDCF research assistant), *The Washington Times*, 5/2/05, p. A17, Excerpted from Howard Phillips Issues & Strategy Bulletin of March 15, 2005

capabilities for use in regional conflict. Vice Adm. Lowell Jacoby, director of the Defense Intelligence Agency said in prepared testimony to the panel that China is adding numbers and more capable ballistic missiles to its arsenal to 'improve their survivability and war-fighting capabilities, enhance their coercion and deterrence value, and overcome ballistic missile defense systems.

This effort is because of with its growing power and more assertive policies, especially with respect to Taiwan. The officials' testimony shows an apparent effort to define the danger posed by China's rising military power, which critics said have been minimized in the past, in part so as not to offend the country with markets coveted by U.S. businesses. The CIA, in particular, has been criticized in the past for underestimating Chinese military and security developments.

Sen. Susan Collins, Maine Republican, yesterday asked Defense Secretary Donald H. Rumsfeld at a Senate Appropriations Committee hearing about Mr. Goss' testimony that 'sounded the alarm about China's modernization of its navy.'

Mr. Rumsfeld said China is boosting defense spending by 'double-digit' rates and most of the buildup is being carried out in secret. 'They're purchasing a great deal of relatively modern equipment from Russia,' Mr. Rumsfeld said. 'And as you point out, they have been expanding their navy and expanding the distances from the People's Republic of China that their navy ventures.'

If Beijing decides that Taiwan is taking steps toward permanent separation that exceed Beijing's tolerance, we assess China is prepared to respond with varying levels of force.

Adm. Jacoby identified three new missile systems, the DF-31, DF-31A mobile intermediate range ballistic missiles (ICBMs) and JL-2 submarine launched missile, noting that by 2015 China will have increased its nuclear warhead arsenal to several times the current level. The DIA estimated in 2000 that China had a total of 157 nuclear warheads for long- and short-range missiles, and will have 464 warheads for its missiles by 2020.

The United States has long focused attention on the Chinese government's threat to use military force against Taiwan if the island, which China views as a renegade province, moves toward independence. Until now, Japan has been content to let the United States bear the brunt of Beijing's displeasure."

But in the most significant alteration since 1996 to the U.S.-Japan Security Alliance, which remains the cornerstone of U.S. interests in East Asia, Japan will join the Bush administration in identifying security in the Taiwan Strait as a 'common strategic objective. And in December, Japan angered China by granting a tourist visa to former Taiwanese president, Lee Tenghui, who was educated in Japan and had an emotional reunion here with a former professor.[54]

China Threaten Japan's Security

Along with the threat of North Korea, which declared itself a nuclear-armed nation, the rise of China has become the primary concern fueling Japan's shift away from nearly six decades of pacifism.

Japan has generally been inclined to sidestep conflict with China. But in recent years, China has dramatically modernized its military while expanding its sphere of influence in Asia on the strength of its booming economy. The effort to extend its reach has

---

[54] Bill Gertz, The Washington Times, 2/18/05, p. A3

included exploring for natural gas near Japanese-claimed waters only 110 miles north of Taiwan and countering Japan's claims to exclusive economic zones in the Pacific.

In response, Japan has also shifted course in the past year, moving to defend its territorial claims in the East China Sea. Last November, Japan dispatched aircraft on a two-day hunt for a Han-class Chinese submarine that briefly intruded into Japan's far southern waters in what many here saw as a test of Japanese resolve in the event of Chinese aggression against Taiwan.

It would be wrong for us to send a signal to China that the United States and Japan will watch and tolerate China's military invasion of Taiwan,' said Shinzo Abe, the acting secretary general of Japan's ruling Liberal Democratic Party who is widely considered a likely successor to Junichiro Koizumi as prime minister. 'If the situation surrounding Japan threatens our security, Japan can provide U.S. forces with support.

Such talk reflects what diplomats and scholars call the defining drama of East Asia for the 21st century – the competition for economic and political dominance in the region between Japan, the world's second-largest economy, and China, the world's most populous nation and a fast-developing economic and military power. The two governments have also battled over the route of a trans-Siberian pipeline for Russian oil and territorial rights in an East China Sea island chain known as the Senkaku in Japanese and the Diaoyu in Chinese.

The Chinese government granted rights two years ago for domestic and foreign oil companies to explore and drill an area only three miles from Japanese-claimed territory – a region rich in natural gas and oil. This month, Japan pushed back, boosting its claims to the area by officially taking over ownership of a 15-foot lighthouse built on the island chain by Japanese nationalist activists in 1978.

But the idea of Japanese military cooperation with the United States in the sea-lanes north of Taiwan has particularly rankled Chinese diplomatic and military planners because it goes to the heart of their Taiwan strategy.

On the one hand, diplomats and other specialists say, the Chinese military has embarked on a buildup of short-range missiles, naval vessels and electronics-aided aircraft to enable it to threaten the island militarily if President Chen Shuibian should take what China considers an unacceptably decisive step toward independence. On the other hand, they added, China has set out to improve and extend its maritime and airborne might in the sea lanes north of Taiwan, with the goal of forcing the United States to think twice about military intervention. Within the next five years, according to U.S. estimates, the Chinese navy is expected to have more than 20 modern attack submarines, including half a dozen nuclear-powered vessels.[55]

Japanese officials said that the official position advocating a peaceful resolution of the Taiwan issue has not changed. They said the constitution limits the level of assistance that Japan could offer in the event of a U.S. confrontation with China over Taiwan. But the joint statement on Saturday could help lay the groundwork for the Japanese to extend as much cooperation as they legally can, including logistical support such as transportation and medical rescue operations behind the lines of combat, officials said. We consider China a friendly country, but it is also unpredictable,' a senior Japanese government official

[55] From Tokyo, Anthony Failoa, *The Washington Post*, 2/18/05, pp. 1, A26

said. 'If it takes aggressive action, Japan cannot just stand by and watch.

China Is a Super Power Because of the United States

Condoleezza Rice lists 'outposts of tyranny,' but Communist China is missing: According to Secretary of State-designate Condoleezza Rice, there are six 'outposts of tyranny' (*Washington Times*): Stalinist North Korea, Iran, Burma, Belarus, Cuba and Zimbabwe. As for Communist China, Rice preferred 'building a candid, cooperative and constructive relationship with China that embraces our common threats but still recognizes our considerable differences about values' (Cybercast News). Never mind that the Communists have several economic and/or military ties to *all six* 'outposts,' and that their treatment of their own people qualifies for nothing *but* tyranny.[56]

China has deployed a brigade of up to eight new road-mobile DF-31 long-range missiles. That's the latest assessment from the authoritative International Institute for Strategic Studies publication, 'The Military Balance.'

China also has 24 DF-5A long-range strategic missiles and 112 intermediate - range DF-4, DF-3A and DF-21 missiles. The assessment that eight DF-31s are operational goes beyond the Pentagon's latest report on Chinese military power made public in May. The Pentagon report stated that the DF-31 is still in development with deployment expected 'later this decade.' The Pentagon stated that China also is working on two longer-range versions of the DF-31, one that is a solid-fuel ground-based mobile missile and a solid-fuel submarine-launched version.

---

[56] China_ e_ lobby *News of the Day*, 1/19/05

China is building up its strategic nuclear forces. It is expected to add 10 intercontinental ballistic missiles (ICBM) to its arsenal this year and 30 more ICBMs by 2010. [57]

China is modernizing its military forces faster than anyone expected, escalating the potential danger to the island of Taiwan, to American forces and bases in Asia, and to the overall balance of power in the region. China adheres to the military strategy of active defense and works to speed up the revolution of military affairs (RMA) with Chinese characteristics,' says the white paper Beijing issued in December. It points to 'leapfrog development' in high-tech weapons for its missile units, navy, and air force. Where many American and Asian analysts said before that China would be able to mount a credible threat between 2010 and 2015, now they are saying it will come earlier, perhaps by 2006 and certainly by 2012.

Behind this military progress has been the rapid growth of the Chinese economy that pays for the military power. China's defense budget is estimated to have ballooned to $80 billion, the world's third largest after the United States and Russia, and almost double that of Japan, which has Asia's second largest defense budget.

The Chinese, who had insisted on self-sufficiency, have bought weapons and technology from abroad, notably from Russia. China could afford those purchases because Beijing's foreign exchange reserves, the world's largest, rose to $610 billion by

---

[57] Bill Gertz and Rowan Scarborough, Inside the Ring, *The Washington Times*, 1/21/05, p. A5 Excerpted from Howard Phillips Issues & Strategy Bulletin of February 28, 2005

the end of 2004, more than 10 times their holdings of $53 billion 10 years ago.

China's missile force, called the Second Artillery, had been deploying 50 to 75 short-range missiles a year; that has increased to more than 100 and in 2006 Second Artillery will have 800 aimed at Taiwan. Accuracy has been doubled so that most missiles would hit within 60 to 90 feet of their targets. Moreover, the missiles have been made mobile to make them less of a target. In a training drill, a brigade moved 360 miles and was ready to fire in two days.

Land-based and air-launched cruise missiles, which are flying torpedoes with stubby wings and advanced navigational devices, have been added to the Chinese inventory to add to their ability to stand off and fire at targets on Taiwan or at U.S. warships at sea.

In the Chinese navy, long the stepchild of the People's Liberation Army, submarines are leading the way. In the event of hostilities, they would be tasked with gaining control of the Taiwan Strait between the island and the mainland, and fending off the U.S. Navy. China has bought eight Kilos diesel-electric submarines from Russia and is planning to buy four more. Beijing is also building its own Song class of diesel-electric boats. Although they lack the range of nuclear-powered submarines, they are quieter and more effective close to shore. For long-range operations, China is building several nuclear-powered attack submarines. China, which has become the world's third largest shipbuilder, has produced about 100 amphibious ships, and four-tank landing ships are under construction. [58]

---

[58] Richard Halloran, *Honolulu Advertiser*, 2/6/05

China can challenge other Super Powers

China's military has launched the first of a new class of ballistic missile submarines in what defense officials view as a major step forward in Beijing's strategic weapons program.

The new 094-class submarine was launched in late July and when fully operational in the next year or two will be the first submarine to carry the under-water-launched version of China's new DF-31 missile, according to defense officials.

A second intelligence official said building submarines is a top priority of the Chinese, and the Type 094 will be 'China's first truly intercontinental strategic nuclear delivery system.' The submarine is (believed to be) based largely on Russian nuclear submarine technology, the officials said. A CIA reports made public last week stated that Russia was a major supplier of technology to China's naval nuclear propulsion programs.

The launching of the new missile submarine appears ahead of schedule. A Pentagon report on Chinese military power made public in May stated that the new Chinese missile submarine would not be deployed until around 2010.

Mobile, solid-fuel missiles and a new ballistic missile submarine will improve the force's ability to survive a first strike,' the report said, 'while more launchers, on-board penetration aids, and possibly multiple warheads will improve its ability to penetrate missile defenses.

Richard Fisher, vice president of the Washington-based International Assessment and Strategy Center, said the launch of the new missile submarine is 'an astounding development.

The 094 has followed 093 developments far more rapidly than the assessments in the annual Pentagon reports on the PLA,' Mr. Fisher said, referring to ... China's People's Liberation Army. China also recently launched a new attack submarine known as the Type 093. Additionally, U.S. intelligence agencies were surprised by China's disclosure in July of a third new type of submarine known as the Yuan-class, a diesel-electric attack submarine.

In the very near future, China will have a secure, second-strike nuclear attack capability that it will use to bolster its nuclear strategy of seeking to deter the United States from aiding Taiwan after a PLA attack.

The new submarine will make it more difficult for the U.S. military to take part in a defense of Taiwan because of the threat of nuclear retaliation.

The Pentagon has deployed a new missile defense system, but a spokesman for the Missile Defense Agency has said the current interceptor system is designed to stop a long-range North Korean missile, but not an attack from Chinese or Russian missiles.

A 1999 report by the House Select Committee on U.S. National Security and Military/Commercial Concerns with the People's Republic of China stated that the new missile submarines will likely benefit from stolen U.S. nuclear warhead designs. ...

The range of the JL-2 is estimated to be about 7,500 miles, enough 'to strike targets throughout the United States,' the report said. Instead of venturing into the open ocean to attack the United States, the Type 094-class submarines could remain near [Chinese] waters, protected by the [People's Liberation Army,] Navy and Air Force,' the report said.[59]

---

[59] Bill Gertz, *The Washington Times*, 12/3/04, pp. 1, A14

Russia Strengthens Chinese Navy / Army

China soon will receive a new Kilo submarine from Russia, part of a naval buildup of modern warships and submarines that has triggered new fears for U.S. military planners.

It is the first of eight advanced Kilos that China is acquiring, and intelligence officials say the submarine will be outfitted with advanced SS-N-27 cruise missiles, which are capable of attacking U.S. warships. ...

Since 2002, China has built 14 submarines, including a new Yuan submarine that was unknown to U.S. intelligence until photos of it appeared on the Internet last year. Other submarines in development include the Type 094 ballistic-missile submarine, known as the Jin class.

At least two Type 093 attack submarines are under construction, as well as additional Jin, Song, Yuan and Shang submarines, the officials said. Other new submarines include one Ming submarine, 10 Song submarines and one Shang class. ...

China's surface-to-surface missile forces also are increasing, including new short and long-range missiles, along with a new warhead that can maneuver to avoid missile defenses.

If you take a step back and look at the entire array of Chinese weapons, the Kilos, the Songs, the Yuans, the ballistic missiles, this (maneuverable warhead) capability, more surface ships with anti-ship cruise missiles, these are all things that are going to give you capability to deal with any kind of naval force that comes toward you.

Russia plans to sell a host of new fighters and transport planes to China in 2005, arms export officials said Friday, and foreign sales of Russian weaponry could exceed $5 billion next year.

Yury Krylov, who heads the air force division of the state agency Roso boron export, said that his agency and the Chinese air force expect to sign several new contracts for Su-30MK2 jet fighters, according to Interfax. Pre-contract work on supplying Il-76 Candid military transports and Il-78 Midas aerial tankers were almost finished.

The Sukhoi Su-27 – a similar twin-engine design to the Su-30 – has been in service since 1985, and has the NATO code name 'Flanker.' Its speed and maneuverability made it one of the key planes in the former Soviet Air Force, and it resembles the U.S. F-15 Eagle fighter with two rear stabilizers and twin engines. Director General Sergei Chemezov said naval contracts are expected to grow, along with upgrading planes and helicopters, missile and artillery armaments, and communication systems and other technologies.[60]

Once-bitter rivals Russia and China would hold a large joint military exercise on Chinese territory in 2005 involving submarines and possibly strategic bombers, Russia's defense minister said yesterday, as the two nations move to bolster burgeoning military ties. Many observers saw the announcement as Russia's response to a spat with the United States and other Western nations over the disputed election in Ukraine, Russia's neighbor, where Kremlin-backed candidate Victor Yanukovych trailed pro-Western Viktor Yushchenko in near-final results.

For the first time in history, we have agreed to hold quite a large military exercise together with China on

---

[60] Combined AP, Bloomberg Reports, *Moscow Times*, 12/28/04, p. 5

Chinese territory in the second half of the year,' Defense Minister Sergei Ivanov said at a cabinet session chaired by President Vladimir V. Putin, according to the ITAR-Tass news agency.

The Russian side will not bring big numbers of servicemen, but mostly state-of-the-art weapons – navy, air, long-range aviation, submarines – to practice interaction with China in different forms of military maneuvers.' After decades of rivalry, Moscow and Beijing have developed what they call a strategic partnership since the Soviet Union's collapse. China has become the No. 1 customer for Russia's struggling defense industry, buying billions of dollars worth of fighters, missiles, submarines and destroyers.

Putin and other Russian officials allege the United States improperly influenced Ukraine's elections by funding democracy-building organizations. A Nov. 21 ballot in which Yanukovych was declared the winner was annulled after allegations of widespread fraud and amid huge public protests.[61]

Chins increases Defense Budget in 2012-2013

China announced its defense budget by 11.2 percent to a whipping **US $ 106.4 billion**, pushing its military spending for the first time to the triple digit, a move that might fuel concerns among neighbours and others about its growing might in Asia Pacific. China, which has the world's largest standing **army of 2.3 million,** had been hiking its defense budget by double digits during most part of the last decade. Analysts believe that China spends much higher than the official figures. (News, March 4, 2012)

---

[61] From Moscow, Vladimir Isachenkov, Associated Press, *Philadelphia Inquirer*, 12/28/04

Israel Is In Good Terms with China

Israel's persistent clandestine military dealings with China have created waves with the U.S., reports *International News Services*. Israel has reportedly concealed from Washington an upgrade of a major weapons system it sold to China more than a decade ago. By assisting in upgrading China's weapons system, Israel violated its commitment not to transfer U.S. technology to China without Washington's permission. Israel is China's second-largest arms supplier, after Russia. Although diplomatic relations between Israel and China were established only in 1992, military ties go back to the early 1980s. Until formal diplomatic ties were established in the early 1990s, the nation's military relationship was covert. Israel sold approximately US$4 billion worth of arms to China during the covert relationship.

During the 1990s, while much of the West penalized Beijing following the Tiananmen Square Massacre, the Sino-Israel military relationship grew rapidly. After Israel was pressured by the U.S. to scrap a $250 million deal to sell China the Phalcon, an airborne radar system, the military relationship soured. Washington claimed that providing Beijing access to the technology would upset the military balance between China and Taiwan and threatens U.S. interests in the region. When the U.S. Congress threatened to cut the $2.8 billion it gives Israel annually if the deal went ahead, Israel buckled and scrapped it.

For years, the U.S. government has expressed concerns over Israel illegally transferring technology to China. During the Gulf War, the U.S. gave Israel Patriot Missiles as protection against Iraqi Scud missiles. In 1992, a U.S. intelligence report revealed that soon after the end of the Gulf War, Israel had sold Patriot anti-missile data to China. Washington has also alleged on several occasions that Israel violated agreements by exporting to China restricted U.S. technology it buys with yearly U.S. subsidies. This was the case with the largely U.S.-funded Lavi fighter-plane program, the technology of which Israel passed to Beijing. China's F-10 fighter jet is believed to be almost identical to the Lavi.

In 2002, a deal for Israeli communication satellites was signed with the United States. Early this year, an Israeli delegation went to China for talks on rebuilding military ties. Beijing's relationship with Israel has enabled it to acquire 'dual-use technology' that the U.S. and Europe have been reluctant to provide. (December 21)[62]

China Is Prepared For Space Fight

For some time now, China has spearheaded an international movement to ban conventional weapons from space. More than a year ago, the Asian superpower – joined by Russia, Vietnam, Indonesia, Belarus, Zimbabwe and Syria – introduced a draft treaty at the United Nations to outlaw the deployment of space-based weapons.

But even as it tries to rally multinational coalitions and public opinion to oppose 'the weapon-fighting of space,' Beijing quietly continues to develop its own space-based weapons and tactics to destroy American military assets.

China's strategy here is to blunt American military superiority by limiting and ultimately neutralizing its existing space-based defense assets, and to forestall deployment of new technology that many experts believe would provide the best protection from ballistic-missile attack.

---

[62] Al Santoli, American Foreign Policy Council's *China Reform Monitor*, 1/12/05

Chinese security experts have a keen appreciation of America's space-based assets and how the military envisions using them in future conflicts. Strategists in the People's Liberation Army have studied our campaigns in the 1991 Gulf War, Kosovo, Afghanistan and this year's war in Iraq. They have observed our overwhelming superiority in the general field of 'C4ISR'.[63] More importantly, they have noted that our superiority in communication, reconnaissance and surveillance depends on what we have up in space.

These lessons have convinced PLA military planners that America's strength can become our Achilles heel. If they can neutralize or destroy our space assets, American forces will lose a critical advantage, leaving them far more vulnerable to China's larger but less-advanced military. But a decade's-worth of technical articles in Chinese science digests discussing how to fight a war in space and analyzing U.S. strengths and vulnerability make it clear that Beijing has a long-running military program designed to challenge America's dominance in – and dependence on – space.

China's Technology Research Academy, for example, has been developing an advanced anti-satellite Weapon called a 'piggyback satellite.' The system is designed to seek out an enemy satellite (or space station or space-based laser) and attach itself like a parasite, either jamming the enemy's communications or physically destroying the unit. The PLA also is experimenting with other types of satellite killers: land-based, directed-energy weapons and 'micro-satellites' that can be used as kinetic energy weapons. According to the latest (July 2003) assessment by the U.S. Defense Department, China will probably be able to field a direct-ascent anti-satellite system in the next two to six years.

---

[63] Note: C41SR = Command, Control, Communications, Computers, Intelligence, Surveillance and Reconnaissance

Such weapons would directly threaten what many believe would be America's best form of ballistic-missile defense: a system of space-based surveillance and tracking sensors, connected with land-based sensors and space-based missile interceptors. Such a system could negate any Chinese missile attack on the U.S. homeland.

China[64] may be a long way from contemplating a ballistic missile attack on the U.S. homeland. But deployment of American space-based interceptors also would negate the missiles China is refitting to threaten Taiwan and U.S. bases in Okinawa and Guam. And there's the rub, as far as the PLA is concerned.

Beijing's draft treaty to ban deployment of space-based weapons is merely a delaying tactic aimed at hampering American progress on ballistic-missile defense while its own scientists develop effective countermeasures. What Beijing hopes to gain from this approach is the ability to disrupt American battlefield awareness – and its command and control operations – and to deny the U.S. access to the waters around China and Taiwan should the issue of Taiwan's sovereignty lead to conflict between the two Chinas.

China and the United States Are Not Friends, But ---

As Hu Jintao – the heir apparent in Beijing – meets President Bush - it is worth asking how much real substance remains in the U.S. - China relationship. Economic ties remain strong, of course, if lopsided. The U.S. is China's largest export market, a major source of investment and an even more important

---

64 Larry Wortzel, www.foxnews.com, 8/11/03, Excerpted from Howard Phillips Issues & Strategy Bulletin of September 30, 2003

source of technology, whether licitly or illicitly acquired. ...

Beijing's top leaders are crisscrossing the globe, visiting anti-U.S. bastions such as Cuba, Iran and Libya, while trying to pry European allies away from their Atlantic ties. China attempted to fill the gap left by Moscow's apostasy and become the cornerstone of an anti-liberal world coalition.

From that decision has flawed a quixotic foreign policy that embraces unsavory regimes, from Burma to Cuba to North Korea. China also supplies advanced weapons to Iraq and Iran and nuclear technology to Pakistan and is undertaking an unnecessary military buildup that has sown suspicion around China's periphery.

China's internal stability is increasingly dependent on good relations with the U.S. and other foreign powers, who pay the bills through imports and investment. Yet Beijing's rhetoric and foreign policy continues to undercut that relationship.[65]

In short, all these reports are newspaper reports and China has never disowned these publications. But China believes that each impossible aim could be fulfilled one day if there is a continuous effort to achieve the goal.

Trilateral Cooperation of China- Japan-ROK

On the occasion of the Tenth Anniversary of China-Japan-ROK Trilateral Cooperation, we, the heads of Government /State of the People's Republic of China, Japan and the Republic of Korea met in Beijing, China on October 10, 2009. They reviewed the course of

---

[65] Arthur Waldron, *Wall Street Journal*, 5/1/02, p. A18, Excerpted from Howard Phillips Issues & Strategy Bulletin of May 15, 2002

trilateral cooperation in the past and drew up plans for its future development. The statement is as follows:

We reached the common understanding that since the launch of the trilateral cooperation in 1999, the common interests of the three countries have continuously grown, the mechanisms for dialogue have been further broadened and the cooperation in a whole range of fields has been promoted, yielding highly fruitful results. The three countries have enhanced political mutual trust through the forging of a future-oriented comprehensive cooperative partnership. With the rapid increase in trilateral economic cooperation as well as trade and investment, the three countries have emerged as important trading partners to one another. Cultural and people-to-people exchanges were dynamic and close, which greatly enhanced the mutual understanding and friendship among the peoples. The three countries remained committed to the development of an East Asia community based on the principles of openness, transparency, inclusiveness as a long-term goal, and to regional cooperation, while maintaining increased trilateral communication and coordination on regional and international affairs.

We expressed the common recognition that the achievements over the past decade proved that to reinforce cooperation among China, Japan and the ROK serves the fundamental interests of the three countries and peoples, and moreover, contributes to regional peace, stability and prosperity. In this context, the three countries also recognized the significance of the "Joint Statement for Tripartite Partnership" issued at the first trilateral Summit in Fukuoka, Japan.

We believe that as the world undergoes major changes and adjustments, China – Japan - ROK cooperation will have many opportunities for development in the coming decade. We will view and approach the trilateral cooperative relationship from a strategic point of view, and will constantly aim to bring our cooperation to higher levels.

We believe that mutual respect, equality, common interests, openness, transparency and respect for our diverse cultures constitute the foundation and guarantee for trilateral cooperation, and these principles should be followed in future trilateral cooperation. In the spirit of facing history squarely and advancing towards the future, the three countries will explore the potential and expand the areas of cooperation. We will push the trilateral relations forward in the direction of good-neighborliness, mutual trust, comprehensive cooperation, mutual benefit and common development. We are convinced that this will contribute to world peace, stability and prosperity.

With this in mind, we have agreed to:

1. Build up mutual trust in the political field. We will step up high-level contacts and strategic dialogues, strengthen mutual understanding, expand common ground and build solid strategic mutual trust. We will regard one another as partners of win-win cooperation. We will support one another's peaceful development and regard it as an opportunity. We will respect one another's major concerns and core interests. We will properly address sensitive issues and seek settlement of disputes through dialogue and consultation.

We will strengthen security dialogue and facilitate exchange and cooperation between the defense and military personnel of the three countries.

2. Deepen mutually beneficial cooperation. We will make full use of the high complementarities and

great potential of the three economies and bring to higher levels our cooperation in key areas such as business, trade, finance, investment, logistics, intellectual property, customs, information, science and technology, energy conservation, environmental protection and circular economy. We will step up our efforts to develop green economy, improve the quality of economic development, oppose trade protectionism in all forms, and uphold a fair, free and open global trading and investment system. We are determined to seek an ambitious and balanced conclusion to the Doha Development Round in 2010, consistent with its mandate, based on the progress already made, including with regard to modalities. By making full use of existing forum, including ASEAN+3, EAS, APEC and G20, we will continuously inject fresh vitality into the recovery and stable development of the economy of Asia and the world.

3. Expand people-to-people exchanges. We will continue to conduct exchanges among all sectors of the three countries, particularly friendly youth exchanges and exchanges among universities. We will consider establishing a long-term mechanism for youth and media exchanges, encourage academic institutions and local authorities, and promote closer trilateral cooperation in areas such as disaster management, healthcare, tourism, human resources, education and sports. We will carry forward the spirit of peace and friendship and promote affinity among our three peoples while respecting each culture so as to enhance popular support for the stable, healthy and friendly development of the trilateral relations.

4. Promote peace, stability and prosperity of Asia. We will further strengthen cooperation so as to promote development of regional and sub-regional cooperation of various mechanisms such as ASEAN integration and community building, ASEAN+3, East Asia Summit, ASEAN Regional Forum and APEC. We will remain committed to dialogue and consultation and

continue to work through peaceful means to pursue the denuclearization of the Korean Peninsula. We will make joint efforts with other parties for an early resumption of the Six-Party Talks, so as to safeguard peace and stability in Northeast Asia, and thereby to build an Asia of peace, harmony, openness and prosperity.

5. Actively respond to global issues. We will strengthen communication and consultation on regional and international affairs such as climate change, financial risks, energy security, public health, natural disasters, terrorism, arms control, disarmament and non-proliferation, and UN reform. We will actively participate in reforms in the international political, economic and financial fields and join the rest of the international community to work unremittingly for global peace, development and prosperity.

Looking ahead to the next decade, we are full of confidence and hope for the consolidation of the tripartite partnership and comprehensive cooperation. We firmly believe that in keeping with the calling of the times and with the development of our three countries, cooperation among China, Japan and the Republic of Korea will embrace an even brighter future, benefiting not only the three countries but also indeed the world. Hence the United Nations should take urgent step to appoint "Boundary Commission" for all the countries, which are now engaged in wars, rebellion, annexation and amalgamation etc. (News)

China and the United States

November 17, 2009

The President of United State and President of China discussed on world affairs and a press communiqué was released on November 17, 2009 in Beijing. These are the major decisions[66]:

China and the United States pledged to work together on a wide range of issues, including anti-terrorism initiatives and law enforcement cooperation and to talk about manned space flights and space exploration.

Agreed to develop a "partnership" to deal with global challenges, including climate change, the economic recovery and nuclear non-proliferation

Agreed that each country and its people have the right to choose their own path, and all countries should respect each other's choice of a development model.

The two sides reiterated that the fundamental principle of respect for each other's sovereignty and territorial integrity is at the core of the three Sino-US joint communiqué that guide China-US relations.

To strengthen communication, dialogue and cooperation on issues related to South Asia and work together to promote peace, stability and development in the region.

The US respects the sovereignty and territorial integrity of China and reaffirmed Washington's commitment to the one-China policy.

They would work together for a "positive outcome" at the Copenhagen Climate Summit.

China has a clear and consistent goal on the nuclear issue on the Korean Peninsula, and Beijing hopes all parties will make the best of the opportunities and return to the negotiating table.

[66] China daily, November 17, 2009

The US also wants to see the resumption of Six-Party Talks and would push for the de-nuclearization of the Korean Peninsula.

Agreed to continue to adopt strategic and long-term perspective, increase dialogue, exchanges and cooperation and work together to build a positive, cooperative and comprehensive China-US relationship for the 21st century

To take concrete action to steadily grow a partnership between the two countries to meet common challenges

Mr. Barack Obama opined that the major challenges of the 21st century - from climate change and nuclear nonproliferation to economic recovery - are challenges that touch both China and US; **challenges that neither can solve by acting alone.** US welcomed China's efforts to play an increasingly important role on the world stage, "a role in which its growing economy is joined by growing responsibility".

Hu also championed more cooperation, stressing the need to steadily increase strategic mutual trust between the countries, which would be preceded by respect and accommodation of each other's core interests and major concerns.

China hopes that the US understands and supports Beijing's stand on issues such as Taiwan and called on Washington to ensure Tibetan and Uygur activists are not allowed to engage in separatist activities on the United State soil. China's development has created opportunities, not challenges, for the world including the United State.

Instead of becoming adversaries, the countries should become interdependent and genuinely cooperative partners.

Hu also called on the US to reduce restrictions on hi-tech exports to China and urged Washington to recognize China's market economy status. He also asked Washington to properly deal with trade disputes. Hu told the press the countries should be firmer in their opposition to trade protectionism.

China is willing to engage in dialogue on issues such as human rights and religion on the basis of mutual respect and non-interference of each other's internal affairs while committing to more high-level and people-to-people exchanges. The countries will restart dialogue on human rights next February 2010.

China and United States headed for Cold War

In China's eyes, the American response – which includes a pledge by Obama to get tougher on trade – is reaction against its rising power. The Global Times has predicted that a cold war will break out between the US and China.

A member of the Chinese people's political consultative conference declared that "We should retaliate with 'an eye for an eye' and sell arms to Iran, North Korea, Syria, Cuba and Venezuela. We have nothing to be afraid of. The North Koreans have stood up to America and anything happened to them? No. Iran stands up to America and does disaster befall it? No."

A military officer says, "This time China must punish the US." Another military officer says, "China would upgrade its military qualitatively over the next 10 years to force a showdown when we are strong enough for a hand-to-hand fight with the United States." The reasons are:

The battles over Taiwan, Tibet, trade, climate change, internet freedom and human rights have poisoned the relations between the United States and China.

In a recent poll, more than half of Chinese people questioned said that china and America are heading for a new 'cold war'.

An independent survey of Chinese language media found army and navy officers predicting a military showdown between the giants and political leader calling china to sell more arms to America's foes.[67]

(B)
United States as a Big Brother

The United States of America faced Independence War, Civil War, Mexico War, World War II, and Cold War with Russia (1940s to the end of 1980s) and Korean War (1950 – 1953).

The US had direct military intervention in Guatemala (1954), Lebanon (1958 and 1983-85), the Dominican Republic (1865), Panama (1968 and 1889) and the Grenade (1983). The US forces attempted to hold back a communist takeover of Indo-China in Vietnam (1964 – 1973) but had withdrawn the war.

The US is now engaged in war against Iraq and Afghanistan as a **Big Brother** either to save democracy or to fight terrorism. The United States of America pokes its nose to all crises in the world, which should have been taken up by the United Nations Organization.

The US controls world economy, world politics, and is the World leader in scientific research, education, industry, and banking and is self sufficient in each sector. But the country produces controls and makes huge profit in international trade of arms, ammunitions, and fighter planes and leads all the countries in defense expenditure. The US is a Super Power. Some of the unwanted wars taken up by the

---

[67] Michael Sheridan in Sunday Times

United States in the past could have been avoided. Let us examine these wars.

The United States and Vietnam War

Although the Cold War was the dominant feature of the post-1945 world, another momentous change in the international system took place concurrently: the end of Europe's five-century-long domination of the non-European world. Some one hundred new sovereign states emerged from the wreckage of European colonialism, and Cold War competition was promptly extended to many of these new states.

The Vietnam War was the legacy of France's failure to suppress nationalist forces in Indochina as it struggled to restore its colonial dominion after World War II.

Led by Ho Chi Minh, a Communist-dominated revolutionary movement - the Viet Minh - waged a political and military struggle for Vietnamese independence that frustrated the efforts of the French and resulted ultimately in their ouster from the region. Vietnam had gained its independence from France in 1954. The country was divided into North and South. The North had a communist government led by Ho Chi Minh. The South had an anti-communist government led by Ngo Dinh Diem.

The Communist victory in the Chinese Civil War in 1949 and Chinese intervention against the United Nations in Korea made U.S.-China policy a captive of Cold War politics. Those events also helped to transform American anti-colonialism into support for the French protectorates in Indochina, and later for their non-Communist successors. American political and military leaders viewed the Vietnam War as the Chinese doctrine of revolutionary warfare in action (using Chinese and Soviet arms, to boot).

The overarching geopolitical aim behind the United States' involvement in Vietnam was to contain the spread of communism in Southeast Asia. To accomplish this aim, the United States supported an anti-communist regime known as the Republic of Vietnam (South Vietnam) in its fight against a communist take-over. South Vietnam faced a serious, dual-tracked threat: a communist-led revolutionary insurgency within its own borders and the military power of its communist neighbor and rival, the Democratic Republic of Vietnam (North Vietnam). Preventing South Vietnam from falling to the communists ultimately led the United States to fight a major regional war in Southeast Asia. The North Vietnamese regime, which received outside assistance from the communist great powers, the Soviet Union and the People's Republic of China, proved a formidable adversary. Whether the United States should have heavily committed itself militarily to contain communism in South Vietnam remains a hotly debated topic. The debate is closely related to the controversy over whether the problems in Southeast Asia were primarily political and economic rather than military. The United States strategy generally proceeded from the premise that the essence of the problem in Vietnam was military, with efforts to "win the hearts and minds" of the South Vietnamese populace taking second place.

To frustrate North Vietnamese and Viet Cong efforts, and in part to "contain" China, the United States eventually fielded an army of over 500,000 men and engaged in extensive air and naval warfare against North Vietnam. The American military effort provoked stiff domestic and international opposition, led to strained civil-military relations at home, and called into question many of the assumptions that had dominated US foreign and military policy since 1945, but failed to compel the enemy to do its will. In short America's strategic culture was fundamentally altered in the jungles of Indochina.

Allied forces in South Vietnam were never organized into a single combined command, but at lower levels many-combined operation were conducted, with varying degrees of success. The war also demonstrated the advantages (and especially disadvantages) of tight operational control by the President, the National Security Council and the Department of Defense in Washington.

US involvement in Vietnam began during the administration of Dwight D. Eisenhower (1953-1961), which sent US military to South Vietnam. Their numbers increased as the military position of the Saigon government became weaker. In 1957 Communist rebels - Viet Cong - began a campaign of terrorism in South Vietnam. They were supported by the government of North Vietnam and later by North Vietnamese troops. Their goal was to overthrow the anti-communist government in the South.

John F. Kennedy (1961-1963) decided to commit American support troops to South Vietnam. Four thousand troops were sent in 1962. There has been an endless debate about what he would have done in Vietnam. He of course, did escalate American involvement by expanding the number of advisors there from 15,000 to 16,000. But there is evidence that he would not have Americanized the war to the extent that Lyndon Johnson did. He was skeptical of the military. He feared that the US could get bogged down in Vietnam. He had Secretary of Defense McNamara in 1962 to lie out plans for American withdrawal by 1965. On the day he left for Dallas Texas in 1963, he asked his policy advisor Mike Forrestall to lay plans for a full discussion of Vietnam including a full discussion on getting the United States out of there. In the fall of 1963, American efforts to build a democratic bulwark against communism in South Vietnam were failing. President Kennedy struggled to get the Diem government and a communist insurgency--under control.

On November 3, 1963 Ngo Dinh Diem died at the hands of his generals.

Less than two weeks after President Diem's death, President Kennedy was assassinated.

After John Kennedy was murdered, Vice President Lyndon B. Johnson served the last fourteen months of Kennedy's term. He then was elected to his own full term. It began in January 1965. Much of his time and energy would be taken up by the war in Vietnam. By early 1964, America had about seventeen thousand troops in Vietnam. The troops were there to advise and train the South Vietnamese military.

Under President Lyndon B. Johnson (1963-1968), US intervention mushroomed both militarily and politically. Johnson asked for a resolution expressing U.S. determination to support freedom and protect peace in Southeast Asia. Congress responded with the Tonkin Gulf Resolution, expressing support for "all necessary measures" the President might take to repel armed attacks against US forces and prevent further aggression.

Under the strategy developed by General William C. Westmoreland, Commander, U.S. Military Assistance Command, Vietnam, American divisions would seek out and destroy North Vietnamese and Viet Cong (South Vietnamese Communist) formations, while air power carried the war to the North, attacking both the will of Hanoi's leaders to continue the fight and, to an increasing extent, their ability to do so. The list of targets expanded to include transportation, oil storage, and the nation's few industries. In theory, Westmoreland's strategy of search and destroy would force the Communists to expend supplies and thus make the logistics establishment in North Vietnam all the more vulnerable to bombing.

In 1966, more than 200,000 troops were committed to Vietnam. The United States escalated its participation in the war to a peak of 543,000 troops in April 1969. American forces in Southeast Asia operated under some stringent restrictions, including being forbidden to invade enemy territory in North Vietnam and, for many years, likewise being barred from ground operations against enemy sanctuaries in bordering Laos and Cambodia. The "body count" of Vietcong killed was the centerpiece of the American approach to waging the war, conducted through search-and-destroy operations in remote jungle regions. By 1966 it became increasingly clear that this strategy of attrition was not working and could not work because of the enemy's capacity to replace losses far higher than those the allies were able to inflict.

The Vietnam conflict wore many faces. It was at once an insurrection by indigenous guerrilla forces and an invasion by the regular army of a neighboring regime. It was a war of snipers and ambushes, booby traps and pitched battles. The location of the fighting ranged from the densely inhabited rice basket of the Mekong Delta to the remote, jungle-mountains of the Central Highlands, It included both platoon-level "pacification" efforts aimed at small bands of Vietcong and corps-level operations targeted against main-force North Vietnamese Army (NVA) regiments and divisions. A determined enemy and brutally difficult terrain combined to negate the effects of American technology and presented a dramatic challenge to a U.S. Army commander's battle command skills.

Vietnam saw changes in employment tactics of artillery. Front lines common in previous wars were replaced by perimeter defenses. The helicopter became a prime mover for artillery giving increased mobility. Artillery units occupied fire support bases and could fire 360 degrees in support of operations. The ability of the artillery to provide rapid and devastating fire support at critical times often spelled the difference between victory and defeat. Very few major engagements were fought without artillery support. American tactics in Vietnam relied on overwhelming firepower -- chiefly close air support and artillery -- to reduce friendly casualties while overcoming the enemy’s advantage in numbers. While fire support contributed significantly, it proved a two-edged sword. Although American firepower created staggering enemy casualties and limited his ability to mass maneuver forces, preparatory fires seldom neutralized the NVA positions. The dense jungle and the sharp relief of the hill attenuated the concentration of firepower, as did the enemy's well-prepared defenses.

The political challenge of the war stemmed from the belief of the rural Vietnamese that the Government of Vietnam will not stay long when it comes into an area, that the Government was indifferent to the people's welfare, that the low-level officials were tools of the local rich; and that the Government was excessively corrupt from top to bottom. The American search-and-destroy military operations didn't solve these problems, and were at best irrelevant to security in rural Vietnamese villages. At worst, indiscriminate aerial attacks and artillery fire exacted a toll on village allegiance to the Saigon government.

When General Creighton Abrams took command of MACV in the spring of 1968 the focus of American ground operations turned to "strategic hamlets" with population security as its goal.

In 1965, US air strikes were ordered against North Vietnam. By late 1965, such air strikes became part and parcel to daily activities of those stationed in Vietnam. But US forces were not permitted to attack some targets for fear of Chinese retaliation. The perceived danger from Communist China influenced President Johnson's choice of means for ensuring the survival of a South Vietnam independent of the North. In 1950, when United Nations forces threatened to overrun North Korea, China had come to the aid of its Communist neighbor. As the Vietnam War intensified in 1965 and 1966, so, too, did the Chinese commitment to the survival of North Vietnam. By the spring of the latter year, some 50,000 Chinese troops served in North Vietnam, a total that may have tripled before China began to withdraw its forces in 1968.

Until President Johnson limited ROLLING THUNDER to southern North Vietnam, effective April 1, 1968, China gave refuge to North Vietnamese fighters when airfields in the North came under aerial attack, and reports surfaced of Chinese pilots flying North Vietnamese interceptors. During this period of involvement, China made no secret of its sympathy for the Hanoi government; prudence therefore required that the Johnson administration consider the possibility of further Chinese intervention. Concern that China might react as it had fifteen years earlier in Korea argued powerfully for relying on air power rather than invasion to convince Hanoi to call off the war in the South. Having turned to air power, the Johnson administration chose to apply it in a gradually escalating fashion. President John F. Kennedy's recent success in compelling the Soviet Union to with draw bombers and ballistic missiles from Cuba bred confidence in the gradual application of force.

The individual services, for the most part, controlled their own air arms. The Army maintained control of its large helicopter fleet as organic air assets. Marines followed their traditional organizational path of assigning an Air Wing to each Marine division. The Navy maintained complete control of its air assets and Admiral Sharp, as Commander in Chief of Pacific Command (CINCPAC), implemented the Route Pack system for all air operations over North Vietnam.

General Clay, the Pacific Air Force (PACAF) commander, was assigned coordinating authority for de-conflicting air operations, but he felt that the existing command arrangements (route packaging and assigning the air component only coordinating authority) did not provide a sound means to control the overall air effort.

The Route Pack system divided responsibility within North Vietnam into seven different geographic areas, with the Air Force and the Navy each receiving responsibility for portions of the route packs. Commander in Chief of Pacific Fleet (CINCPACFLT), the naval component of Pacific Command (PACOM), maintained control of carrier air assets. Even within the Air Force there was no single air commander. Seventh Air Force was responsible for Air Force air operations in Vietnam, while Thirteenth Air Force was responsible for Thailand, and Strategic Air Command (SAC) never relinquished command or control of its B-52 bombers.

The targeting process further complicated this patchwork of responsibility. Targets were selected in Washington by a small team on the joint staff and approved only at the presidential level. The result was a major misuse of air power. Air power application came to be simply the servicing of targets, with little regard for whether or not they were the "right" targets, and without an air campaign plan. Service parochialism dominated the air effort. Lacking a single responsible air commander, a clear set of objectives, and a common concept of operations, even the most skilled operations of the separate components tended to work at cross-purposes and give respite to the enemy. The total number of US Military Personnel in Vietnam was only 900 by 31st December 1960, but it increased to 536,100 by 31st December 1968 and was 250,900 in June 9, 1971.

Initially, most Americans backed Washington's Vietnam policy. A dangerous situation seemed to be developing; one, which the US government referred to as the "domino theory". If South Vietnam were allowed to fall to communism, so eventually would the rest of Southeast Asia. But as the war dragged on and a military victory appeared more and more elusive, public opposition became more vocal.

President Johnson believed that the United States had to support South Vietnam. Many other Americans agreed. They believed that without American help, South Vietnam would become communist. Then, all of Southeast Asia would become Communist, too. As Johnson's term began, his military advisers told him the Communists were losing the war. They told him that North Vietnamese troops and Viet. cong forces would soon stop fighting. On February sixth, however, the Viet Cong attacked American camps at Pleiku and Qui Nhon. The Johnson administration immediately ordered air attacks against military targets in the north.

Some observers in the United States questioned the administration's policy. For example, a leading newspaper writer, James Reston, said President Johnson was carrying out an undeclared and unexplained war in Vietnam. Johnson defended his policies. He said withdrawal would not bring an end to the conflict. He said the battle would continue in one country, and then another.

In March 1965 the first American ground troops arrived in South Vietnam. Congress supported the president's actions at that time. However, the number of Americans who opposed the war began to grow. These people said the war was a civil war. They said the United States had no right, or reason, to intervene. For six days in May, the United States halted air attacks on North Vietnam. The administration hoped this would help get the North

Vietnamese government to begin negotiations. The North refused. And the United States began to build up its forces in the South. By July, 125, 000 Americans were fighting in Vietnam.

Some Americans became angry. Anti-war demonstrations took place in the cities of San Francisco and Chicago. More and more students began to protest. They wanted the war to end quickly. Writer James Reston commented that the anti-war demonstrations were not helping to bring peace to Vietnam. He said they were postponing it. He believed the demonstrations would make Ho Chi Minh think America did not support its troops. And that, he said, would make President Ho continue the war.

In December 1965 the United States again halted air attacks against North Vietnam. Again, it invited the North Vietnamese government to negotiate an end to the fighting. And again, the North refused. Ho Chi Minh's conditions for peace were firm. He demanded an end to the bombing and a complete American withdrawal. Withdrawal would mean defeat for the South. It would mean that all of Vietnam would become Communist. President Johnson would not accept these terms. So he offered his own proposals. The most important was an immediate cease-fire. Neither side would compromise, however. And the fighting went on.

In 1966 President Johnson renewed the bombing attacks in North Vietnam. He also increased the number of American troops in South Vietnam. He condemned those who opposed his policies. He said: "The American people will stand united until every soldier is brought home safely. They will stand united until the people of South Vietnam can choose their own government."

Local and state elections were held in the United States in late 1966. The war in Vietnam had an effect on those elections. The opposition Republican Party generally supported the President's war efforts. Yet it criticized him and other Democrats for economic problems linked to the war. The war cost $ 2 billion every month. The price of many goods in the United States began to rise. The value of the dollar began to drop. The result was inflation. Then economic activity slowed, and the result was recession.

To answer the criticism, Administration officials said progress was being made in Vietnam. But some Americans began to suspect that the government was not telling the truth about the war. Several news writers, for example, said the number of enemy soldiers killed was much lower than the government reported. Opposition to the war and to the Administration's war policies led to bigger and bigger anti-war demonstrations in United States.

Studies were done to measure Americans' opinion on the issue. In a study in July 1967 a little more than half the people questioned said they did not approve of the President's policies. Yet most Americans believed he would run again for President the next year.

Johnson strongly defended the use of American soldiers in Vietnam. In a speech to a group of lawmakers he said: "Since World War II, this nation has met and has mastered many challenges -- challenges in Greece and turkey, in Berlin, in Korea, in Cuba. We met them because brave men were willing to risk their lives for their nation's security. And braver men have never lived than those who carry our colors in Vietnam this very hour."

Between 30 January and the end of February 1968, the North Vietnamese military launched a series of devastating attacks against South Viet Nam's major cities, extending from Khe Sanh in the north to Ca Mau on the country's southern tip. Now known as the Tet Offensive, this operation was timed to coincide with the beginning of Tet, an annual celebration of the lunar New Year and the most festive of Vietnamese holidays. Previously, the combatants had observed a cease-fire during Tet. Hence the American forces and their South Vietnamese allies, relaxing and celebrating as in years past, were caught completely off guard. The results, writes historian George C. Herring (in America's Longest War), were the bloodiest battles of the war: "in the first two weeks of the Tet campaigns, the United States lost 1,100 killed in action and South Vietnam 2,300. An estimated 12,500 civilians were killed, and Tet created as many as one million new refugees".

Thirty-six of 44 provincial capitals and 64 of 242 district towns were attacked. They even struck at the American embassy in the capital, Saigon. Once the shock and confusion wore off, most attacks were crushed in a few days. During those few days, however, the fighting was some of the most violent ever seen in South Vietnam. 50,000 Communist soldiers were killed during the tet offensive. 14,000 South Vietnamese soldiers were killed. And 2000 American soldiers were killed. Thousands of Vietnamese civilians were killed, too.

The Tet Offensive was particularly tragic for the South Vietnamese populace. It also reverberated loudly back home in America. In particular, it negatively impacted American public opinion, calling into question Pentagon and Johnson Administration claims that America was winning the war.

Americans at home saw a different picture. Many Americans were surprised, even shocked, that the Communists could launch such a major attack against South Vietnam. For several years, they had been told that Communist forces were small and were losing badly. Claims of progress in the war, already greeted with skepticism, lost more credibility in both public and official circles. As a result, popular support for the Administration fell even more.

Democrats who opposed President Johnson seized this chance. Several ran against him in the primary elections held before the party's presidential nominating convention. These included Senator Robert Kennedy of New York and Senator Eugene McCarthy of Minnesota. Kennedy and McCarthy did well in the early primary elections. Johnson did poorly.

On 31st March 1968, the President spoke to the American people on television. He told of his proposal to end American bombing of North Vietnam; the appointment of a special ambassador to start peace negotiations; and his decision about his own future:

"I do not believe that I should devote an hour or a day of my time to any personal partisan causes or to any duties other than the awesome duties of this office -- the presidency of your country. Accordingly, I shall not seek, and I will not accept, the nomination of my party for another term as your president."

Hanoi had suffered a military defeat in the Tet Offensive, but had won a political and diplomatic victory by shifting American policy toward disengagement.

Richard M. Nixon (1969-1974) was elected on the claim that he had a "secret plan" for honorably disengaging American troops, which succeeded initially only in intensifying the conflict. This last phase of American involvement in South Vietnam was carried out under a broad policy called Vietnamization. Its main goal was to create strong, largely self-reliant South Vietnamese military forces.

Vietnamization also meant the withdrawal of a half-million American soldiers.

By 1969 the unsatisfactory results in Vietnam compelled U.S. leaders to reconsider their approach to the Cold War. Consequently, assumptions regarding Cold War adversaries were revised. In their own strategic innovation, Nixon and Kissinger transformed the nature of superpower relations, inaugurating détente with the Soviet Union and rapprochement with the People's Republic of China.

Recognizing the United States' altered economic and strategic position; Kissinger introduced the concept of "interdependence" to explain significant changes in American relations with the less-powerful countries of the world. Such developments led many observers to conclude that the Cold War had ended. Others believed that the change was one of form rather than substance. Some Cold War assumptions and appearances had changed, in their view, but superpower confrontation remained the basis of international affairs.

By the spring of 1972 the Vietnam War was at low ebb. The 1968 Communist Tet Offensive had given way to a gradual winding down by mid-1969, and after the invasion of Cambodia in May 1970, there was little fighting in South Vietnam. Yet, while the United States was in the process of withdrawing it's forces from a war that was becoming increasingly unpopular with its citizens, the North Vietnamese were rebuilding their forces in preparation for another massive offensive in hopes of overrunning the southern half of the divided country. In April 1972, heavily armed North Vietnamese divisions crossed into the South at several points, including from out of Cambodia.

Beginning in late 1972, National Security Advisor Henry A. Kissinger's negotiations with North Vietnam began to move seriously towards a settlement. To build up the military of South Vietnam, Secretary of Defense Melvin R. Laird initiated Project Enhance Plus on 20 October 1972. The Pentagon ordered rush deliveries of some $2 billion worth of military equipment, including over 600 aircraft. The program gave South Vietnam the fourth largest air force in the world, with over 2,000 aircraft. Only the United States, the Soviet Union, and the Peoples' Republic of China maintained larger air forces. By this time South Vietnam also floated the fifth largest navy in the world (with 1,500 ships) and fielded the fourth largest army in the world (with 1.1 million troops).

Nixon resumed bombing of North Vietnam in response to the North Vietnamese 1972 Easter offensive and mined North Vietnamese ports and bombed Hanoi and Haiphong in late 1972. Such pressure was intended, at least in part, to force North Vietnam to sign an armistice. In early 1973 the United States, North and South Vietnam, and the Viet Cong signed an armistice. American military activities in Cambodia and Laos, which had continued after the cease-fire in South Vietnam, went into effect, ended in 1973 when Congress cut off funds.

During the early months of 1974, the North Vietnamese army advanced from the north and west on the southern capital. They soon surrounded Saigon with an ever-tightening perimeter. Saigon fell to the Communists on 29 April 1975. On the morning of April 30, 1975, the last Marine boarded a CH-46 helicopter atop the American Embassy in Saigon and took off eastward disappearing into the blue horizon. It was 21 years after the first advisors arrived in country and nearly three years after the last combat troops withdrew.

South Vietnam's military defeat tended to obscure the crucial inability of this massive military enterprise to compensate for Saigon's political shortcomings. Over a span of nearly two decades, a series of regimes failed to mobilize fully and effectively their nation's political, social, and economic resources to foster a popular base of support. North Vietnamese main force units ended the war, but local insurgency among the people of the South made that outcome possible and perhaps inevitable.

The setback suffered by the United States in the Vietnam War was rooted in a failure of strategy. Indeed, perhaps no war in American history shows more clearly both the difficulties of making sound strategic judgments and the dire consequences of a lack of clear strategic vision. The Vietnam War thus provides a cautionary tale for American political and military decision-makers about the crucial importance of thinking clearly about strategy. By incorrectly relating military strategy to national policy and by improperly understanding the nature of the conflict, the United States exhausted itself against a secondary enemy in South Vietnam.

The American failure in Vietnam also stemmed from trying to fight a traditional conventional war when the conflict's nature demanded a counterinsurgency effort. Top military commanders, unable to fathom the problem, refused to implement such a strategy despite evidence of its effectiveness.[68]

The United States and the Afghan War

October 7, 2009

This year had special significance for US President Barrack Hussein Obama. It was his first Afghan war anniversary. For the United States, it was the eighth.

But for both Obama and the US, the anniversary was not a happy one. It was only last week, eight US soldiers — whom the Taliban branded as invading

---

[68] Global Security Org

terrorists — died in a single attack that reminded the Americans that the enemy was as strong as it was eight years ago, if not stronger.

The fact that the war entering its ninth year is itself a damning indictment that underscores the US failure in Afghanistan, which in the past had become a graveyard for many invaders, from the ancient Macedonians to the Soviets in the 1980s and 1990s.

History shows that nations drunk with power take little or no lesson that history teaches.

Determined to fight what is increasingly becoming an unpopular war to the end, Stanley McChrystal, the top US General who commands 100,000 NATO troops, including some 68,000 American forces, in Afghanistan, in a recent statement called on the Obama administration to send in some 40,000 more troops.

The request came months after Obama increased the US troop presence in Afghanistan by 12,000 in tune with his campaign rhetoric to defeat the Taliban. But now the Obama administration urges other NATO members to contribute more troops — a request which has not drawn a favourable response. In an obvious reference to the Obama administration's reluctance to commit more US troops to Afghanistan, McChrystal warned that a war strategy that was narrower than the one he was advocating would be ineffective and short-sighted.

His comments or warning apparently did not go down well with the Obama administration. But Obama is not President Harry Truman to fire McChrystal. Truman in 1951 had the courage to relieve General Douglas MacArthur, when, during the height of the Korean War, he felt the highly decorated World War II hero was overstepping his limits and trying to dictate policy. MacArthur disagreed with Truman's decision not to extend the Korean War to China. He sent an ultimatum to China without consulting the President. Truman saw his actions not only as a violation of the US constitutional principle that made the military subservient to the civilian leadership but also an attempt to usurp the President's authority to make foreign policy. General Mathew Ridgway replaced him. But in the case of McChrystal, Obama had a one-on-one meeting with him aboard Air Force One. The meeting took place in Copenhagen where Obama sought Denmark's support in a botched attempt to win the 2016 Olympic venue for Chicago, his home base. Like victory eludes him in Afghanistan, Obama failed in his Olympic bid. The IOC decided on Brazil's Rio de Janeiro.

Not much is known about the Obama-McChrystal meeting. The White House was initially critical of McChrystal's remarks but after the Air Force One meeting, it tried to downplay the controversy. The Washington Post quoted a White House official who wished to remain anonymous as saying that McChrystal was simply speaking of the situation on the ground as he saw it and how he would execute the President's current strategy. "He was not pushing his views or in any way trying to influence policy."

The mood change at the White House from anger to compromise may indicate either Obama's weakness or his administration's desire to put the McChrystal issue behind and get going with Afghanistan. Perhaps, there was a realization that any action against McChrystal at this stage would only push the US deeper into the Afghan quagmire. The Obama administration surely does not want to take such a risk at a time it is struggling to bail itself out of the economic crisis. The administration feels that the economy can suffer no more shocks. But the shock is coming.

In an article in the London-based Independent this week, veteran journalist Robert Fisk said that West Asian oil producing countries, including staunch US allies such as Saudi Arabia and Kuwait, and emerging economic powers such as China and Russia had been meeting secretly for the past two years to de-dollarize the oil economy. Wary of the dollar's future, the article said, these countries wanted to use currencies such as the euro, yen and even the ruble for oil transactions. Though the story drew a Saudi denial, Fisk in a follow-up article and in his comments to al-Jazeera television stood by his story. Imagine China and the Arab countries releasing trillions of dollars in their reserves to the market to buy other currencies. This will no doubt deal a killer punch to the US dollar, probably setting off another major financial crisis, with the United States being the worst hit.

Against this backdrop, one wonders whether a financially weak United States can sustain two major wars — Iraq and Afghanistan. If Obama heeds the call of McChrystal and sends 40,000 additional troops, he would be traveling along the path that Lyndon B. Johnson trod during the Vietnam War. Johnson escalated the war — and as a result, his administration neglected domestic issues. One of the casualties was his "Great Society Program" a social reform package aimed at poverty alleviation. If the Afghan war continues — and escalates — Obama, like Johnson, will also find it difficult to push through his health care reforms and deal with domestic issues such as unemployment, which stood at 9.8 percent last month, the highest in 26 years.

A wise Johnson, sensing his unpopularity, did not contest for a second term. Will Obama also be a one-term president? Or is the move to escalate the Afghan war part of a conspiracy to make Obama a one-term president? The sooner Obama realizes that the Afghan war is becoming unpopular with the US masses, the better his chances of re-election in 2012.

No wonder, at Tuesday's meeting between Obama and US lawmakers, the Republicans insisted that the President follow the generals' advice and send in reinforcements to Afghanistan. In contrast, some of the Democrats were wary of any moves that would escalate the war, which Obama's predecessor and the Republican President George W. Bush started in Texas cowboy style. If Obama who is to announce his Afghan policy today or tomorrow chooses the Bush hubris, then he will be digging his own political grave.

Whatever path he chooses, he might do well to take into account the large-scale fraud that helped the incumbent Hamid Karzai win the presidency. A UN report leaked on Tuesday said the number of votes that Karzai polled in some districts was more than the number of people who cast their votes. That Karzai, a pro-US puppet president, had to rely on fraud to win the election is an indication of widespread public discontent with the occupation.

The Afghans may be equally discontent with the Taliban, but many people see them as freedom fighters and extend their support to them. Armed with the growing public desire to rid the country of the occupation forces, the Taliban on Wednesday issued a statement saying they posed no threat to the West and their struggle was only to oust the occupying foreign troops.

"We had and have no plan of harming countries of the world, including those in Europe ... our goal is the independence of the country and the building of an Islamic state," said the Taliban whose growth and the fighting capability have baffled even US and NATO military commanders.

In these circumstances, the options before the US are few. If the US withdraws from Afghanistan, it will be seen as a defeat. If it doesn't withdraw, the war would escalate and aggravate the human suffering and the US economic crisis. Given these two options, the wise person may go for the first because one can always devise a face-saving exit. The US only needs to say that it has achieved its objectives and get the hell out of Afghanistan.

A little soul-searching may also help. It may show that after eight years of war and occupation in Afghanistan, hardly anything has changed there. In October 2001, the US went into an Afghanistan that was beset with problems such as illiteracy, insecurity, and oppression of women, drugs and warlords. Has the US or its puppet Karzai regime succeeded in addressing these issues? The ground reality is that the same old problems remain or have grown worse.

The War engaged 67,700 troops and 1446 troops were killed in action.

The US Commander in Afghanistan has requested additional 40,000 troops for a successful operation. The numbers of troops contributed by the countries are as follows: United States (31,855), Britain (9,000), Germany (4,245), France (3,070), Canada (2,830), Italy (2,795), Nether land (2,160), Poland (2,025), Australia (1200), Spain (1000), Romania (990), Turley (820), Denmark (700), Norway (6oo), Belgium (510) and other countries (3,894) as on October 2009.

Backgrounder

The war in Afghanistan was begun on October 7, 2001 with the aim of eliminating al-Qaeda terrorists, whom the United States accused of carrying out the September 11, 2001 attacks on New York's World Trade Center and the Pentagon. The US vowed to capture al-Qaeda leader Osama bin Laden and remove the Taliban regime, which had given him refuge.

The Taliban was ousted within weeks. The war saw the United States and Britain carrying out an indiscriminate bombing campaign that **killed some 3,500 civilians** in the first few days of the operation codenamed "Enduring Freedom" Eight years after the war; bin Laden is still at large. [69]

Afghanistan in 2010

The United States would take all steps to punish Al Qaeda in 2010 with higher defense expenditure and deployment of 30,000 more military personnel. Al Qaeda has left Afghanistan but they maintain direct ties with the Taliban of Afghanistan. Deployment of troops in southern Afghanistan and in the tribal areas along the Afghanistan-Pakistan border may take three to six months by the US Army. The president's commitment to withdraw US troops from Iraq this year and finally all troops by the end of 2011 is a wise decision. The US is aware that Al Qaeda is helping Laskar–e-Toiba to provoke Indo-Pak conflicts. By this, it can destabilize Pakistan and gain access to its nuclear arsenal. The US is taking all steps that the N-arms do not reach the Terrorists. A corrupt and inefficient government governs Pakistan. It receives US $7.5 billions assistance in 2010 from the US to fight terrorism, but it would encourage crisis in the region. The Army officials and politicians in Pakistan are more interested to earn US $ as compared to their assigned duties.

USA and Russia

Presidents Bush and Putin have committed to combating the threat of nuclear terrorism and

---

[69] Daily Mirror October 9, 2009

pursuing the necessary steps with other willing partner nations to combat nuclear terrorism. The resolutions are as follows:

The U.S. and Russia have invited initial partner nations to attend an initial meeting to elaborate and endorse a Statement of Principles for this Initiative. The U.S. and Russia have also invited the IAEA to serve as an observer.

The International Convention on the Suppression of Acts of Nuclear Terrorism is an important, although not the exclusive, legal basis for the work of the Initiative. Other important legal bases include the Convention on the Physical Protection of Nuclear Material and Nuclear Facilities, and UN Security Council Resolutions 1373 and 1540, as well as national legal authorities.

The activities of the Initiative should include national efforts and could include *inter alias* multinational exercises, expert-level meetings to share best practices, and the provision of assistance from those nations in a position to offer such assistance to those nations requiring it.

Taking into account the global character of the Initiative, the participants will seek to mobilize the largest possible number of nations to improve national capabilities to combat nuclear terrorism. To this end, both agree that outreach to related industries and the public is necessary to effect the full implementation of the Initiative.

In launching this Global Initiative to Combat Nuclear Terrorism, both the U.S. and Russia reaffirm their commitment to non-proliferation while promoting legitimate cooperation in peaceful nuclear activities for the prosperity of all nations. The Initiative will not address issues related to safeguarding nuclear weapons and other nuclear facilities, installations, and materials used for military purposes remain strictly the national prerogative of the nuclear weapons state parties to the Non-Proliferation of Nuclear Weapons Treaty (NPT), for which they bear special responsibility. [70]

Defense Restructuring in Russia

US President Barack Obama and Russia President Dmitry Medvedev have signed the 'Global Zero' campaign for a world free of nuclear arms.

Under the plan, the number of defense officers in Russia would be slashed from 355,000 to 150, 000 and the overall manpower will fall from 1.2 million to one million. The scheme calls for reducing the Russian Army units from the present 1,890 to just 172 by 2012. Russia currently deploys 2,780 strategic warheads, which may come down to 1,500 under new deal – plus another 2,000 tactical weapons.

Mr. Nikolai Patrushev, the Chief of Kremlin Security Council, has expressed that Russia is drafting a new military doctrine which may authorize the Armed Forces to use nuclear weapons not only to counter a massive conventional attack but even to launch a pre-emotive strike against a small regional adversary, such as neighbouring Georgia or Ukraine, that might be deemed a threat to Russia. The country proposes to use nuclear weapons after the collapse of Soviet Union and the evaporation of its military alliance, the Warsaw Pact and the growth of NATO in the eastern European countries.

It seems that the impact of World War II is still in the minds of all political leaders. The use of nuclear weapons would not solve the problems rather it would increase the problems and effects of the devastating wars. The civilized nations may plan their defense

---

[70] G-8 Summit 2006, Saint Petersburg

strategies but they should organize and work for 'world peace movement' to save their money, people, country and the world. Therefore the world leaders should try to save the humanity through brotherhood, cooperation, mutual understanding and in making a stronger United Nations Organization, which could be impartial, effective, and must be able to solve the crisis at the earliest.

US and Russia Sign Nuclear Arms Pact

April 9, 2010

With flourish and fanfare, President Obama and President Dmitri A Medvedev of Russia signed a Nuclear Arms Treaty on April 9, 2010 in Prague and opened what they hoped would be a new era in the tumultuous relationship between former cold war adversaries. They agreed to bring down their arsenals and restore an inspection regime that expired in December 2009. Along the way, they sidestepped unresolved disputes over missile defense and other issues.

Mr. Obama said, 'when the United States and Russia are not able to work together on big issues, it is not good for either of our nations nor is it good for the world. Together, we have stopped the drift, and proven the benefits of cooperation. Today is an important milestone for nuclear security and nonproliferation, and for US – Russia relations. The President of Russia Mr. Medvedev expressed, "The treaty is a historic event that 'open a new page' in Russia- American relations. What matters most is 'this is a win-win situation.' No one stands to lose from this agreement. I feel this is a typical feature of our cooperation. Both parties have won. He also supported the sanctions on Iran. We cannot turn a blind eye to Teheran's nuclear program. The sanction should be smart and avoid hardship for the Iranian people.

US defends Taiwan arms deal; China threatens sanctions - February 1, 2010

Unmindful of china's shrill reaction and threat to slap sanctions, the United States has strongly defended its proposed $6.4 billion arms sales package for Taiwan. Pentagon's Defense Security Cooperation Agency notified the US Congress that five planned arms sales include 60 UH-60M Black Hawk helicopters, 114 advanced Patriot air defense missiles, a pair of Osprey mine-haunting ships and a command-and-control enhancement known as Multifunctional Information Distribution Systems. Such sales would contribute in maintaining security and stability to the Taiwan Strait.

China would slap sanctions on American companies participating in the sale. Beijing has suspended plans for visits between Chinese and US militaries and postponed a high level arms control meeting. China is aggrieved because of long-running disputes over trade and currency, human rights and the Tibet problem. But the US follows commitment to provide Taiwan with defensive weapons as provided in the Taiwan Relations Act, 1979. (News Pioneer)

Defense Budget of the USA

The United States of America provided the highest defense budget in fiscal year 2009. The budget provided $515.4 billion in discretionary authority for the Department of Defense (DOD), a $35.9 billion or 7.5 percent increase over the enacted level for fiscal year 2008.

The Fiscal Year 2009 budget reflects the President's priorities and sustains his commitment to prevail in the Global War on Terror; increase ground combat capabilities; improve force readiness; develop the combat capabilities needed to meet future threats;

and improve the quality of life for Service members and their families.

Defense Secretary Robert M. Gates appreciated the budget because it provides the resources necessary to maintain an agile, highly trained, and lethal fighting force, increase Army and Marine Corps end strength, and sustains the United States' technological advantage over current and potential enemies.

This budget would assist in the following objectives:

(a) Maintains a highly trained fighting force of 2.2 million soldiers, sailors, airmen, and Marines;
(b) Recruits, trains and equips 65,000 additional active duty soldiers and 27,000 additional Marines over five years;
(c) Provides pay increases of 3.4 percent for military members, improves benefits for the all-volunteer force, and increases pay 2.9 percent for the civilian workforce;
(d) Provides world-class health care for 9.2 million eligible Service members, families, and retirees;
(e) Procures and maintains an arsenal of the world's most advanced weapon systems;
(f) Improves war fighting capabilities and invests in science and technology to maintain U.S. advantage over the Nation's enemies;
(g) Maintains 545,000 facilities at 5,300 sites in the U.S. and around the globe; and
(h) Maintains vital intelligence capabilities.

The Fiscal Year 2009 Defense budget request sustains the President's commitment to growing U.S. ground forces that are needed to prevail in the current conflicts in Iraq and Afghanistan, to sustain a high rate of military readiness and prepare for a wide range of threats that face the Nation now and in the years ahead, and to care for Service members and their families.

This year's request increases investments in five areas: prevailing in the Global War on Terror (GWOT); increasing ground combat capabilities; improving force readiness; developing future combat capabilities; and improving quality of life for Service members and families.

Deficit Budget

Congress should consider the sobering fact that the Chinese hold billions of dollars of U.S. debt. The dollars the Chinese acquire by selling us goods and services eventually must be returned to the United States. Since the Chinese are not buying an equivalent amount of American goods and services, they use dollars to finance our extravagant spending.

In fact, our ability to continue funding the welfare-warfare state without destroying the American economy depends on foreigners buying our debt.[71]

Global War on Terror

The global threat posed by violent extremists is the pre-eminent danger of our time. To ensure freedom and security and advance peace and stability throughout the world, the United States took steps in Iraq and Afghanistan to prevent Terrorism with its allies and partners

In addition to the $515.4 billion request, the Administration requests $70 billion as an emergency allowance for the Global War on Terror. Details will be provided to Congress once the specific requirements of our troops on the ground are better known.

---

[71] Rep. Ron Paul, M.D. (R-Tex.), *LewRockwell*.com, 11/4/03

In fiscal year 2008, Congress appropriated $86.8 billion or 46 percent of the President's $189.3 billion request for GWOT. Congress has not yet appropriated the remaining balance – $102.5 billion – of funds requested and needed for U.S. forces currently in combat.

These additional funds are required to pay our military personnel, continue operations in Iraq and Afghanistan, reconstitute our forces, and provide force protection for the troops, and fund the Iraqi and Afghan security forces.

Build Partnership Capacity: Recognizing that threats to U.S. security exist beyond the war on terror in Iraq and Afghanistan, the U.S. must also build and strengthen the military and security capabilities of our global partners to increase the effectiveness of U.S. forces. To strengthen the military and security capabilities of global partners, the fiscal year 2009 budget provides $750 million: (a) $500 million for the Global Train and Equip Program, (b) $200 million for security and stabilization assistance, and (c) $50 million for the Combatant Commander Initiative Fund for Urgent Humanitarian Relief and Reconstruction.

Africa Command: To strengthen U.S. security and promote peace and stability in Africa, DoD requests $389 million in FY2009 to establish the U.S. Africa Command. The new geographical command will focus primarily on building partnership capacities, conducting theater security cooperation, building important counter-terrorism skills and, as appropriate, supporting other U.S. Government agencies in implementing programs that promote regional stability.

Increase Ground Combat Capability: The Nation's security demands a ready and available war fighting force. To that end, the U.S. is increasing its ground forces to meet current and projected needs and to sustain a high state of military readiness and support. The growth in ground combat forces will increase the potential for longer time at home station between deployments for soldiers and Marines.

Increase Ground Forces: The FY 2009 budget provides $20.5 billion, an increase of $8.7 billion or 73 percent over the FY 2008 enacted level of $11.9 billion, to increase the size of the Army and Marine Corps to meet operational demands and to increase the average time that soldiers and Marines are home between deployments.

The FY 2009 budget provides $15.5 billion to increase Army active end strength to 532,400, which includes an increase of 7,000 over the fiscal year 2008 request. The Army plans to increase active end strength by a total of 65,000 to 547,400. In fiscal year 2009, the number of active Army Brigade Combat Teams (BCT) will increase by two BCTs, from 40 to 42, toward a goal of 48 BCTs.

Similarly, increasing the number of Marines in the operating forces is expected to reduce stress on the force. The fiscal year 2009 budget provides $5.0 billion, an increase of $.9 billion over the fiscal year 2008 enacted level, to increase Marine Corps end strength to 194,000, which includes an increase of 5,000 Marines over the Fiscal Year 2008 request. To achieve three balanced Marine Expeditionary Force units, and to increase time at home station between deployments, the Marine Corps plans to increase end strength by a total of 27,000 to 202,000 by fiscal year 2011.

Improve Force Readiness: Sustaining critical combat and support operations, the Fiscal Year 2009 budget provides $158.3 billion, an increase of $14.9 billion or 10.4 percent over the Fiscal Year 2008 enacted level of $143.4 billion, to maintain DoD operations at levels consistent with those of Fiscal Year 2008. To maintain combat readiness, the Fiscal Year 2009 budget requests $68.0 billion to keep our force of soldiers, sailors, airmen, and Marines at the highest levels of proficiency. The budget invests in readiness measured in terms of tank miles driven per month, ship steaming days underway per quarter, and flying hours per month. Also included is $33.1 billion for logistical, intelligence, and Service-wide support activities.

The budget also requests $10.7 billion for training, recruiting, and retention to attract and retain Service members possessing critical skills needed to meet tomorrow's defense requirements; $11.8 billion for equipment maintenance and to increase repair and refurbishment of equipment, and the transition of systems from development to fielded systems; and $32.6 billion for facility and base support.

Develop Future Combat Capabilities: In addition to strengthening the combat readiness of America's armed forces, the Nation continues to invest in the strategic modernization necessary to meet current and future threats from land, sea, air, or space. The United States must also maintain its significant advantages in war fighting capabilities and work to prevent adversaries from acquiring or using weapons of mass destruction.

Continue Modernization: The FY2009 budget requests $183.8 billion in modernization to meet future threats, an $8.3 billion increase or 4.7 percent over the fiscal year 2008 enacted level of $175.5 billion. This includes procurement, as well as research and development.

The Fiscal Year 2009 budget provides $9.2 billion, an increase of $0.4 billion, to maintain and strengthen joint ground capabilities and to continue development of the Army's Future Combat System -- including manned and unmanned vehicles, the non-line-of-sight launch system, and the joint network communications system -- system upgrades to the Stryker weapons system, and chemical weapons destruction. The Fiscal Year 2009 budget requests $16.9 billion to strengthen joint maritime capabilities including: the CVN-21 Carrier; one DDG-1000, the next generation surface combatant; two littoral combat ships; two joint high speed vessels; two auxiliary cargo ships (T-AKEs); and one Virginia Class submarine.

Joint Air Capabilities are strengthened in the Fiscal Year 2009 budget that provides $45.6 billion, a $4.9 billion increase over Fiscal Year 2008 enacted levels, for F/A 18 Hornet and E/A-18G Growler fighters, the F-35 Joint Strike Fighter, V-22 vertical lift aircraft, additional unmanned aerial vehicles, and the re-capitalization of various missiles and other weapons.

The fiscal year 2009 budget provides $10.7 billion, an increase of $1.6 billion, to strengthen joint space-based capabilities in several categories, including Space-Based Infrared Systems, communications satellites, Global Positioning System satellites, environmental satellites, Advanced Extremely High Frequency satellites, and launch vehicles. The Fiscal Year 2009 budget also provides $79.5 billion for an array of modern command, control, communications, computers and intelligence ($16.4 billion); procurement of advanced munitions and missiles ($11.0 billion); and mission support ($52.1 billion) such as ammunition, portable generators, cooling equipment, field medical supplies, hospital equipment, and night vision goggles.

Sustain Research and Development: Changes in the 21st century threat environment create strategic challenges from irregular warfare, potential adversaries having weapons of mass destruction, and disruptive technologies. The fiscal year 2009 budget provides $11.5 billion to sustain ongoing science and technology efforts, including $1.7 billion for basic research, an increase of $300 million over the fiscal year 2008 budget request.

Improve Missile Defense Capabilities: To improve missile defense capabilities, the 2009 budget provides $10.5 billion, an increase of $0.6 billion, for continued development of a multi-layered system to protect the U.S. and its allies from tactical and strategic ballistic missile attack.

Base Realignment and Closure: Current and future national security challenges require a more flexible, expeditionary force projection capability.

Consequently, units stationed overseas will be brought back to bases in the United States. The fiscal year 2009 budget requests $9.5 billion to continue Base Realignment and Closure (BRAC). For the approved FY 2005 Base Realignment and Closure recommendations, the Budget fully funds 24 major realignments, 25 base closures, and 765 lesser actions.

Improve Quality of Life for Service Members and Families: Recognizing that success in everything we do depends upon the dedication and skill of the men and women who willingly sacrifice their own comfort and safety to safeguard the freedom that all Americans enjoy every day, the Fiscal Year 2009 budget includes the resources necessary to provide the finest training, equipment and force protection for those who serve in harm's way; the best possible care and medical facilities for the wounded, ill, and injured; a high quality of life for Service members and their families; and various incentives to recruit and retain the all-volunteer force.

Improve Quality of Life for Personnel and Families: With significant emphasis on the quality of life for personnel and families, the fiscal year 2009 budget provides $107.8 billion in pay and benefits for 2.2 million active and reserve members, an increase of $9.6 billion or 9.7 percent over the Fiscal Year 2008 enacted level of $98.2 billion.

The fiscal year 2009 budget increases military pay by 3.4 percent. Since 2001, military pay has increased by an average of 37 percent. In 2009, the average enlisted E-6 (Army Staff Sergeant) will see a pay increase of $1,289. The pay of the average O-3 (Army Captain or Navy Lieutenant) increases by $1,943 in FY 2009.

Sustain High Quality Health Care: To maintain exceptional health care benefits for 9.2 million eligible military members and their families, working-age retiree members and their families, and Medicare-eligible beneficiaries, the FY 2009 budget provides $41.6 billion in fiscal year 2009 for the military health system. Our forces deserve and can expect world-class health care in the future, despite the rising cost of health care and congressionally expanded benefits. The Department will submit legislation to enact the recommendations of the Task Force on the Future of Military Health Care. These recommendations will help keep the generous military health benefits affordable and sustainable for current and future retired Service members and their families.

Further, recognizing the compelling and critical need to provide world-class health and rehabilitative care to all war fighters who are wounded, ill, or injured in service to the Nation, the Department has begun and will continue to take action on the recommendations made by the President's Commission on Care for America's Returning Wounded Warriors.

Family Housing and Facilities: The budget also includes $3.2 billion, an increase of $300 million above the Fiscal Year 2008 enacted level, which will construct new family housing, improve existing housing, eliminate inadequate housing overseas, operate and maintain government-owned housing, and fund the privatization of 12,324 additional homes.

In short, the request for $515.4 billion in the Fiscal Year 2009 budget sustains the President's commitment to prevail in the Global War on Terror; sustain a high rate of military readiness and support; prepare for the wide range of current and future dangers that threaten the Nation in the years ahead; and improve the quality of life for Service members and their families.[72]

Space Plan: China Broadens Challenge to U.S.

Broadening its challenge to the United States, the Chinese government on Thursday announced an ambitious five-year plan for space exploration that would move China closer to becoming a major rival at a time when the American program is in retreat.

A rocket carrying a Nigerian communication satellite blasted off at the Xichang Satellite Launch Center in China's Sichuan Province on Dec. 20.

Coupled with China's earlier vows to build a space station and put an astronaut on the moon, the plan conjured up memories of the cold-war-era space race between the United States and the Soviet Union. The United States, which has de-emphasized manned spaceflight in recent years, is now dependent on Russia for transporting its astronauts to the International Space Station. Russia, for its part, has suffered an embarrassing string of failed satellite launchings.

---

[72] United States, Department of Defense News 2009

China has been looking for ways to exert its growing economic strength and to demonstrate that its technological mastery and scientific achievements can approach those of any global power. The plan announced Thursday calls for launching a space lab and collecting samples from the moon, all by 2016, along with a more powerful manned spaceship and space freighters.

In recent years, China has also sought to build a military capacity in keeping with its economic might, expanding its submarine fleet and, this year, testing its first aircraft carrier, a refurbished Soviet model. Under the new space plan, it would vastly expand its version of a Global Positioning System, which would have military as well as civilian uses. The plan shows how the government intends to draw on military and civilian resources to meet the goals, which the government is betting will also produce benefits for the Chinese economy. "This approach offers lessons for other advanced space powers, including the U.S., which needs to make sure it sustains its high-level investment in various aspects of space development across the board," said Andrew S. Erickson, a professor at the United States Naval War College who has studied the Chinese space program. While a leader in the business of launching satellites, China is still years behind the United States in space. Its human spaceflight accomplishments to date put it roughly where the United States and the Soviet Union were in the mid-1960s.

But China has consistently stuck to a development timeline for its program and met the realistic goals set out in its five-year plans, which are mainstays of the Communist Party's authoritarian system.

For human spaceflight, the plan lays out a continuation of China's steady but unrushed efforts to develop technologies and extend its capacities. It says that China will begin the work to land its astronauts on the moon, but it does not provide a target date for when they will go.

"I think it is a comprehensive, moderately paced program," said John M. Logsdon, former director of the Space Policy Institute at George Washington University. "It's not a crash program."

By contrast, NASA's direction tends to shift with every change of presidency. President George W. Bush called on NASA to return to the moon by 2020. President Obama canceled that program and now wants the agency to send astronauts to an asteroid. NASA shut down its 30-year space shuttle program after a final flight in July.

"The one thing that is admirable about their program is they don't have fits and starts," said Joseph R. Fragola, a space safety expert who has visited the space facilities in China. "Their program is low budget but it is laid out, and they follow it in an orderly process, and we don't do that."

Experts say Beijing is approaching its space program the way it did its military modernization. In addition to the aircraft carrier, which it bought from Ukraine, China has also made a progress on an anti-ship ballistic missile, which could be deployed to ward off foreign warships. Last January, the Chinese military tested a stealth fighter hours before Robert M. Gates, the defense secretary at the time, met in Beijing with President Hu Jintao.

Unlike in the United States, where there are separate military and civilian space programs, in China the People's Liberation Army is the driving force behind development of the Chinese space program. Civilian institutions, including various universities and laboratories, are part of the military-led efforts. In the white paper that laid out the plan, released by the State Council, China's cabinet, the authors took pains to say that Beijing was not seeking to challenge any nation militarily with its space program. "China always adheres to the use of outer space for peaceful purposes, and opposes weaponization or any arms race in outer space," the paper said. [73]

The US- Russia Arms Talks

The next round of U.S.-Russian nuclear arms talks is likely to focus on the delicate task of reducing a much broader range of atomic weapons, U.S. negotiators said on Friday as they discussed the first anniversary of the New START treaty.

Ted Warner, senior adviser to the undersecretary of defense for arms control, said the United States and Russia had reached a point where negotiations needed to include strategic and tactical weapons, regardless of whether they are in storage or mounted on delivery vehicles.

New START, which went into force in February last year, commits the two sides to reducing their strategic, or longer-range, deployed nuclear weapons to 1,550 per side, down from the previous ceiling of 2,200.

The treaty did not address tactical, or shorter-range, nuclear weapons, or even stockpiles of strategic warheads held at storage facilities apart from their delivery vehicles. The United States said in 2010 that its total nuclear stockpile, including deployed and non-deployed, tactical and strategic nuclear weapons was 5,113.

---

[73] Edward Wong and Kenneth Chang (2011), "Space Plan From China Broadens Challenge to U.S.", The New York Times, December 29, 2011

Russia has not made public its total arsenal, but is believed to have a stockpile "in shouting distance of that," Warner told a forum at the Brookings Institution think tank in Washington.

Warner said President Barack Obama made it clear when he signed New START that he hoped to move ahead with another round of nuclear arms talks that would look at the full range of atomic weapons.

"What the president said is ... the next time we look at this, we really ought to look at the total operational inventory, the nuclear stockpile of operational weapons," he said. "And that would be strategic and nonstrategic, and both deployed and non-deployed." Rose Gottemoeller, assistant secretary of State for arms control, said work on New START over the past year had helped lay the groundwork for a new round of arms control talks but "the next treaty will be one that I think takes us in some more challenging directions."

A treaty dealing with non-deployed weapons would require opening sensitive storage facilities to inspection and verification, she said. A treaty incorporating tactical nuclear arms would require greater openness and transparency about conventional systems like missile defense or U.S. plans for "Prompt Global Strike," a conventional weapon that could hit any target on Earth in about an hour. With Russia and the United States in the process of holding presidential elections, neither side is in a position to move ahead with a new round of nuclear arms talks right away.

For now, the sides are carrying out what Warner described as "homework" as they attempt to set the stage for a renewal of arms control discussions once elections are over. The United States is conducting a Nuclear Posture Review implementation study, which will allow Obama to issue guidance to the Pentagon about the future size and scope of the country's nuclear arsenal. The implementation study informed the Pentagon's strategic review issued in early January, which said the administration believes it can maintain an effective nuclear deterrent with fewer warheads. NATO is conducting a similar review looking at the nuclear, conventional and missile defense forces it believes will be needed to protect the Western alliance over the next decade.

The aim is to have NATO leaders formally approve the Deterrence and Defense Posture Review at their summit in Chicago in May. Meanwhile, U.S. and Russian negotiators are holding regular Strategic Stability Talks this year on a range of issues in an effort to lay the groundwork for new arms control talks. "The Russians have made clear if we're going to move on to further nuclear reductions, there are a set of issues that need to be addressed at least in parallel as this goes along," Warner said. Those issues include the Prompt Global Strike weapon and the European missile defense system being assembled by the United States and its NATO allies. Russia views both as a threat to its nuclear deterrent.[74]

NATO Needs a Tighter Focus

U.S. Secretary of Defense Leon Panetta and Secretary of State Hillary Clinton have an opportunity this weekend as they address the Munich Security Conference to suggest ways to stabilize NATO's ailing defense capabilities. European nations have slashed their defense budgets to record low levels without much regard for NATO's overall defense requirements. And last week the United States announced that it would remove two of its four Brigade Combat Teams from Europe. Those European

[74] David Alexander (2012), "Next US - Russia Arms Talks", Political and Business daily, February, 14, 2012 – Principal source is Reuters.

reductions are beginning to weaken NATO's core military capabilities. Most European defense cuts have been across the board, creating the potential for hollow forces with low readiness and low sustainability levels. More recently key allies like the British and Dutch have eliminated entire military categories such as carrier aviation and armor.

The alliance is certainly not doomed. In 2011, Europe still had two million personnel under arms and spent about €215 billion on defense; those numbers are declining. NATO emerged victorious in Libya without losing a man; and maritime operations are having a positive impact against pirates and terrorists. The Afghanistan coalition was shaken recently with France's decision to withdraw early, but NATO Secretary General Anders F. Rasmussen has since said that the United States and its allies would step back from a combat role in Afghanistan in mid-2013. The real long-term risk to NATO is that gaps will appear in the European force structure that the United States won't be able to fill, and that the alliance will be unable to act in a future crisis. That risk needs to be faced squarely at the NATO summit in Chicago in May.

Panetta and Clinton might consider a five-part plan to deal with this looming problem. First, NATO needs to define more precisely what military capabilities are needed to meet its three agreed tasks: collective defense, crisis management and cooperative security. NATO's Allied Command Transformation has been unable to design such a "must have" priority list. The U.S. National Defense University has just completed a major study on this which might serve as a starting point for prioritization. Skilled military personnel, technology and deployable capability are more important than massed armies and large installations. Ideally, at the Chicago summit, heads of state would pledge that as they consider their national defense budgets, they would protect these "must have" military capabilities. They might also pledge to build back beyond this minimal requirement after the economic recession has passed.

Second, NATO must take a bolder approach to Rasmussen's concept of Smart Defense. The alliance has identified some 16 current multinational defense projects where military assets are pooled or shared by several nations. That is a good start, but it will not deal with the magnitude of this crisis. The level of specialization and cooperation needs to be raised to the mission level in order to maximize efficiency and political attractiveness. Clusters of willing nations might form what has been called "mission focus groups" that prepare for certain types of missions, such as fighting piracy, policing the air and special operations. Those nations would self-organize under the general guidance of the NATO secretary general. Rewiring the alliance around a mission focus group concept may be a bridge too far for Chicago, but the concept should consider there.

Third, the United States European Command, Eucom, needs reorientation. During the past decade, U.S. forces in Europe have followed a "lily pad" strategy by which they sit waiting to jump to another theater. Given the nature of NATO's coming capabilities crisis and U.S. reductions, Eucom needs to work more closely with its European allies to maintain European skills and trans-Atlantic interoperability. A recent American decision to dedicate a U.S. based Brigade Combat Team to work with the NATO Response Force is precisely the kind of close U.S.-European military interaction that is needed.

Fourth, NATO's partners need to play enhanced roles and even consider dividing some of the labor with NATO. For example, the European Union might agree to take the lead on certain missions, such as peacekeeping in Africa. Russia might form a close cooperative arrangement with NATO on counterterrorism. Historically non-aligned European nations like Sweden and Finland might integrate even more with NATO for missions like Baltic defense. The most capable partners can be closely associated with Smart Defense efforts and take a leadership role in training and education.

Finally, to reassure our Eastern allies, NATO needs to exercise its contingency plans for so-called Article 5 missions using U.S.-based forces and to retain its current nuclear posture in Europe. With NATO's conventional capabilities in decline, this is no time to remove the remaining handful of U.S. nuclear bombs in Europe that both reassure allies and deter potential adversaries. Any future nuclear reductions need to be part of a broad negotiation with Russia. Therefore, NATO must keep up its guard even in times of austerity. It may also need to lower its level of ambition and focus on priority missions. These five measures can maximize military efficiencies and maintain basic confidence that the Alliance will be able to deal with the uncertain challenges that lie ahead.[75]

Conclusion

China claims that its territorial waters engulf three million sq. kilometers out of 3.5 million sq. km. in the South China Sea. China is engulfed in maritime disputes with Philippines, Malaysia, Vietnam, Brunei, Indonesia, Japan, North Korea and South Korea. In the beginning,

China claims others' land and sea; then it raises war against that country. China claims a state of Arunachal Pradesh of India, and then it would raise war against India. It fought with India in 1962; has occupied thousands acres of land till today. China

[75] Hans Binnendijk (2012), "A leaner NATO needs a tighter focus", International Held Tribune, February 4, 2012

violates its promises. It encourages Maoism in Nepal. It has forcefully occupied Tibet since 1959. China declares war against any country without any valid reason.

China may challenge countries like Russia, India and Japan in Asian continent anytime.

China is not included in South East Asia, but the country tries to start ASEAN conferences in Beijing. China has become a terror state in the Asian region. The US has accepted China as a super power not only in Asia but also in the whole world. The President Mr. Barack Obama revealed this during his visit to Beijing in November 2009.

China's policy of Maoism alerts to the whole world that 'everything is possible by killing others'. The US is a democratic country. So the US and China can never be friends in true sense forever. But the friendship started by both the countries is a good attempt for inviting WORLD PEACE.

The US should watch their friendship each moment as a warmonger country cannot be believed upon always, as China would challenge the US someday.

The United States should influence the United Nations to act on the erring country for a solution (war or peace) as a big brother but should not take up the matter unilaterally.

The US should not finance Pakistan with a donation of US $7.5 billions to work against the al-Qa'da and Oascar-e-Toiba as Pakistan government depends upon these organizations to run the administration. Pakistan would not solve the problem rather it would finance these Terrorist organizations to commit more harm to the neighbouring countries.

Both Pakistan and Afghanistan need food aid and healthcare aid. These countries earn money through opium cultivation and trade in arms and ammunitions. They have accepted terrorism as a profession.

Islam means peace; but they kill others in the name of heaven.

The United States should not work in partnership with China in Defense, Nuclear Research, trade in arms and ammunitions and employ Chinese people in these establishments, as China would quickly take negative actions against the US.

A warmonger country can try to do any harm to its enemy country/countries anytime.

Tomas Magnusson (Sweden) laments:

How can this wonderful world accept that nations are preparing to repeat the mistakes of yester years?

These countries stockpile deadly arsenals, build up nuclear capacity and increase weapons of mass destruction. Moreover, these countries waste resources on conventional weaponry instead of tackling global problems and resolving conflicts, through peaceful means!

-- Speech in Japan 2007

+++++

Chapter V

RE-ORGANIZATION OF THE UNITED NATIONS

You can't shake hands with a clenched fist.
---- Indira Gandhi, Former Prime Minister of India

Military invasion is a crime against peace. The international law specifically explains that waging war is against the integrity, independence, or sovereignty of a territory or state, or else a military violation of relevant international treaties, agreements or legally binding assurances. An important exception to the forgoing is defensive military actions taken under Article 51 of the UN Charter. Such defensive actions are subject to immediate Security Council review, but do not require UN permission to be legal within international law. "Nothing in the present Charter shall impair the inherent right of individual or collective self-defense if an armed attack occurs against a Member of the United Nations." (UN Charter, Article 51).

Generally a rich country attacks a poor country to satisfy its land hunger. Claiming Tibet as a part of China is a bright example of annexing a small kingdom by force.

Tibet is situated in the Himalayan region. On March 14, 2008, the Chinese troops and Buddhist monks fought in the streets of Lhasa against Communist rule in Tibet. The UK and USA have voiced deep concern over the escalating violence.

Wars are fought between soldiers of opposite countries; but the twenty-first century witnesses wars are being fought between soldiers and Buddhist monks in Tibet and Myanmar. In terrorists' countries, wars are caused between the governments and voters.

How can thousands of military persons equipped with guns and bullets fight with monks without arms? Wars cannot be fought among civilians and military. In both the wars, in Rangoon and Lhasa, deaths and injuries to hundreds of innocent religious people were caused, who protested the imposition of anti-democratic rule over their land.

Perhaps the Communist government of China and military Government of Myanmar and the soldiers, who killed the monks, buried **humanity** in cemetery at the time of execution of the rule of land. Even the offices of the United Nations are attacked in Kabul or elsewhere intermittently. On October 28, 2009, only three Taliban militants wearing suicide vests and police uniforms equipped with grenades and machine guns stormed at the UN staff guesthouse in the heart of the Afghan capital and killed 12 people including six UN staff.

Wars are caused because of a number of reasons. But it can be stopped if appropriate actions are taken at the earliest. This chapter deals with suggestions by researchers and international organizations for checking wars and activating the United Nations for advancing peace everywhere by stopping wars, that has become the greatest government pioneered disasters to humanity and civilization. We have emphasized how the UN can stop war and strengthen peace all over the world. Let the UN be activated to function as the world government to award peace to all living beings. Let the UN act as the World Peace Organization and it is possible.

Causes of War

Professor Robin Hahnel opines that different trajectories of the anti-Vietnam and anti-Iraq war movements are not primarily due to differences in leadership. The anti-Vietnam war movement was part of a rising tide of progressive social activism in the United States during the 1960s and 1970s that began with the civil rights and black power movements, spread to the new left student movement, and led to the re-birth of the women's liberation movement and birth of the environmental movement. The anti-Iraq war movement, on the other hand, has struggled to grow in a political era when conservative social activism and power has reached its zenith. It is pointless to blame the leadership of today's anti-war movement for this underlying problem. The important lesson to draw is that an anti-war movement on its own will not accomplish turning the United States away from the path of empire. Only in combination with powerful movements pushing progressive agendas forward in every sphere of social life can the peace movement secure its goal. Nonetheless, it's high time the US anti-war movement kicked some butt! He emphasizes on "participatory economics," is not only feasible but highly desirable.

A participatory economy is designed to promote:

(a) Economic justice, defined as economic reward commensurate with effort, or sacrifice;
(b) Economic democracy, or self-management, defined as decision making power in proportion to the degree one is affected by a decision; and
(c) Solidarity, defined as concern for the well being of others—all to be achieved without sacrificing economic efficiency while promoting a diversity of economic life styles.

Institutions used to achieve these goals are:

(a) Democratic councils of workers and consumers,
(b) Jobs balanced for empowerment and desirability,
(c) Remuneration according to effort as judged by one's work mates, and
(d) A participatory planning procedure in which councils and federations of workers and consumers propose and revise their own activities under rules designed to yield outcomes that are efficient and equitable.

Participatory Planning:

The participants in the participatory planning procedure are the worker councils and federations, the consumer councils and federations, and an Iteration Facilitation Board (IFB). Conceptually, the planning procedure is quite simple.

(a) The IFB announces current estimates of the social opportunity costs for all goods, resources, categories of labor, and capital stocks.
(b) Consumer councils and federations respond with consumption proposals. Worker councils and federations respond with production proposals listing the outputs they propose to make and the inputs they need to make them.

(c) The IFB then calculates the excess demand or supply for each final good and service, capital good, natural resource, and category of labor, and adjusts the estimate of the opportunity cost for the good up, or down, in light of the excess demand or supply.

(d) Using the new estimates of opportunity costs, consumer and worker councils and federations revise and resubmit their proposals. Individual worker and consumer councils must continue to revise their proposals until they submit one that is accepted by the other councils. The planning process continues until there are no longer excess demands for any goods, any categories of labor, any primary inputs, or any capital stocks -- in other words, until a feasible plan is reached.

But it would be a mistake to reduce the logic of empire to economic calculus alone. Many who fight in imperial wars do so because they believe their country is threatened. Many who fight believe they are helping those whose country they invade and occupy. Many who fight do so because they believe those they kill or subjugate are racially inferior to themselves. Many who fight believe there must always be wars and warriors, and being a warrior is part of what it means to be a man. And finally, many who fight, or who work in the military industrial complex, do so because they have few alternatives and that is where jobs are to be found. In other words, imperial war is as much the result of misguided patriotism, racism, sexism, militarism, and individual self-preservation as it is the result of corporate self-interest.

Participatory Economics is based on the conviction that people can manage their own economic activities and cooperate with others efficiently through fair and democratic procedures. Moreover, when we do so we can be more effective than when small elite tells the vast majority of us what to do. That lesson applies to the peace movement as well. The peace movement is made up of millions of individuals and tens of thousands of peace groups and organizations. When peace groups initiate their own activities, and when peace groups form organizations and coalitions governed by participatory, democratic procedures to coordinate their efforts, the peace movement is more powerful. But this is not the way most people are used to working together.

People are used to hierarchy. People come into the peace movement with racist and sexist attitudes whether or not they realize it. Just as participatory economics builds institutional correctives for habits that are socially dysfunctional -- like balanced job complexes and minority and women's caucuses -- the peace movement also needs to develop correctives for predictable weaknesses people bring with them from their life experiences outside the movement. [76]

The UN can stop killing

Bianca Jagger explains that UN General Assembly has a unique opportunity to make a real difference to the lives of people all over the world. The opportunity is a draft resolution for an international Arms Trade Treaty that would place tough controls on arms sales, put forward by the UK, Finland, Japan, Argentina, Australia, Costa Rica, and Kenya.

If this resolution is approved, it will help to stop human rights abuses, limit the threat of terrorism, and reduce suffering for millions of people. But once again, there is also a real chance that some countries will block progress. The Arms Trade Treaty would make it illegal to sell weapons to human rights

[76] Robin Hahnel and Marla Renn (2006), " An Interview with Robin Hahnel: Looking Inside the Anti-war Movement", Vancouver Parecon: July 07, 2006,

abusers. It would make it harder for weapons to end up in the hands of criminals and terrorists. It would help regulate a trade that is spiraling beyond control.

The world spends US $900 billion on defense and only US $60 billion on aid and fuels unimaginable human suffering. Every day, over 1,000 people loss their lives through armed violence.

We have recently seen the appalling consequences of the conflict in Lebanon: the Israeli army flattening civilian targets with precision–guided 1,000 lb "bunker-buster bombs" killing 1,393 people, leaving 5,350 injured and forcing 1,150,000 to flee their homes, 215,413 are still homeless. Hezbollah rockets fired into civilian areas in northern Israel killed 43 and forcing ten of thousands to leave. Both are War Crimes. And both are largely perpetrated with weapons that have been imported from other countries. Israel's military hardware including its deadly cluster bombs and the lethal precision-guided "bunker buster" 5,000 lb GBU-28 " a special weapon developed for penetrating hardened command centers located deep underground" is overwhelmingly American-made, with hi-tech British components used in the Apache helicopters that have fired rockets at cars on crowded streets, and the F-16s and F-15 that devastated southern Lebanon. Neither is Hezbollah manufacturing the Katyushas or longer-range "Khaibar-1" missiles, they used to fire indiscriminately into Israeli towns.

Tens of thousands of unexploded cluster munitions have created *de facto* minefields in Lebanon's streets, fields and playgrounds. According to a report from the United Nations 90 percent of Israeli cluster bomb strikes occurred in the last 72 hours of the conflict when a ceasefire was in sight. The U.N. Mine Action Coordination Center has so far identified more than 400 bomb strike areas that are contaminated with as many as 100,000 unexploded bombs lets. Abbas Yusef Shibli, a six-year-old, picked up a cluster munitions while playing with friends because it looked "like a perfume bottle". When it exploded in his hand, Abbas suffered a ruptured colon, ruptured gall bladder, perforated lung, and torn medial nerve and has so far undergone two blood transfusions. Over a thousand civilians in Lebanon have been killed in this recent conflict.

He has seen for himself the horrifying effects of arms proliferation in countries all over the world. From Nicaragua, his birthplace, still awash with weapons left over from a bloody conflict fuelled by the US arming the Contras, the country had a toll of more than 40,000 civilian killed. Nicaragua has never completely recovered from the war. It is now one of the poorest nations in the Western hemisphere.

For decades, the US government provided millions of dollars in military aid to military dictatorship and oppressive governments in Latin America, many of those countries now have appallingly high levels of armed violence. As a human rights campaigner, he has campaigned on behalf of countless victims of conflicts throughout the world from Latin America, to the Balkans to the Middle East; I can attest to the devastating effect that armed conflicts have on the civilian population particularly on women and children.

Some nations will try to block the treaty's progress; however, their arguments are fundamentally flawed. An Arms Trade Treaty would not undermine states' sovereignty or their ability to act lawfully to defend themselves. It would not hamper legitimate law enforcement to provide security for their citizens. Arms importers and exporters would have a clear set of rules to abide by with every arms transfer, rather than the current hotchpotch of uneven and conflicting regulation that fails to control the trade today.

What the treaty would do is promote security – real security. It would prevent armed groups and militia, which pay no heed to international law, from acquiring weapons that cause carnage and misery. An Amnesty International report last year detailed shipments of over 240 tonnes of weapons, from Eastern Europe to governments in Africa's war-torn Great Lakes region, including millions of rounds of Kalashnikov ammunition, Amnesty traced the supply of weapons and ammunition to the governments of the Democratic Republic of Congo, Rwanda and Uganda and their subsequent distribution to armed groups and militia in the eastern DRC that have been involved in massacres, mutilation and mass rapes of civilians.

Given some governments' obsession with the "War on Terror" and the 'security agenda', what on earth is holding them back? The only people who benefit from an unregulated arms trade are the bad guys – repressive governments, who terrorize their own people, armed groups looking for RPGs and warlords who put AK47s in the hands of children. And of course, the people who sell them the hardware: the pilot who runs guns into Central Africa, and the broker who takes a fat commission and never even sees the damage caused by the goods on delivery. There has been a positive response from many countries to calls for an Arms Trade Treaty. Over 50 states have voiced their support – but to make it happen we need a majority of 192-member state to support the treaty. Britain hosts a meeting of world diplomats to discuss the need for tougher arms controls.

Bianca Jagger urges people throughout the world to take this message directly to those states that are holding back progress, to take real, concrete action to make their communities safer. Today is the Control Arms Campaign's Day of Action, In the UK; people from Brazil, India, Pakistan, Nigeria and South Africa are going to their embassies in London and calling on them to support the Arms Trade Treaty. Similar events are happening around the world. This month the international community and the UN has an opportunity to make a real difference to people's lives. It can make people safer. For once it can act pre-emptive to prevent carnage, not be forced to mop up afterwards. It is an opportunity that the UN must seize.[77]

Iraq War

The Baker-Hamilton report is right to advocate creation of a broad International Support Group; it should comprise the five permanent Security Council members and Iraq's six neighbours. But its purpose cannot be to support the Iraqi government. It must support Iraq, which means pressing the government, along with all other Iraqi constituents, to make the necessary compromises. It also means agreeing on rules of conduct and redlines regarding third party involvement in Iraq. This does not entail a one-off conference, but sustained multilateral diplomacy.

A new, more equitable and inclusive national compact needs to be agreed upon by all relevant actors, including militias and insurgent groups, on issues such as federalism, resource allocation, de-Baathification, the scope of the amnesty, and the timetable for a U.S. withdrawal. This can only be done if the International Support Group brings all of them to the negotiating table, and if its members steer their deliberations, deploying a mixture of carrots and sticks to influence those on whom they have particular leverage.

---

[77] http://www.amnesty.org.uk/arms

A new U.S. regional strategy, including engagement with Syria and Iran, an end to efforts at regime change, revitalization of the Arab-Israeli peace process has altered strategic goals.

Polite engagement of Iraq's neighbours will not do; rather, a clear redefinition of Washington's objectives in the region will be required to enlist regional, but especially Iranian and Syrian help. The goal is not to bargain with them, but to seek agreement on an end-state for Iraq and the region that is no one's first choice, but with which everyone can live.

There is no magical solution for Iraq. But nor can there be a muddle-through. The choice today could not be clearer. An approach that does not entail a clean break vis-à-vis both Iraq and the region at best will postpone what, increasingly, is looking like the most probable scenario: Iraq's collapse into a failed and fragmented state, an intensifying and long-lasting civil war, as well as increased foreign meddling that risks metastasizing into a broad proxy war. Such a situation could not be contained within Iraq's borders.

With involvement by a multiplicity of state and non-state actors and given that rising sectarianism in Iraq is both fuelled by and fuels sectarianism in the region, the more likely outcome would be a regional conflagration. There is abundant reason to question whether the Bush administration is capable of such a dramatic course change. But there is no reason to question why it ought to change direction, and what will happen if it does not.

Baker–Hamilton Recommendations:

1. **Steps to establish an International Support Group,** composed of the five permanent members of the Security Council, Iraq's neighbours and the UN,

represented by its Secretary General, with the objective of:

(a) Agreeing on rules of the game for outside parties' vis-à-vis Iraq;
(b) Reaching agreement on broad goals and key compromises for Iraq;
(c) Appointing an empowered UN special envoy to begin work with all Iraqi constituents on a reconciliation process; and
(d) Convening a conference of all of Iraq's political stakeholders (including insurgent groups and other disenfranchised but politically significant elements of society).

2. **Steps to ensure regional cooperation**

U.S. Government:

(a) Alter regional strategy, renouncing in particular ambitions to forcibly remodel the Middle East.
(b) Refrain from referring to Iraq as a "model" for the region or the new "front" in the anti-terrorism war.
(c) Engage in discussions with Iran and Syria in a direct and sustained manner that acknowledges they have legitimate interests in Iraq's and the region's future.
(d) In the context of the Quartet, and together with Arab countries, revitalize the search for a comprehensive Arab-Israeli peace.

Government of Syria:

(a) Enhance control at the Iraqi border.
(b) Facilitate achievement of a national Iraqi compact by
(c) Using its extensive intelligence on and lines of communication with insurgent groups to facilitate negotiations; and

(d) Drawing on its wide-ranging tribal networks to reach out to Sunni Arabs in the context of such negotiations.

Government of Iran:

(a) Enhance control at the Iraqi border.
(b) Facilitate achievement of a national compact by using its leverage to control SCIRI and its channels in southern Iraq to influence the Sadists.

Government of Saudi Arabia:

Facilitate achievement of a national compact by using its influence with insurgent groups, in particular by cutting off funding from private Saudi sources to those that refuse to cooperate.
Government of Turkey:

(a) Facilitate achievement of a national compact by using its influence with all Iraqi actors, including insurgent groups.
(b) Continue to develop peaceful economic and political relations with Iraqi Kurdistan.

3. **Steps to achieve a new Iraqi political compact**

(a) To the Iraqi Government, Political Parties, and Insurgent and Militia Groups
(b) Work with the UN special envoy and attend the International Support Group's conference to reach agreement on a political compact focused on power and wealth sharing, including:
(c) An asymmetric federal system providing a separate status for the Kurdish region, as currently defined and with powers broadly described in the constitution, and an Arab Iraq divided into fifteen decentralized governorates that reflect present boundaries

(d) Acceptance of Kirkuk governorate as a decentralized governorate with an interim power-sharing arrangement to last at least ten years; and a UN envoy appointed to facilitate this arrangement and help create a mechanism to determine the governorates final status

(e) A process for equitable revenue sharing, under which income from oil, gas and other natural resources would accrue to a federal trust fund operated by an independent federal authority and would be distributed according to each region's demographic share

(f) A relaxation of de-Baathification measures, with the principal criterion for exclusion being past proven crimes, not past party membership

(g) Passage of broad amnesty-covering individuals, who agree to put down their arms and subscribe to the national compact

(h) Reintegration of officers of the former army unless proven to have committed human rights abuses or other crimes

(i) Negotiation with the U.S. of a relatively rapid timetable for the full withdrawal in stages of its forces;

(j) Agreement on a status of foreign forces, with rules of engagement focusing on the need to protect populations and respond to immediate threats against troop security, while requiring prior Iraqi command authorization for any manoeuvres, offensives, arrest campaigns or other military actions outside this framework; and

(k) Agreement on a new electoral law providing for direct, constituency-based elections

4. **Members of the Recommended International Support Group:**

Guide Iraqi participants in a peace conference towards accepting a national compact along the lines described above.

Condition further and augmented economic support on quick agreement on and implementation of elements of the national compact

Government of Iraq: Organize, assuming agreement on a national compact is reached and reflected in a revised constitution, a referendum for its approval.

5. **Urgent steps to stem the violence**

Government of Iraq: Seek to reduce sectarian and ethnic polarization and violence by:-

(a) Stating publicly its commitment to work toward a new, more inclusive national compact, as described in this report,
(b) Condemning and seeking to halt the killing of civilians and torture by security forces, investigating allegations of abuse and prosecuting offenders;
(c) Suspending police units suspected of serious human rights abuses and participation in sectarian violence;
(d) Urging all government officials to desist from ethnic, sectarian or otherwise inflammatory statements, and pressing members of the council of representatives to do the same;
(e) Making a deliberate and widely announced effort to provide health services, opening bank branches and fixing power supply in predominantly Sunni Arab towns and neighborhoods; and
(f) Making a commitment to a peaceful solution to the Kirkuk question, and postponing referendums to determine its and other disputed areas' status.

U.S. Government: Adopt a less aggressive military posture in Iraq by:-

(a) Redirecting resources to a program of embedding U.S. troops in Iraqi units
(b) Moving away from fighting the insurgency to focusing on protecting the civilian population, and in particular halting blind sweeps that endanger civilians, antagonize the population and have had limited effect on the insurgency.
(c) Re-deploy troops along the frontlines of the unfolding civil war, notably by filling in the current security vacuum in Baghdad
(d) Focus on limiting the militias' role to protecting civilians in places where government forces cannot, rather than seek to forcibly disband them, while taking strong action against political assassinations, sectarian attacks, or attempts to overrun government offices.
(e) Avoid steps to engineer a cabinet reshuffle aimed at sidelining Muqtada al-Sadr, which would further inflame the situation.
(f) Shelve plans to hurriedly expand the Iraqi security apparatus and focus instead on vetting, restructuring, and retraining existing units.
(g) Free and compensate Iraqi prisoners detained by the U.S. without charge.
(h) Compensate Iraqis who have suffered as a result of the U.S.-led counterinsurgency campaign.
(i) Condition short-term financial support on the government reversing its policy of serving certain constituencies at the expense of others (most notably with regard to salary payment and basic service delivery)
(j) Abandon the super-embassy project and move a reduced embassy to a more neutral location.

(k) Publicly deny any intention of establishing long-term military bases or seeking to control Iraq's oil.[78]

Middle East Conflicts

The G-8 Leaders, St Petersburg, 2006 (15-17 July 2006) expressed their deepening concern about the situation in the Middle East, in particular the rising civilian casualties on all sides and the damage to infrastructure. They are united to pursue efforts to restore peace. They offered full support for the UN Secretary General's mission in the region.

The root cause of the problems in the region is the absence of a comprehensive Middle East peace plan. The immediate crisis results from efforts by extremist forces to destabilize the region and to frustrate the aspirations of the Palestinian, Israeli and Lebanese people for democracy and peace. In Gaza, elements of Hamas launched rocket attacks against Israeli territory and abducted an Israeli soldier. In Lebanon, Hizbollah, in violation of the Blue Line, attacked Israel from Lebanese territory and killed and captured Israeli soldiers, reversing the positive trends that began with the Syrian withdrawal in 2005, and undermining the democratically elected government of Prime Minister Fuad Siniora.

These extremist elements and those that support them cannot be allowed to plunge the Middle East into chaos and provoke a wider conflict. The extremists must immediately halt their attacks. It is also critical that Israel, while exercising the right to defend itself, be mindful of the strategic and humanitarian consequences of its actions. We call

---

[78] After Baker-Hamilton: What to Do in Iraq", International Crisis Group, Working to Prevent Conflict Worldwide, Middle East Report Number 60, Baghdad/Amman/Damascus/Brussels, 19 December 2006

upon Israel to exercise utmost restraint, seeking to avoid casualties among innocent civilians and damage to civilian infrastructure and to refrain from acts that would destabilize the Lebanese government. The most urgent priority is to create conditions for a cessation of violence that will be sustainable and lay the foundation for a more permanent solution. This requires:

(a) The return of the Israeli soldiers in Gaza and Lebanon unharmed;
(b) An end to the shelling of Israeli territory;
(c) An end to Israeli military operations and the early withdrawal of Israeli forces from Gaza;
(d) The release of the arrested Palestinian ministers and parliamentarians.

The framework for resolving these disputes is already established by international consensus. In Lebanon, UN Security Council Resolutions 1559 and 1680 address the underlying conditions that gave rise to this crisis. G8 urged the UN Security Council to develop a plan for the full implementation of these resolutions. G8 extends to the Government of Lebanon full support in asserting its sovereign authority over all its territory in fulfillment of UNSCR 1559. This includes the deployment of Lebanese Armed Forces to all parts of the country, in particular the South, and the disarming of militias. G8 would welcome an examination by the UN Security Council of the possibility of an international security/monitoring presence. G8 also supports the initiation of a political dialogue between Lebanese and Israeli officials on all issues of concern to both parties. In addition, G8 will support the economic and humanitarian needs of the Lebanese people, including the convening at the right time of a donor's conference.

In Gaza, the disengagement of Israel provided an opportunity to move a further step toward a two state solution under the Road Map. All Palestinian parties should accept the existence of Israel, reject violence, and accept all previous agreements and obligations, including the Roadmap. For its part, Israel needs to refrain from unilateral acts that could prejudice a final settlement and agree to negotiate in good faith. G8's goal is an immediate end to the current violence, resumption of security cooperation and of a political engagement both among Palestinians and with Israel. This requires:

(a) An end to terrorist attacks against Israel;
(b) A resumption of the efforts of President Abbas to ensure that the Palestinian government complies with the Quartet principles;
(c) Immediate expansion of the temporary international mechanism for donors established under the direction of the Quartet;
(d) Israeli compliance with the Agreement on Movement and Access of November 2005 and action on other steps to ease the humanitarian plight of the people of Gaza and the West Bank;
(e) Resumption of security cooperation between Palestinians and Israelis;
(f) Action to ensure that the Palestinian security forces comply with Palestinian law and with the Roadmap, so that they are unified and effective in providing security for the Palestinian people;
(g) Resumption of dialogue between Palestinian and Israeli political officials.

These proposals are G8's contribution to the international effort underway to restore calm to the Middle East and provide a basis for progress towards a sustainable peace, in accordance with the relevant UN Security Council Resolutions. The Quartet will continue to play a central role. The G-8 welcomes the positive efforts of Egypt, Saudi Arabia and Jordan as well as other responsible regional actors to return the region to peace. We look forward to the report of the Secretary General's mission to the Security Council later this week which we believe could provide a framework for achieving our common objectives.[79]

Arab World: past versus future

IN 2001, a book came out about George Mitchell's diplomatic work in Northern Ireland that was entitled "To Hell with the Future, Let's Get on with the Past." One hopes that such a book will never be written about today's Arab awakenings. But watching events unfold out there makes it impossible not to ask: Will the past bury the future in the Arab world or will the future bury the past?

I am awed by the bravery of the Syrian and Egyptian youths trying to throw off the tyranny of the Assad family and the Egyptian military. The fact that they go into the streets — knowing they face security forces who will not hesitate to gun them down — speaks of the deep longing of young Arabs to be free of the regimes that have so long choked their voices and prevented them from realizing their full potential.

But I am deeply worried that the longer the fighting continues in Syria and Egypt, the less chance that any stable, democratizing order will emerge anytime soon and the more likely that Syria could disintegrate into civil war. You can't exaggerate how dangerous that would be. When Tunisia was convulsed by revolution, it imploded. When Egypt was convulsed by revolution, it imploded. When Libya was convulsed by revolution, it imploded. If Syria is convulsed by revolution, it will not implode. Most Arab states implode. Syria explodes.

---

[79] The statement of G-8 Leaders, St Petersburg, 15-17 July 2006

Why? It is because Syria is the keystone of the Levant. It borders and balances a variety of states, sects and ethnic groups. If civil war erupts there, every one of Syria's neighbors will cultivate, and be cultivated by, different Syrian factions — Sunnis, Alawites, Kurds, Druse, Christians, pro-Iranians, pro-Hezbollahites, pro-Palestinians, pro-Saudis — in order to try to tilt Syria in their direction. Turkey, Lebanon, Hezbollah, Iraq, Iran, Hamas, Jordan, Saudi Arabia and Israel all have vital interests in who rules in Damascus, and they will all find ways to partner with proxies inside Syria to shape events there. It will become a big Lebanon-like brawl.

Syria needs a peaceful democratic transition set in motion now. Ditto Egypt. But that is easier said than done. Events in both countries are a reminder of the multidimensional struggle for power across the Middle- East — what I once described as the struggle between "The Lexus and the Olive Tree."

On one level, you have the very modern, deeply felt and truly authentic longing by Syrians and Egyptians for freedom, for the skills to thrive in modernity and for the rights of real citizens.

Outsiders often underestimate just how much these Arab youths are determined to limit the powers of their militaries as a necessary step for achieving true democracy. What you see in Egypt today are young people from across the political spectrum and classes who are willing to join forces, break ranks with their own parties and return to Tahrir Square to press for real freedom. This is a generational rupture. It is the old versus the young. It is the insiders (the adults) versus the outsiders (the youth). It is the privileged old guard versus the disadvantaged young guard. These young Egyptians, and Syrians, who have stopped fearing their military masters, are determined to unleash a true transformation in their world. We should be on their side.

But the weight of their history is so heavy. The new Lexus-like values of "democracy," "free elections," "citizen rights" and "modernity" will have to compete with some very old Olive Tree ideas and passions. These include the age-old civil wars within Islam between Sunnis and Shiites, over who should dominate the faith, the heated struggle between Salafists and modernists over whether the 21st century should be embraced or rejected, as well as the ancient tribal and regional struggles playing out within each of these societies. Last, but not least, you have the struggle between the entrenched military/crony elites and the masses. These struggles from the "past" always threaten to rise up, consume any new movement for change and bury "the future."

This is the grand drama now being played out in the Arab world — the deeply sincere youth-led quest for liberty and the deeply rooted quests for sectarian, factional, class and tribal advantage. One day it looks as though the revolutions in Egypt, Syria and Tunisia are going to be hijacked by forces and passions from the past while the next day that longing of young people to be free and modern pushes them back.

The same drama played out in Iraq, but there the process was managed, at a huge cost, by an American midwife — managed enough so that the communities were able to write a new, rudimentary social contract on how to live together and, thereby, give the future a chance to bury the past. But we still do not know how it will end in Iraq. [80]

We know, though, that there will be no impartial outside midwife to guide the transitions in Egypt, Syria, Tunisia, Libya and Yemen. Can they each make it without one? Only if they develop their own Nelson Mandela — unique civic leaders or coalitions who can

---

[80] Thomas L. Friedman (2011), " In the Arab world, it's past versus future", the New York Times, November 26, 2011

honor the past, and contain its volcanic urges, but not let it bury the future.

Peoples Millennium Forum,
Declaration and Agenda for Action (22 –26 May 2000)

The United Nations organized the Peoples Millennium Forum at the UN headquarters in New York from 22 - 26 May 2000. 1,350 representatives of over 1,000 non-governmental organizations (NGOs) and other civil society organizations from more than 100 countries attended the conference to build upon a common vision. The work begun at civil society conferences in 1990's and the UN world conferences of the 1990's were again discussed to draw the attention of governments to the urgency of implementing the commitments they have made, and to channel collective energies by reclaiming globalization for and by the people.

Their Agenda for Action included steps that should be taken by civil society, governments, and the United Nations. One of the objectives was Peace, Security, and Disarmament, which is described as follows:

Peace, Security and Disarmament

The UN and its member states have failed to fulfill their primary responsibility of maintaining peace and preserving human life. Organized armed violence is depriving millions of people all over the world - 95 percent of them civilians -- of their lives, and many millions more of their right to peace. The victims of Hiroshima/Nagasaki A-bombs and of the century's other wars have vehemently warned us that the errors of the 20th century must not be repeated in the 21st. However, the killing is continuing. Six million people have died in over 50 wars in the last decade. There have been some successes, but many of these conflicts have lasted for decades with millions of dead. The cycle of violence begins with cultures that glorify violence and warrior virtues, and may be manifest in domestic violence.

Despite over fifty years of effort, no decisive progress has yet been made in eliminating nuclear weapons, still capable of destroying all life on this planet, and the circle of their possessors is expanding. For mainly commercial reasons, there is no adequate verification for treaties prohibiting biological weapons, while knowledge of how to produce them spreads. Rape continues to be used as a weapon of war. Space has been militarized, and space weapons are being actively developed. For the moment, the problem is centered in a small group of eight states that are claiming for themselves the right to possess weapons that could destroy all of humankind.

Disarmament alone is not the way to peace; it must be accompanied by genuine human security. It is imperative that NGOs be included in the dialogue for peace. The world community -- civil society, including younger and older people, and governments -- has the resources and knowledge to move from a culture of violence to a culture of peace.

The time has come to carry out the primary mission set forth in the United Nations Charter, "to preserve future generations from the scourge of war," and to apply the principle of non-use of force, which is fundamental to the UN Charter. Working together, both civil society and governments can make armed conflict increasingly rare and can move, step by step, to the abolition of war. The Forum urges:

To The United Nations

To carry out the objective of moving toward the abolition of war by practical means, the UN Secretariat and interested governments, or a separate group of governments, should develop a draft proposal for global disarmament to be discussed in a fourth Special Session of the General Assembly for Disarmament. This proposal would be aimed specifically at reducing the level of armed violence throughout the world through continuing improved conflict prevention, peace keeping, conventional disarmament, and nuclear weapons abolition, in a program designed to be promoted by a broad coalition of civil society organizations, particularly youth organizations, and by interested governments.

1. To establish a corps of at least 50 professionally trained mediators for more effective conflict prevention, to assist in conflict warning, mediation, and conflict resolution.

2. To authorize, through the General Assembly, the establishment of an international, non-violent, inclusive, standing Peace Force of volunteer women and men to deploy to conflict areas to provide early warning, facilitate conflict resolution, protect human rights, and prevent death and destruction.

3. To draw on legal systems for conflict prevention and resolution, such as those of indigenous peoples which have conflict resolution mechanisms of their own?

4. To ensure that any military force uses no "non-discriminatory" weapons, such as landmines and sub-munitions, in particular by any force or coalition acting under a UN mandate.

5. To assist the Security Council on conflict prevention in a more flexible way, the General Assembly should establish an open-ended Conflict Prevention Committee to serve a rapid action conflict prevention and early warning function. It should give the world public, civil society, the UN, and national governments balanced, timely information on potential conflicts and promote possible solutions.

6. To respect national sovereignty and the prohibition of the use of force, which are fundamental in the UN Charter? This principle must not be undermined. In the solution of conflicts, all peaceful methods in accordance with the UN Charter must be tried before measures of force are undertaken. The UN General Assembly should set up a broad commission to analyze standards for forceful action in cases where crimes against humanity, war crimes, or genocide are committed.

7. To expand the UN Arms register in order to show production and sale of small arms and light weapons. It should include specific names of their producers and traders.

8. To reopen the Peace Education Unit in the Department of Political Affairs (UN-DPA) with provisions for continuous liaison with NGOs.

9. To establish a humanitarian commission composed of independent experts to work with the Security Council and Secretary General and other UN agencies. The mandate of this commission would be to assess humanitarian needs and recommend protective measures for civilian populations in times of armed conflicts.

10. To establish ready police and peacekeeping forces Sensitivity and respect for civilians, especially women and children, should be included in the training of all peacekeepers.

11. To establish an annual youth peace prize for signal accomplishments in this field.

To the Governments

The governments should promptly carry out their obligations in the Non-Proliferation Treaty to eliminate all nuclear weapons and to ban them. So, governments should, by the beginning of the year 2001, convene the conference to eliminate nuclear dangers, as proposed by Secretary-General Kofi Annan. Governments should immediately undertake to close laboratories that research and develop new nuclear weapons, to de-alert nuclear weapons, and to withdraw nuclear weapons from foreign states.

Together with nearly all governments that participated in the recent Nuclear Proliferation Treaty (NPT) review conference, Forum participants consider that unilateral deployment of nationwide missile defense by any country could have dangerously destabilizing effects and create pressures to permanently retain high levels of nuclear weapons or even to increase existing levels. The deployment of theater missile defenses in Asia or other regions could have serious regional destabilizing effects. Such plans should be relinquished in favor of a worldwide missile launch warning system and a conference to review methods of ending production of long-range surface-to-surface missiles and long-range bombers. The objectives are:

12. To expand the network of nuclear free zones until they cover all areas other than territory of weapons states and to complement that network by maritime measures that close ports to naval vessels unless they certify that they are not carrying nuclear weapons. Civil society should energetically promote all these measures to control nuclear weapons.

13.To initiate a worldwide freeze on armed forces and a 25 per cent cut in production and export of major weapons and small arms, and, to this end, to adopt an international Code of Conduct on arms exports, as the beginning of worldwide build-down of conventional forces.

14. To implement the International Anti-Personnel Landmines Convention of 1997, also known as the Ottawa Treaty, to ban anti-personnel landmines

15. To establish a commission at the UN to devise ways of stopping the technological development of new and more advanced weapons that create new imbalances in global power relationships. The Conference on Disarmament should also establish a working group on this subject.

16. To establish peace education, including coping with domestic conflict, covering all ages from young children to older adults, at all levels from pre-school through university and non-formal community education. Education for peace and conflict avoidance is essential for moving toward sustainable peace. An appropriate treaty should assure implementation of this obligation of each national government.

17. To increase their efforts to promote and to comply with international humanitarian laws, limiting the methods and means of war and protecting non-combatants, civilian populations and humanitarian personnel.

18 The international community--civil society, governments and the UN--has a responsibility to stop promptly any genocide, war crimes, or any massive violations of human rights. All those involved should seek to avoid any confusion between humanitarian help and military intervention.

19. To immediately adopt measures to implement the Optional Protocol to the Convention on the Rights of the Child, so that children up to the age of 18 will be prohibited from participation in armed conflict.

Civil Society

20.To give special attention and support to those disabled and injured by violent conflict, to children, and the elderly, and to the re-integration into society of former combatants. Protection of war-affected children in conflict zones must become a worldwide campaign.

21.To maintain the impartiality and independence of all NGOs working for peace, security, disarmament and humanitarian issues from political, military and economic powers and institutions. At the same time NGOs should organically link with popular movements promoting equity, justice, and diversity (such as the labor movement, women's movements, and civil rights movements).

22. To protect the humanitarian principles those are linked with human rights and reject all attempts to transform the field of humanitarian assistance into a new market open to private companies.[81]

International Arms Trade Treaty:

An international Arms Trade Treaty would make a major improvement to the lives of those suffering from armed violence if it was properly elaborated and implemented effectively. Many other things must also be done - from bolstering institutions that respect fundamental human rights (including economic, social and cultural rights) and conducting effective conflict resolution and peacekeeping, to providing livelihoods for thousands of ex-combatants and ensuring development in countries and regions emerging from armed conflict. Much also depends on the success of two vital new institutions, both founded in June 2006: the UN Human Rights Council and the UN Peace Building Commission.

---

[81] Peoples Millennium Forum Declaration and Agenda for Action: Strengthening the United Nations for the 21st Century, UN Headquarters, New York, 22-26 May, 2000

But in the attempt to make people around the world more secure and prosperous, the Arms Trade Treaty is indispensable. It should be part of the rule of law, of international law, and is necessary to guarantee the protection of human rights and security of all people.

More than 50 governments have already given explicit public support for an Arms Trade Treaty. Now is the time for all governments to join that movement and begin negotiations that can bring such a Treaty to reality. The globalised arms trade already has a huge head start.

In October 2006, all governments have the opportunity, at the First Committee of the UN General Assembly, to launch a process to negotiate an Arms Trade Treaty, based on full respect for international law when governments decide whether or not to allow specific international arms transfers. The UN General Assembly is the world's highest global forum for disarmament and security affairs.

Already a group of states led by Argentina, Australia, Costa Rica, Finland, Japan, Kenya and the UK have given notice that they will table a resolution this October to start a process to develop an Arms Trade Treaty. Their draft resolution calls for a Group of Government Experts to consider the issue in 2008. While this welcome initiative rightly refers to better respect for international law, including the UN Charter and international humanitarian law, there is no reference so far to international human rights law, and this must be corrected if there is to be an effective treaty that will save a significant number of lives.

Those who suffer the daily effects of armed violence need a tough Arms Trade Treaty. And they need it as swiftly as humanly possible. Worldwide, the hundreds of thousands of members of civil society groups who are supporting the call for an Arms Trade Treaty through the Control Arms campaign are expecting governments to act. Time has come to do so.[82]

Global Principles for Arms Transfers:
Suggestions of Non-Government Organizations

The following Principles bring together States' existing obligations in respect of international transfers of arms and ammunition. The Principles are proposed by a diverse group of non-government organisations. The Principles reflect the content of a variety of international instruments including: international and regional treaties, declarations and resolutions of the United Nations and other multilateral and regional organisations, and model regulations intended for national legislation. Some of the Principles reflect customary and treaty law, while others reflect widely accepted emerging norms. The compilation indicates the best general rules for effective control of international transfers of all conventional arms and ammunition. The rules reflect States' obligations under international law while also recognizing States' right to legitimate self-defense and law enforcement in accordance with international standards. The principles are explained as follows:

Principle 1: **Responsibilities of states**

All international transfers of arms and ammunition shall be authorized by all States with jurisdiction over any part of the transfer (including import, export, transit, transshipment and brokering) and carried out in accordance with national laws and procedures that reflect, as a minimum, States' obligations under international law. Authorization of each transfer shall be granted by designated State officials in writing only if the transfer in question first conforms to the Principles set out below in this instrument and shall

[82] www.controlarms.org

not be granted if it is likely that the arms or ammunition will be diverted from their intended legal recipient or re-exported contrary to the aims of these Principles.

Principle 2: **Express limitations**

States shall not authorize international transfers of arms or ammunition that violate expressed obligations under international law. These obligations include:

A. Obligations under the Charter of the United Nations – including:

(a) Binding resolutions of the Security Council, such as those imposing arms embargoes
(b) The prohibition on the threat or use of force;
(c) The prohibition on intervention in the internal affairs of another State

B. Any other treaty or decision by which that State is bound, including:

(a) Binding decisions, including embargoes, adopted by relevant international, multilateral, regional, and sub-regional organisations to which a State is party
(b) Prohibitions on arms transfers that arise in particular treaties which a State is party to, such as the 1980 UN Convention on Prohibitions or Restrictions on the Use of Certain Conventional Weapons Which May be Deemed to be Excessively Injurious or to Have Indiscriminate Effects, and its Protocols, and the 1997 Convention on the Prohibition of Anti-Personnel Mines.

C. Universally accepted principles of international humanitarian law including:

(a) The prohibition on the use of arms that are of a nature to cause superfluous injury or unnecessary suffering;
(b) The prohibition on weapons or munitions incapable of distinguishing between combatants and civilians

Principle 3: **Limitations based on use or likely use**

States shall not authorize international transfers of arms or ammunition where they will be used or are likely to be used for violations of international law, including:

(a) Breaches of the UN Charter and customary law rules relating to the use of force;
(b) Gross violations of international human rights law;
(c) Serious violations of international humanitarian law;
(d) Acts of genocide or crimes against humanity.

Principle 4: **Factors to be taken into account**

States shall take into account other factors, including the likely use of the arms or ammunition, before authorizing an arms transfer, including the recipient's record of compliance with commitments and transparency in the field of non-proliferation, arms and munitions control, and disarmament.

States should not authorize the transfer if it is likely to:

(a) Be used for or to facilitate terrorist attacks
(b) Be used for or to facilitate the commission of violent or organized crime;
(c) Adversely affect regional security or stability;
(d) Adversely affect sustainable development
(e) Involve corrupt practices
(f) Contravene other international, regional, or sub-regional commitments or decisions made,

or agreements on non- proliferation, arms control, and disarmament to which the exporting, importing, or transit States are party.

Principle 5: **Transparency**

States shall submit comprehensive national annual reports on all their international arms and ammunition transfers to an international registry, which shall publish a compiled, comprehensive, international annual report. Such reports should cover the international transfer of all conventional arms and ammunition including small arms and light weapons.

Principle 6: **Comprehensive controls**

States shall establish common standards for specific mechanisms to control:

(a) All import and export of arms and ammunition;
(b) Arms and ammunition brokering activities;
(c) Transfers of arms and ammunition production capacity; and
(d) The transit and trans-shipment of arms and ammunition

States shall establish operative provisions to monitor enforcement and review procedures to strengthen the full implementation of the Principles.[83]

The International Crisis Group is a voluntary research organization which studies the conflicts arising in different parts of the world. Its suggestions bear high values for resolving crises.

---

[83] www.controlarms.com

The International Crisis Group

The International Crisis Group has recommended the following suggestions for bringing normalcy in Niger Delta State. The recommendations are:

To Nigeria's Federal Government

(a) Initiate a credible, sustained dialogue on control of resources with Niger Delta civil society groups, including militants, activist leaders, religious leaders, women and youth drawn from nominees submitted by councils of ethnic groups in the Niger Delta states.

(b) Institute while this dialogue is preceding a derivation formula of between 25 and 50 per cent of mineral resources, including oil and gas, to all Nigerian states, and phase this in over five years in order to avoid budgetary shock to non-oil producing states and to encourage exploration and production of other mineral resources throughout Nigeria.

(c) Amend or repeal the 1978 Land Use Act to expand the opportunity for communities to seek compensation for land through legal means and to allow a more transparent adjudication process of potential land seizures.

(d) Seek in parallel with the dialogue on control of resources an agreement with militants that includes a phased withdrawal of troops from Delta towns, concurrent with a weapons-return amnesty program that pays militants and gang members market rates for guns and enrolls them in skills and job training and that pays attention as well to the needs of girls and women who may not carry guns but have roles within those bodies (such as forced wives or cooks).

(e) Bring the increasing number of quasi-independent local government institutions formally into federal structures as part of an effort to rationalize local governments in Niger Delta states, particularly in areas where these are unworkably large or combine substantively distinct ethnicities or communities.

(f) Ensure that security force personnel are paid on time and in full in order to help prevent dependency on oil company payments and illicit and corrupt practices; increase enforcement of penalties for corruption and consider raising salaries; clarify the chain of command; and change the uniform of the "supernumerary police" that provide security services for the energy companies.

(g) Refashion the government/transnational oil company joint ventures that control production to offer residents a substantial ownership stake along the lines of what corporate majors have done in Canada's Arctic.

To the State Governments

Engage more fully with professional, non-governmental organisations that demonstrate a capability and willingness to assist communities to take responsibility for their own development.

Accelerate steps to implement poverty reduction strategies outlined in State Economic Empowerment and Development Strategies (SEEDS) that have been developed in conjunction with Nigeria's national umbrella anti-poverty strategy,

NEEDS

Make budget details publicly available and respond to queries about specific spending patterns and projects.

To the Energy Companies

Improve measures to ensure transparency of contracts and other community payments, including for surveillance, development projects and compensation for land use and pollution, and in particular

Honour company commitments and ensure that payments are made in full, by bank transfer – not in cash – to the intended recipients;

Conclude agreements wherever possible that provide for individuals and local communities to be compensated for land use and pollution; and

Seek independent mediation or arbitration when agreements are in dispute.
Prioritize long-term ability to operate in Nigeria over short-term production goals and seek community assent before proceeding with production-related projects.

Develop partnerships with non-governmental, community-based bodies with a demonstrated ability to provide skills training and capacity building for development projects, including women's and religious groups that have played significant roles in mediating among various ethnic groups and actors in the past decade.

To the US, EU, and EU Member States
With major interests in Nigeria (UK, France and Italy)

Press the Nigerian government to institute resource-control reforms and negotiate in good faith with Niger Delta groups, and encourage oil companies headquartered in their countries to be transparent about revenue and payments.

Conditional assistance to the government upon greater transparency in federal and state budgets, particularly with regard to energy revenues

Lobby China and India to sign the Extractive Industries Transparency Initiative.

To the UN and the wider International Community:

Offer the good offices of a neutral country without oil interests in Nigeria to mediate between the federal government and Delta groups, an idea already accepted in principle by MEND.

Consider delaying or postponing cooperation with state governments that have a poor record for delivering public services or controlling graft, and do not work with government or party officials who provide weapons or funding to armed groups for political purposes.[84]

The UN Security Council shows its weakness

For decade after decade, diplomats at the United Nations have had on-again, off-again talks on how to reform the Security Council, the supreme decision-making panel on international security. The crisis in Syria shows that progress has been minimal and that power politics often trump human rights.

At issue is the composition of a body "frozen in amber since the end of World War II," in the words of Stewart Patrick, a fellow at the Council on Foreign Relations, a New York-based foreign policy think tank. The biggest difficulty in unfreezing it is the veto power wielded by the five permanent members of the 15-nation council – the United States, Russia, China, Britain and France.

---

[84] The Swamps of Insurgency: Nigeria's Delta Unrest, Africa Report N°115, International Crisis Group, Working to Prevent Conflict World Wide, Dakar/Brussels, 3 August 2006, http://www.crisisgroup.org

A veto by one permanent member is enough to sink a resolution. On February 4, two veto-wielders, Russia and China, banded together to vote against a resolution that provided for Syria's president, Bashar al-Assad, to step aside, halt a ruthless crackdown on dissidents, and begin a transition to democracy. Assad saw the veto as a green light to crack down even harder. A week before the vetoes, the U.N. estimated the death toll at 5,400.

On February 28, it was revised to more than 7,500, the result of a merciless artillery and tank bombardment of the central city of Homs, an opposition stronghold. In the weeks between those body counts, there has been a growing chorus of condemnation of the Assad government, including a United Nations General Assembly vote (by 137 to 12) criticizing "widespread and systematic human rights violations by Syrian authorities." Russia, China and 10 other countries voted against that resolution. It has no legal force, unlike council resolutions.

More international condemnation came from a "Friends of Syria" meeting that brought together Western and Arab foreign ministers whose calls for ending the violence and allowing access for humanitarian aid fell on deaf ears in Damascus.

Russia and China stayed away from the Tunis gathering and were showered with blistering criticism from U.S. Secretary of State Hillary Clinton for their "despicable" Security Council vetoes.

Why the make-up of the council and the way it operates has remained unchanged since 1945 is a question that merits more vigorous public debate than there has been in the past. The case for re-thinking the system becomes stronger every time a veto frustrates the will of the majority. Clinton complained that the council had been "neutered" by the vetoes on Syria but the neutering is a logical consequence of the power wielded by the permanent five.

They have the privilege to ignore the rest, push their own interests and protect their allies, as Russia did on Syria and as the United States (the most active veto-wielder in the past four decades) has done often to shield Israel from censure. None of the five have shown eagerness to change the veto system but that doesn't mean it will never happen.

Ideas on what to change and how to do it have been tossed around since 1993 in the bureaucratic obscurity of the bureaucratically-named "Open ended Working Group to consider all aspects of the question of an increase in the membership of the Security Council and other matters related to the Council."

An expansion of the top UN decision making body is more likely in the foreseeable future than "other matters", a phrase that embraces abolishing the veto. In February, the four countries that have lobbied most energetically to become veto-wielding Security Council members (Germany, Japan, India, Brazil) issued a statement urging tangible progress before September, when the current session of the U.N. General Assembly ends.

Japan and Germany are the second and third-biggest financial contributors to the U.N., India is a nuclear power and the world's second-most populous country, and Brazil is becoming a regional superpower in Latin America. Their inclusion would be a big step towards a Security Council that reflects the world as it is now, not as it was in 1945.

Skeptics tend to argue that expansion of the council would result in a decision-making process even more difficult and time-consuming than it is now. Perhaps, But adding four stable, liberal democracies to the lineup would probably also result in better decisions.

Members of the UN General Assembly vote endorse the Arab league's plan for Syria's president Basher al-Assad to step aside, at the UN headquarters in New York on February 16, 2012. The 193-nation UN General Assembly on Thursday overwhelmingly approved a non-binding resolution endorsing an Arab league plan that urges Syria president Basher al-Assad to step aside.[85]

(B) The United Nations

The United Nations is an organization of countries/states formed in 1945 as the successor to the League of Nations.

Its main aims are to maintain international peace and security and to cooperate in finding solutions for political, economic, social, cultural and humanitarian problems on an international level.

The UN has six main organs such as: (1) The General Assembly; (2) The Security Council; (3) The Economic and Social Council; (4) The Trusteeship Council; (5) The International Court of Justice; and (6) The Secretariat. All these organs have formed many Committees, Agencies, Centers, Commissions, Missions, Specialized Agencies, Temporary Bodies, and Country Offices.

The UN has also agreement of mutual co-operation with International Monetary Fund (IMF), International Atomic Energy Agency (IAEA), International Labour Organization (ILO), Food and Agriculture Organization (FAO), United Nations Educational, Scientific and Cultural Organization (UNESCO), World Health Organization (WHO), IBRD, IDA, IFC, ICAO, UPU,

---

[85] Bernd Debusmann (2012), " UNSC shows weakness", www Reuters com, March 2, 2012

ITU, WMO, IMO, WTO, WIPO, IFAD, UNIDO, and other organizations

The United Nations Charter

The Charters of the United Nations are:

Article 1: To maintain international peace and security, and to that end: to take effective collective measures for the prevention and removal of threats to the peace, and for the suppression of acts of aggression or other breaches of the peace, and to bring about by peaceful means, and in conformity with the principles of justice and international law, adjustment or settlement of international disputes or situations which might lead to a breach of the peace;

To develop friendly relations among nations based on respect for the principle of equal rights and self-determination of peoples, and to take other appropriate measures to strengthen universal peace;

Article 2: The interdiction of aggressive war was confirmed and broadened by the United Nations' Charter, which states in paragraph 4 that "All Members shall refrain in their international relations from the threat or use of force against the territorial integrity or political independence of any state, or in any other manner inconsistent with the Purposes of the United Nations."

Article 33: The parties to any dispute, the continuance of which is likely to endanger the maintenance of international peace and security, shall, first of all, seek a solution by negotiation, enquiry, mediation, conciliation, arbitration, judicial settlement, resort to regional agencies or arrangements, or other peaceful means of their own choice. The Security Council shall, when it deems necessary, call upon the parties to settle their dispute by such means.

Article 39: The Security Council shall determine the existence of any threat to the peace, breach of the peace, or act of aggression and shall make recommendations, or decide what measures shall be taken in accordance with Articles 41 and 42, to maintain or restore international peace and security.

Article 51: Nothing in the present Charter shall impair the inherent right of individual or collective self-defence if an armed attack occurs against a Member of the United Nations, until the Security Council has taken measures necessary to maintain international peace and security. Measures taken by Members in the exercise of this right of self-defence shall be immediately reported to the Security Council and shall not in any way affect the authority and responsibility of the Security Council under the present Charter to take at any time such action as it deems necessary in order to maintain or restore international peace and security.

Article 102: Every treaty and every international agreement entered into by any Member of the United Nations after the present Charter comes into force shall as soon as possible be registered with the Secretariat and published by it.

After World War I, an attempt was made to establish such a new international law of peace, of which the League of Nations was considered to be one of the cornerstones, but this attempt failed unfortunately. The Charter of the United Nations (1945) in fact reflects the fact that the traditional notion of state sovereignty remains the key concept in the law of nations.

The League of Nations

Following World War I, as after the Thirty Years' War, there was an outcry for rules of warfare to protect civilian populations, as well as a desire to curb invasions. The League of Nations, established after the war, attempted to curb invasions by enacting a treaty agreement providing for economic and military sanctions against member states that used "external aggression" to invade or conquer other member states. An international court was established, the Permanent Court of International Justice, to arbitrate disputes between nations without resorting to war. Meanwhile, many nations signed treaties agreeing to use international arbitration rather than warfare to settle differences. International crises, however, demonstrated that nations were not yet committed to the idea of giving external authorities a say in how nations conducted their affairs. Aggression on the part of Germany, Italy and Japan went unchecked by international law, and this caused a Second World War to end it.

The postwar era

After World War II, as after the First World War and the Thirty Years' War, there was a strong desire to never again endure the horrors of war endured by the civilian populations. The League of Nations was re-attempted through another treaty organization, the United Nations.

The postwar era has been a highly successful one for international law. International cooperation has become far more commonplace, though of course not universal. Importantly, nearly two hundred nations are now members of the United Nations, and have voluntarily bound themselves to its charter. Even the most powerful nations have recognized the need for international cooperation and supports, and have routinely sought international agreement and consent before engaging in acts of war.

International law is, of course, only partly about the conduct of war. Most rules are civil, concerning the delivery of mail, trade, shipping, air travel, and the like. Most countries obey most rules routinely, because the rules make life easier for all concerned. The rules are rarely disputed. But some international law is extremely political and hotly debated. This includes not just the laws of warfare but also such matters as fishing rights.

Modern customary international law

An important development in modern international law is the concept of "consent." Before World War II, a nation would not have been considered to be bound by a rule unless it had formally agreed to be bound by it, or it was already customarily abiding by that rule. Now, however, merely consenting to an international practice is sufficient to be bound by it, without signing a treaty. An evolution of the positivist approach of Grotius, the concept of consent is an element of customary international law. Customary international law is essentially what states actually do, plus the *opinio juris* of what states believe international law requires them to do.

Customary international law applies to every country, regardless of whether they have formally agreed to it. At the same time, all countries take part in forming customary international law by their practices and decisions. As new rules arise, countries accept, reject or modify them. When most countries are following a rule, everyone else will be held to it. Therefore, doing nothing is the same as consenting. Nations that did not take action may find themselves bound by an international law that is not to their advantage. Customary international law can be overruled, however, by a treaty. For this reason, much customary international law has been agreed to formally by treaties between nations.

Modern treaty law

Treaties are essentially contracts between countries. They are agreements by which the parties intend to be bound. If treaties are broken, their effectiveness is weakened because there is no guarantee that future promises will be kept. So there is a strong incentive for nations to take treaties very seriously. Modern nations engage in a two-step procedure for entering into treaties. The first step is signing the treaty. Being a signatory to a treaty means that a country intends to enter into the agreement. The second step is ratifying the treaty. A country that has ratified a treaty has gone beyond merely intending to enter into the agreement, and is now bound by it. This is a critical distinction, and sometimes a point of confusion. A nation may be a signatory to a treaty for many years without ever having ratified it. Each country ratifies treaties its own way. The United States requires the two-thirds support of the Senate, the upper body of its legislature, for a treaty to be ratified; both the executive and the legislature must agree.

In Canada, on the other hand, ratification is strictly an executive action, and no parliamentary approval is required before the nation is bound. Modern treaties are interpreted according to the 1969 Vienna Convention on the Law of Treaties. This convention is so widely accepted that even nations that are not parties to the convention follow it. The convention's most important and sensible rule is that a treaty should be interpreted according to the plain meaning of its language, in the context of its purpose, and in good faith. This prevents much squabbling and unnecessary nit-picking. It also makes treaty authors spell out what they are trying to accomplish, to make interpretation easier, in a non-binding "preamble." In the modern world, international law is more important than ever. Even the most powerful countries rely on it, and seek to comply with it- and suffer consequences if they ignore it.[86]

---

[86] History of public international law, http://enwikipedia.org,

The primary aim of the United Nations is to establish world peace. Therefore, the first and foremost duty of the UN is to stop war and activate the peace process. It should also try to enact international laws for the benefits of all countries.

But the UNO is increasing its supplementary activities and is incurring deficit budgets. The UN can endorse responsibilities to the willing countries to bear expenses, management and do needful as per requirement of the sufferer country; and can only supervise the supplementary activities.

The UN should act as the 'World Government' for peace, progress, perpetuity and performance.

It should not bow down to a country or group of countries; it should be loyal to the humanity, countries and a future world.

The UN should convince the industrialized countries to stop researches on nuclear weapons, biological weapons and chemical weapons, which could convert the world into ashes and a graveyard. These countries should not undertake arms trade with low-income countries and other developing countries. The UN is facing tough challenges to solve insurgencies and wars.

The UN has not yet taken steps to dethrone the military rulers. The UN peacekeeping forces are being utilized to pacify and delay the war. It can create world opinion to punish the rulers/governments of the warmonger countries by announcing expulsions of these countries from the UN, imposing trade barriers and through awarding strictures on the default governments. The UN can declare the military rulers, President/Prime Ministers of the warmonger countries as "Criminals of Human Rights". The first step to achieve world peace is to declare that 'Persons in Military Dresses' cannot hold the posts of Chairman, President, Prime Minister or Administrator of any country with immediate effect or from a specified date.

Many low-income countries are engaged in wars, conflicts, crises and violence even after achieving independence. It happens when the revolutionaries are not satisfied with the administration or they are aspirants of the chairs. The political situation of these countries continues to be morbid because of poverty, corruption, lack of transparency and excessive political power. Politics has become a profitable business in lieu of social service or a chance to serve the country or its people. These warmonger countries have lost peace and are pushed into war or insurgency.

The World faces crises in most of the developing countries. The media is publishing news on violence, wars, and brutal killings and carries news analyses, which has terrified the common men of the entire world. It predicts that the worst terror of World War III is approaching very fast. Some of the religious people are predicting the time of this disaster.

It is predicted that the year of disaster for the world would be 2018 or 2027.

But it can be safely avoided for a century or more. It is, therefore, needed that the political leaders should try to **'replace confrontation with cooperation'** and **'settle conflict through dialogue'** for the benefit of human civilization.

Each day the world faces the disaster of war; each day the world produces arms and ammunitions; each day international trade in arms continues; and each day brave soldiers and common people are killed.

Why we cannot stop massive production and trade of arms?

Arms production is necessary for internal security; but not for international trade or invasion.

The developed countries can make the world free of war, if these countries reduce the production of war arsenals, fighter planes, and stop researches on nuclear, biological, and chemical weapons.

It is a fact that World War II has caused millions of deaths; resulted environmental hazards; buried humanity in the graveyard; Germany was divided; and created Guerrillas, Tigers (Sri Lanka), Terrorists, Maoists and Naxalites. During the last six and half decades (from 1945 till date), **the world has only seen 26 days without war.** The world leaders have not yet been successful in resolving the ongoing wars. The arms trade with the low-income countries has resulted in easy availability of latest weapons to the private hands through black marketers.

More over, powerful bombs are produced and sold even in forest areas of war prone countries. There occurred several incidents all over the world, which speaks that the world organizations and world leaders are incapable of providing security to the people. The long-term wars are caused between the neighbor countries. For example, Burundi, Central African Republic, Democratic Republican of Congo, Rwanda, Uganda, Chad, Ethiopia, Eritrea, Somalia, Somaliland (Somalia) located in central Africa is fighting among them for grabbing land of other countries or capturing power. But innocent people are leaving their birthplace for employment elsewhere and to avoid war hazards each day. The governments in different countries have not yet changed their mindsets even during the twenty-first century. Military rulers of different countries like Myanmar are more interested to stabilize their positions at the cost of peace of the people and country. They spend massive quantum of own funds and borrowed funds for military expenses and military research. But peace can be achieved when wars can be stopped or decreased. War and peace cannot move together; development and destruction cannot march together. We have the power to bid good-bye to war forever.

The first step to achieve peace and to avoid war is to minimize arms production and a ban on international trade of arms arsenals and fighter planes etc. In this chapter, the world scenario of crises and arms trade have been analyzed to focus how the countries are sincerely trying to wage wars and underscoring world peace. However, we feel that world peace can be revived and crises can be solved through the world organisations, world leaders, religious centers, and the intelligentsias.

Reorganization of the United Nations

The aims of the United Nations are to maintain international peace and security and to cooperate in finding solutions for international problems. So this highest organization should undertake all possible steps to stabilize WORLD PEACE and solve all problems leading to WORLD WAR. It should prioritize and promulgate international laws with approval of member states. The United Nations should not be a poster organization; it should act as the WORLD GOVERNMENT of the 21st Century. The United Nations should be stronger legally, politically and economically. The UN should have four organs instead of six organs. The organs are:

(1)The United Nations Peace Council
(2)The United Nations War Council
(3)The United Nations Law Council, and
(4)The United Nations Secretariat

All the four organizations should be strengthened with statutory powers for ensuring permanent world peace. The present organs of the United Nations such as the General Assembly, the Security Council, the Economic and Social Council, the Trusteeship Council, the International Court of Justice should be accommodated in the above four organs or dismantled.

(1) The United Nations Peace Council would be represented by each country/state through its Permanent Members sponsored by the respective Governments to form the General Assembly. The working of the General Assembly should be limited to only 40 days in a year. But the Peace Council, War Council and Law Council should work round the year.

The United Nations Peace Council would nominate or appoint one UN Peace Representative in each state/ country to act on behalf of the UN for that state/country with an office. Moreover, the Peace Council may appoint or nominate special Representatives in problematic areas for specific purposes. The Peace Representatives would keep constant touch with the Government, people and sufferers. The United Nations Peace Council would constitute 40 percent of Members of General Assembly as its permanent Members, who would try to popularize and stabilize the peace process.

(2) The United Nations War Council would adopt all steps to stop war between nations. The UN is now unable to stop ongoing wars, conflicts, annexations and military rule in many countries.

The UN was unable to rescue Ms. Aung San Suu Kyi (A Nobel Laureate in Peace, 1991) in Myanmar (Burma) since last two decades. The UN is unable to recognize Tibet as a country since 1950 and its religious leader His Holiness the Dalai Lama (A Nobel Laureate in Peace, 1989) has taken asylum in India since 1959 (for the last half century). It is necessary to activate and energize the United Nations for very survival of humanity. Now Ms Suu Kyi is free and is active in politics in Myanmar.

The UN can make requisition of army from member states to wage war against any unruly country in order to achieve peace and humanity in the entire world. But it cannot be a spectator if a country attacks another country even for peace. The UN must save the World; must stop War and award peace to people. The UNO must stop 'religion-based war' through persuasion, aid, and warning or by force. The UN should control and regulate the production of Nuclear Weapons or it should ban Nuclear Weapons. The War Council should immediately form a Commission on International Boundaries. The International Atomic Energy Commission should function under this council.

The United Nations War Council would constitute 40 percent of Members of General Assembly as its permanent Members, who would try to stop and dissuade the warmonger countries not to wage war against the weak countries or face consequences. Even the terrorists attack the UN offices in Afghanistan and other places. On October 28, 2009, Taliban militants wearing suicide vests and police uniforms stormed a guesthouse used by UN staff in the heart of the Afghanistan capital Kabul, and killed 12 people including six UN staff. They also used grenades, rockets and machine guns. In short, the Taliban challenges the United Nations.

(3) The United Nations Law Council would promulgate international laws pertaining to economy, trade, commerce, banking, defense, investment, military cooperation, international organizations, acquisition of land and property, conversion of religion, bribery and corruption for awarding peace to the people. The International Court of Justice should be a part of this Council.

The United Nations Law Council should take up the problem of 'Debt Relief' and award a verdict provided the donors do not agree for 100 per cent debt relief within a specified period. The problem is that the donors have misled the debtor countries; governments of low-income countries have mis-utilized funds; and the numbers of hungry people have crossed one billion and other poor people have exceeded over two billion. Now, the allocation of funds for debt repayment is more than the budgetary expenses for education and healthcare in all the low-income countries. The United Nations Law Council would constitute 20 percent of Members of General Assembly as its permanent Members, who would try to make suitable laws for the unity of mankind and for enjoying peace, progress and prosperity of all countries.

(4)**The United Nations Secretariat** should be the main office of the UN for coordinating all offices and activities of the UN. All the UN Organizations on education, development, labour, agriculture, culture and health etc should be occluded sine die. Only committees may be formed for a purpose. The UNDP, UNESCO, UNIDO, UNCTAD, UNITAR, UNICEF, FAO, IFAD and other organizations are unwanted or less wanted appendages of the UN. These organizations work without achievements. The UN bears heavy expenditure for these unnecessary institutions. The UN can set up subsidiary World Committees on anti-illicit drugs trade, permanent settlement of international boundaries, settlement of refugees and internally displaced persons, anti-trafficking in persons and utilization of atomic energy to make a peaceful and secured world. The Member-States could revise the UN Charter at the earliest to make it more functional for the world community.

Conclusion

Military invasion is a war crime. The UN charter has incorporated war crimes and can appoint other UN organs or independent commissions to enquire; if there is war or warlike situations anywhere. The latest uprising is in Tibet. The UN should interfere in the matter. The UN is the highest organ in the world and 192 countries are voluntarily bound to the UN charter. So the UN can usher world peace by protecting human civilization, culture, peace and people.

The Iraqi problem could be solved through multilateral approach with a new political compact and Arab-Israel peace process with participation of UN Security Council, and governments of US, Syria, Iran, South Arabia, and Turkey. All international crises can be solved through adoption of middle path. We have to achieve something by sacrificing something. Achievements through this procedure would render long-term benefits and peace.

The UN should be made more powerful and impartial to render justice to all. The VETO power vested on different countries should be withdrawn to render justice to the poor countries and poor people. Let their voices be heard by the General Assembly and let them feel that justice has been awarded to them.

The developed countries would enjoy peace throughout if they show sympathy to the poor countries and assist them in crises. These countries should not force the poor countries to borrow funds for infrastructure development and should avoid revenge on countries, which do not surrender to them. The developed countries should give a call **'March towards World Peace'** instead of 'War on Terrorism'. World peace could be achieved without high expenditure, human sacrifice and tension. We feel that World Peace is possible and inevitable.

Chapter VI

BAN NUCLEAR WEAPONS TO AVOID WORLD WAR III

A MARCH TOWARDS WORLD PEACE

Peace is the whole truth that wishes to enrapture humanity. War is the whole falsehood that wants to capture humanity. Peace begins in the soul and ends in the heart. War begins in the mind and ends in the body.

Sri Chinmoy in 'Songs of the Soul'

The world in the twenty-first century faces the greatest challenge to world peace because of a mad rush for acquiring the title of 'Nuclear state' even by poor countries like Iran, India and Pakistan. The USA, Russia, United Kingdom, France, Japan, Israel, and Germany are advanced nuclear countries. Scientific advances have contributed the threats of nuclear weapons, which are made simply for nuclear warfare. The world knows that nuclear explosion causes damage through intense thermal radiation, a blast wave, and widespread contamination of the environment, genetic damage. The biological warfare causes incurable diseases and chemical warfare could cause blindness, madness and deaths not only in the area of blast but also in the non-belligerent states. The lives of future generations become more bleak and harmful. The destruction of humanity and civilization would be immeasurable, if nuclear research is continued. When 850 million of people are underfed, illiterate, and live in slums, a single country spends more than US $ 350 billon on research for biological warfare. The world needs peace and not war. It is astonishing that developed countries are spending more funds for nuclear, biological and chemical research for defense purposes and undertake international trade in weapons of mass destruction.

A number of Conventions were organized and Treaties were signed to save the world from nuclear devastations. Some of these are: Geneva Protocol, 1925, Biological Conventions, Treaty on Non-Proliferation Nuclear Weapons, US/Russia Bilateral agreement, Comprehensive Test Ban treaty, Anti-Ballistic Missile Treaty, START I and START II.

Moreover, Commission reports have been published for elimination of nuclear weapons to save the human species and human civilization. In 1982, a commission headed by Prime Minister Olof Palme of Sweden submitted a report entitled 'Common Security'. In 1996, the Australian Government published 'Report of the Canberra Commission on Elimination of Nuclear Weapons'. In 1999, the Tokyo Forum for Nuclear Non-Proliferation and Disarmament published 'Action Plan' dealing with nuclear disarmament, non-proliferations and terrorism. All the reports aim at elimination of nuclear warfare and establishment of world peace for welfare of international community and common man.

In the chapter only 4 reports are cited on nuclear weapons. These are:

(a) Nuclear weapons around the world
(b) The Canberra Commission on the Elimination of Nuclear Weapons and
(c) Weapons of Terror Freeing the World of Nuclear, Biological and Chemical Arms
(d) Growing Nuclear stock piles require new security measures

The first information sheet is presented to highlight the danger that could cause immense damage to the people of the whole world.

The other two reports on 'Elimination of Nuclear Weapons' could possibly save the living beings on earth. So the United Nations must have to take up specific actions on these valuable reports. The last report on 'growing nuclear stockpiles' highlights the need for urgent solutions. Moreover, an immediate action on 'Towards a world without nukes' highlights the grave situation the world faces now. Unless nuclear weapons are banned, the earth cannot be saved and world peace cannot be anticipated. Let us hope that the world leaders would take up steps to stop destruction and to build and strengthen WORLD PEACE on permanent basis.

(A)
Nuclear weapons around the World

Today there are nine nuclear-armed states: the United States, Russia, the United Kingdom, France, China, Israel, India, Pakistan and North Korea. The first five of these states were declared as nuclear-weapon states when the Nuclear Non-Proliferation Treaty entered into force. Israel, India and Pakistan, which are not NPT parties, acquired their nuclear weapons subsequently, although Israel has never acknowledged the existence of its arsenal.

North Korea tested a nuclear device in 2006 and declared itself a nuclear-weapon state, and tested another in 2009. In addition to these nine states, US nuclear weapons are deployed in six European states: Belgium, Germany, Italy, the Netherlands, Turkey and the United Kingdom. However, recent reports suggest that the last remaining US nuclear weapons in the United Kingdom were removed from Lake Heath Air Force Base in 2008.

Nuclear weapons are also aboard warships on international water.

There are approximately 23,300 nuclear weapons in the world's arsenals.

Of these almost 96 per cent are in the United States and Russia. Forty-four states in the world have the capacity to develop nuclear weapons through their nuclear power reactors and research reactors.

Nuclear forces in 2009
United States — 9400
Russia — 13,000
United Kingdom — 160
France — 300
China — 186
India — 60–70
Pakistan — 60
Israel — 80
North Korea — 1–10
Total — 23,330 [87]

American nuclear forces: In January 2009, the US nuclear arsenal was estimated at 9400 nuclear warheads. Of these 2700 were operational. The US nuclear programme consists of three parts: intercontinental ballistic missiles, submarine-launched

[87] Source: SIPRI

ballistic missiles and bombers. The United States also holds approximately 500 tactical nuclear weapons.

Russian nuclear forces: Russia has the largest nuclear weapons arsenal in the world. As of early 2009, Russia was estimated to have approximately 4834 nuclear warheads in its operational stockpile and 8166 in reserve or awaiting dismantlement, for a total of approximately 13,000 nuclear weapons. The Russian nuclear programme, like the US programme, consists of three parts: intercontinental ballistic missiles, submarine-launched ballistic missiles and bombers.

British nuclear forces: The UK arsenal consists of one nuclear weapon system: a fleet of nuclear-powered submarines equipped with ballistic missiles. Each submarine is equipped with 48 nuclear warheads, each of which can be fired in a separate direction. Each warhead has a firepower equivalent to 100 kilotons, which equals eight times the yield of the atom bomb dropped over Hiroshima in 1945. The British government announced in 2005 that it has fewer than 200 operationally available nuclear warheads.

French nuclear forces: The French nuclear arsenal is estimated at 300 nuclear warheads. The Federation of American Scientists notes that France, like other nuclear-weapon states, probably has inactive nuclear warheads in a reserve. The French arsenal consists of two nuclear weapon systems: submarine-launched ballistic missiles and air-launched, intermediate-distance missiles. Three of France's nuclear submarines are equipped with 16 ballistic missiles each, and each missile has a capacity to launch six warheads. A fourth nuclear submarine, Le Terrible, was inaugurated in March 2008. France also has about 60 nuclear warheads for delivery from bombers.

Chinese nuclear forces: China has a total stockpile of about 240 nuclear warheads, of which 186 are operational. China's nuclear arsenal consists of approximately 80 land-based missiles with the capacity to carry one nuclear warhead each. The state also has one nuclear submarine equipped with 12 single warhead missiles. A small number of nuclear warheads—approximately 40 —can be launched by bombers.

Indian nuclear forces: India tested a nuclear device in May 1998. The state is not party to the Nuclear Non-Proliferation Treaty and is considered a de-facto nuclear-weapon state. The number of warheads in the Indian nuclear arsenal has not been made public by the Indian government, making an estimate difficult. India has produced enough weapons-grade plutonium to produce some 100 nuclear warheads. It is estimated that India's arsenal consists of 60 to 70 nuclear warheads, mainly air-borne.

Pakistani nuclear forces: In May 1998, after India's nuclear-weapon tests, Pakistan tested a series of nuclear weapons over two days to show its nuclear capability. Like India, Pakistan is not a party to the NPT. The country is quickly developing and upgrading its nuclear arsenal. It is difficult to state the exact size and composition of the Pakistani arsenal, as the government has not made any information public. It is estimated that Pakistan's nuclear arsenal holds 60 warheads, for delivery by bombers and land-based ballistic missiles.

Israeli nuclear forces: Israel's nuclear weapons have been called "the world's worst-kept secret". It is generally accepted that Israel possesses nuclear weapons, although Israeli officials have never confirmed their existence. The nuclear doctrine of Israel is based on the concept of ambiguity. The exact size of the Israeli nuclear arsenal is unknown. It has been estimated that the Israeli arsenal holds approximately 80 warheads.

North Korean nuclear weapons: There is a great level of uncertainty surrounding the North Korean nuclear weapon program. The country has operated a reactor producing nuclear weapons-grade plutonium since 1986. Independent experts claim it has produced about 43kg of separated plutonium. Depending on technical knowledge and the desired yield, North Korea may have produced something between 5 and 10 nuclear warheads. It is uncertain if it has produced nuclear warheads that actually can be delivered by a missile.

North Korea conducted its first underground nuclear test on October 9, 2006. The expected blast was less than 1 kiloton, which can be compared to the bomb dropped on Hiroshima in 1945 with a blast effect of 19 kiloton. The test most likely did not achieve the expected effect, yet showed that North Korea has mastered the nuclear fuel cycle and has the capacity to produce at least more primitive nuclear weapons. It conducted a second nuclear test in 2009.

North Korea was a member of the Non-Proliferation Treaty but announced its withdrawal in early 2003. Only a few months later, North Korean officials revealed for the first time during a roundtable talk with the United States that the country had produced nuclear weapons. It also stated that it possessed and would consider exporting plutonium rods unless the United States would accept bilateral negotiations. Negotiations with North Korea, which have been ongoing for many years with long periods of standstills and cooperation problems, have been conducted under the so-called Six-Party Talks among North Korea, the United States, Japan, South Korea, China and Russia.

Nuclear-weapon programmes: In 2003 Libya revealed that it had a far-reaching nuclear-weapon programme and enough uranium centrifuges to produce enough highly enriched uranium for nuclear weapons within a few years. Libyan leader Muammar al-Gaddafi, however, made clear that his country would give up its nuclear weapons plans. With the assistance of the United States, the United Kingdom and the International Atomic Energy Agency, the Libyan nuclear-weapon programme was dismantled.

Iraq also had a clandestine nuclear-weapon programme during the 1990s, which was revealed by IAEA inspectors. The nuclear-weapon programme was dismantled and, in its final report of 1998, the IAEA announced that no material or technological prerequisites existed for Iraqi resumption of its nuclear-weapon programme.

After the dissolution of the Soviet Union, nuclear weapons were deployed in four newly independent states: Russia, Belarus, Ukraine and Kazakhstan. The latter three decided to surrender the nuclear weapons on their territories and joined the NPT as non-nuclear-weapon states. All former Soviet nuclear weapons were inherited by Russia.

South Africa is the only state ever to possess nuclear weapons and voluntarily give them up in order to join the NPT as a non-nuclear-weapon state. The country had a nuclear-weapon programme during the 1970s and 1980s. It produced six nuclear devices and had a seventh under development when it abandoned the nuclear option in the 1990s.

NATO nuclear sharing: Under the NATO nuclear-sharing programme, the United States today has about 350 nuclear weapons deployed in six European NATO Member States. One of these, the United Kingdom, is a nuclear-weapon state, while the other five—Belgium, Italy, the Netherlands, Germany and

Turkey —are non-nuclear-weapon states. The NATO nuclear doctrine has hardly changed during the last decades, despite the changes in the security situation after the end of the Cold War. NATO conducted a review of its nuclear policy in 2003 and concluded that the nuclear weapons deployed in Europe were still necessary to protect European security.

NATO's non-nuclear members are, to different extents, involved in the nuclear policy of the military alliance. Some states do not allow the placement of nuclear weapons on their territories in times of peace. Other states have US nuclear weapons deployed on their territories to be used if needed by the United States and/or its own air force. All NATO member states participate in the NATO Nuclear Planning Group, where implementation of the nuclear policy and organization of exercises are discussed. France is an exception, having pulled out of the NATO military structure in 1966.

NATO's nuclear cooperation has been criticized for violating the NPT, or at least going against the spirit of the treaty. Article I of the NPT establishes that the five nuclear-weapon states parties — the United States, Russia, the United Kingdom, France and China — are not allowed to transfer nuclear weapons to "any recipient whatsoever".

Under Article II, non-nuclear-weapon states are not allowed to produce or in any other way acquire nuclear weapons. Many states parties believe that NATO nuclear cooperation is a violation of these provisions of the NPT. The United States and NATO contest this conclusion. NATO states are also criticized for violating the NPT, as European non-nuclear-weapon states under the NATO nuclear sharing can be allowed access to and control over US nuclear weapons placed in Europe.

Nuclear weapon free zones: Nuclear-weapon-free zones at a minimum prohibit the stationing, testing, use and development of nuclear weapons inside a particular geographical region, whether that is a single state, a region or an area defined solely by international agreements. Such zones have been described in many fora, including the Non-Proliferation Treaty and the UN General Assembly, as positive steps towards nuclear disarmament.

Today there are nuclear-weapon-free zones in Latin America and the Caribbean, the southern Pacific, Southeast Asia, Central Asia and Africa. More than 50 per cent of the Earth's surface today comprises such zones (including 99 per cent of all land in the Southern Hemisphere). One hundred and nineteen of the world's approximately 195 states belong to a nuclear-weapon-free zone, and 1.9 billion people live in such zones. States that belong to a nuclear-weapon-free zone are prohibited from producing, testing, stockpiling or acquiring nuclear weapons, and they cannot have nuclear weapons deployed in their territories.

Nuclear weapons in space: There is a big difference between militarization and weaponization of outer space. Space has been militarized since the first communication satellite was launched, and today armed forces all over the world rely on satellites for surveillance, warning systems and navigation. While space is heavily militarized, so far it is not weaponized. The Outer Space Treaty of 1967 prohibits the placement of nuclear weapons and other weapons of mass destruction in orbit in outer space. Nuclear - weapons testing in outer space is prohibited, and celestial bodies such as the moon and the planets may only be used for peaceful purposes.

Even if the existing legally binding agreements limit deployment of weapons, use of force and military activities in certain parts of outer space to some extent, these are seen by some states as too limited to prevent weaponization of outer space. Scientific development and technological progress call for strengthening existing instruments or negotiating new treaties. The Weapons of Mass Destruction Commission recommended a Review Conference of the Outer Space Treaty to strengthen it and extend its scope. Some states argue for a new treaty on the Prevention of an Arms Race in Outer Space (PAROS). The United States argues that an arms race in outer space does not yet exist, and it is therefore unnecessary to take action on the issue. Some delegations and experts have thus argued that PAROS is not the most relevant treaty to pursue. Discussion in the Conference on Disarmament has recently focused instead on prevention of the placement of weapons in outer space. Changing the language in this way circumvents the US argument against PAROS.[88]

(B)
The Canberra Commission on the Elimination of Nuclear Weapons

The Nuclear Weapon Debate

The Canberra Commission is persuaded that immediate and determined efforts need to be made to rid the world of nuclear weapons and the threat they pose to it. The Commission acknowledges that the debate between those for and against the elimination of nuclear weapons is not new. Both sides claim that their positions are rational and moral. But the circumstances that created and sustained the nuclear arms race of the Cold War have all but disappeared, and an uncertain global strategic future lies ahead. This uniquely favourable moment should be seized to eliminate the class of weapons, which, alone, can destroy all life on earth.

---

[88] ICAN around the World

The Commission believes that to be compelling, the case for a nuclear weapon free world must be convincingly argued from two sides of the issue: why these weapons should be eliminated; and a rebuttal of the rationale most commonly cited for retaining them. Simultaneously the security concerns of the present day including, in particular, nuclear proliferation must be addressed.

The case for elimination of nuclear weapons is based on three major arguments:

(a) The destructiveness of nuclear weapons is so great they have no military utility against a comparably equipped opponent, other than the belief that they deter that opponent from using nuclear weapons. Use of the weapons against a non-nuclear weapon opponent is politically and morally indefensible.
(b) The indefinite deployment of the weapons carries a high risk of their ultimate use through accident or inadvertence.
(c) The possession of the weapons by some states stimulates other nations to acquire them, reducing the security of all.

The destructive power of nuclear weapons dwarfs that of any conventional weapon or non-nuclear weapon of mass destruction. More energy can be released in one microsecond from a single nuclear weapon than all the energy released by conventional weapons used in all wars throughout history. The atomic bombs detonated over Hiroshima and Nagasaki in August 1945, while by today's standards of relatively low yield, in a matter of seconds erased both cities. In 1945 nuclear weapons became a new part of the international context and the world had to cope as best it could with a radically changed calculus of national and international security.

The world has lived under the shadow of the mushroom cloud continuously since 1945, and the cumulative psychological impact has been overwhelmingly negative. The threat that the existence of nuclear weapons poses to the future of the human species and the global environment remains undiminished. It must not be ignored or forgotten by the international community.

In the 1960s, the world looked at the prospect of dozens of nuclear weapon states, recoiled and rejected it. The result was the Treaty on the Non-Proliferation of Nuclear Weapons (NPT) of 1968 with its promise of a world free of these weapons. The overall success of the NPT and other nuclear non-proliferation regimes has been gratifying, but it has been hard won, and is by no means guaranteed. The prospects of a renewal of horizontal proliferation have become real.

The US decision in 1991 to terminate entirely the 30-year practice of maintaining a portion of its strategic bomber force on peacetime alert further reduced the exposure of these unsheltered forces to the likelihood of accident or deliberate damage. However salutary these steps to reduce alert levels, and despite the transformation of relations between the United States and Russia, the fact remains that both of these states, and other nuclear weapon states, maintain thousands of nuclear warheads on continuous alert. This perpetuation of the most overtly hostile and risky aspects of the Cold War defies logic. It needlessly prolongs an atmosphere of mistrust and the potential for accidents. It is entirely out of keeping with the urgent interest of fully integrating Russia into the institutions and norms of a global community moving rapidly toward democratic government and free and open markets.

Limited Military Utility

Nuclear weapons have long been understood to be too destructive and non-discriminatory to secure discrete objectives on the battlefield. They came increasingly to be regarded as weapons to be employed only in extremis, and then with the dismaying knowledge that the ensuing consequences would obviate whatever military or political objective prompted their use. As early as the 1970s, under the provisions of the Strategic Arms Limitation Treaties (SALT) and subsequently according to the obligations of the Strategic Arms Reduction Treaties (START), the United States and Russia began to constrain and reduce the capabilities and size of their strategic forces. In addition, they began to reduce the dangers of tactical nuclear weapons. These weapons have been largely withdrawn from overseas deployment and removed from ships and sea-based aircraft to stockpiles on their own territory.

Even at the height of the Cold War, the ostensible use of tactical or battlefield nuclear weapons to prevail against a conventional attack; the 'flexible response' strategy, never satisfied the conflicting concerns of NATO allies nor was perceived as guaranteeing either a controllable nuclear exchange or ensuring an automatic link to United States strategic nuclear forces. Indeed, whether nuclear weapons were the decisive factor in or superfluous to the deterring of Warsaw Pact aggression against Western Europe has been a matter of contention for some time. What is clear, however, is that possession of nuclear weapons has not prevented wars, in various regions, which directly or indirectly involve the major powers. They were deemed unsuitable for use even when those powers suffered humiliating military setbacks (as in Korea) and, ultimately, defeat (as in Vietnam and

Over the period of the Cold War, deterrence proved to be an open-ended, highly risky and very expensive strategy for dealing with the reality of nuclear weapons in a world of nation states with enduring, deep-seated animosities. Conversely, given the origins and peculiar ideological character of the East-West conflict, the extreme alienation of the principal antagonists, the vast infrastructures put in place and the sense of imminent, mortal danger on both sides, deterrence may have served to at least introduce a critical caution in superpower relationships. Whatever the final judgement may be with respect to this era of unprecedented threats and risks, in the post-Cold War environment, the argument for deterrence is largely circular. Its utility implies and indeed flows from an assumption of the continued existence of nuclear weapons, but in a world of dramatically reduced global tensions. The only military utility that remains for nuclear weapons is in deterring their use by others. That utility implies the continued existence of nuclear weapons. It would disappear if nuclear weapons were eliminated.

Reversing Nuclear Proliferation

The proliferation of nuclear weapons is amongst the most immediate security challenges facing the international community. It is a palpable threat to the security of both nuclear weapon states and non-nuclear weapon states. The inherent risks attending the possession of nuclear weapons as recounted above can only multiply should the possession of nuclear weapons expand.

Security without Nuclear Weapons

For all the reasons outlined above, the world would be a much more secure place for everyone if there were no nuclear weapons. For forty years the two superpowers made Herculean efforts, at great cost, to integrate nuclear weapons into their respective national security postures - bigger warheads, smaller warheads, a greater diversity of delivery systems and launch platforms, and all manner of innovations in deterrence doctrine and declaratory postures. But nothing could alter the reality that each depended for its very existence on the rationality as well as the technical and organizational competence of its most bitter foe.

Nuclear weapons are either powerless to address or in some cases simply exacerbate the most prevalent threats to national security in today's world, including terrorism, ethnic conflicts, state disintegration, humanitarian disasters and economic crises. To help counter these security threats, states are crafting new cooperative strategies, institutions and mechanisms, both at the global and regional levels. Several states, most notably Argentina, Brazil, South Africa and Sweden, have revised their earlier assessment that a nuclear option provided a route to enhanced national security and international influence. Meanwhile, the vast majority of states have voluntarily rejected the nuclear weapon option while maintaining and enhancing their national security.

Nuclear weapons to some degree influence the security outlook of a wide range of states, not just the nuclear weapon states and other states with a nuclear weapon capability. The elimination of nuclear weapons will contribute to and facilitate important changes in the international security environment. Individual states can be reassured that the process of elimination does not undermine their security. Practical steps to achieve a nuclear weapon free world can be agreed and verified. In sum, the safe and verifiable elimination of nuclear weapons would make a major contribution to prospects for a more secure global community in the century to come.

A New Opportunity

The end of the Cold War has created a new climate for international action to eliminate nuclear weapons, a new opportunity. It must be exploited quickly or it will be lost. There has been no better opportunity since the beginning of the nuclear age. Permanent arsenals and proliferating nuclear powers will be the fate of the world if this opportunity is ignored. Nuclear weapons have not been used for 50 years but the risk is likely to become greater as time goes on. Nuclear weapons should not be nor should they be seen to be a natural or inevitable feature of the human society. If, on the other hand, nuclear weapons are accepted as a permanent feature of the international system, then states will inevitably develop new nuclear weapons and their associated delivery systems. The whole global community has a direct and fundamental interest in the elimination of nuclear weapons, and the regime, which manages that process and its outcome. The key responsibility lies with the nuclear weapon states themselves and in particular with the United States and Russia. The invigoration of the elimination process will depend on decisions, which they alone can make.

Rebutting the Case for Retaining Nuclear Weapons

The case for retaining nuclear weapons as instruments of national power continues to be very influential; people of great experience and authority remain unconvinced about the wisdom of elimination. Accordingly, the following rebuttal deals at some length with the arguments for retention. Nuclear Weapons have prevented and will continue to be needed to prevent war between the major powers. Perhaps the most important role claimed for nuclear weapons - beyond deterring the use of other nuclear weapons, is that they discourage recourse to war among the major powers and are thus a force for stability. The empirical evidence appears strong. The period 1870-1945 saw two World Wars and several briefs, confined but full-scale clashes between major states such as France and Germany in 1870, China and Japan in 1894-95, and Japan and Russia in 1904-5. Since 1945 there has been no direct clash between the recognized major powers (although China and the Soviet Union fought a brief border war in 1969). Many therefore contend that, for better or worse, it has taken the unique sobering capacity of nuclear weapons to break the entrenched cycle of war between the world's most powerful states.

This broad historical correlation between nuclear weapons and the absence of war between the major powers is seen as being decisively reinforced by the belief of some that nuclear weapons played a vital part in deterring the Soviet Union from pushing the Iron Curtain in Europe further to the West. The experience in Europe in 1945-90 in fact lies at the heart of the view that nuclear weapons have, on balance, played a positive role. While it must be accepted the beliefs were deeply held that the Soviet Union aspired to invade and occupy Western Europe, and that nuclear weapons deterred it from doing so, the evidence for those beliefs is now unclear.

Nuclear weapons protect the credibility of security assurances to Allies.

It is argued that the credibility of security assurances extended to third parties requires the continued existence of nuclear weapons. Extended deterrence was formulated in the first instance to address circumstances in Western Europe, as a means of transposing United States power and negating the proximity and ready reinforcement capability of the Soviet Union's larger conventional forces. The gravity of the United States' political commitment to defend its allies in Europe and also in Asia and the Pacific lay in its declared preparedness to expose its own territory to nuclear attack. One consideration never formally declared but not disguised with any vigour, was to dampen incentives in Germany and Japan to become nuclear weapon states themselves.

The Canberra Commission does not propose that any nuclear weapon state should eliminate its nuclear forces unilaterally. Moreover, extended deterrence assurances in the form of collective defense arrangements will remain as part of stable security arrangements. Extended nuclear deterrence, however, cannot be used as a justification for maintaining nuclear arsenals in perpetuity, and the security and non-proliferation function of extended nuclear deterrence in any case will no longer apply in a nuclear weapon free world. Allies of the United States have lent their strong support to the NPT's stated objective of nuclear disarmament. Their interest in collective security arrangements based on conventional forces is sure to continue after nuclear weapons have been eliminated.

Nuclear Weapons Deter the Use of other Weapons of Mass Destruction

Weapons of mass destruction embrace chemical and biological as well as nuclear weapons. The claim is still sometimes made that nuclear weapons are an effective deterrent against them all and constitute the only guarantee of national security against threats posed by such weapons. All the nuclear weapon states have formulated negative security assurances, statements that set out the circumstances in which they would not use nuclear weapons. The United States declared in 1982 that it would "not use nuclear weapons against any non-nuclear weapon state except in the case of an attack on the United States, its territories or armed forces, or its allies, by such a state allied to or associated with a nuclear weapon state in carrying out or sustaining the attack". The clear inference that can be drawn from this statement, which, together with that of the United Kingdom, is the most conditional negative assurance offered by a nuclear weapon state, is that a non-aligned non-nuclear weapon state acting on its own but using biological weapons or chemical weapons against the United States should not fear retaliation with nuclear weapons. In other words, the US and the other nuclear weapon states signaled, through these security assurances that the only circumstances in which, it would be appropriate to use or threaten to use nuclear weapons was when nuclear weapons were present, directly or indirectly, on the opposing side.

The United States has not failed to capitalize on the fact that it has nuclear weapons and that a non-nuclear adversary might doubt its ordinances of self-denial. In 1990 the United States did not discourage Iraq from the view that it might be subject to nuclear retaliation if it used chemical weapons to protect its occupation of Kuwait. Iraq's Foreign Minister subsequently asserted that the nuclear capability of the coalition forces cast a shadow over the means the regime determined it could sensibly employ to resist eviction from Kuwait. But the United States had means other than veiled nuclear retaliation to deter Iraq from using weapons of mass destruction, for example, the prospect of Iraq's utter devastation through massive conventional bombings or changing the main objective of the war from liberating Kuwait to toppling the Iraqi Government. Furthermore, the United States would have been aware that, if Iraq had raised the stakes and used chemical weapons, the consequences of nuclear retaliation by the United States might have been even more far reaching than the threat it was seeking to deter.

No nuclear weapon state has been or is prepared to declare as a matter of national policy that it would respond to the use of biological or chemical weapons with nuclear weapons. Whatever incidental contribution they might consider nuclear weapons to make in deterring the use of biological and chemical weapons (and it is not difficult to find high-level statements short of formal policy declarations seeking to establish this connection), the nuclear weapon states have not specifically included this in rationales for the maintenance of nuclear forces. They have evidently also taken full account of the fact that use of nuclear weapons in response to use or threat of use of other weapons of mass destruction would cross an important psychological as well as military threshold, making the management of future conflicts even more uncertain. The remarkable advances in the capabilities of conventional armaments both already achieved and in prospect, can be expected on the whole to confirm this self-imposed limitation on the utility of nuclear weapons.

An increasing number of states have in recent years come to be concerned at the threat of chemical and biological weapons. The issue has become enmeshed with policy responses to proposals for nuclear weapon free zones. The 1996 Treaty of Pelindaba provided an opportunity for nuclear weapon states to reaffirm to African states the assurances they have previously given. As argued in the case for the elimination of nuclear weapons, the solution to these concerns lies in the strengthening and effective implementation of and universal adherence to the Chemical Weapons Convention and the Biological Weapons Convention, with particular emphasis on early detection of untoward developments. The response to any violation should be a multilateral one.

Nuclear Weapons Confer Political Status and Influence

It is said of nuclear weapons, with some justification, that their possession delivers important benefits in the form of status, influence and autonomy in world affairs. All of these are strong motives for states as well as individuals. Pressures to retain or acquire nuclear weapons for these reasons must be taken seriously. Yet the growth in influence of several non-nuclear weapon states tends to refute this proposition.

The example most frequently cited of the correlation between nuclear weapons and status is the fact that the five permanent members of the United Nations Security Council, the only members with the power of veto, are also the nuclear weapon states. None of the five, however, secured this status because of nuclear weapons. Not even the United States was a confirmed nuclear power when the Charter of the United Nations was signed on 26 June 1945. And today, it is beyond doubt that any expansion of the permanent membership of the Security Council will not be on the basis of preserving the nexus between such membership and the possession of nuclear weapons.

Nuclear weapons cannot exclusively be relied on for defense, especially if potential adversaries also have them. So the cost of the nuclear forces, including their continued modernization, must essentially be added to conventional means of defense. In the cases of the United Kingdom, France and China, the need to support extensive nuclear programs has taken resources and skilled personnel away from conventional forces. The diversion to military purposes of a disproportionately large share of a country's research and development capability is a significant factor in explaining differences in the rate of economic growth that states can sustain over the medium and longer term. In part it explains the pronounced shifts that have occurred over the post-war period in the relative economic weight of the major states, and how Japan and Germany, in particular, have improved their position markedly relative to all the nuclear weapon states. The pressures to refine and update delivery systems have eased although missiles, aircraft and ballistic missile submarines will require expensive maintenance and replacement from time to time. On the other hand the outlook for the medium and longer term is less optimistic. In the absence of a commitment to eliminate nuclear weapons more countries are likely to acquire them, prompting costly competition for at least a qualitative edge. And even a modest increase in the membership of the nuclear club must sharply diminish whatever benefits these weapons are felt to deliver in terms of status.

Nuclear Weapons Provide Effective Defense at Lower Cost

It is sometimes argued that nuclear weapons are cost-effective and make possible a more economical defense posture. This view was briefly entertained in the early years of the nuclear era when the United States had a nuclear monopoly or a huge preponderance in deliverable nuclear weapons and when there was a temptation to discount the horror of Hiroshima and Nagasaki and regard nuclear weapons as an important but basically evolutionary development p; just a bigger bomb.

While the US/NATO strategy of 'massive retaliation' was an echo of this view, it is important to note that the United States simultaneously decided to reverse the drastic demobilization that occurred after World War II and to maintain indefinitely large standing conventional forces. The Korean War strongly reinforced this policy position. Much the same happened in the other nuclear weapon states. It was quickly recognized that the circumstances in which nuclear weapons could beneficially be employed were extremely narrow if, indeed, they existed at all. Rather than nuclear weapons being regarded as a substitute for conventional forces, the overwhelmingly dominant line of reasoning has been to maintain the strongest practicable conventional capabilities and thereby maximize the firebreak between conventional war, should it break out, and nuclear war.

No accurate data exists on the recurring or cumulative cost of the nuclear posture for any of the nuclear weapon states, though without doubt a realistic full costing would yield staggering figures. Such a costing would embrace the production of fissile material; the fabrication of nuclear weapons; environmental clean up; testing; the design, development, production and operation of delivery systems; the command, control and communications architecture; and the panoply of early warning systems.

Nuclear Weapons Deter and if Necessary Can Defeat Large Scale Conventional Aggression by Regional Powers

The view is held that in a prospective multi-polar world with a significant diffusion of economic, technological and military power, nuclear weapons could prove valuable in deterring and if necessary defeating large scale conventional aggression by regional powers, perhaps occurring in more than one theatre at the same time. This presupposes that a nuclear weapon state would find it morally and politically acceptable to use nuclear weapons against a non-nuclear foe.

This contention is unrealistic. Even in the most favourable circumstances, where there has been no prospect of retaliation, political, moral and military inhibitions have excluded the use of nuclear weapons. Twice during the Korean War, when US forces were in desperate straits and when North Korea and China had no nuclear capability and the Soviet Union only a relatively small one, the US President recoiled from the moral and political costs of resorting to nuclear weapons. When French forces were besieged at Dien Bien Phu in 1954, serious consideration was given in the United States to providing assistance through use of low-yield nuclear weapons. But in these and other instances, including in the later American involvement in Vietnam, self-deterrence proved as effective as mutual deterrence.

The nuclear weapon states have concluded that it is in their interests to formulate negative security assurances that formally proclaim the inadmissibility of the use or threat of use of nuclear weapons in circumstances where the aggressor is not a nuclear weapon state and is not being actively supported by a nuclear weapon state. It is also plain that any attempt to unshackle nuclear weapons through contemplating a role for them in conventional regional conflicts would be shortsighted in the extreme. This would inevitably and significantly intensify proliferation pressures.

Deep-Seated Regional Disputes Will Always Frustrate Universal Agreement on the Elimination of Nuclear Weapons

It is sometimes contended that even if the nuclear weapon states saw net advantage in the complete elimination of nuclear weapons, the necessary universal commitment to this goal would be frustrated by the states involved in the most intractable regional disputes. The two key examples given are the disputes between Israel and the Arab states, and between India and Pakistan. But, without question, the overt nuclearisation of these disputes would complicate them further and make any genuine reconciliation vastly more difficult. The states concerned would be locked into very expensive and dangerous nuclear deterrent relationships, with the familiar incessant pressures to increase and diversify the nuclear arsenals. The actual use of nuclear weapons, whether by design or by accident, would exacerbate these disputes beyond measure and make more likely the direct involvement of the major powers.

It is clearly in the interests of the nuclear weapon states, and substantially within their capacity and that of the international community, to address the concerns of the few states that may believe that a nuclear capability is indispensable to their security. Strengthening conflict mediation procedures and providing additional security assurances will be in the interests of both nuclear and non-nuclear weapon states.

The striking development, post-Cold War, of increasing global interdependence has led most states to appreciate the potential of seeking security in cooperation with rather than in confrontation against their neighbours. Though cautiously in some cases, many states are now exploring the potential for dialogue, transparency and other trust and confidence building measures with their neighbours as a more reliable and effective means of providing for their security than confrontation or deterrence. Furthermore, the commitment to the goal of a nuclear weapon free world should reinforce the determination of states to strengthen collective and cooperative means of addressing their security concerns.

The Elimination of Nuclear Weapons is Unverifiable; Cheating and Breakout Will Occur:

The elimination of nuclear weapons will not be possible without the development of adequate verification. A political judgement will be needed on whether the levels of assurance possible from the verification regime are sufficient. All existing arms control and disarmament agreements have required political judgements of this nature because no verification system provides absolute certainty. This situation has not prevented the international community acting in the area of nuclear and other weapons of mass destruction first with the NPT and the International Atomic Energy Agency (IAEA) safeguards system, then the CWC and the Comprehensive Test Ban Treaty (CTBT).

The nature of nuclear weapons, the secrecy that has surrounded their development and uncertainties about total amounts of nuclear material produced for weapons, will make it very difficult, or in the view of some impossible, to be confident that states which have operated large scale military nuclear programs have made full declarations of their holdings of nuclear weapons and fissile material. The possession by a state of a number of nuclear weapons and the means to deliver them in an otherwise nuclear weapon free world would present the state concerned with a powerful coercive instrument. While such a development is considered a significant risk it is hard to envisage the nuclear weapon states totally eliminating their arsenals. Confidence in the verification arrangements will have to apply to the nuclear programs of the declared nuclear weapon states and the undeclared and threshold nuclear weapon states.

Nuclear disarmament will be achieved in stages, and the decision point on whether verification is adequate for complete elimination is unlikely to be reached for some time. The potential uncertainty about whether a verification regime can be developed to provide sufficient confidence for final elimination should not be allowed to divert attention from the benefits of making an early start on practical steps toward a nuclear weapon free world. Development and implementation of the verification arrangements is needed for each step toward elimination will provide immediate benefit through reducing the dangers posed by nuclear weapons and the threat of nuclear proliferation including nuclear terrorism. If it were to take a long time for the verification system to deliver the levels of confidence needed for total elimination, a world of small residual arsenals would, in the meantime, be a safer place than at present although the dangers of nuclear proliferation and a renewed arms race would remain. Movement to this penultimate stage of nuclear disarmament would establish circumstances in which states could conclude, with increasing conviction over time, that nuclear weapons are not relevant to their security, thereby eliminating any remaining incentive to cheat.

It should be recognized that a verification regime is composed of both its material and technical features, which should be of the highest order attainable, and the common political and legal commitments, which support it. This creates the climate of confidence essential to any verification regime. An inclusive approach to verification can increase levels of assurance. In the case of verification for a nuclear weapon free world, technical verification can be supplemented by measures such as transparency in nuclear activity, relevant national intelligence information passed to verification bodies, an enhanced role for individuals in verification and application of effective export controls.

A number of factors can be identified which will act in favour of development of adequate verification arrangements for a nuclear weapon free world. First, because the nuclear weapon scientific industrial complex is a tightly regulated governmental enterprise, there is an increased probability that extensive records of nuclear weapons and weapons fissile material production will be available. This is not to diminish the magnitude of the task of verifying the completeness of states' declarations of holdings of weapons and weapons nuclear material, and records can of course be destroyed or falsified.

A second consideration is the nearly thirty years of experience accumulated in verifying compliance with the NPT. The IAEA safeguards system offers a proven and evolving system for delivering a high degree of assurance that safeguarded nuclear material remains in peaceful use. Action necessary to improve the IAEA's capacity to detect undeclared nuclear activity is being taken and the Agency has expertise in verifying declarations of previously un-safeguarded nuclear programs, including its work in Iraq, the DPRK (North Korea) and South Africa after that country renounced nuclear weapons.

Third, there is the experience of the SALT, START, INF, CFE and CWC agreements that individually and collectively demonstrate the powerful influence that political will can exert over what is desirable and possible in terms of verification. In the 1980s, the arms control agenda was transformed by the negotiation, in particular, of the INF (Intermediate-range Nuclear Forces) and the CFE agreements. Prior to these treaties, the scope of arms control was, with the major exception of IAEA safeguards inspections, basically limited to arrangements that could be verified by so-called 'national technical means', that is, by the information that each side could extract without the cooperation of the other.

Once it had been determined politically that both sides really wanted the outcomes in question, the realm of verification expanded beyond recognition to include on-site inspections and voluntary transparency and cooperative measures. In a similar vein the verification regime supporting the CWC broke significant new ground in response to the scale and complexity of the challenge, the harnessing of new technologies for verification purposes and the forging of a partnership, worldwide, between governments and the chemical industry. These agreements show that verification capabilities can grow to support the objective when that objective is determined unequivocally to be in the political and security interests of all concerned.

In short, the world community has had 50 years of experience with nuclear weapons. In this period much of its effort, including of those members of the community, who have owned nuclear weapons, has been directed towards protecting itself from their destructive power. Vertical proliferation, the urge of nuclear weapon states to add to and perfect their arsenals has been a major cause of the problem of living with nuclear weapons. Horizontal proliferation, the urge of other states to acquire this perceived means of enhancing their security, has also been and remains of great concern. It has been argued that nuclear weapons have reinforced caution in the conduct of relationships between the major powers. But their existence carries the inherent risk of their use, which would inevitably have catastrophic results. The only complete defence against such catastrophe is the elimination of nuclear weapons and the assurance that they will never be produced again. Inertia and complacency should not be permitted to prevent the international community from reaching this goal.

Steps to Eliminate Nuclear Weapons

The elimination of nuclear weapons must be a global endeavour involving all states. The impetus and driving force however must come from the nuclear weapon states and particularly the United States and Russia. A decisive signal from these longstanding nuclear powers that the risks associated with nuclear weapons far outweigh the presumed benefits would be of historic importance. Indeed, such a definitive commitment to a nuclear weapon free world would accelerate a course of events set in motion well before the Cold War ended.

Movement toward a nuclear weapon free world has begun. That movement rests fundamentally on the Anti-Ballistic Missile Treaty and was significantly advanced with the ratification of the Intermediate-range Nuclear Forces Treaty. The INF was unprecedented in that it was the first negotiated treaty to actually reduce nuclear weapons. More to the point of this report, it was also the first agreement to eliminate an entire class of nuclear weapons. In more recent years the United States and Russia have agreed to deep cuts to their nuclear arsenals, which today in total approximate 40,000 to 50,000 warheads. The START-I and START-II agreements require a two-thirds reduction in US and Russian strategic nuclear arsenals from pre-START levels of approximately 10,000 deployed strategic warheads each to 3000-3500 by 2003.

Both the United Kingdom and France have unilaterally reduced their nuclear postures by measures including withdrawal from deployment and elimination of elements of their nuclear forces. Tactical nuclear weaponry has been mostly withdrawn from deployment and removed from ships and sea-based aircraft. China has reiterated its support of the goal of the elimination of nuclear weapons, and its declaration of no first use of nuclear weapons. The experience the United States and Russia have accumulated through decades of negotiating and implementing nuclear arms control agreements will prove invaluable both as a basis for further bilateral reductions and as a store of knowledge that can be drawn upon by the other nuclear weapon states.

The first requirement for movement towards a nuclear weapon free world is for the five nuclear weapon states to commit themselves unequivocally to proceed with all deliberate speed to a world without nuclear weapons, not as an objective for the far distant future, but as an objective, which deserves action from the time, the commitment is given. A commitment of this kind would transform the whole process. The process followed must ensure that no state feels, at any stage, that further nuclear disarmament is a threat to its security. To this end nuclear weapon elimination should be conducted as a series of phased, verified reductions that allow states to satisfy themselves, at each stage of the process, that further movement toward elimination can be made safely and securely. Political commitment and allocation of adequate resources will be needed to overcome technical constraints such as the current slow rate of weapons dismantlement p; around 2000 per year each by the United States and Russia.

The rate of present dismantlement should not be the factor, which determines the rate of elimination. The important condition is to have agreed procedures for establishing new targets, which drive the process forward to the ultimate objective of total elimination. While the nuclear weapon states have a special responsibility, all states must contribute to development of and support for an environment favourable to nuclear weapons elimination, including an end to nuclear testing and prevention of further horizontal nuclear proliferation. The Commission reaffirms its strong conviction that immediate and consequential steps are possible. These would both convey a powerful signal of commitment to elimination by the nuclear weapon states, and enhance global security by widening the firebreak between the onset of a crisis engaging a nuclear weapon state and the risk of a deliberate or inadvertent nuclear detonation. Progress towards a nuclear weapon free world should not be made contingent upon other changes in the international security environment. Successful nuclear weapon negotiations will benefit other security related negotiations and progress in regional and other political and security related negotiations would enhance the prospect of building a nuclear weapon free world.

Nuclear Weapon State Commitment to a Nuclear Weapon Free World:

The nuclear weapon states should commit themselves unequivocally to the elimination of nuclear weapons and agree to start work immediately on the practical steps and negotiations required for its achievement. This commitment should be made at the highest political level. Non-nuclear weapon states should support the commitment by the nuclear weapon states and join in cooperative international action to implement it.

Such a commitment would constitute a concrete expression of the intention of the nuclear weapon states to implement the 'Principles and Objectives for Nuclear Non-Proliferation and Disarmament' agreed at the 1995 Review and Extension Conference of the Treaty on the Non-Proliferation of Nuclear Weapons (NPTREC). It would receive the enthusiastic support of an overwhelming majority of states. High-level political commitment has proven time and again to be the crucial condition for the resolution of seemingly intractable situations and reconciling embittered foes. A declaration by the nuclear weapon states, in clear and unambiguous terms, would have a dramatic impact on the way the world thinks about nuclear weapons. It would change instantly the tenor of debate, the thrust of war planning, and the timing or indeed the necessity for modernization programs. It would transform the nuclear weapons paradigm from the indefinite management of a world fraught with the twin risks of the use of nuclear weapons and further proliferation, to one of nuclear weapons elimination.

Finally, much as the end of the Cold War greatly accelerated the broad agenda of arms control, a commitment now to eliminate nuclear weapons would generate the necessary political momentum and give a new coherence to the entire spectrum of non-proliferation, disarmament and arms limitation efforts currently being pursued at global and regional levels.

The Commission recommends that negotiation of the nuclear weapon states' commitment to a nuclear weapon free world should begin immediately, with the aim of first steps in its implementation being taken in 1997.

Additional Immediate Steps:

The commitment by the nuclear weapon states to a nuclear weapon free world must be accompanied by a series of practical, realistic and mutually reinforcing steps. There are a number of such steps that can be taken immediately. They would significantly reduce the risk of nuclear war and thus enhance the security of all states, but particularly that of the nuclear weapon states. Their implementation would provide clear confirmation of the intent of the nuclear weapon states to further reduce the role of nuclear weapons in their security postures.

These steps would also signal that the nuclear weapon states were unequivocally of the view that continued possession of nuclear weapons was incommensurate with the risks they pose.

The recommended steps are:

(a) Taking nuclear forces off alert
(b) Removal of warheads from delivery vehicles
(c) Ending deployment of non-strategic nuclear weapons
(d) Ending nuclear testing
(e) Initiating negotiations to further reduce US and Russian nuclear arsenals
(f) Agreement among the nuclear weapon states of reciprocal no first use undertakings, and of a non-use undertaking by them in relation to the non-nuclear weapon states
(g) Taking Nuclear Forces Off Alert

The continuing practice of maintaining nuclear-tipped missiles on alert, whether on land-based or sea-based platforms, is a highly regrettable perpetuation of Cold War attitudes and assumptions. It needlessly sustains the risk of hair-trigger postures. It retards the critical process of normalizing United States-Russian relations. It sends the unmistakable and, from an arms control perspective, severely damaging message that nuclear weapons serve a vital security role. It is entirely inappropriate to the extraordinary transformation in the international security environment achieved at such staggering cost. Taking these missiles off alert is a natural counterpart to the stand-down of bombers from nuclear alert, which was implemented, in late 1991.

Terminating nuclear alert would reduce dramatically the chance of an accidental or unauthorized nuclear weapons launch. It would have a most positive influence on the political climate among the nuclear weapon states and help set the stage for intensified cooperation. Taking nuclear forces off alert could be verified by national technical means and nuclear weapon state inspection arrangements. In the first instance, reductions in alert status could be adopted by the nuclear weapon states unilaterally.

Removal of Warheads from Delivery Vehicles:

The physical separation of warheads from delivery vehicles would strongly reinforce the gains achieved by taking nuclear forces off alert. This measure can be implemented to the extent that nuclear forces can be reconstituted to an alert posture only within known or agreed upon timeframes, much as is the case with bomber forces today. Adequate response to nuclear threats would remain certain, but the risk of large scale preemptive or surprise nuclear attack and the imperative for instantaneous retaliation would be obviated. Further, the barriers against inadvertent or accidental use would be greatly strengthened. The range of verification procedures, which are already in place between the United States and Russia, could likely be applied as the basis of a regime to ensure that no state would have a meaningful advantage in terms of the ability to reassemble its nuclear force for a first strike capability.

Ending Deployment of Non-Strategic Nuclear Weapons:

The nuclear weapon states should unilaterally remove all non-strategic nuclear weapons from deployed sites to a limited number of secure storage facilities on their territory. This would be a logical follow-on to the 1991 unilateral declarations of the United States and the Soviet Union, whereby each pledged to remove all non-strategic nuclear weapons from ships and submarines and store them on shore. As regards NATO, with the dissolution of the Warsaw Pact and all that has followed in its wake, the nuclear threat long felt by the alliance has evaporated. United States tactical nuclear weapons deployed in Western Europe serve no security purpose. To the contrary, they send a subtle but unmistakable message that Russia is still not to be trusted, thus feeding the fears that NATO harbours aggressive designs against it. These nuclear weapons can be returned to US territory and stored so that, much like strategic forces removed from alert, they cannot be readily redeployed.

Ending Nuclear Testing:

The Comprehensive Test Ban Treaty will be a major impediment to the development of new generations of nuclear weapons by the nuclear weapon states. It will perform an equally vital non-proliferation function by inhibiting nuclear weapons development by potential new nuclear weapon states, including the undeclared nuclear weapon states and nuclear threshold states. Most important, the CTBT obligation permanently to cease or forgo nuclear testing sets the psychological stage for moving toward elimination of nuclear weapons. Pending universal application of the CTBT, all states should observe at once the moratorium it imposes on nuclear testing.

Further US/Russian Bilateral Reductions:

The nuclear arms race was driven by competition between the United States and the former Soviet Union. The United States and Russia must continue to show leadership in reversing the nuclear accumulations of the Cold War. Their purpose should be to move toward nuclear force levels for all the nuclear weapon states, which would reflect unambiguously the determination to eliminate these weapons when this step can be verified with adequate confidence. The immediate steps discussed above deal with the manner in which residual nuclear forces are deployed that diminish to the greatest possible extent both the risk of inadvertent or accidental use and the adverse political signals transmitted by poised nuclear forces. With respect to the size of arsenals, there are two notional targets. First, the United States and Russia should, in consultation with the other nuclear weapon states, establish the relative force levels that would allow all five nuclear weapon states to proceed in concert with reductions beyond that point. Second, the five nuclear weapon states should agree on the minimum residual forces to be retained until the stage had been set for complete elimination.

The Commission considers it inappropriate to try and forecast the stages involved in reaching these targets. Clearly, there will have to be at least one further reduction agreement on the part of the United States and Russia. It should be noted in this context that the entry into force of the START II agreement is in some doubt because Russia may be required to invest in new nuclear weapon systems in order to reach parity. To obviate this undesirable development, and to facilitate the ratification of START II, lower ceilings could be promptly negotiated in a START III agreement. President Yeltsin has already proposed the figure of 2000 (compared with the 3000, 3500 the agreement currently specifies) but lower levels should be considered to hasten the achievement of force levels that would bring all the nuclear weapon states into the process.

Similarly, the Commission considers it presumptuous to try and specify from its present vantage point the minimum residual forces that the nuclear weapon states would regard as the appropriate final way station pending complete elimination. It would observe, however, that the considerations that the nuclear weapon states would bring to bear in determining this level would be profoundly different from those, that has shaped these negotiations to this point. While of signal importance, the existing START agreements do not require that withdrawn warheads be disassembled and destroyed. Hence actual stockpiles of warheads in the United States and Russia post-START II are likely to be much higher than the figures set by the agreement. Nor do the START agreements address disposition of the fissile material content of warheads removed from deployment. This material represents the core element of a 'virtual arsenal' existing outside the START framework, and which would be available to the United States and Russia if ever a political decision were taken to reassemble dismantled warheads.

This concern was mitigated in part by agreements reached at the 10 May 1995 US/Russian summit to develop procedures for ensuring that excess nuclear warheads are dismantled and the reduction process made irreversible. The 1996 Moscow Nuclear Safety and Security Summit also underscored a need to identify appropriate strategies for the management of fissile material designated as no longer required for defense purposes. The summit undertook to convene by the end of 1996 an international meeting of experts to examine available options and identify possible development of international cooperation in the implementation of national strategies. The knowledge gained from implementation of these undertakings should prove valuable for development of systems for verification of warhead dismantlement and fissile material control. The Commission considers arrangements for the control and verification of the dismantlement to be essential for the stability and sustainability of the process of reducing nuclear weapons.

The security benefits of the START agreements and their value as a staging point to wider nuclear disarmament would be increased if START III or a separate agreement required the verified dismantlement of warheads withdrawn under past and future US/Russian bilateral reduction agreements, tactical warheads withdrawn unilaterally and reserve warheads. This would establish warhead numbers (strategic and tactical, active and in reserve) as the basic unit of account in US/Russian reductions and provide a common basis for considering relative force levels when nuclear disarmament moves beyond the bilateral phase.

Agreements on 'No First Use' and on 'Non-Use of Nuclear Weapons'

In the post-Cold War world the only conceivable residual role of nuclear weapons is to pose a threat of retaliation against nuclear aggression. It follows that a joint no-first use undertaking would be at no strategic cost to the nuclear weapon states. Indeed as a significant confidence building measure it would in fact enhance their security. As one of the immediate steps, the nuclear weapon states should agree and state that they would not be the first to use or threaten to use nuclear weapons against each other and that they would not use or threaten to use nuclear weapons in any conflict with a non-nuclear weapon state. The Commission considers that such an agreement should be brought into operation as soon as possible.

Reinforcing Steps:

The recommended nuclear weapon states' political statement of commitment and other 'Immediate Steps' would firmly orient the defence and bureaucratic establishments of all nuclear weapon states to the goal of elimination and to the development of a practical program of nuclear disarmament. The following steps would build on the solid foundation of commitment, accomplishment and goodwill established through implementation of the steps recommended for immediate action:

(a) Action to prevent further horizontal proliferation
(b) Developing verification arrangements for a nuclear weapon free world
(c) Cessation of the production of fissile material for nuclear explosive purposes
(d) Action to Prevent Further Horizontal Proliferation

The problem of nuclear proliferation is inextricably linked to the continued possession of nuclear weapons by a handful of states. As long as any state has nuclear weapons, there will be others, state or sub-state actors, who will seek to acquire them. Other national security reasons also motivate states to acquire nuclear weapons. The task of preventing further proliferation becomes even more urgent as existing nuclear arsenals are being eliminated. A world environment where proliferation is under control will facilitate the disarmament process and movement toward final elimination and vice versa. The emergence of any new nuclear weapon state during the elimination process would seriously jeopardize the process of eliminating nuclear weapons. It would not, of course, rule out forever the possibility of elimination, although it would probably retard it. Action is therefore needed to ensure effective non-proliferation controls on civil and military nuclear activities, and to press for universal acceptance of non-proliferation obligations.

At the level of national action, states have the fundamental obligation, under a variety of treaties and in moral terms, to ensure that sensitive nuclear material, equipment and technology under their jurisdiction and control do not find their way into the hands of those who would misuse them. A breakdown in national nuclear controls could lead to nuclear material coming into the possession of would-be proliferate states or sub-state groups, including terrorists. States must have competent systems of nuclear materials accountancy to keep track of nuclear material. Nuclear establishments and the transport of nuclear material need appropriate physical protection and states need to have effective procedures to control what leaves their territory, know where it is going and for what purpose. All member states of the International Atomic Energy Agency and the future Comprehensive Test Ban Treaty Organization should ensure that they meet in full their financial obligations so these bodies can properly perform their functions.

The Treaty on the Non-Proliferation of Nuclear Weapons remains the cornerstone of the international nuclear non-proliferation regime. It is the legal and political means by which almost all states give effect to their decisions to renounce nuclear weapons. Because of the near universality of the non-proliferation regime those states operating significant nuclear programs without comprehensive safeguards stand exposed to the international community as being of possible proliferation concern. Application of IAEA NPT or equivalent full scope safeguards in non-nuclear weapon states promotes national, regional and global security and stability by providing a high level of assurance that nuclear material remains in peaceful, non-explosive use.

A small number of states continue to refuse to join the NPT or accept equivalent non-proliferation commitments. Bringing these states into the non-proliferation regime through acceptance of internationally verifiable, legally binding non-proliferation obligations will be an essential step in the process of eliminating nuclear weapons. The NPT Review and Extension Conference identified universal adherence to the NPT as an urgent priority and called upon all states not yet party to the treaty to accede to it at the earliest date, particularly those states that operate unsafeguarded nuclear facilities. This process would be enhanced by the unequivocal commitment of the nuclear weapon states to the elimination of nuclear weapons and concrete movement towards that goal.

Proliferation pressures in South Asia, the Middle East and the Korean peninsula may prejudice the prospects for eliminating nuclear weapons. Determined efforts, particularly on the part of the states in these regions and the nuclear weapon states, are urgently needed to address the long-standing differences that fuel proliferation in these regions. Just as the nuclear weapon states need to be convinced that giving up nuclear weapons will not harm their security so too will the undeclared weapon states and threshold states need to be convinced that ending their nuclear ambiguity will not damage their interests.

Past experience points to a variety of ways in which such situations can be resolved. Unilateral action is possible, as in the case of South Africa's unilateral dismantlement of its nuclear weapons. In this case, close attention was needed by the IAEA to ensure completeness of initial inventories preparatory to the application of full scope safeguards to South Africa's remaining nuclear activities.

Bilateral negotiations can also be successful as in the case of Argentina and Brazil. After decades of nuclear competition and uncertainty about the direction of their nuclear programs these states took joint action. Both now accept comprehensive IAEA safeguards and have established a bilateral nuclear inspection agency, the Argentina-Brazil Accounting and Control Commission. Both have ratified the Treaty of Tlatelolco and Argentina has joined the NPT. Of particular note is that safeguards are applied bilaterally and by the IAEA. Each state thereby has direct access to information about the other's nuclear program, providing high transparency and confidence.

A combination of bilateral and multilateral approaches is also possible. The De-nuclearisation Declaration between the ROK and the DPRK coupled with the US-DPRK Agreed Framework and the Korean Peninsula Energy Development Organization (KEDO) is an example of how dialogue, encouragement, assistance, some security guarantees (in this case negative nuclear security assurances) and give and take on both sides can help to wind back nuclear weapon ambitions on the part of an insecure state.

In situations of regional tension, such as India and Pakistan in South Asia and Israel and its neighbours, the security needs of all parties involved have to be identified, acknowledged and addressed systematically to find solutions. Action should be taken as a matter of urgency, and if necessary discretely, to prevent a regional dispute acquiring a nuclear dimension. This indicates to a multilateral approach involving relevant regional and possibly neighbouring powers. Bilateral or regional involvement could be employed as a means of providing additional assurance and confidence building above and beyond international inspections. The overall security environment, including conventional armaments and other weapons of mass destruction, would be highly relevant to a negotiated solution. There could be a role in this regard for assistance and assurances from outside powers, particularly the nuclear weapon states, covering such matters as security assistance, positive and negative nuclear security assurances, assurances about access to imported technologies and agreed restraint in arms exports to the region.

Developing Verification Arrangements for a Nuclear Weapon Free World:

Effective verification is critical to the achievement and maintenance of a nuclear weapon free world. Before states agree to eliminate nuclear weapons they will require a high level of confidence that verification arrangements would detect promptly any attempt to cheat the disarmament process whether through retention or acquisition of clandestine weapons, weapon components, means of weapons production or undeclared stocks of fissile material. Formal legal undertakings should be accompanied by corresponding legal arrangements for verification. To maintain security in a post-nuclear weapon world the verification system must provide a high level of assurance as to the continued peaceful, non-explosive use of a state's civil nuclear activity.

To be adequate, the verification regime must provide a high probability that cheating of proliferation significance would be detected promptly. This is essential to provide confidence that nuclear weapons have been eliminated and to discourage potential violators. A political judgement will be needed on whether the level of assurance possible from the verification regime is sufficient. All existing arms control and disarmament agreements have required judgements of this nature because no verification system can provide absolute certainty. The likelihood that the verification regime for a nuclear weapon free world will involve a small probability that attempted breakout might go undetected does not alter the fact that a nuclear weapon free world would be, fundamentally, a safer place. Development and implementation of the verification arrangements, needed for each step toward elimination, will provide immediate benefit through reducing the dangers posed by nuclear weapons and the threat of nuclear proliferation including nuclear terrorism.

Verification is likely to involve bilateral US/Russian measures, verification among the nuclear weapon states and multilateral verification during various stages of the dismantlement and elimination of nuclear weapons. Bilateral or regional involvement in inspections on nuclear facilities and in monitoring the dismantlement of any nuclear weapons could be employed as a means of providing additional assurance and confidence building above and beyond international inspections particularly during the early stages of disarmament while states develop confidence that multilateral verification is operating effectively. The verification regime will take many years to develop. To ensure that movement toward a nuclear weapon free world is not held up by lack of adequate verification, higher priority should be given to the development of the verification techniques that will be needed.

The following are some of the main components of a possible verification regime:

(a) Effective, cost-efficient non-proliferation controls on the civil nuclear industry in all states
(b) Detection of undeclared nuclear activity
(c) Ceasing production of fissile material for nuclear weapons
(d) Nuclear warheads dismantlement and elimination
(e) Disposition of warhead uranium and plutonium

(f) Controls on nuclear weapons components other than nuclear material
(g) Dismantlement of nuclear weapons infrastructure

A key element of non-proliferation arrangements for a nuclear weapon free world will be a highly developed capacity to detect undeclared nuclear activity at both declared and undeclared sites. Progressive extension of safeguards to nuclear activity in the nuclear weapon states, the undeclared weapon states and the threshold states will be needed with the end point being universal application of safeguards in all states. Few facilities in the nuclear weapon states are safeguarded at present and a number of other states operate unsafe guarded nuclear facilities. The first stage of extending safeguards in these states is likely to be verification of facilities and material covered by a convention to end fissile material production for weapons.

Systems will be needed to verify that nuclear warheads are dismantled and destroyed and their fissile material content safeguarded to provide maximum confidence that such material cannot be reintroduced to weapons use. Controls on important components of nuclear weapons other than fissile material such as tritium and non-nuclear components will need to be considered. To ensure that a nuclear force of strategic significance cannot be reconstituted quickly a staged process for verified destruction of the nuclear weapons infrastructure is likely to be considered necessary.

Even allowing for future developments it seems unlikely that technical verification alone can provide the levels of assurance needed for the elimination of nuclear weapons. Supplementing technical verification by other measures such as transparency in nuclear activity, relevant information obtained by national technical means and passed to verification bodies, exchange of information between verification bodies and application of effective export controls can increase the levels of assurance from technical measures. Societal verification or citizen's reporting may prove to be an additional means of supporting the verification system for a nuclear weapon free world.

The political commitment to eliminate nuclear weapons must be matched by a willingness to make available the resources needed for nuclear disarmament including effective verification. The amounts involved are likely to be considerable, especially for the dismantlement of weapons and disposition of their fissile material content, but very much less than developing, maintaining and upgrading nuclear arsenals. In addition, the costs of the verification system should be weighed against the substantial contribution to global, regional and national security that effective verification of a nuclear weapon free world would make. Consideration should be given to creating an international fund for this purpose.

As the verification regime is developed it will be necessary to ensure that institutional arrangements are appropriate. Some probable institutional elements such as the IAEA and the CTBT verification organization exist or soon will be. Other institutional requirements should be considered as the disarmament process develops. Elaboration of technical aspects of verification should be initiated without delay within the framework of the Conference on Disarmament.

States must also be confident that any violations detected will be acted upon. In this context, the Security Council should continue its consideration of how it might address, consistent with specific mandates given to it and consistent with the Charter of the United Nations, violations of nuclear disarmament obligations which might be drawn to its attention. This should demonstrate that the collective security system enshrined in the Charter would operate effectively in this field.

Cessation of the Production of Fissile Material for Nuclear Explosive Purposes:

Ending the production of fissile material for nuclear weapons or other nuclear explosive devices (cut-off) would require the dismantlement or placement under international safeguards of all enrichment and reprocessing plants in the nuclear weapon states and in undeclared weapon states and threshold states. A cut-off convention would contribute to nuclear disarmament by capping the amount of nuclear material available for nuclear weapons use and by extending safeguards coverage over currently unsafeguarded sensitive nuclear facilities. The Conference on Disarmament has agreed a mandate for negotiation of a production cut-off convention and the negotiations should proceed as a matter of urgency.

Final Steps

Final steps towards elimination will require a negotiating process involving all nuclear weapon states and any remaining undeclared weapons states and threshold states. The detail of how this might be achieved will principally be a matter for the states involved at the time, but some general comments can be offered. Steps suggested are:

A. Other Nuclear Weapon States Joining the Process
B. Further START agreements and nuclear confidence building measures should establish a receptive international climate for negotiations on global reduction of nuclear arms. Following the achievement by the United States and Russia of appropriate force levels, the next step might be to reduce the levels of

all nuclear weapon states to 100 warheads each. The United Kingdom, France and China have given undertakings that they will join nuclear arms reductions when the arsenals of the United States and Russia are reduced sufficiently. These undertakings would need to be given concrete form and acted upon.

Preparations for negotiations involving all nuclear weapon states need not await the achievement by the United States and Russia of the appropriate force levels. The United States and Russia could commence a process for bringing the United Kingdom, France and China into the nuclear disarmament process. For example, early exploration of a comprehensive exchange of information on each state's nuclear arsenal and stocks of fissile material will be needed to establish baseline data for nuclear weapon state negotiations. Further early steps could be for the United States and Russia to prepare the ground for verification of nuclear weapon state reductions including by sharing information and expertise on START verification, on weapons dismantlement and on verification and control of fissile material from dismantled weapons. US/Russian experience on nuclear confidence building should be extended to the other nuclear weapon states, and new measures developed which involve them.

With respect to reductions involving all nuclear weapon states, as their arsenals are substantially reduced, the levels of warheads or warheads components thought to be held by any remaining undeclared nuclear weapon states and threshold states will become a more serious concern. It is therefore essential that states with presumed nuclear weapons potential take early action and enter into international legal constraints, as they will have to resolve their ambiguous nuclear status before the nuclear weapon states will finally move to zero nuclear weapons. As part of the process, it will be necessary for these states to acknowledge the progress made toward nuclear disarmament and to demonstrate their own intentions in this regard including through cessation of production of fissile material until production facilities are subject to international monitoring.

During the early part of nuclear weapon state reductions there are likely to be asymmetries in the arsenals which would reflect the different starting points of the participants. Progressive reductions in these asymmetries could be expected, leaving all nuclear weapon states with similar residual stocks of weapons as they approach the elimination stage. For nuclear disarmament to be genuine and stable it should not be easily or unevenly reversible. There must be confidence that any attempt by a state to reverse disarmament would be a drawn out, highly visible, resource-intensive exercise. As nuclear disarmament extends beyond US / Russian bilateral reductions, so too must arrangements to provide a high degree of assurance that it would not be reversible. These arrangements include verified dismantlement and destruction of warheads and ending fissile material production for weapons purposes.

Getting to Zero

Each successive phase toward elimination of nuclear weapons will provide a guide to possible legal arrangements for a nuclear weapon free world. These measures could include further US/Russian bilateral agreements, a Comprehensive Test Ban Treaty, a cut-off convention and any no-first-use treaty that may have been negotiated. Further new treaties will be needed at the global or regional level and existing instruments may have to be modified or replaced.
Separate but mutually reinforcing instruments could be one way to give legal effect to nuclear disarmament. As nuclear disarmament nears the

elimination stage, consideration should be given to whether the legal obligations to sustain a nuclear weapon free world would be best given effect by the incremental approach of a number of separate instruments or through a comprehensive approach which would combine all relevant instruments into a single legal instrument, a nuclear weapons convention.

A comprehensive treaty would be a fresh start, removed from acrimonious debate, such as that over the NPT. It may also be possible to include in a new treaty provisions, which would minimize any danger to the NPT such as a requirement that the new treaty would enter into force only after all states party had ratified it to the NPT.

In any reflection on the legal regime required as a basic part of the architecture for a nuclear weapon free world, it is fundamental to recognise that the legal regime supports but cannot itself bring about such a world. The prospective components of the nuclear weapon free world legal regime will play an important role in the political negotiations through which a nuclear weapon free world will be established. But it is these political negotiations and the determination to make them effective, which are central to the elimination of nuclear weapons. The maintenance of a nuclear weapon free world will require an enduring legal framework, linked to the Charter of the United Nations, possibly in the form of a convention on nuclear weapons.

Building Environment for a Nuclear Weapon Free World:

A world ready to eliminate nuclear weapons would be very different from today's world. The absence of nuclear weapons and related activity would become an internationally accepted norm, obviously including in all five declared nuclear weapon states. National arguments that nuclear weapons are needed because others have them would not apply. States' commitment to a nuclear weapon free future would be codified in international legal documents. Nuclear weapons would by then have to be seen as having no part to play in assuring any state's national sovereignty and independence. The world would have to live in the knowledge that cheating could spark the return of a nuclear-armed world and the threat of a nuclear war, but the basic changes, which would have occurred, would buttress, substantially, the technical barriers against breakout and collective interest in maintaining them.

Concurrent with the central disarmament process, there will be a need for activity supported by all states, but particularly the nuclear weapon states, to build an environment conducive to nuclear disarmament and non-proliferation. Progress in each track will influence the other. It is essential that the international nuclear and security agenda should move forward on a broad front in ways supportive of nuclear disarmament so that the process does not lose momentum.

Ballistic Missiles

Aside from warheads, missile delivery systems are of the greatest concern in seeking to ensure that a meaningful nuclear force cannot be reconstituted quickly. Reductions in strategic nuclear missile numbers should therefore track reductions in warhead numbers closely. The provision of START agreement for verified destruction of launchers and platforms is a possible model for strategic nuclear ballistic missile reductions involving the nuclear weapon states. Missile capabilities in the Middle East, South Asia and on the Korean peninsula also need to be addressed. The Anti-Ballistic Missile Treaty concluded in 1972 by the United States and the Soviet Union recognized the potential for strategic missile defense systems to fuel the offensive arms race as both sides sought to counter the other's defensive systems. By limiting strategic missile defense sites to one per side the ABM Treaty removed a strong incentive to increase offensive forces and paved the way for the START I and II reductions.

Proliferation of missiles and their use in conflicts such as the Gulf War have intensified interest, particularly in the United States, in missile defense systems. While Cold War missile defense proposals centered on strategic ballistic missiles, the present focus is on defenses against shorter-range theatre missiles. In practice it is likely to become increasingly difficult to draw a clear line between systems to defend against strategic ballistic missiles and those which defend against sub-strategic and particularly theatre ballistic missiles. The deployment of some ballistic missile defense systems during the transition to a nuclear weapon free world could threaten seriously the continuation of the process, particularly as technology capabilities in this field vary significantly.

It will be extremely important for the pursuit of the elimination of nuclear weapons to protect fully the integrity of the ABM Treaty. A global treaty controlling longer-range ballistic missiles would provide a universal means of addressing the dangers to international security posed by ballistic missiles; it would also avoid the potential destabilizing effect of ballistic missile defense systems. It would increase the confidence of nuclear weapon states that nuclear disarmament will not damage their security, and it would improve the security environment in a number of regions by eliminating destabilizing missile arms races.

Pending development of such a regime, confidence-building measures such as a multilateral ballistic missile launch notification agreement and a ballistic missile flight test ban could be explored.

Nuclear Weapon Free Zones:

Nuclear weapon free zones are part of the architecture that can usefully encourage and support a nuclear weapon free world. The spread of such zones around the globe, with specific mechanisms to answer the security concerns of each region, can progressively codify the transition to a world free of nuclear weapons.

Nuclear weapon free zones are an effective means of addressing regional nuclear tensions in a cooperative way and provide ongoing assurance that nuclear activity in a region is confined to peaceful purposes. Their potential contribution to global and regional peace and security was reaffirmed at NPTREC, which encouraged development of nuclear weapon free zones, especially in regions of tension such as the Middle East, as a matter of priority. There are also proposals for the establishment of such zones in South Asia, in Central Europe and from the Black Sea to the Baltic Sea.

The cooperation of the nuclear weapon states is necessary for the maximum effectiveness of nuclear weapon free zones. To increase the likelihood that nuclear weapon states will become party to nuclear weapon free zones they should be consulted early in the negotiation process. Equally, because of the contribution nuclear weapon free zones can make to disarmament and non-proliferation, the nuclear weapon states should support them including through signing nuclear weapon state protocols.

About half of the earth's surface is already covered by nuclear weapon free zones, comprising the Latin American and the Caribbean countries (Treaty of Tlatelolco), the South Pacific (Treaty of Rarotonga), the ASEAN countries (Southeast Asian Nuclear Weapon Free Zone) and African countries (the Treaty of Pelindaba).

Once the ASEAN and African agreements come into force, most of the southern hemisphere (and some parts of the northern hemisphere) will be covered by nuclear weapon free zones.

The Canberra Commission encourages development of linkages between all existing and prospective southern hemisphere nuclear weapon free zones to create a southern hemisphere free of nuclear weapons.

Nuclear Trade and Export Controls:

All states have an obligation to ensure that their nuclear trade does not contribute, wittingly or unwittingly, to nuclear weapons proliferation by either states or sub-state groups. Meeting this obligation is assisted by a common understanding of what items are sensitive in the nuclear proliferation process and has resulted in development of internationally agreed standards for nuclear exports. Such standards support the non-proliferation regime and foster legitimate trade and cooperation in the peaceful uses of nuclear energy by contributing to the climate of confidence essential for international nuclear cooperation. The importance of nuclear export controls is acknowledged in the NPTREC 'Principles and Objectives for Nuclear Non-Proliferation and Disarmament'. These state that new supply arrangements should require acceptance of full scope safeguards 'as a necessary precondition', thereby clearly specifying the full scope safeguards supply standard as the accepted global norm for nuclear supply.

States looking to develop nuclear weapons also need delivery systems, and a close correlation exists between nuclear weapons proliferation and missile proliferation. More broadly, states seeking to develop weapons of mass destruction may try to develop several categories of weapons simultaneously.

Effective export controls on items that could contribute to development of non-nuclear weapons of mass destruction are therefore important to establishing and sustaining an international climate favourable to the elimination of nuclear weapons. It is essential that export control regimes are transparent in their operation and do not impede legitimate trade and technology transfer.

Eliminating Other Weapons of Mass Destruction:

The Commission does not accept the view that nuclear weapons need to be retained to serve as a deterrent against other types of weapons of mass destruction, particularly chemical and biological weapons. Implementation of effective measures to eliminate both types of weapons would significantly enhance global security and provide more conducive circumstances for the elimination of nuclear weapons. While there have been longstanding efforts to prohibit both chemical and biological weapons, these efforts have not yet reached the stage where the international community can be confident that the menace of such weapons has been finally removed.

One hundred and sixty countries have signed the Chemical Weapons Convention since it was opened for signature in Paris in January 1993. The CWC will enter into force 180 days after the 65th country has ratified the convention. The CWC promises to be an effective instrument for controlling chemical weapons but will face a variety of challenges when it becomes operational. A key issue will be universality, a number of important countries in the Middle East and in other regions of tension have not yet signed the convention. The US and Russia, two largest possessors of chemical weapons, have yet to ratify. It will be vital that the CWC achieve comprehensive participation if its promise is to be realized. Signatories, who have not yet ratified, the CWC should give high priority to ratification, and non-signatories, particularly in regions of tension, should join this new regime as soon as possible.

The 1925 Geneva Protocol sought to ban use of biological weapons, but a more comprehensive ban was established in the Biological Weapons Convention, which came into operation in 1975. The BWC has been hampered by the lack of formal provisions and machinery to verify compliance, a major deficiency, which has been underlined by suggestions that a number of countries have maintained programs to develop such weapons despite the convention's provisions. Negotiations to develop a legally binding instrument to reinforce the BWC, which is expected to contain verification provisions, were commenced only in 1995. These negotiations will need to come to an early conclusion to preserve the BWC's value in maintaining a global norm against biological weapons. Assisted by the rapid advance in biotechnology, these weapons, more so than chemical weapons, have the potential to cause damage on a widespread, strategic scale and could become the new scourge for the next century if current arms control efforts are not successful.

Timing Considerations

The Commission considered carefully the merits of setting out a precise timeframe for the elimination of nuclear weapons, but elected not to do so. However, this does not imply that it accepts the extended timelines imposed by such current constraints as limited warhead dismantlement facilities. Those constraints could obviously be relieved by political decisions and the allocation of resources required advancing dismantlement. Another limiting factor may prove to be establishing the necessary confidence in the verification regime, which would be required to take the final step to complete elimination. In this context the Canberra Commission remains convinced of the basic importance of agreed targets and guidelines which would drive the process inexorably toward the ultimate objective of final elimination, at the earliest possible time.

The Canberra Commission on Elimination of Nuclear Weapons has dealt in detail the catastrophe it would cause to the human beings and the world. It has suggested how the race for nuclear arms could be controlled and trade in missiles and nuclear missiles could be abandoned. The report must be discussed and analyzed in the United Nations Security Council and international laws must be promulgated to save the world. But till date no specific laws have been enacted; even terrorists are expecting to own nuclear arms in near future.

(C)
BLIX COMMISSION REPORT or Report on "Weapons of Terror Freeing the World of Nuclear, Biological and Chemical Arm"

The Blix Commission Report or the Report on " Weapons of Terror Freeing the World of Nuclear, Biological and Chemical Arms' chaired by Dr. Hans Blix puts forward a number of proposals on how the world could be freed of nuclear, biological and chemical weapons.[89]

The Commission's 14 members unanimously endorsed the report and it was submitted to the Secretary-General, United Nations Organization. The copies of the report were presented to Governments, nongovernmental organizations and the general public around the world. The Commission was convened by the Swedish Government, which also

---

[89] United Nations A/60/934, General Assembly, Distr.: General, 10 July 2006, Sixtieth session, Agenda items 97 and 120, General and complete disarmament Follow-up to the outcome of the Millennium Summit, Letter dated 29 June 2006 from the Permanent Representative of, Sweden to the United Nations addressed to the Secretary-General

provided the main funding for the secretariat and the work of the Commission. The report on "Weapons of Terror Freeing the World of Nuclear, Biological and Chemical Arms" has incorporated excellent suggestions to save the world from destruction and to secure permanent world peace. The implementation of suggestions prescribed by the Commission needs neither investments nor criticisms. It simply requires 'will power' for the benefits of all people living in our planet.

Chairman's preface

In September 2003, the Swedish Foreign Minister, Anna Lindh, was brutally killed. Inspirational, young and full of initiative, she would have had much more to contribute to making the world a better place. During the first months of 2003, Anna phoned me from time to time to inform herself about the United Nations inspection work in Iraq, for which I was responsible. She and many of her colleagues were very unhappy about the drift towards military action against Iraq and felt that the inspectors should be given more time for their search for weapons of mass destruction. She also felt, however, that a skeptical attitude to armed action was not enough. It had to be matched by more active policies on the issue of non-proliferation. I fully agreed with her and was pleased to see that in June 2003 she and her colleagues in the European Union declared new joint policies.

These policies, in my view, started from sensible premises: that the best solution to the problem of the proliferation of weapons of mass destruction was that countries should no longer feel that they needed them and those violators should be encouraged to walk back and rejoin the international community. These policies stressed the need for a cooperative approach to collective security and a rule-based international order. They highlighted the role of international verification and effective multilaterally.

They also supported, as a last resort, however, the position that coercive measures under Chapter VII of the United Nations Charter could be taken, with the Security Council as the final arbiter.

By the end of June 2003, when the occupation of Iraq was a fact and I was leaving the United Nations, Anna Lindh contacted me again.

She thought that the time was right not only for the new European policies but also for an idea first advanced by Jayantha Dhanapala, then United Nations Under-Secretary-General for Disarmament: the creation of an independent international commission to examine how the world could tackle the problem of weapons of mass destruction. She asked if I would chair such a commission. I said I would.

After Anna Lindh's death, Swedish Prime Minister, Göran Persson, and Anna's successor as Foreign Minister, Laila Freivalds, gave me a free hand to establish the Commission. I have been fortunate to secure the participation of high calibre members, who have contributed their ideas, knowledge, judgement — and texts. The Commissioners consisted of Dewi Fortuna Anwar, Alexei G. Arbatov, Marcos de Azambuja, Alyson J. K. Bailes, Jayantha Dhanapala, Gareth Evans, Patricia Lewis, Masashi Nishihara, William J. Perry, Vasantha Raghavan, Cheikh Sylla, Prince El Hassan bin Talal, Pan Zhenqiang and Hans Blix, Chairman. They have all taken part in practical political, diplomatic or military work related to the maintenance of peace and the reduction of armaments. The Commission has not aimed at utopian goals but has ardently and jointly sought to exercise judgement and point to constructive avenues out of difficulties that are still with us. While this preface is mine, the report and its recommendations reflect the joint effort of the Commission.

The Swedish Government has generously financed most of the costs of the Commission and — as separately acknowledged — several other Governments and other sources have kindly contributed, especially the Simons Foundation in Vancouver, Canada. Three previous independent international commissions have presented valuable reports in the same field. In 1982, a commission headed by Prime Minister Olof Palme of Sweden submitted a report entitled *Common Security*. It argued that the nuclear arms race and mutual assured destruction (MAD) could destroy human civilization and that security could only be attained through cooperation and disarmament. It pinned its hopes on the strong antiwar opinion, which feared nuclear annihilation. Although the cold war continued, significant bilateral arms-control agreements were concluded between the United States and the Soviet Union, and the Helsinki Conference on Security and Co-operation in Europe was a harbinger of a new climate.

In 1996, there appeared the Australian Government-sponsored *Report of the Canberra Commission on the Elimination of Nuclear Weapons*. After the end of the cold war, this was a period of bright hope. After the successful United Nations authorized Gulf War in 1991, which stopped Iraq's aggression against Kuwait, United States President George H. W. Bush talked about "a new world order". The indefinite extension of the Non-Proliferation Treaty was achieved in 1995, after the five Nuclear weapon States had reaffirmed commitments to the Treaty to nuclear disarmament. The Canberra Commission urged that practical steps to eliminate nuclear weapons should be taken immediately.

In August 1998, just months after Pakistan's and India's nuclear tests, the Government of Japan organized the independent Tokyo Forum for Nuclear Non- Proliferation and Disarmament. Its final report, issued a year later, presented an "Action Plan" dealing with nuclear disarmament, non-proliferation and terrorism. Soon thereafter, however, the United States Senate declined to support ratification of the Comprehensive Nuclear-Test-Ban Treaty. With little or no progress on nuclear disarmament, with nuclear proliferation an ongoing reality and with growing fears of the dangers of terrorism, the post-cold war window of opportunity was closing, despite other more positive trends.

In the ten years that have passed since the Canberra Commission report was published, global economic interdependence has accelerated. All States of the world have come to face the same environmental threats and risks of contagious diseases. There have been no serious territorial or ideological conflicts between the major military Powers. Yet, amazingly, the climate for agreements on arms control and disarmament has actually deteriorated. Efforts to consolidate global treaties, like the Nuclear Non-Proliferation Treaty and the Biological and Toxin Weapons Convention, have stagnated, ratifications of the Comprehensive Nuclear-Test-Ban Treaty remain lagging, and negotiations have not even opened on the much needed treaty to stop the production of fissile material for weapons. There are even some waves of new armaments: the United States missile shield may be triggering countermeasures by China and Russia in the nuclear weapons area; and nuclear weapons with new missions may be under development in the United States and elsewhere. While the peaceful uses of space and satellites are developing at a dizzying pace, which facilitates global information exchange and communication, the most advanced military Powers are calculating how they can most effectively pursue war in this environment.
In spite of all this, Governments and world public opinion are paying less attention to the global regimes for arms control and disarmament. One reason is the intense and justified focus on the war

on terrorism and the handling of specific cases of actual or potential nuclear proliferation. Another reason may be that global treaties did not help to prevent the terrorist attack on the United States on 11 September 2001 and constituted insufficient barriers against the efforts of Iraq, North Korea and Libya to acquire nuclear weapons and against Iran to conceal a programme for the enrichment of uranium. While the reaction of most States to the treaty violations was to strengthen and develop existing treaties and institutions, the United States, the sole super-Power, has looked more to its own military power for remedies.

The United States National Security Strategy of 2002 made it clear that the United States would feel free to use armed force without the authorization of the United Nations Security Council to counter not only an actual or imminent attack involving WMD but also a WMD threat that might be uncertain as to time and place. The declared United States policy — reaffirmed on this point by the strategy issued in March 2006 — has, as I see it, parted ways with the United Nations Charter provisions on self-defense. The aim of the strategy is said to be "to help make the world not just safer but better", indicating that the United States believed that this policy had benefits for all.

No one underestimates the difficulties on the road to disarmament and to outlawing nuclear weapons in the same manner as the way in which other weapons of terror — biological and chemical weapons — have been outlawed. Some of the current stagnation in global arms control and disarmament forums is the result of a paralyzing requirement of consensus combined with an outdated system of bloc politics. However, a more important reason is that the nuclear weapon States no longer seem to take their commitment to nuclear disarmament seriously — even though this was an essential part of the NPT bargain, both at the Treaty's birth in 1968 and when it was extended indefinitely in 1995. The devaluation of international commitments inherent in these positions risks undermining the credibility and effectiveness of multilateral treaty commitments. Against a generally gloomy short-term outlook for arms control and disarmament, some positive features can be discerned in the broader field of security. The number of inter-State armed conflicts has been declining. Peacekeeping operations have prevented and continue to prevent shooting wars in many places. Efforts to reform the United Nations have borne some fruit and more may be hoped for. The new United Nations Peace building Commission will assist States emerging from conflicts, thereby reducing the risk of their relapse into violence.

The Security Council recently adopted an important resolution obligating Member States to adopt domestic legislation designed to prevent the proliferation of weapons of mass destruction (WMDs). The precedent is constructive. But if the Council were to further use and develop its quasi-legislative potential, it would need to ensure that it acts with the broad support of United Nations Members. In the longer run, this would entail making the Council more representative of the United Nations membership.

Lastly, in today's rapidly integrating world community, global treaties and global institutions, like the United Nations, the International Atomic Energy Agency and the Organization for the Prohibition of Chemical Weapons (OPCW), remain indispensable. Even with their shortcomings they can do some important things that States acting alone cannot achieve. They are, therefore, essential instruments in the hands of the international community to enhance security, jointly operate inspection systems and reduce the threat of weapons of mass destruction. Governments that have shown disenchantment with global treaties and institutions will inevitably return and renew their engagement.

When there is a greater general readiness to return to a cooperative multilateral system in the sphere of arms control and disarmament, the Commission's report will, I hope, contribute to the practical agenda. Some ideas and recommendations are new, but the Commission also espouses and argues in favour of some well known existing proposals.

Indeed, at the present time it seems to me that not only successes in the vital work to prevent proliferation and terrorism but also progress in two additional areas could transform the current gloom into hope. Bringing the Comprehensive Nuclear- Test-Ban Treaty into force would significantly impede the development of new nuclear weapons. The weapons that exist today are bad enough. Negotiating a global treaty to stop the production of fissile material for weapons would close the source for new such material and help hinder possible arms races — notably in Asia. In both of these areas the United States has the decisive leverage. If it takes the lead, the world is likely to follow. If it does not take the lead, there could be more nuclear tests and new nuclear arms races.

Weapons of Terror Freeing the World of Nuclear, Biological and Chemical Arms:

Nuclear, biological and chemical arms are the most inhumane of all weapons. Designed to terrify as well as destroy, either States or non- State actors, can cause destruction on a vastly greater scale than any conventional weapons, and their impact is far more indiscriminate and long lasting. So long as any State has such weapons — especially nuclear arms — others will want them. So long as any such weapons remain in any State's arsenal, there is a high risk that they will one day be used, by design or accident. Any such use would be catastrophic. Notwithstanding the end of the cold war balance of terror, stocks of such weapons remain extraordinarily and alarmingly high:

some 27,000 in the case of nuclear weapons, of which around 12,000 are still actively deployed.

Weapons of mass destruction (WMDs) cannot be un-invented. But, they can be outlawed, as biological and chemical weapons already have been, and their use made unthinkable. Compliance, verification and enforcement rules can be effectively applied with the requisite will. And with that will, even the eventual elimination of nuclear weapons is not beyond the world's reach. Over the past decade, there has been a serious, and dangerous, loss of momentum and direction in disarmament and non-proliferation efforts. Treaty making and implementation have stalled and, as a new wave of proliferation has threatened, unilateral enforcement action has been increasingly advocated. In 2005 there were two loud wake-up calls in the failure of the NPT Review Conference and in the inability of the World Summit to agree on a single line about any WMD issue. It is critical for those calls to be heeded now.

Procedure for Freezing 'Weapons of Terror'

The Weapons of Mass Destruction Commission makes many specific and detailed recommendations throughout its report. The most important of them are summarized below.

1. Agree on general principles of action

Disarmament and non-proliferation are best pursued through a cooperative rule-based international order, applied and enforced through effective multilateral institutions, with the United Nations Security Council as the ultimate global authority.

There is an urgent need to revive meaningful negotiations, through all available intergovernmental mechanisms, on the three main objectives of reducing the danger of present arsenals, preventing proliferation and outlawing all weapons of mass destruction once and for all.

States, individually and collectively, should consistently pursue policies designed to ensure that no State feels a need to acquire weapons of mass destruction.

Governments and relevant intergovernmental organizations and nongovernmental actors should begin preparations for a world summit on disarmament, non-proliferation and terrorist use of weapons of mass destruction to generate new momentum for concerted international action.

2. Reduce the danger of present arsenals: no use by States — no access by terrorists

(a) Secure all weapons of mass destruction and all WMD-related material and equipment from theft or other acquisition by terrorists.
(b) Take nuclear weapons off high-alert status to reduce the risk of launching by error; make deep reductions in strategic nuclear weapons; place all non-strategic nuclear weapons in centralized storage; and withdraw all such weapons from foreign soil.
(c) Prohibit the production of fissile material for nuclear weapons and phase out the production of highly enriched uranium.
(d) Diminish the role of nuclear weapons by making no-first-use pledges, by giving assurances not to use them against non-nuclear-weapon States and by not developing nuclear weapons for new tasks.

3. Prevent proliferation: no new weapon systems — no new possessors

(a) Prohibit any nuclear-weapon tests by bringing the Comprehensive Nuclear- Test-Ban Treaty into force.

(b) Revive the fundamental commitments of all NPT parties: the five nuclear weapon States to negotiate towards nuclear disarmament and the non-nuclear weapon States to refrain from developing nuclear weapons.

(c) Recognize that countries that are not party to the NPT also have a duty to participate in the disarmament process.

(d) Continue negotiations with Iran and North Korea to achieve their effective and verified rejection of the nuclear-weapon option, while assuring their security and acknowledging the right of all NPT parties to peaceful uses of nuclear energy.

(e) Explore international arrangements for an assurance of supply of enriched uranium fuel and for the disposal of spent fuel, so as to reduce incentives for national facilities and diminish proliferation risks.

4. Work towards outlawing all weapons of mass destruction once and for all

(a) Accept the principle that nuclear weapons should be outlawed, as are biological and chemical weapons, and explore the political, legal, technical and procedural options for achieving this within a reasonable time.

(b) Complete the implementation of existing regional nuclear-weapon-free zones and work actively to establish zones free of WMDs in other regions, particularly and most urgently in the Middle East.

(c) Achieve universal compliance with, and effective implementation of, the Chemical Weapons Convention, and speed up the destruction of chemical weapon stocks.

(d) Achieve universal compliance with, and effective implementation of, the Biological and Toxin Weapons Convention, and improve cooperation between industry, scientists and Governments to reinforce the ban on the development and production of biological weapons and keep abreast of developments in biotechnology.
(e) Prevent an arms race in space by prohibiting any stationing or use of weapons in outer space.

Recommendations of Blix Commission

(a) Nuclear weapons

Preventing the proliferation of nuclear weapons

1. All parties to the Non-Proliferation Treaty need to revert to the fundamental and balanced non-proliferation and disarmament commitments that were made under the Treaty and confirmed in 1995 when the Treaty was extended indefinitely.

2. All parties to the Non-Proliferation Treaty should implement the decision on principles and objectives for non-proliferation and disarmament, the decision on strengthening the Non-Proliferation Treaty review process and the resolution on the Middle East as a zone free of nuclear and all other weapons of mass destruction, all adopted in 1995. They should also promote the implementation of the "thirteen practical steps" for nuclear disarmament that were adopted in 2000.

3. To enhance the effectiveness of the nuclear non-proliferation regime, all Non-Proliferation Treaty non-nuclear-weapon States parties should accept comprehensive safeguards as strengthened by the International Atomic Energy Agency Additional Protocol.

4. The States parties to the Non-Proliferation Treaty should establish a standing secretariat to handle administrative matters for the parties to the Treaty. This secretariat should organize the Treaty's Review Conferences and their Preparatory Committee sessions. It should also organize other treaty-related meetings upon the request of a majority of the States parties.

5. Negotiations with North Korea should aim at achieving a verifiable agreement including, as a principal element, North Korea's manifesting its adherence to the Non-Proliferation Treaty and accepting the 1997 Additional Protocol, as well as revival and legal confirmation of the commitments made in the 1992 Joint Declaration on the De-nuclearisation of the Korean Peninsula: notably, that neither North nor South Korea shall have nuclear weapons or nuclear-reprocessing and uranium-enrichment facilities. Fuel-cycle services should be assured through international arrangements. The agreement should also cover biological and chemical weapons, as well as the Comprehensive Nuclear-Test-Ban Treaty, thus making the Korean peninsula a zone free of weapons of mass destruction.

6. Negotiations must be continued to induce Iran to suspend any sensitive fuel cycle- related activities and ratify the 1997 Additional Protocol and resume full cooperation with the International Atomic Energy Agency in order to avoid an increase in tensions and improve the outlook for the common aim of establishing a Middle East zone free of weapons of mass destruction. The international community and Iran should build mutual confidence through measures that should include: reliable assurances regarding the supply of fuel-cycle services; suspending or renouncing sensitive fuel-cycle activities for a prolonged period of time by all States in the Middle East; assurances against attacks and

subversion aiming at regime change; and facilitation of international trade and investment.

7. The nuclear weapon States parties to the Non-Proliferation Treaty should provide legally binding negative security assurances to non-nuclear-weapon States parties. The States not party to the Non-Proliferation Treaty that possess nuclear weapons should separately provide such assurances.

8. States should make active use of the International Atomic Energy Agency (IAEA) as a forum for exploring various ways to reduce proliferation risks connected with the nuclear fuel cycle, such as proposals for an international fuel bank; internationally safeguarded regional centres offering fuel-cycle services, including spent-fuel repositories; and the creation of a fuel-cycle system built on the concept that a few "fuel-cycle States" will lease nuclear fuel to States that forgo enrichment and reprocessing activities.

9. States should develop means of using low-enriched uranium in ships and research reactors that now require highly enriched uranium. The production of highly enriched uranium should be phased out. States that separate plutonium by reprocessing spent nuclear fuel should explore possibilities for reducing that activity.

10. All States should support the international initiatives taken to advance the global clean out of fissile material. Such support should encompass the conversion of research reactors from highly enriched to low-enriched uranium fuel, storing fissile material at centralized and secure locations and returning exported nuclear materials to suppliers for secure disposal or elimination.

11. All Non-Proliferation Treaty nuclear weapon States that have not yet done so should ratify the

protocols of the treaties creating regional nuclear-weapon-free zones. All States in such zones should conclude their Comprehensive Safeguards Agreements with the IAEA and agree to ratify and implement the Additional Protocol.

12. All States should support continued efforts to establish a zone free of weapons of mass destruction in the Middle East as a part of the overall peace process. Steps can be taken even now. As a confidence-building measure, all States in the region, including Iran and Israel, should commit themselves for a prolonged period of time to a verified arrangement not to have any enrichment, reprocessing or other sensitive fuel-cycle activities on their territories. Such a commitment should be coupled with reliable assurances about fuel-cycle services required for peaceful nuclear activities. Egypt, Iran and Israel should join the other States in the Middle East in ratifying the Comprehensive Nuclear-Test-Ban Treaty (CTBT).

13. India and Pakistan should both ratify the CTBT and join those other States with nuclear weapons that have declared a moratorium on the production of fissile material for weapons, pending the conclusion of a treaty. They should continue to seek bilateral détente and build confidence through political, economic and military measures, reducing the risk of armed conflict, and increasing transparency in the nuclear and missile activities of both countries. Eventually, both States should become members of the Nuclear Suppliers Group and the Missile Technology Control Regime, as well as parties to International Atomic Energy Agency safeguards agreements under the terms of the 1997 Additional Protocol.

Preventing nuclear terrorism:

14. States must prevent terrorists from gaining access to nuclear weapons or fissile material. To achieve this, they must maintain fully effective accounting and control of all stocks of fissile and radioactive material and other radiological sources on their territories. They should ensure that there is personal legal responsibility for any acts of nuclear terrorism or activities in support of such terrorism. They must expand their cooperation through inter alia the sharing of information, including intelligence on illicit nuclear commerce. They should also promote universal adherence to the International Convention for the Suppression of Acts of Nuclear Terrorism and to the Convention on the Physical Protection of Nuclear Material and implementation of United Nations Security Council resolution 1540 (2004).

Reducing the threat and the numbers of existing nuclear weapons:

15. All States possessing nuclear weapons should declare a categorical policy of no-first-use of such weapons. They should specify that this covers both pre-emptive and preventive action, as well as retaliation for attacks involving chemical, biological or conventional weapons.

16. All States possessing nuclear weapons should review their military plans and define what is needed to maintain credible non-nuclear security policies. States deploying their nuclear forces in triads, consisting of submarine-launched missiles, ground-based intercontinental ballistic missiles and long-range bombers should abandon this practice in order to reduce nuclear-weapon redundancy and avoid fuelling nuclear arms races.

17. Russia and the United States should agree on reciprocal steps to take their nuclear weapons off hair-trigger alert and should create a joint commission to facilitate this goal. They should

undertake to eliminate the launch-on-warning option from their nuclear war plans, while implementing a controlled parallel decrease in operational readiness of a large part of their strategic forces, by:

(a) Reducing the number of strategic submarines at sea and lowering their technical readiness to launch while in port
(b) Storing nuclear bombs and air-launched cruise missiles separately from relevant air fields;
(c) Storing separately nose cones and/or warheads of most inter-continental ballistic missiles or taking other technical measures to reduce their readiness.

18. Russia and the United States should commence negotiations on a new strategic arms reduction treaty aimed at reducing their deployments of strategic forces allowed under the Moscow Treaty on Strategic Offensive Reductions by at least half. It should include a legally binding commitment to irreversibly dismantle the weapons withdrawn under the Moscow Treaty. The new treaty should also include transparent counting rules, schedules and procedures for dismantling the weapons and reciprocal measures for verification.

19. Russia and the United States, followed by other States possessing nuclear weapons, should publish their aggregate holdings of nuclear weapons on active and reserve status as a baseline for future disarmament efforts. They should also agree to include specific provisions in future disarmament agreements relating to transparency, irreversibility, verification and the physical destruction of nuclear warheads.

20. All States possessing nuclear weapons must address the issue of their continued possession of such weapons. All nuclear weapon States parties to the Non-Proliferation Treaty must take steps towards

nuclear disarmament, as required by the Treaty and the commitments made in connection with the Treaty's indefinite extension. Russia and the United States should take the lead. Other States possessing nuclear weapons should join the process, individually or in coordinated action. While Israel, India and Pakistan are not parties to the Non-Proliferation Treaty, they, too, have a duty to contribute to the nuclear disarmament process.

21. Russia and the United States should proceed to implement the commitments they made in 1991 to eliminate specific types of non-strategic nuclear weapons, such as demolition munitions, artillery shells and warheads for short-range ballistic missiles. They should agree to withdraw all non-strategic nuclear weapons to central storage on national territory, pending their eventual elimination. The two countries should reinforce their 1991 unilateral reduction commitments by developing arrangements to ensure verification, transparency and irreversibility.

22. Every State that possesses nuclear weapons should make a commitment not to deploy any nuclear weapon, of any type, on foreign soil.

23. Any State contemplating replacement or modernization of its nuclear-weapon systems must consider such action in the light of all relevant treaty obligations and its duty to contribute to the nuclear disarmament process. As a minimum, it must refrain from developing nuclear weapons with new military capabilities or for new missions. It must not adopt systems or doctrines that blur the distinction between nuclear and conventional weapons or lower the nuclear threshold.

24. All States possessing nuclear weapons, notably Russia and the United States, should place their excess fissile material from military programmes

under International Atomic Energy Agency safeguards. To facilitate the reduction of stocks of highly enriched uranium, States possessing such stocks should sell uranium blended to enrichment levels suitable for reactor fuel to other Non-Proliferation Treaty States or use it for their own peaceful nuclear energy needs.

25. All States possessing nuclear weapons should adopt strict standards for the handling of weapons-usable fissile material deemed to be in excess to military requirements or recovered from disarmament activities, as exemplified in the United States stored-weapon and spent-fuel standards.

26. The Conference on Disarmament should immediately open the delayed negotiations for a treaty on the cut-off of production of fissile material for weapons without preconditions. Before, or at least during, those negotiations, the Conference on Disarmament should establish a group of scientific experts to examine technical aspects of the treaty.

27. To facilitate fissile material cut-off negotiations in the Conference on Disarmament, the five Non-Proliferation Treaty Nuclear Weapon States, joined by the other States possessing nuclear weapons, should agree among themselves to cease production of fissile material for weapon purposes. They should open up their facilities for such production to International Atomic Energy Agency safeguards inspections, building on the practice of Euratom inspections in France and the United Kingdom. These eight States should also address the issue of verifiable limitations of existing stocks of weapons-usable nuclear materials.

28. All States that have not already done so should sign and ratify the Comprehensive Nuclear-Test-Ban Treaty unconditionally and without delay. The United States, which has not ratified the Treaty, should

reconsider its position and proceed to ratify the Treaty, recognizing that its ratification would trigger other required ratifications and be a step towards the Treaty's entry into force. Pending entry into force, all States with nuclear weapons should continue to refrain from nuclear testing. Also, the 2007 conference of Comprehensive Nuclear-Test-Ban Treaty signatories should address the possibility of a provisional entry into force of the Treaty.

29. All signatories should provide financial, political and technical support for the continued development and operation of the verification regime, including the International Monitoring System and the International Data Centre and its secretariat, so that the Comprehensive Nuclear Test Ban Treaty Organization (CTBTO) is ready to monitor and verify compliance with the Treaty when it enters into force. They should pledge to maintain their respective stations and continue to transmit data on a national basis under all circumstances.

From regulating nuclear weapons to outlawing them

30. All States possessing nuclear weapons should begin planning for security without nuclear weapons. They should start preparing for the outlawing of nuclear weapons through joint practical and incremental measures that include definitions, benchmarks and transparency requirements for nuclear disarmament.

(b) Biological and toxin weapons

31. All States not yet party to the Biological and Toxin Weapons Convention should adhere to the Convention. The States parties to the Convention should launch a campaign to achieve universal adherence by the time of the Seventh Review Conference to be held in 2011.

32. To achieve universal adoption of national legislation and regulations aimed at full and effective implementation of the Biological and Toxin Weapons Convention, the States parties should offer technical assistance and promote best-practice models of such legislation. As a part of the confidence-building process and in order to promote transparency and harmonization, all States parties should make annual biological-weapon-related national declarations and make them public.

33. States parties to the Biological and Toxin Weapons Convention should enhance the investigatory powers of the United Nations Secretary-General, ensuring that the Secretary-General can rely upon a regularly updated roster of experts and advice from the World Health Organization and a specialist unit, modeled on the United Nations Monitoring, Verification and Inspection Commission, to assist in investigating unusual outbreaks of disease and allegations of the use of biological weapons.

34. States parties to the Biological and Toxin Weapons Convention should establish a standing secretariat to handle organizational and administrative matters related to the Treaty, such as review conferences and expert meetings.

35. Governments should pursue public health surveillance to ensure effective monitoring of unusual outbreaks of disease and develop practical methods of coordinating international responses to any major event that might involve bio-weapons. They should strengthen cooperation between civilian health and security-oriented authorities at the national, regional and global levels, including in the framework of the new International Health Regulations of the World Health Organization. Governments should also review their national bio-safety and bio-security measures to protect health and the environment from the release

of biological and toxin materials. They should harmonize national bio-security standards.

36. At the Sixth Review Conference, in 2006, the States parties to the Biological and Toxin Weapons Convention should reaffirm common understandings reached at previous review conferences and take action on all subjects addressed at Convention meetings since 2003. They should also establish a work programme on additional topics for future meetings. States parties should ensure more frequent reassessment of the implications of scientific and technological developments and reaffirm that all undertakings under article I of the Biological and Toxin Weapons Convention apply to such developments.

This Review Conference should reaffirm that all developments in the life sciences fall within the scope of the Convention and that all developments in the life sciences for hostile purposes are prohibited by the Convention.

(c) Chemical weapons

37. States parties to the Chemical Weapons Convention must provide adequate resources to ensure that there are no undue delays in the agreed destruction of chemical weapon stockpiles.

38. The Organization for the Prohibition of Chemical Weapons and States parties to the Chemical Weapons Convention should continue their efforts to secure universal adherence to the Convention. States parties should fully implement the rules on trade and transfer of chemicals that are precursors to chemical-weapon agents. They should further develop regulations regarding the trade and transfer of chemicals that can be used to produce chemical weapons. The Organization for the Prohibition of Chemical Weapons and States parties should continue to offer States

positive incentives, including technical assistance, to join and implement the Chemical Weapons Convention. When providing such assistance or transferring relevant technologies, they should consider steps to ensure safe and responsible handling by the recipient.

39. States parties to the Chemical Weapons Convention should confirm that, like the use of riot control agents, the use of toxic chemical agents for purposes of law enforcement is banned as a method of warfare. Accordingly, each State party must declare any such agent under article III.

40. States parties should ensure that the Organization for the Prohibition of Chemical Weapons has the resources, experience and legal authority needed to carry out challenge inspections in a timely and effective manner, including the taking and removal of samples for testing.

41. Through their domestic laws and policies, all States should prohibit the production, possession and use of toxic chemicals and technologies for purposes that are banned by the Chemical Weapons Convention. States should ensure the security of chemical facilities and security within such facilities through legislation and agreement with industry. States should also develop national means to monitor that security standards are met.

42. States parties to the Chemical Weapons Convention should use the Organization for the Prohibition of Chemical Weapons as a coordinating center in the development of global standards for a chemical industry security culture. The Organization should offer evaluation and security assistance at declared sites. States parties should also strengthen the capacity of the Organization for the Prohibition of Chemical Weapons to provide practical assistance

against chemical weapons, for instance detection equipment, alarm systems and medical antidotes.

(d) Control of Weapons

WMD delivery means, missile defenses, and weapons in space

43. Member States of the Missile Technology Control Regime should make new efforts to better implement and expand export controls on relevant materials and technology. States subscribing to 'The Hague Code of Conduct' should extend its scope to include cruise missiles and unmanned aerial vehicles. They should establish a multilateral data exchange center, based on the Russian-United States initiatives for the exchange of data on missile launches from early-warning systems. Regional and international non-proliferation measures should include information exchanges; launch notification and restrictions or bans on specific items or capabilities.

44. States should not consider the deployment or further deployment of any kind of missile defence system without first attempting to negotiate the removal of missile threats. If such negotiations fail, deployments of such systems should be accompanied by cooperative development programmes and confidence-building measures to lower the risk of adverse effects on international peace and security, including the risk of creating or aggravating arms races.

45. All States should renounce the deployment of weapons in outer space. They should promote universal adherence to the Outer Space Treaty and expand its scope through a protocol to prohibit all weapons in space. Pending the conclusion of such a protocol, they should refrain from activities inconsistent with its aims, including any tests against space objects or targets on earth from a space

platform. States should adapt the international regimes and institutions for space issues so that both military and civilian aspects can be dealt with in the same context. States should also set up a group of experts to develop options for monitoring and verifying various components of a space security regime and a code of conduct, designed inter alias to prohibit the testing or deployment of space weapons.

46. A review conference of the Outer Space Treaty to mark its 40th year in force should be held in 2007. It should address the need to strengthen the Treaty and extend its scope. A special coordinator should be appointed to facilitate ratifications and liaise with non-parties about the reinforcement of the Treaty-based space security regime.

Export controls, international assistance, and non-governmental actors:

47. All States should conduct audits of their export-control enforcement agencies (customs, police, coast guard, border control and military) to ensure that they can carry out their tasks effectively. States should seek to establish a universal system of export controls providing harmonized standards, enhanced transparency and practical support for implementation. Members of the five export control regimes should promote a widening of their membership and improve implementation in view of current security challenges, without impeding legitimate trade and economic development.

48. The Group of Eight Global Partnerships (G8) should expand the geographical and functional scope of its non-proliferation assistance. The G-8 should guarantee full funding for the Elimination of Weapons-Grade Plutonium Production programme. Potential donors should consider how technical assistance; training, equipment and financing could be brought to bear to help States of all regions

implement United Nations Security Council resolution 1540 (2004).

49. Companies engaged in activities relevant to weapons of mass destruction have the ability and responsibility to help prevent the proliferation of such weapons and an interest in demonstrating that they are fulfilling that responsibility, including full compliance with national and international obligations and public transparency. Trade associations should also promote such objectives.

50. States, international organizations and professional associations should encourage the appropriate academic and industrial associations to adopt and effectively implement codes of practice and codes of conduct for science and research in weapons of mass destruction-relevant fields.

51. Governments possessing any weapons of mass destruction should keep their parliaments fully and currently informed of their holdings of such weapons and their activities to reduce and eliminate them. Parliaments should actively seek such information and recognize their responsibility in formulating policies relevant to weapons of mass destruction issues. Greater inter-parliamentary cooperation on weapons of mass destruction issues is needed.

52. States should assist non-governmental organizations to participate actively in international meetings and conferences and to inform and campaign in the weapons of mass destruction field. Private foundations should substantially increase their support for organizations that are working to eliminate global weapons of mass destruction threats.

53. Organizations with security-relevant agendas should re-examine the 2002 United Nations study on disarmament and non-proliferation education and should consider ways in which they could foster and

support such education and an informed public debate. Governments should fund student internships at multilateral institutions working on weapons of mass destruction issues.

Compliance, verification, enforcement and the role of the United Nations:

54. As the strengthened safeguards system adopted by the International Atomic Energy Agency through the Additional Protocol should become standard for parties to the Non-Proliferation Treaty, supplier States should make acceptance of this standard by recipient parties a condition for contracts involving nuclear items.

55. Governments should instruct their intelligence authorities to assist international inspection agencies by providing relevant information without compromising the independence of the inspection systems.

56. The United Nations Security Council should establish a small subsidiary unit that could provide professional technical information and advice on matters relating to weapons of mass destruction. At the request of the Council or the Secretary- General, it should organize ad hoc inspections and monitoring in the field, using a roster of well-trained inspectors that should be kept up-to-date.

57. International legal obligations regarding weapons of mass destruction must be enforced. International enforcement action should be taken only after credible investigation and authoritative finding of non-compliance with legal obligations.

58. In orders for the Conference on Disarmament to function, it should be able to adopt its Programme of Work by a qualified majority of two thirds of the members present and voting. It should also take its

other administrative and procedural decisions with the same requirements.

59. The United Nations General Assembly should convene a world summit on disarmament, non-proliferation and terrorist use of weapons of mass destruction, which should meet after thorough preparations. This world summit should also discuss and decide on reforms to improve the efficiency and effectiveness of the United Nations disarmament machinery.

60. The United Nations Security Council should make greater use of its potential to reduce and eliminate threats of weapons of mass destruction — whether they are linked to existing arsenals, proliferation or terrorists. It should take up for consideration any withdrawal from or breach of an obligation not to acquire weapons of mass destruction. Making use of its authority under the Charter to take decisions with binding effect for all members, the Council might, inter alias:

(a) Require individual States to accept effective and comprehensive monitoring, inspection and verification;
(b) Require Member States to enact legislation to secure global implementation of specific rules or measures; and
(c) Decide, as instance of last resort, on the use of economic or military enforcement measures. Before United Nations reform has made the Security Council more representative of the United Nations membership, it is especially important that binding decisions should be preceded by effective consultation to ensure that they are

supported by the membership of the United Nations and will be accepted and respected.[90]

Growing Nuclear Stockpiles Require New Security Measures

Today 2,000 metric tons of separated highly enriched uranium and plutonium stockpiled in civilian and military programs pose a significant proliferation risk. These stockpiles could grow if plans for an expansion in civilian nuclear energy materialize. Since 2005, more than 20 countries that do not now have nuclear power have expressed interest in installing nuclear reactors. With more reactors, it is likely that additional uranium enrichment and possibly plutonium reprocessing plants would also be built. Current efforts to restrict the expansion of such sensitive technologies are competing with efforts to promote plutonium as an energy resource. The systems that guard against state diversion of and terrorist access to sensitive materials that could be used in nuclear weapons are already under duress. New measures will be needed to provide confidence that fissile material is adequately secured and safeguarded.

To address these issues, the Stanley Foundation brought together a group of leading experts at its 48th annual Strategy for Peace Conference October 25-27 at the Airlie Center in Warrenton, Virginia. Participants in a roundtable on securing, controlling, and capping of nuclear materials recommended, among other things:

(a) New approaches to reducing the spread of uranium enrichment and plutonium

---

[90] Hans Blix, Chairman of the Weapons of Mass Destruction Commission, May 2006: Anders Lidén, Permanent Representative of Sweden, http://wmdcommission.org

reprocessing facilities that address the complete range of states' incentives

(b) Measures to improve transparency across the board.

(c) Identification of subsidies to the nuclear industry to encourage the application of economic criteria to nuclear energy development

(d) Pursuit of an agreement to halt the production of fissile material for nuclear weapons, either in the Conference on Disarmament (CD) in Geneva, or outside the formal CD forums via informal discussions among the five permanent UN Security Council members and the three de facto nuclear weapons states of Pakistan, India, and Israel.

(e) Consideration of a "proliferation tax/user fee" that could be used to finance advances in safeguards and physical protection.

Reducing enrichment and reprocessing

Recent proposals (fuel assurances via a global, centralized fuel bank) only target one or two incentives for states to develop indigenous enrichment plants and, depending on implementation, could subsidize the further spread of power reactors and material subject to theft or diversion. Other solutions are needed. Examples:

(a) Devaluing fissile material production through clarifying the environmental hazards.

(b) Stronger and purposeful efforts by the US, and perhaps other major powers, to strip the prestige away from nuclear technology by de-emphasizing their own national reliance on enrichment and reprocessing.

Measures to improve transparency: There should be better dissemination of information about materials, including material that the IAEA considers "material unaccounted for." The IAEA's Safeguards Implementation Report should be declassified, and illicit trafficking databases should be linked together (e.g., IAEA, Interpol, Salzburg University).

Identify subsidies: Nuclear expansion depends heavily on government support, particularly in the form of tax incentives, loan guarantees, and streamlined licensing. There is currently no data on the extent of subsidies to the US nuclear industry. There has also been no attempt to apply economic criteria to nuclear development. A useful step would be to identify subsidies going to nuclear industries both in the United States and abroad, to be used as a baseline against other energy source cost.

A proliferation tax/user fee: In a world with a carbon tax, could there be an analogous proliferation tax? If nuclear energy is being promoted in the context of reducing global carbon emissions, the proliferation risks of nuclear energy need to be given equal emphasis. The user fee could be applied to improved and expanded physical protection measures and safeguards on fissile material.

Fissile Material Production Cut-off (FMCT): FMCT is a critical nonproliferation and disarmament step, but efforts in the CD have yielded little progress. A strategy is needed for bringing in Pakistan, and there is a need to pursue additional channels for progress outside the CD. This should begin with a declared fissile material production moratorium for the 5 nuclear weapons states (United States, United Kingdom, Russia, China and France) as well as India, Pakistan, and Israel.

Additionally, roundtable participants identified the following gaps in current programs:
(a)The challenges posed by failing states: Current measures in the areas of safeguards against fissile material diversion and physical protection of

materials do not address the problems raised by potential state failure and ungoverned areas.

(b)Improving physical protection: Implementation of physical protection goals needs to be universalized through an enforcement protocol or norm. How does the international community track or verify the effective adherence of states to their obligations on physical protection of materials and facilities—an issue that challenges traditional sovereign rights of states to police and secure their own territory? Also, there is a gap between how direct-use material is handled in the military versus the civilian sector, particularly in research reactors at academic institutions.

(c)Reducing use of highly enriched uranium and plutonium (HEU/Pu) in the civil sector: While there is widespread agreement on avoiding HEU/Pu in the civil sector, there is not similar agreement on plutonium because of the use of mixed oxide fuel in some states' reactors.

(d)Inadequacy of safeguards against diversion: IAEA safeguards at bulk handling facilities need to be strengthened, particularly for enrichment plants.

(e)Nonproliferation systems do not track nuclear expertise, which could provide critical information about proliferation-related activities.[91]

Towards a world without nukes

The two of us have joined a number of our colleagues on both sides of the Atlantic in discussing a threatening development: the accelerating spread of nuclear weapons, nuclear know-how and nuclear

---

[91] THE STANLEY FOUNDATION: 31/10/2007 Maxims News Network, United Nations - 31 October 2007 -- Muscatine, Iowa

material. We now face a very real possibility that the deadliest weapons and materials ever invented could fall in to dangerous hands.

We believe the United States and Germany, NATO and all of Europe, including Russia, have a special leadership role to play in support of global efforts to reduce reliance on nuclear weapons, to prevent their spread into dangerous hands, and ultimately to end them as a threat to the world.

We are encouraged by a growing recognition that in order to deal decisively with the nuclear threat and stop nuclear proliferation, nations must embrace both the vision of a world free of nuclear weapons and the urgent practical steps necessary to overcome the nuclear dangers that we all face.

Over the past few years, statesmen from several European countries have published articles in support of the "vision and steps" as originally set forth by George Shultz, William Perry, Henry Kissinger and Sam Nunn. Governments are also embracing this approach. In September 2009, heads of state met at the U.N. Security Council and passed a strong resolution in support of this direction. The United States and Russia concluded a New Start treaty in 2010, and leaders from around the world met in Seoul in March 2012 to continue the work to secure nuclear materials begun at the 2010 Washington Nuclear Security Summit.

These efforts both inside and outside of governments are important, as the key to achieving these urgent near-term steps and realizing the long-term vision is cooperation.

In May, NATO leaders will meet in Chicago, preceded by a meeting of foreign and defense ministers this coming week in Brussels. The urgent question facing the alliance is how NATO can make a positive contribution to nuclear threat reduction in light of these converging developments. While America bears a special responsibility, nuclear policy must also be addressed within Europe, and NATO allies should strive to move together with a sense of urgency on core nuclear issues.

In this context, we believe the drafting of NATO's Deterrence and Defense Posture Review tasked at the 2010 Lisbon summit provides an opportunity to set a solid foundation for NATO nuclear policy. Importantly, it would also provide a basis for a new process of engagement with Russia and other nuclear-weapons-capable states. Negotiations aimed at substantially reducing the number of nuclear weapons must continue, initially between the United States and Russia, in order to encourage and ensure that the other countries possessing such weapons will join this process.

In Chicago, NATO should state that it now believes the fundamental purpose of its nuclear weapons is to deter the use of nuclear weapons by others, and it should plan for further reductions of U.S. tactical nuclear weapons in Europe. The target of completing consolidation to the United States should be within five years, with the timing and pace determined by broad political and security developments between NATO and Russia, including but not limited to Russian tactical nuclear deployments near NATO's border.

This can be accomplished in ways that ensure that NATO will remain a nuclear alliance for as long as nuclear weapons exist, and that America's extended nuclear deterrent will continue — but in a form that is safer and more credible. The alternative — maintaining the nuclear status quo in Europe — runs a high cost and unacceptable risk.

Russia retains a large stockpile of tactical nuclear weapons, estimated at about 2,000, and many of these are deployed in Europe. Russia, too, has a vital interest in the security of tactical nuclear weapons — its own and those of others. A dialogue among the United States, NATO and Russia focused on accountability, transparency, reductions and elimination should be a high priority and should not await formal agreements.

Global security and stability can only be achieved through stable and reliable cooperation among America, Russia, Europe and China. Thus, cooperation should become the keyword of this century on the way to a nuclear-weapon-free world.

A broader NATO-Russia discussion of Euro-Atlantic security is necessary if we are to make political and practical progress on nuclear threat reduction. Cooperation on missile defense is another long-overdue area where Russia, the United States and NATO can and should be working together rather than building separate and uncoordinated systems.

Failure to develop a cooperative approach to missile defense in Europe would fuel charges of unilateralism and contribute to the risk of returning to the era of confrontation with Russia, leading to a new arms race and new tensions. This must be avoided by an agreement on missile defense, including reliable arrangements or understandings necessary for cooperation.

One approach to framing a new process on European security that should also be endorsed in Chicago must be to deepen consultations aimed at reliable arrangements or understandings with Russia on the full range of Euro-Atlantic security issues, including missile defense and conventional and nuclear arms.

Steps to increase warning and decision time for political and military leaders should be central to this dialogue, so that no nation fears a short-warning conventional attack or perceives the need to deter or defend against such an attack with tactical nuclear arms. Progress including action on these issues can be made separately, as long as all issues are being seriously addressed in parallel and within a common framework. Military-to-military discussions mandated by political leaders are essential.

The common interests of the United States, Europe and Russia are more aligned today than at any point in modern history. We must seize this historic opportunity and act accordingly.[92]

Conclusion

The most brilliant proposals for elimination of nuclear, chemical and biological weapons have been explained, which could avoid the World War III provided all nations follow the guidelines incorporated in these two reports.

If we can avoid these catastrophic weapons, the WORLD PEACE program would be successful. The developed countries and the arms manufacturing countries must consider humanitarian approach to safeguard the life of human beings, animals and plants of this planet.

These two reports should be sincerely discussed and accepted by the UN member countries to save this planet. But there is no information that the nuclear countries have accepted all proposals enumerated in these scholarly reports.

---

92 Helmut Schmidt and Sam Nunn (2012), "Towards a world without nukes", The New York Times, Opinion Page, April 13, 2012, Notes: Helmut Schmidt served as chancellor of the Federal Republic of Germany. Sam Nunn is a former chairman of the U.S. Senate Armed Services Committee.

The UN should prevail upon the developed and other nuclear countries to accept the suggestions. The UN should fight terrorism and should also ban researches on Nuclear, Chemical and Biological weapons.

Global security and stability can only be achieved through stable and reliable cooperation among America, Russia, Europe and China. Thus, cooperation should become the keyword of this century on the way to a nuclear-weapon free world.

The terrorists create problems to the whole world as they can kill thousands of innocent people anywhere, anytime and in any country. But the nuclear countries can make the whole world the largest graveyard any time just to prove that their country/ countries are super powers and they can destroy the God's Kingdom at anytime.

The developed countries can solve both the problems by reducing arms production and reducing nuclear research. These countries should immediately stop international trade of arms and related scientific know-how.

The United Nations Organization should hold annual conference on 'World Peace' in Sweden or Australia with Presidents of at least 15 countries for a meaning full dialogue to award permanent peace to the people of the world. But it should be held annually outside the UN HQs.

Japan is the only major power that can afford no enemies. - Marius S. Jansen, Japan and Its World

+++++

Chapter –VII

WORLD PEACE IS POSSIBLE

Our team of experts found highly radioactive materials stored in open fields without any security. Hillary Rodham Clinton:
In a speech delivered at the University of Louisville, Kentucky on April 9, 2010

GOD, NATURE, LUCK, and TIME have different dictionary meanings. But these words control life of each living being jointly and independently. The Almighty God blesses or punishes individuals on the basis of his / her work and devotion. Nature favours individuals or a country to prosper and allows them to live in peace; but sometimes it becomes so rough that individuals, society or country or even a continent starve and perish. Good luck can make a man a king, President of a country and even the Secretary General of the United Nations. Time rewards and harms to each living being. Inauspicious time can cause assassination of Mahatma Gandhi, Abraham Lincoln and John Fitzgerald Kennedy; and auspicious time can adorn an unknown man as President or Prime Minister of a country. These four factors can award peace to individuals, people, society, country and the world. We must remember that life flows within. Whatever we achieve, it is the reward of our activities. If we fall into holes, it is because we make holes for others. We draw advances from the Banks as others have deposited their surplus in the bank. We feel we are lonely but we make the human society.

The shortcut way to attain peace in life is adhering truth, sacrifice, courage and strength, which we possess. We should not blame others for our pain or suffering or frustration. If we try to attain peace in life – it is possible. Similarly world peace is possible and it can be made permanent.

War or revenge is not the solution for a long lasting problem. World peace cannot be restored through war or revenge. The peace attained through war or revenge can never be permanent; it is simply a silence over a graveyard, which can become more dangerous after some time. The World War II is the cause and effect of World War I. So to avoid World War III, we must analyze the history of World War II. The causes of World War III will not be the rivalry among the countries, but the terrorists, fundamentalists, Maoists and Naxalites, may initiate it. Cannot we convince them to join the peace process? The nuclear countries must remember that war equipments manufactured by them reaches the hands of the terrorists easily. Hence it is possible that terrorists and other organizations may mis-utilize the nuclear, biological and chemical weapons against the manufacturing countries and other targeted countries.

It is time for creation of 'United Nations Peace Organization' to activate the peace process in each human settlement all over the world.

Can we stop manufacturing of nuclear, biological and chemical weapons for the greater cause of WORLD PEACE?

Can we reduce defense expenditure? Can we utilize the defense personnel's to protect the land only and not to utilize them to attack other countries?

World peace costs nothing but it can save our earth. The governments just need patience but the United Nations need immediate action.

Understanding Peace:

- **(a) Peace is a state of harmony and the absence of hostility.**
- **(b) Peace is a cessation of violent international conflict.**
- **(c) Peace is antonyms of war.**
- **(d) Peace results in respect, justice, and goodwill.**
- **(e) Peace is influenced by environment.**
- **(f) Peace describes calm, serenity, and silence.**
- **(g) Peace awards God-Realization.**

The symbol of the Campaign for Nuclear Disarmament has become a widely recognized peace symbol. The traditional political definition of peace and the very word itself originated among the ancient Romans who defined peace, *pax*, as *absentia belli*, the absence of war.

Today, peace is often understood as the absence of war between two or more state-organized armies. Nonetheless, the concept of peace also applies to the state of people within their respective geopolitical entities, as civil war, state-sponsored genocide, terrorism, and other violence are all threats to peace on an international level. Since World War II, wars among states have become less common, while violent internal conflicts have become a more central concern. Present day Sudan, for example, is the site of widespread suffering and violence, despite its not being engaged in war with another sovereign state. Peace, in this context, is understood as the absence of violence among groups, whether part of a state apparatus or not. This concept of peace as a mere absence of overt violence, however, is still challenged by some as incomplete.

Lord Gautama Buddha has taught the human beings that the real and lasting victories are those of peace and not of war.

Mahatma Gandhi suggested that if an oppressive society lacks violence, the society is nonetheless not peaceful, because of the injustice of the oppression. Gandhi articulated a vision of peace in which justice is an inherent and necessary aspect; that peace requires not only the absence of violence but also the presence of justice.

Influential peace researcher **Johan Galtung** has described this former conception of peace as "negative peace", suggesting that underlying conflict must be resolved in order to achieve true peace. Galtung described peace with justice as "positive peace," because hostility and further violence could no longer flourish in this environment.

During the 1950s and 60s, when Martin Luther King Jr. and the civil rights movement carried out various non-violent activities aimed at ending segregation and racial persecution in America, they understood peace as more than just the absence of violence. They observed that while there was not open combat between blacks and whites, there was an unjust system in place in which the government deprived African-Americans of equal rights. While some opponents criticized the activists for "disturbing the peace",

Martin Luther King observed that "True peace is not merely the absence of tension: it is the presence of justice."Galtung coined the term structural violence to refer to such situations, which although not violent on the surface, harbor systematic oppression and injustice.

Peace Movement: In a participatory discussion on peace, Hahnel[93] explains that Peace movements cannot stand idly by and wait for the economics of competition and greed to be replaced by the economics of equitable cooperation. Peace movements must rage against war and all its causes in societies waging unjust wars, which are most often societies who also practice the economics of competition and greed. This means one job of the peace movement is to dispel the myth that empire benefits the average citizen. It is pointless to deny that there are material benefits of empire. But it is usually the case that the distribution of the benefits and costs of empire is such that, on balance, ordinary citizens are worse off. Moreover, the dynamics of empire invariably shift the internal balance of power further in favor of the ruling elite. So it is important for peace movements to explain that an accurate material calculus reveals that ordinary people are usually worse off and further dis-empowered when their governments pursue imperial ambitions.

However, peace movements should never make this material calculus their major argument against empire. It is the first responsibility of citizens to prevent a government that purports to speak for them from engaging in imperial policies because imperialism is wrong. It is wrong to subvert the sovereignty of other nations. It is wrong to intervene

---

[93] R. Hahnel and Marla Renn (2006), " A Participatory Peace – An Interview with Robin Hahnel: Looking Inside the Anti-war Movement", July 7, 2006; http://www.vanparecon.resist.ca

in the domestic affairs of other countries -- undermining regimes that strive for sovereignty and propping up regimes that acquiesce to domination. It is wrong to use military, economic, and political power to seize the lion's share of the benefits from international investment and trade from less developed countries. Moreover, empires never last forever, and chickens always come home to roost. And we can all live much better in a world of peaceful coexistence ruled by international law where the benefits of international economic cooperation are shared equitably than we do in a world of rising and falling empires.

There is no reason to believe ridding the world of war is an easy task. Humans have waged war on one another from time immemorial. As we become more numerous, and our weaponry becomes more deadly and environmentally destructive, the consequences of failing to kick this uniquely human habit become ever more frightening. But we are a species capable of reason and we can and do learn from our mistakes. Nor is the peace movement without its troops. Phyllis Bennis, who heads a team of anti-war activists at the Institute for Policy Studies in Washington DC, likes to point out that there are still two super powers in the world today. The Soviet Union is gone, but the United States is not a super power without a world-class challenger. The world peace movement is the other super power, and we should never underestimate our potential and our power.

World Peace Council condemns Israeli attacks:

The World Peace Council condemned the Israeli government's attacks against the Palestinian and Lebanese peoples, calling it genocide. In a statement declaration, the council said that the bombings of Gaza and the recent Israeli actions in Lebanon was a clear sign of Tel Aviv's interest in worsening the Middle East crisis. Such actions also corroborated deliberate support for the US´ plans to take possession of the entire area, as clearly stated by Israeli Prime Minister Ehud Olmert, who threatened to attack Syria.

This is just the prelude to the imperial aggression of the entire Middle East because, apart from the threat to Syria, there is also the warmongering campaign against Iran for its peaceful use of nuclear energy, the statement added. Orlando Fundora, the president of the council has stated for members and those opposing war, hegemony, and imperialism, to censure Israel's actions. A strong world front against this new round of Israeli genocide in complicity with US imperialism must be created.[94]

Civilizations and World Peace:

Algerian President Abdelaziz Bouteflika opines that:

(a) Better understanding and respect for other civilizations is the key to improving a world full of skepticism and violence.
(b) Today's world is plagued by unjustness and power politics. More communication between civilizations is essential to easing tension and promoting world peace.
(c) China and Arab nations have enduring friendship, and the way that the two ancient civilizations get along with each other can be a model for other civilizations.
(d) The concept of **multiculturalism** must be developed, as youth are the future of the world.
(e) Over emphasis (of the idea) may isolate some people and push them to extremism and terrorism.
(f) Terrorism is not confined to a certain religion, race or region.

---

[94] NNN – Prensa Latina, Havan, July 15,2006

(g) He is optimistic about the future of relations between China and the Arab world, including relations between China and Algeria.
(h) Algerian people will not forget that China was the first Asian country to recognize the new Algeria in 1958.
(i) Poverty, illiteracy and infectious diseases are considered the three major problems for Africa. To bring a decent life to all African people is the priority for the entire continent.

Xu Shuying, a freshman from the University's International Studies Department, opines that many conflicts today are results of misunderstandings among civilizations,"[95]

Nuclear Realities

Given the worrying over nuclear Iran, it is timely to review the rules of nuclear proliferation. Otherwise insignificant nations and failed states gain credibility by shorting their own people to divert billions of dollars to acquiring a bomb. Take away that fact from Pakistan, and the United States would probably have reduced aid to such a de facto belligerent long ago. Without the ongoing appearance of possessing nukes, North Korea would probably earn about as much foreign aid as Chad or Niger. What makes France a world player, in a way that the much larger and richer Germany is not, is not just the burdens of German guilt, but also the fact of a nuclear France. The bomb sometimes achieves what even GDP, population, strategic location, or natural resources cannot.

Madness as force multiplier: Presumed madness is a force multiplier of nuclear capability, especially in an Islamic apocalyptic context. Under conventional nuclear deterrence, rough nuclear parity, and the assurance that neither side has a first-strike

---

[95] China Daily

capability sufficient to render its opponent nuclear impotent, prevent both wars and nuclear blackmail. But if a head of state can feign insanity, or, better yet, convincingly announce a wish for the apocalypse, then he can, in theory, circumvent some traditional rules of deterrence. An Iranian theocrat's supposed willingness to use his sole nuclear weapon to wipe out tiny Israel — at the cost of losing 30 million Iranians from retaliation — yields a cheap way to obtain not just parity with Israel, but potentially a nuclear advantage.

Advertisement: In any given Middle Eastern crisis, a soon-to-be-nuclear Iran will always talk of the return of the hidden imam while threatening to repeat the Holocaust. By these means, it hopes to reap political concessions that its paltry array of nukes would not otherwise warrant. Acting as if one had nothing to lose is an advantage in nuclear poker — analogous to the supposedly prison-bound high-school dropout picking a fight with his graduating, Harvard-bound counterpart.

Sort, kind nuclear: All intelligence concerning the current status of the world's nuclear club is inexact at best. Therefore, to achieve nuclear deterrence, it may not even be necessary for a rogue state to provide conclusive proof that it has nuclear weapons on hand and that they actually work.

Iraq might well never have been able to produce enough weapons-grade plutonium from its Osirak reactor to make a bomb, even had Israel not destroyed the plant in 1981. No matter: Had we known in 1991 that the reactor was intact and had been working for a decade, there is real doubt whether the United States would have dared to invade Iraq during the first Gulf War.

Moammar Qaddafi reportedly gave up his nuclear-weapons program for fear of meeting the same fate as Saddam Hussein. But he may have wrongly surmised, on the basis of our claim that we had invaded Iraq in part to stop Saddam's WMD program, that the existence of such a program would have prompted a U.S. preemptive response. He might have been more accurate had he concluded that uncertainty about the status of his nuclear acquisition might have convinced the U.S. of the dangers of attacking such a potential nuclear power. Had Qaddafi instead accelerated work on his nuclear program from 2003 to 2011 — even falsely claiming at key intervals that he had a bomb — there is less likelihood that NATO would have bombed him out of power last year?

Syria, after the fall of Saddam, apparently better understood these realities and therefore was racing to enrich uranium and obtain one or two bombs. Israel destroyed its enrichment facility near Deir ez-Zor in 2007 when it was unequivocally clear that Syria was not yet nuclear. Note, as in the case of Saddam Hussein in 1981, that Bashar al-Assad did not retaliate against Israel in 2007 — apparently afraid to engage a nuclear Israel over a matter of nuclear weapons. Had the reactor not been bombed then, today, nearly five years later, Assad might well have been able to at least feign nuclear capability in a way that might have shielded him against foreign pressures.

To this day, we do not know whether North Korea has successfully detonated a nuclear bomb that is easily deliverable. But it does not matter; we need to know only that it has achieved some sort of nuclear reaction that suggests the ability to repeat it a few times. That fact prevents any sort of preemptive attack on a North Korean reactor, giving North Korea the sort of exemption that Iraq, Libya, and Syria never quite achieved.

Nuclear stockpiles are not all equal: The United States, in well-meaning fashion, is supposedly considering unilaterally reducing its nuclear force, perhaps even well below the limits agreed on with the Russians. Rumors circulate that a few in the administration are pondering a more radical reduction, to 400 nukes or even fewer — about what China or India may possess.

If true, the logic is bewildering. There is little danger that the size of the U.S. nuclear stockpile per se will ever encourage an American preemptive nuclear strike. There is even less likelihood that terrorists will get their hands on American bombs. In a defense budget of over $600 billion, maintenance of our nuclear stockpiles is not an inordinate expense. Nor is there any evidence that spontaneously reducing stockpiles will encourage the same from others.

Most important, what is forgotten is the reason why the post–Cold War American stockpile is still so large. Unlike Russia or China, the U.S. has several key allies that are non-nuclear and whose security needs are met by our nuclear umbrella — in the sense that we pledge to defend them to the last nuke from any existential attack.

Advertisement: But there is more to it than that. Our allies themselves, unlike the rogue states we have been considering, have the capability to become nuclear overnight. The reason why Germany, Japan, South Korea, and Taiwan are not nuclear is not a matter of technology or finance; indeed, all four could this year alone create nukes as they do BMWs or Hondas. It is not just an American nuclear umbrella but rather a large American nuclear umbrella that assures such countries that they can rest secure without their own deterrent stockpiles.

In other words, if the Obama administration were to take us down to a few hundred bombs, it might send a signal to our allies that we could not possibly deter all their enemies simultaneously — and that they would be wiser to fend for themselves by obtaining their own nuclear arsenals. For each dozen bombs we retired, our allies might feel it necessary to make up the difference on their own.

Democratic bombs: The danger is not the bomb per se, but rather who has it. Most of us do not worry about a democratic Britain, France, India, or Israel possessing nuclear weapons. The fright instead is over a Communist authoritarian China, an unhinged North Korea, an Islamist Pakistan, or an unstable Russia having nuclear weapons. Transparent democracies, in other words, are mostly reliable nuclear guardians; non-transparent autocracies are less so. Should Australia or Canada wish to acquire nuclear weapons, few privately would care; should Cuba or Zimbabwe, everyone publicly would care. It is always wise to limit the nuclear club, given the chance of accident or change of government; but wiser still to limit the non-democratic nuclear club.

Preemptive Attacks: There have been a handful of efforts to preempt and stop nuclear programs. Israel, as we have seen, has done it twice, against Iraq and Syria. America in 2003 claimed it was ensuring that Saddam did not have weapons of mass destruction. Note that all preemptive attacks so far have occurred in the Middle East — no surprise, given the rivalry of Israel, the Arab states, and Iran, the ubiquity of madmen, lots of cash, and 40 percent of the world's oil.

What is strange is that Iran itself, the likely target of any future preemptive effort, was the first nation to attack another nation's nuclear reactor. (Reports of Soviet efforts to target the Israeli reactor at Dimona during the Six-Day War are probably unfounded.) In 1980, Iran sent planes into Iraq to attack the Osirak facility; for fear that Saddam might develop a bomb during the Iraq-Iran War. That mostly failed mission damaged but did not destroy the facility, which was demolished a year later by the Israeli air force. For all the present Iranian talk of sovereignty, it was Iran that established the precedent that unhinged enemies cannot be allowed to have nuclear weapons. In the very first days of its war with Saddam Hussein it sought to ensure that Iraq would not go nuclear — perhaps with some help from Israeli intelligence. As a general rule, preemption against a nuclear facility is as immediately denounced as it is over time quietly appreciated — so long as the mission was successful.

IRAN: **How do all these rules apply to Iran?**

Tehran knows that it has enough natural gas for over a century of electrical-power production. It builds nuclear facilities only to gain prestige, expand its influence beyond what it otherwise would be, and engage in blackmail — always exaggerating the pace of its nuclear acquisition to convince potential preemptors that it may already have the bomb and therefore will retaliate in nuclear fashion. Likewise, it believes that the loonier and more suicidal it sounds, the more likely other countries are to grant concessions — successful states cannot afford to wager all that they have created on the likely hunch that a failed state like Iran is bluffing. If we cannot guarantee our allies deterrence from a nuclear Iran, then they will find a way to obtain it on their own — whether through preemption in the case of Israel or through nuclear acquisition in the case of the Gulf monarchies. Finally, Iranians understand the importance of knocking out an enemy's nuclear facility — not least because they were the first ones to try it themselves.[96]

---

[96] Victor Davis Hanson (2012), "Nuclear Realties", National Review Online, February 21, 2012

Nuclear Exit

Germany's decision to shut down its nuclear power plants latest by 2022 is a historic response to rising public opinion after the Fukushima disaster. It is momentous because it comes from a conservative, business-oriented coalition that earlier viewed nuclear power as vital for competitiveness. It is worth recalling that Chancellor Angela Merkel's government legislated last year to overturn a similar commitment on closure made by its centre-left predecessor. But the nuclear accident in Japan and the swelling tide of public protests led to the dropping of the plan to extend the lifespan of 17 nuclear power stations until 2033. What is more, seven old reactors were retired. Chancellor Merkel's bold move clearly derives much confidence from a forward-looking energy plan that emphasizes cleaner and better power from natural gas and coal, and an expanded role for renewable energy sources such as solar and wind.

The prospect of doing away with nuclear power has worldwide appeal although the imperatives are not the same in every country. The German story is one of an industrialized society that has no compulsion to meet the energy needs of robust economic growth and rapidly rising living standards. In fact, nuclear energy meets 29 per cent of its needs and now requires alternatives. India, on the other hand, needs a safe and efficient mix of sources to cater to massively expanding demand. It must, in parallel, reduce the energy intensity of growth. The way to go would be to actively cooperate with countries like Germany on building efficient coal-fired power plants, tapping newer technologies such as river turbines, and aggressively expanding solar-based technologies. Multiple options are necessary also to stay aligned to carbon emission goals. [97]

---

[97] Editorial - The Hindu Editorial Tuesday June 2, 2011

Peace: Tending Positive

Gareth Evans, the President emeritus of the International Crisis Group and Chancellor of Australian National University delivered the keynote address at the United States Institute of Peace for the second annual conference on "Preventing Violent Conflict" on June 1, 2011. He opined the following observations for a march for World Peace.

Peace Statistics: Doing Better – Despite two major wars that have dominated the past decade, and the addition of the conflict in Libya, the first years of this new century have actually seen a higher "success rate" for ending conflict around the globe.

Only about 55 percent of the peace settlements brokered in the 1990s remained intact after their first five years. But in the first several years of this century, there has been a much higher success rate of sustained peace – roughly 85 percent success rate. Negotiators trying to put together international peace building missions that won't fall apart, and those then charged with holding them together. I think now very conscious of five basic imperatives, and we are getting better at delivering them in practice. Evans cited data from the Human Security Report, compiled by a team led by Andrew Mack, now affiliated with Simon Fraser University in Canada.

Imperative for Peace: Evans said there are five such precepts for ending or preventing conflict:

(a) Determine who should do what and when.
(b) Commit the necessary resources, and sustain that commitment for as long as it takes.
(c) Understand the local political dynamics, and the cultural and other limits within outsiders must operate.

(d) Recognize that multiple objectives have to be pursued simultaneously (from security to rule of law to economic governance and others).
(e) All intrusive peace operations need an exit strategy.

Why Gareth Evans is optimistic: Since the early 1990s, there has been "an extraordinary decrease in the number of wars, the number of episodes of mass killings and the number of people dying violent battle deaths. According to the latest Human Security Report, serious conflicts, for example, which are defined with 1,000 or more reported battle deaths per year, and mass killings have seen an 80 percent decline since the early 1990s. Though a number of significant new conflicts did commence, and a number of apparently successfully concluded conflicts did break out again within a few years – though less recently than in the 1990s – many more conflicts have stopped than started.

Battle Deaths – A Striking Decrease – In most years between the 1940s and 1990s, there were over 100,000 reported battle deaths, and sometimes as many as 500,000. But the average for the first few years of the 2000s has seen fewer than 20,000. The total death for Iraq and Afghanistan coalition military deaths is about 7,300 since 2001, according to icasualties.org. Civilian and deaths of insurgents and militants are far harder to calculate, but are considered to be in the tens of thousands for each war.

What is driving the trend? – The decline in wars and battle deaths that Evans spoke of is partly attributable to the end of the colonial era in regions that had generated two-thirds or more of all the wars from the 1950s to the 1980s. And over the long term, the end of the Cold War also brought a decline in these trends, despite an initial rise in deaths due to the war in the Balkans and elsewhere. The "best explanation" for the trend is the large increase in "international activism" across the spectrum of conflict prevention, management and post-conflict peace building activity over the last 15 years. Many more conflicts have been negotiated to conclusion than have newly erupted, including a tenfold increase from 1991 to 2007 in the number of groups that support peacemaking and follow-on initiatives.

Evans on preventing conflicts – There are three basic stages of a conflict's cycle – Preventing its outbreak, preventing its continuation and preventing its recurrence. If we absorb and apply the half dozen or so main lessons we should by now have clearly learned in each of these areas... we can do better still.

Sometimes, No alternative to military action – Despite the best efforts of those in conflict resolution, there are circumstances when there will simply be no alternative to taking coercive military action. Military action was justified when Iraq invaded Kuwait in 1991, for example, and also after 9/11 when the U.S. and others acted in genuine self-defense. And there is now a third context in which military force may be perfectly defensible – that of the international 'responsibility to protect' those, within the borders of a sovereign state, at risk of genocide and other mass atrocity crimes, the issue raised squarely for us by events in Libya and the wider Middle East.

U. N. mandate in Libya: reaching breaking point? Evans worries that while military action was justified in Libya, that NATO could go too far as the military operations wear on. He said that he is now concerned, like a number of others, that the NATO operation – understandably impatient to avoid a protracted stalemate – will stretch the U.N. mandate to breaking point.

Peace work: no wastage of time – But Evans ended his remarks on an upbeat note: So those of us who have been devoting large chunks of our professional and personal lives to preventing and resolving deadly conflict, my final message is clear, simple and I hope encouraging: **we are not all wasting our time.**[98]

Countries without War:

Since 1945 the world has only seen **26 days** without war. But there is war in a number of countries each day. At least, the soldiers are alert to start war within minutes in those countries. Although history is rife with conflict, some peoples, regions and nations have enjoyed periods of peace that have lasted generations. It is a fact that these countries donot wage war. These ideal countries should be honoured by the world organizations. The following countries[99] are some examples:

Sweden (1814–present): Sweden is the present-day nation state with the longest history of continuous peace. Since its 1814 invasion of Norway, the Swedish kingdom has not engaged in war.

Switzerland (1848–present): A hard stance on neutrality has given Switzerland fame as a country for its long-lasting peace.

Costa Rica (1949–present): Following a 44-day civil war in 1944, 1949, Costa Rica abolished its army. Since then, its history has been peaceful, especially relative to those of neighboring Central American states. This has earned the country the nickname, "Switzerland of the Americas."

---

[98] Gareth Evans (2011), "Peace: Tending Positive", A speech delivered at the United States Institute of Peace", June 1. 2011

[99] www.wikipedia.com

Pennsylvania (1682–1754). The colony of Pennsylvania enjoyed 72 years of peace, maintaining no army or militia and fighting no wars. Under the proprietorship of William Penn (1644–1718), a member of the Religious Society of Friends, the colony earned a reputation for religious and personal freedom, as well as for respectful dealings with Native Americans. Although somewhat a utopian experiment, the colony was not a utopia, marred with slavery, indenture ship and class conflict.

In addition, William Penn's heirs dealt less fairly with the Native Americans, especially in the Walking Purchase of 1737. Nevertheless, the colonial experience of Pennsylvania bears study as an example of a peaceful society.

Amish (1693–present): A sect of Anabaptists or Mennonites of predominantly Swiss/German descent, the Amish practices a peaceful lifestyle that includes religious devotion, resistance to technological advancement, and nonresistance. They rarely defend themselves physically or even in court; in war time, they take conscientious objector status. Today over 150,000 Amish live in close-knit communities in 47 states in the United States, as well as Canada and Belize.

Challenges to peace:

War and violence seem to be organic, and perhaps inevitable, features of human society, although generosity and altruism are perhaps predominant. In this vein, a desire for peace can be seen as a product of the evolution of human interrelations; clearly, peace is the self-sustaining choice for humankind.

Nonetheless, peace and justice may be viewed as contradictions in practical terms. If one believes that the only way to prevent injustice and create justice is by force, then one believes that justice requires hostilities, which precludes peace. Similarly, the clash of political interests has often been identified as a justification of war.

The desire for power and advantage puts groups in opposition. This opposition naturally escalates as one side, and then the other, tries to gain advantages, sometimes culminating in violence and war. This effect is also seen in religious and ethnic groups. These groups see themselves as being oppressed and violence and war have often been rationalized as justified in defense of a culture or religion.

International Creed for Peace:

The International Creed for Peace, created by Chika Sylva-Olejeme and the International Peace Institute, sets forth an agenda and moral code for the advancement of peace for all humans and nations. The creed suggests that based on realization that independence, freedom and justice is inherent to all, peace is achieved when people fulfill their duty to choose, live and respect others.

Annexation of Princely States in India

India achieved independence on August 15, 1947 from the British government under the leadership of Mahatma M. K. Gandhi. The first Prime Minister of India was Mr. Jawaharlal Nehru. The British India was freed from foreign rule but as many as 562 Princely States in India were left free and these states became independent states /countries as per legal authority.

Dr. Hare Krishna Mahtab, popularly called as 'Lion of Orissa State' (Utkal Keshari), the then Industry Minister of Government of India initiated the proposal of merger of these princely states to India just after the Independence. Dr. HK Mahtab could convince Mahatma M. K. Gandhi, Mr. J. Nehru and Mr. Ballav

Bhai Patel for their approval of this dangerous venture. The first 'Princely State of Nilagiri' in Orissa state voluntarily opted for merger to the Indian Union. Other 35 Princely states of Orissa followed the peaceful path of merger with Orissa state. As a result, the number of districts increased from 6 districts to 13 districts when Mr. Naba Krishna Choudhury was the Chief Minister.

Out of 562 Princely States of British India, 557 Princely States merged with Indian union and 5 Princely States merged with Pakistan voluntarily. The 'Iron Man' of India, Sardar Ballav Bhai Patel, then Home Minister, took all steps for the merger of Princely States without bloodbath of soldiers and common people and without war. India boasts that the country got independence and became a great country by merger of Princely States through peaceful activities rather than waging war against these small states.

The World is over-armed, but Peace is Under-funded

IN November 2012, competing interests prevented agreement on a much-needed treaty that would have reduced the appalling human cost of the poorly regulated international arms trade. Meanwhile, nuclear disarmament efforts remain stalled, despite strong and growing global popular sentiment in support of this cause.

The failure of these negotiations and this month's anniversaries of the atomic bombings at Hiroshima and Nagasaki provide a good opportunity to explore what has gone wrong, why disarmament and arms control have proven so difficult to achieve, and how the world community can get back on track towards these vitally important goals.

Many defence establishments now recognize that security means far more than protecting borders. Grave security concerns can arise as a result of demographic trends, chronic poverty, economic inequality, environmental degradation, pandemic diseases, organized crime, repressive governance and other developments no state can control alone. Arms can't address such concerns.

Yet there has been a troubling lag between recognizing these new security challenges, and launching new policies to address them. National budget priorities still tend to reflect the old paradigms. Massive military spending and new investments in modernizing nuclear weapons have left the world over-armed – and peace under-funded.

Last year, global military spending reportedly exceeded $1.7 trillion – more than $4.6 billion a day, which alone is almost twice the UN's budget for an entire year. This largesse includes billions more for modernizing nuclear arsenals decades into the future.

This level of military spending is hard to explain in a post-Cold War world and amidst a global financial crisis. Economists would call this an "opportunity cost". I call it human opportunities lost. Nuclear weapons budgets are especially ripe for deep cuts.

Such weapons are useless against today's threats to international peace and security. Their very existence is de-stabilizing: the more they are touted as indispensable, the greater is the incentive for their proliferation. Additional risks arise from accidents and the health and environmental effects of maintaining and developing such weapons.

The time has come to re-affirm commitments to nuclear disarmament, and to ensure that this common end is reflected in national budgets, plans and institutions.

Four years ago, I outlined a five-point disarmament proposal highlighting the need for a nuclear weapon convention or a framework of instruments to achieve this goal.

Yet the disarmament stalemate continues. The solution clearly lies in greater efforts by States to harmonize their actions to achieve common ends. Here are some specific actions that all States and civil society should pursue to break this impasse.

(a) Support efforts by the Russian Federation and the United States to negotiate deep, verified cuts in their nuclear arsenals, both deployed and un-deployed.
(b) Obtain commitments by others possessing such weapons to join the disarmament process.
(c) Establish a moratorium on developing or producing nuclear weapons or new delivery systems.
(d) Negotiate a multilateral treaty outlawing fissile materials that can be used in nuclear weapons.
(e) End nuclear explosions and bring into force the Comprehensive Nuclear-Test-Ban Treaty.
(f) Stop deploying nuclear weapons on foreign soil, and retire such weapons.
(g) Ensure that nuclear-weapon states report to a public UN repository on nuclear disarmament, including details on arsenal size, fissile material, delivery systems, and progress in achieving disarmament goals.
(h) Establish a Middle East zone free of nuclear weapons and other weapons of mass destruction.
(i) Secure universal membership in treaties outlawing chemical and biological weapons.
(j) Pursue parallel efforts on conventional arms control, including an arms trade treaty, strengthened controls over the illicit trade in small arms and light weapons, universal membership in the Mine Ban, Cluster Munitions, and Inhumane Weapons Conventions, and expanded participation

in the UN Report on Military Expenditures and the UN Register of Conventional Arms.

(k) Undertake diplomatic and military initiatives to maintain international peace and security in a world without nuclear weapons, including new efforts to resolve regional disputes.

And perhaps above all, we must address basic human needs and achieve the Millennium Development Goals. Chronic poverty erodes security. Let us dramatically cut spending on nuclear weapons, and invest instead in social and economic development, which serves the interests of all by expanding markets, reducing motivations for armed conflicts, and in giving citizens a stake in their common futures. Like nuclear disarmament and non-proliferation, such goals are essential for ensuring human security and a peaceful world for future generations.

No development, no peace. No disarmament, no security. Yet when both advance, the world advances, with increased security and prosperity for all.

These are common ends that deserve the support of all nations.[100]

Pursue peace, destroy weapons

In July 2012, competing interests prevented agreement on a much-needed treaty that would have reduced the appalling human cost of the poorly regulated international arms trade. Meanwhile, nuclear disarmament efforts remain stalled, despite strong and growing global popular sentiment in support of this cause.

---

[100] Ban Ki-moon (2012), " World is over-armed, peace under-funded", Deccan Herald, August 28, 2012

The failure of these negotiations and this month's anniversaries of the atomic bombings at Hiroshima and Nagasaki provide a good opportunity to explore what has gone wrong, why disarmament and arms control have proven so difficult to achieve, and how the world community can get back on track toward these vitally important goals.

Many defense establishments now recognize that security means far more than protecting borders. Grave security concerns can arise as a result of demographic trends, chronic poverty, economic inequality, environmental degradation, pandemic diseases, organized crime, repressive governance and other developments no state can control alone. Arms can't address such concerns.

Yet there has been a troubling lag between recognizing these new security challenges, and launching new policies to address them. National budget priorities still tend to reflect the old paradigms. Massive military spending and new investments in modernizing nuclear weapons have left the world over-armed – and peace under-funded.

Last year, global military spending reportedly exceeded US$1.7 trillion – more than $4.6 billion a day, which alone is almost twice the United Nations' budget for an entire year. This largesse includes billions of dollars more for modernizing nuclear arsenals decades into the future.

This level of military spending is hard to explain in a post-Cold War world and amid a global financial crisis. Economists would call this an "opportunity cost". I call it human opportunities lost. Nuclear weapons' budgets are especially ripe for deep cuts.

Such weapons are useless against today's threats to international peace and security. Their very existence is destabilizing: The more they are touted as indispensable the greater is the incentive for their proliferation.

Additional risks arise from accidents and the health and environmental effects of maintaining and developing such weapons.

The time has come to re-affirm commitments to nuclear disarmament, and to ensure that this common end is reflected in national budgets, plans and institutions.

Four years ago, I outlined a five-point disarmament proposal highlighting the need for a nuclear weapon convention or a framework of instruments to achieve this goal.

Yet the disarmament stalemate continues. The solution clearly lies in greater efforts by states to harmonize their actions to achieve common ends. Here are some specific actions that all states and civil society should pursue to break this impasse:

Support efforts by the Russian Federation and the United States to negotiate deep, verified cuts in their nuclear arsenals, both deployed and un-deployed.

(a) Obtain commitments by others possessing such weapons to join the disarmament process.
(b) Establish a moratorium on developing or producing nuclear weapons or new delivery systems.
(c) Negotiate a multilateral treaty outlawing fissile materials that can be used in nuclear weapons.
(d) End nuclear explosions and bring into force the Comprehensive Nuclear-Test-Ban Treaty.
(e) Stop deploying nuclear weapons on foreign soil, and retire such weapons.
(f) Ensure that nuclear-weapon states report to a public UN repository on nuclear disarmament, including details on arsenal size, fissile material,

delivery systems and progress in achieving disarmament goals.

(g) Establish a Middle East zone free of nuclear weapons and other weapons of mass destruction.

(h) Secure universal membership in treaties outlawing chemical and biological weapons.

(i) Pursue parallel efforts on conventional arms control, including an arms trade treaty, strengthened controls over the illicit trade in small arms and light weapons, universal membership in the Mine Ban, Cluster Munitions and Inhumane Weapons Conventions, and expanded participation in the UN Report on Military Expenditures and the UN Register of Conventional Arms.

(j) Undertake diplomatic and military initiatives to maintain international peace and security in a world without nuclear weapons, including new efforts to resolve regional disputes.

(k) And perhaps above all, we must address basic human needs and achieve the Millennium Development Goals.

Chronic poverty erodes security. Let us dramatically cut spending on nuclear weapons, and invest instead in social and economic development, which serves the interests of all by expanding markets, reducing motivations for armed conflicts, and in giving citizens a stake in their common futures. Like nuclear disarmament and non-proliferation, such goals are essential for ensuring human security and a peaceful world for future generations.

No development, no peace. No disarmament, no security. Yet when both advance, the world advances, with increased security and prosperity for all. These are common ends that deserve the support of all nations.[101]

---

[101] Ban Ki-moon (2012), "Pursue peace, destroy weapons", China daily, USA, August 29, 2012

Towards a Global Parliament

A transnational representative body would make the international system more fair and democratic. Upon the country's Independence in 1947, Indian democracy was perceived by many, particularly in the West, as an impossible dream. Perhaps most famously Winston Churchill, an avowed colonialist, derisively conjectured that India would "fall back quite rapidly through the centuries into the barbarism and privations of the middle Ages". Such doubters pointed to India's huge income disparities, linguistic and religious divisions, lack of a common national identity, and the independent nature of its provinces and princely states.

In sum, such doubters pointed out that with about one-seventh of the world's population, the governance challenges facing India were of the same nature as those facing the planet as a whole. And indeed, there was fresh evidence in 1947 that governance on such a scale was chaotic, prone to be cataclysmic, and certainly not democratic. Gandhi, Nehru and their dedicated entourage of followers who created modern India were not dissuaded. They succeeded in launching India on a democratic path, and as we all know over 60 years later, their vision has endured.

Today, as many of our core challenges, ranging from environmental stewardship to economic and financial governance, must be decided globally, we on the planet are collectively confronted with the same question faced by India's founding generation: What role for democracy?
Once again naysayers insist that any proposal to scale democracy is a doomed utopian project. But is a campaign to establish global democracy today more implausible than the dreams of Indian democracy in

1947? Developments already taking place within the global system give us hope that it is not.

Though their creation has largely been under the radar of public awareness, over a hundred transnational parliamentary organisations exist in the world today. Among the most notable are the popularly elected Central American Parliament that has been functioning for over 20 years, and the eight-year-old Pan-African Parliament whose delegates though presently elected by national parliaments are intended to be eventually elected by the African citizenry.

Many specialized international organisations now also have a parliamentary dimension. These include assemblies of parliamentarians that function under the auspices of the Council of Europe, the Organisation for Security and Cooperation in Europe, the North American Treaty Organisation and the South American, Mercosur.

Without doubt the most advanced experiment in transnational parliamentarianism is the European Parliament. Established in the early period of European integration, as an advisory body composed of representatives of national parliaments, it has steadily evolved over the decades. Today, the European Parliament possesses veto power over much European Union legislation, and its members are directly elected by the over 500 million persons living within EU boundaries. Despite these many developments in transnational parliamentarianism, a parliamentary body that represents global citizenry as a whole is still missing. We believe that the case for such a parliament is strong.

First, by its very existence a global parliament would make the international system more fair and democratic. There is no principled reason why the establishment of citizen representative institutions should be the litmus test for legitimate governance at the local, provincial and national levels, but not at the global level. Surely, the ethical imperative behind democracy – that all citizens be given a say regardless of ethnicity or local affiliation and that officials be democratically accountable to those citizens – does not carry with it an exception for the increasingly important global polity as a whole.

Second, present fragmented global governance of states, by states, and for states is increasingly unable to solve humanity's common problems. Even in such vital areas as climate change and the control of weapons of mass destruction, the current system seems unable to achieve sufficient consensus to implement appropriate policy initiatives. Though a global parliament would most likely be limited initially to a largely consultative role, the experience of the European Parliament suggests that the parliament's claim to democratic authority will contribute to its empowerment, allowing it over time to assume legislative powers.

Finally, a global parliament would hopefully make the world less prone to war and other forms of political violence. A functioning assembly of elected delegates from around the world would help discredit belligerent and fundamentalist ideologies. In addition, if experience in existing multi-polity parliaments such as India, Belgium, or the European Union is indicative, national delegations would tend to fragment based on differing class interests and policy priorities, replacing dangerously nationalist worldviews with far more fluid transnational parliamentary coalitions.

A credible organizational initiative, the Berlin-based Campaign for a United Nations Parliamentary Assembly, is now mobilizing grassroots support for a global parliament, and the recently released manifesto of the International Assembly of the

Occupy Movement calls for a parliamentary assembly at the global level. Indians who know first-hand that aspirations to scale democracy can be realized are poised to help lead the campaign for a global parliament.[102]

WORLD PEACE IS POSSIBLE

The authors have identified some of the key tools by which people of the whole world can breathe, work, take food and take rest and feel that we, the people of the world can also solve the greatest catastrophe the world facing today. Simply we have to adjust our mind for a greater cause to save the living world. We have the capacity to achieve world peace. The suggestions are as follows:

The United Nations

In this turbulent world, world peace is not remote; it is possible. The United Nations can be made more powerful to usher an era of peace and tranquility. There are seven billions of people, innumerable animals and plant kingdom which live in this world. We all should think and work for world peace to make our mother planet safe and prosperous.

The United Nations should act as the world government. It should revitalize the UN Peace Council, the UN War Council, and The UN Law Council and the UN head quarters. All the UN appendages should be closed.

The United Nations should try to stabilize the peace process in all countries by organizing peace organizations in each state, district or even at grass root level.

---

[102] Andrew Strauss and Richard Falk (2012), "Towards a global Parliament", The Times of India, August 23, 2012

The UN should award '100 Peace Prizes' for dedicated peace workers each year.

The UN War Council must take all steps to stop war through request, letters, and negotiations or by force.

Boundary Commission should be created at the earliest to suggest the boundary line between countries / states. The boundary disputes of the countries must be finalized by the United Nations with a high-powered committee consisting of five Ex-Presidents and five Ex-Prime Ministers and five Noble Laureates in the committee. The committee may recommend to the United Nations the justified boundary line of all the countries as on New Year day of 2010.

The UN Security Council should take a decision that no country can fight with unarmed civilians.

Any country facing military attack from another country should be assisted by the United Nations politically, legally, financially and physically. The decision could be taken at once.

The UN Military Regiment consisting of military soldiers and ranks can force a country to stop aggression, attack a country to stop a war, but in no case it will fight with the civilians.

The UN Security Council should take a decision by which no military ruler can be permitted to be the President of a Country in uniform.

The UN peacekeeping volunteers should distribute religious books, food materials and medicines to the affected people.

Governments

A general rule may be promulgated for fixing the number of years an individual can hold the post of President or Prime Minister of a country. This should be applicable to all countries. This should be one term only.

A number of small countries are prone to military rule, which can be avoided. No military person can be a President or ruler of a country in uniform. If he desires to become the President of a country, he has to resign the military post and form a political party and can contest in election after a gestation period of two years from the date of resignation or pay roll.

The low-income countries should adopt pro-poor, pro-rural and pro-agricultural policies to activate peace process among the poor brethrens.

Governments should not measure their achievements by Newspapers or TV advertisements. The politicians in administration should not weigh their popularity by garlands awarded to them in seminars or at aerodromes.

Governments should undertake **"Suresh – Pritam Model for assessing Gross Domestic Peace of a Country (GDPC)"** each year to evaluate their achievements. (Ref: World Peace Volume I)

Each country must ensure that none dies through starvation. But administration hides the real cause of death for survival of the government. They mislead the people, which cause anger among the vulnerable.

Government should protect nature (environment); but the political parties in power make massive corruption through granting leases of mines and agricultural land to the international industrialists, whose main purpose is to garner more funds to their purse.

Let the whole world remain in peace. No individual should be allowed to declare himself as the man with supreme power. No country can remain in safe by waging war against another country or all other countries. Partnership in war / defense collaboration must be declared anti-human policies. History speaks that military forums encourage war and do not create peace.

Each government should hear and accept public grievances. The state laws should be impartial to caste, colour, faith or religion. The administration should respect judiciary; similarly judiciary should not give anti-people verdict. Judgments should not vary for exact cases and should not be delayed.

Terrorists, Maoists, and Naxalites have terrorized the governments of many countries. These groups fight with the government as the rich– poor gap is widening among countries and among different classes of people. So the intelligentsias, political scientists and economists should find ways to reduce the disparity. We feel that all low-income countries and middle-income countries should accept and implement pro-poor, pro-rural and pro-agricultural policies to uplift the poor agricultural labourers, peasants, small farmers and rural people. The rich countries should eliminate subsidy to agriculture in their countries to bring parity of agricultural prices in international markets. Those who create problems for others are also not getting peace in life. All problems can be solved through mutual understanding, sacrifice and humanity.

Defense Expenditure

When we can't give life to the dead, we have no right to kill the innocent civilians and deploy the brave soldiers to die. The soldiers are recruited to save the country and not to attack other countries.

History should not repeat in waging wars. Much blood has already flown into the rivers and oceans. No country should aspire to rule the planet, environment, time and people as Germany has failed and suffered.

There should be ban on nuclear, biological and chemical defense research for all the countries. All nuclear, biological and chemical weapons manufactured and stored should be immediately destroyed.

Defense budget of each country should be made public for information of the general public. The defense budget of each country should be reduced to 75 percent of the present budget in order to pave the way for world peace.

Every one of us needs peace in life. So our ability of making the world a peaceful planet will be possible if all the governments do not appoint fresher to the army for a period of five years. There should be a 5-year-war holiday to restore peace.

The retired army officials may be engaged in social security organizations for internal security and peace. Defense expenditure should be reduced and can be utilized for education and healthcare of unprivileged people.

The military rulers are interested to stick to their chair for indefinite period through waging wars continuously. This can be broken through world bodies. For restoring world peace permanently, war against military rulers can be declared with sufficient time or notice to allow them for vacating the chair peacefully; or they should face election in presence of UN nominated observers.

World War III can be avoided if military associations are declared illegal. But the UN should be assured military help by each member countries as and when necessary. The UN peacekeeping force should be renamed as UN force.

There is no reason for India and Pakistan to fight wars. The organizations, which advocate unification of Kashmir, should think that an independent Kashmir surrounded by China, Russia, Pakistan and India (all nuclear countries) cannot ensure peace to the people of united Kashmir. They should not allow another Israel on the Indian sub-continent. Therefore India should be advised to pump more funds to the Jammu & Kashmir state for healthcare, education, employment opportunities and horticultural development. Similarly, Pakistan should develop Pak occupied Kashmir through higher budgetary provisions for road construction, elementary education, goat rearing, healthcare and employment opportunities. Money spent for defense can be reduced and that money can be utilized for economic growth of the people.

Both the rebel group of soldiers should better be utilized in construction and animal husbandry with government patronage. The quarter-century old civil war must be ended at the earliest. Sudan government must assure safe return of refugees, internally displaced persons and persons remaining in government camps to their villages for peaceful living. **It is estimated that more than 10,000,000 civilians need resettlement in Sudan.**

The Sudan government should request the UN for deputing military personnel for start of peace process of the country. Sudan should undertake fresh appointments of youths as soldiers and others military officers.

The ongoing wars have killed hundreds of thousands of soldiers and innocent people in the name of religion, boundary line or military rule. The ongoing wars can be stopped and world peace can be possible through patronage of UN and peace loving countries.

Productions and International Trade in Arms

In the Twenty-first century, international law is more important than ever. All countries should accept the 1969 Vienna Treaty. The United Nations should make treaties on production and trade of arms, which would cause to avoid war, decrease human sacrifice and strengthen world peace.

There should be total ban on Nuclear, Chemical and biological warfare and total ban on researches on nuclear, chemical and biological weapons to avoid or long delay the emergence of World War III, which can destroy the human civilization, global environment and animal and plant kingdom.

There should be total ban on international arms trade. As a result, all the 35 ongoing wars would be stopped paving the way for a peaceful world. Moreover, this amount can be better utilized for education and healthcare of the poor persons residing in low-income countries. Each country might be permitted to produce guns, machine guns, pistols, bullets, and gunpowder and vehicles for internal security only.

Banning international trade of arms will also limit the availability of arms and ammunitions to the Terrorists, Maoists and Naxalites. The transaction of arms and ammunitions should be controlled by defense and internal security only. As a result, theft, burglary, dacoit, robbery and murder can be reduced in civil areas.

Peace Organizations and individuals:

The force of arms cannot do what peace does. If you can gain your desired end with sweets, why use poison?

The United Nations, all countries, states, conglomerates and even small hamlets should constitute PEACE FORUMS to seek permanent peace in each human settlement.

The International Peace Organizations should have TV channels, newspapers, journals, and magazines for world coverage. The common man should be linked to each peace organization. Active membership of each peace organization should be increased.

A peace worker may be honored, if he/she has contributed a single step towards world peace. Peace movement should be mass based. Only praying for 5-minutes each day for world peace by millions of people will make the 'world peace movement' a success. Each individual should fix a time for peace prayer as per his / her convenience as a daily practice.

Each peace organization should hold at least an annual 'Peace Meet' for three days, wherein it should hold peace rally, mass prayer to the Lord by chanting His Glory, peace seminar, and award of peace certificates and prizes to peace lovers.

Conclusion

Countries want independence, nations want liberation, and people want revolution.

- Mr. Chou En-lai, Former Premier of CHINA

War causes untold economic and social damage; reduces food production; causes famines; imposes poverty; losses peace and converts development assistance into purchase of arms and ammunitions. It results in untold human sufferings including starvation deaths, child pornography, child sale, increase of widows and early old age.

Let the philosophers, saints, intelligentsia, planners and University Professors and peace-lovers of the world find ways how to stop the on-going wars completely and make suggestions for a world free of wars for enjoying peace everywhere.

The whole world is a family. We have the capacity to make this planet an 'Abode of Peace' through our inner quality of humanity, truth, sacrifice and love. We must remember that Alexander the Great has told all of us, "When I die, keep my hands open, so that people will see that I carry nothing (wealth) with me."

The United Nations should be revitalized to function as the '**World Government or World Parliament'**. It should undertake adequate steps for ensuring peace to all; try to stop war between countries and promulgate international laws for safety, peace and prosperity of countries and people. War does not solve a problem; it creates more problems. War kills humanity; kills human beings and destroys a divine-blessed world. We do not need war; we need peace.

We can avoid World War III successfully forever. We are confident that World War III would never occur on this Earth. And World Peace is possible.

+++++

AUTHOR INDEX

+++++

SUBJECT INDEX

THE END

A MOVEMENT FOR A PEACEFUL WORLD

AUTHORS

Professor Suresh Chandra Mallick (b 1944) was a faculty member of the OUAT, Bhubaneswar (India) during 1968 - 2004. He is a researcher, writer, thinker and social worker. He is an Agricultural Economist with specialization in Agriculture, Poverty, Marketing, Policy and World Peace to motivate people's involvement in peace process. He held the post of Vice President, Indian Society of Agricultural Marketing during 2003 - 05. At present, he is the Chairperson of the Institute of Development Studies & Policy Research, Bhubaneswar.

Pritam Mallick (1975–2006) was extremely noble, friendly and knowledgeable and possessed extraordinary memory. He received B.A. (Honors) from Utkal University, M.A. from Central University, Hyderabad and M. Phil. Degree from JNU and completed Ph. D. courses in JNU. He was a specialist in Monetary Economics and Econometrics. He remembered the Oxford Dictionary and Roget's Thesaurus to master English literature. He acquired deep knowledge in Astrology, Palmistry, Mathematics and Statistics. He contributed enormously for WORLD PEACE manuscripts as co-author. But his heavenly demise occurred on August 4, 2006.